Fragile Rise

The Belfer Center Studies in International Security book series is edited at the Belfer Center for Science and International Affairs at the Harvard Kennedy School and is published by the MIT Press. The series publishes books on contemporary issues in international security policy, as well as their conceptual and historical foundations. Topics of particular interest to the series include the spread of weapons of mass destruction, internal conflict, the international effects of democracy and democratization, and U.S. defense policy.

A complete list of Belfer Center Studies appears at the back of this volume.

Fragile Rise

Grand Strategy and the Fate of Imperial Germany, 1871–1914

Xu Qiyu

Foreword by Graham Allison

Translated by Joshua Hill

Belfer Center Studies in International Security
The MIT Press
Cambridge, Massachusetts
London, England

The MIT Press, One Rogers Street, Cambridge, MA 02142-1209, USA

Printed and bound in the United States of America.

This volume was originally published in Chinese
by Xinhua Publishing House.

Cover illustration: Draner [Jules Jean Georges Renard], "L'homme a la boule." Collection de caricatures et de charges pour servir à l'histoire de la guerre et de la révolution de 1870-1871, [s.l.], [ca. 1872], Bd. 3, S. 140. Universitätsbibliothek Heidelberg. Reproduced under Creative Commons license CC BY-SA 3.0 DE.

Library of Congress Cataloging-in-Publication Data

Names: Qiyu Xu, 1974- author. | Hill, Joshua, (historian), translator.
Title: Fragile rise : grand strategy and the fate of Imperial Germany, 1871-1914 / Xu Qiyu ; foreword by Graham Allison ; translated by Joshua Hill.
Other titles: Grand strategy and the fate of Imperial Germany, 1871-1914
Description: Cambridge, MA : The MIT Press, [2016] | Series: Belfer Center studies in international security | Includes bibliographical references and index.
Identifiers: LCCN 2016041048 | ISBN 9780262036054 (hardcover : alk. paper)
Subjects: LCSH: Germany--Foreign relations--1871- | Europe--Politics and government--1871-1918. | Germany--Politics and government--1871-1918. | Geopolitics--Germany--History. | Germany--Strategic aspects. | Balance of power--Case studies. | Strategy--Case studies.
Classification: LCC DD221.5 .X83 2016 | DDC 355/.03354309034--dc23
LC record available at https://lccn.loc.gov/2016041048

10 9 8 7 6 5 4 3 2 1

Contents

Foreword vii
Graham Allison

Translator's Note xi
Joshua Hill

Preface xvii
Xu Qiyu

1. A Low-Posture Rise 1
2. "Active Shaping" and the Foundation of a Grand Staretegy 33
3. Working to Maintain the Grand Strategy 67
4. Entering the Post-Bismarckian Era 95
5. Institutions, Society, Popular Opinion, and Grand Strategy. . . . 127
6. From *Weltpolitik* to Encirclement 155
7. An Obsession with Command of the Seas 191
8. The Schlieffen Plan and the Retreat of Grand Strategy. 227
9. Crisis Management on the Path to World War, 1908–1914 259

Notes 293
About the Author 329
Contributors 331
Index 333
Belfer Center Studies in International Security 343
About the Belfer Center for Science and International Affairs 346

Foreword

Graham Allison

EIGHT YEARS BEFORE the outbreak of World War I in Europe, Britain's King Edward VII asked his prime minister why the British government was becoming so unfriendly to his nephew Kaiser Wilhelm II's Germany rather than keeping its eye on the United States, which he saw as the greater threat. The prime minister instructed the Foreign Office's chief Germany watcher, Eyre Crowe, to write a memo answering this question. Crowe delivered his memorandum on New Year's Day, 1907. The document is a gem in the annals of diplomacy.

The logic of Crowe's analysis echoed Thucydides's insight about the Peloponnesian War in ancient Greece. About the cause of the war, Thucydides wrote: "it was the rise of Athens, and the fear that this inspired in Sparta, that made war inevitable." As Henry Kissinger's *On China* paraphrased Crowe's central question about Germany: Did increasing hostility between Britain and Germany stem more from German capabilities or German conduct? In Crowe's words, did Germany's pursuit of "political hegemony and maritime ascendancy" inevitably pose an existential threat to "the independence of her neighbors and ultimately the existence of England?"

Crowe's answer was unambiguous—capability was key. As Germany's economy surpassed Britain's, it would not only develop the strongest army on the continent but also "build as powerful a navy as she can afford." To quote Kissinger again, German naval supremacy "would be an objective threat to Britain, and incompatible with the existence of the British Empire," whatever German intentions. In Crowe's summary: "a vigorous nation cannot allow its growth to be hampered by blind adherence to the status quo." It was with Crowe's memo in 1907, Xu Qiyu contends in *Fragile Rise*, that the British policy of containing Germany began to come into focus.

In 1910, three years after reading Crowe's memo, Edward VII died. Attendees at his funeral included two "chief mourners"—the new king of Great Britain, George V, and his cousin, Germany's Kaiser Wilhelm. Theodore Roosevelt represented the United States. At one point, Roosevelt—an avid student of naval power and leading champion of the buildup of the U.S. Navy—asked the kaiser whether he would consider a moratorium in the budding German-British naval arms race. Wilhelm replied that Germany was unalterably committed to having a powerful navy. But he asserted that this would not be a problem because war between Germany and Britain was simply unthinkable. "I was brought up in England," he said, "I feel myself partly an Englishman. Next to Germany I care more for England than for any other country." He then added, with emphasis, "I ADORE ENGLAND!"

World War I provides many lessons for statesmen today. None is more relevant for current leaders than the stark reminder that however unimaginable conflict seems, however catastrophic the consequences for all would-be actors, however deep the cultural empathy among leaders, and however economically interdependent states may be—none of these factors was sufficient to prevent war in 1914. Nor would they be today.

The centennial of World War I has inspired a spirited discussion in the West about lessons to be learned from Germany's rise and the reactions of other powers, especially Great Britain. In China, too, historians have been called on to help illuminate the present. Indeed, in 2003, the Chinese Politburo commissioned a lengthy study on the trajectories of the nine nations that had become great powers in modern history (Portugal, Spain, the Netherlands, Great Britain, France, Germany, Japan, Russia, and the United States). This study, entitled *The Rise of the Great Powers*, was later presented in the form of a twelve-part television series which was broadcast on China's leading channel, China Central Television (CCTV), with a companion eight-volume book series. Both enjoyed considerable popularity and sparked a national conversation. This book can be seen as a further extension of that debate.

Unfortunately, much of that conversation in China has failed to reach the West. In sponsoring the translation of a new book which has been praised by Chinese scholars as the best account by a Chinese historian of Germany's rise, The Belfer Center for Science and International Affairs hopes to make this Chinese perspective available to a broader audience.

Xu begins his account of Germany's rise with the unification of the German Empire in 1871. He argues that since unification meant the emergence of Germany as a great power, it also created the central paradox that came to define German foreign policy: As Germany's power grew, so too did its neighbors' apprehensions. To address this paradox, Germany initially adopted a low profile in foreign affairs. By 1878, however, Otto von Bismarck, the guiding hand behind German foreign policy, had become active and visible in shaping European politics. The objective of his grand strategy was to sustain Germany's rise. In Xu's view, despite severe pressure from abroad as well as within the country, his combination of strategic and diplomatic skills allowed him to overcome opponents or keep them off balance.

Bismarck's successors, Xu argues, were not up to the challenge he left them. A preeminent land power by the mid-1890s, Germany's pursuit of a commanding navy brought it into predictable, unavoidable, but unnecessary conflict with Britain. Germany's obsession with naval preeminence became a major strand in the recklessness of "*Weltpolitik.*" This increasing German aggressiveness, according to Xu, was the primary cause of the world war that destroyed Germany's "fragile" rise.

Xu's analysis of German policy and emphasis on the naval race and the Schlieffen Plan as significant contributors to the war complements one of the mainstream schools of Western thought about World War I, alongside authors like Fritz Fischer, Margaret MacMillan, and Paul Kennedy. Unlike Fischer, however, he does not argue that the Great War stemmed from deliberate and strategically coherent German aggression. Nor does he argue that Germany's growing material capabilities inevitably led to war, as some Western scholars have claimed. Rather, Xu's nuanced analysis finds that while Germany's rise created structural stresses that moved the actors toward war, those stresses could have been negotiated by good strategy and statesmanship (as Bismarck had demonstrated). It was the absence of such strategy and statesmanship in Bismarck's successors that allowed inconsequential events in the Balkans to spark war throughout Europe. In this respect, Xu's analysis can be compared to Henry Kissinger's in *Diplomacy.*

Although Xu refrains from stating them explicitly, *Fragile Rise* holds a number of important lessons for the rise of China in our own time. First, China's rapidly growing economic and military power will inevitably create structural stress between China and the United States—a phenomenon that I have labeled the "Thucydides Trap." Whatever the intentions of leaders of both nations, they will have to recognize and manage the risks that inevitably accompany changes in the international balance of power.

Second, this structural stress does not mean that war is inevitable. As Xu notes, prudent diplomacy and astute statesmanship can meet this challenge, as Bismarck demonstrated. Significantly, while compromises will be needed on both sides, Xu's emphasis on the "fragility" of the rising power suggests the burden may fall disproportionately on Chinese leaders.

The defining question for this generation is whether these Chinese leaders and their counterparts in the United States will be up to the challenge. In this regard, *Fragile Rise* provides an important clue for Chinese leaders hoping to negotiate the structural stress created by their country's ascendance. As noted above, Germany's growing capabilities after unification in 1871 led it to turn its attentions to the sea. Under Bismarck's successors, that ambition turned into an obsession that eclipsed all other strategic imperatives and put it on a collision course with the dominant sea power of the era, Great Britain.

Today, the rise of another traditional land power, China, is propelling its leaders to build military capabilities proportionate to its economic power: on land, at sea, and in every other domain. This potentially puts China on a collision course with the world's reigning power, the United States. The strategic imperative for both Washington and Beijing must be to avoid the mistakes made a century ago that led to a war that destroyed not only the fragile rising power, but proved catastrophic for the whole of Europe.

Translator's Note

Joshua Hill

As Xu Qiyu wrote on the original cover of his *Fragile Rise: Grand Strategy and the Fate of Imperial Germany*, "When it is difficult to see clearly into the future, looking back to history, even the history of other peoples, might be the right choice." Although he does not repeat those words inside his book, their spirit is present throughout his text. Xu's *Fragile Rise* is implicit policy advice in the form of an extended historical analogy. This approach has a long tradition in Chinese scholarship—nearly fifteen hundred years ago, a Tang dynasty emperor praised a counsellor adept at using "antiquity as a mirror to understand the rise and fall of states [*yi gu wei jing, ke yi jian xing ti*]" and the metaphor of "history as a mirror" remains part of the Chinese language even today—and represents a profound cultural inclination toward using history as a tool for thinking about the present.[1]

For that emperor, history primarily consisted of canonical tales of Chinese dynasties, both actual and mythical. That purely domestic history still remains a powerful source of insight and inspiration for Chinese leaders. Some analysts, indeed, argue that an awareness of this tradition holds the key to understanding contemporary policymaking.[2] Xu Qiyu participates in an expansive descendant of this longstanding predisposition that seeks value in the histories of other nations beyond China. This was radical when first proposed by early twentieth-century journalist and political theorist Liang Qichao, who saw the histories of various "lost nations," from India to Poland, as relevant for a China beset by Western and Japanese imperialism. It has long since entered the intellectual mainstream. At various points in the twentieth century, Japanese, Soviet, and Singaporean historical experiences have been seen to have special relevance for China. Cosmopolitan reasoning of this sort is common enough to be unremarkable today. The prevalence of these ecumenical discussions in a country convinced of its own uniqueness perhaps should inspire emulation in other nations that pride themselves on the "exceptional" nature of their histories.

German history, too, has served as a "mirror" for Chinese intellectuals and political leaders to reflect on their country's situation. Over a century ago, many viewed Germany as a model for China's future. In 1905, officials appointed by the Qing, China's final dynasty, visited Germany to study its constitutional monarchy, with an eye toward adopting a similar system at home. A second scholarly mission followed in 1908, and substantial aspects of late Qing political reform, including the laws used in China's first authorized legislative elections, bore the mark of German influence. A decade later, after a republican revolution in China and Germany's defeat in the Great War, Chinese observers saw Germany's post-war recovery as an inspiration for their own reconstruction. Chiang Kai-shek, who governed China after 1927, admired Germany enough that he sent his adopted son there for military training in the late 1930s, explaining to him that "Germany is the only country from which we can learn something. They can give us the base from which to develop our own style: firm and solid."[3] Chiang looked to Germany for more than mere spiritual sustenance, however. German military advisors helped train his army in the 1920s and 1930s, while trade in strategic minerals linked the economies of the two nations.

Xu Qiyu, working within the very different geopolitical context of the early twenty-first century, discerns within German history a warning for contemporary China. Like many others eager to think through the implications of China's rise in the twenty-first century, he has drawn a comparison with Wilhelmine Germany between 1871 and 1914. The parallels between the two seem irresistible—then, as now, the emergence of a new power, fueled by a dynamic, fast-growing economy, dramatically reshaped the global strategic balance. Wilhelmine Germany also serves as a cautionary tale of an emerging power that failed to find a place within the existing international order; its rise ultimately resulted in a total war that imposed ruinous consequences for all combatants, victors and defeated alike. The analogy is deeply imperfect, as virtually all who explore it admit, yet it is so powerfully frightening that it compels serious attention.

In recent years, the parallel drawn between contemporary China and Wilhelmine Germany (along with its corollary, the equation of today's United States and the pre-1914 British Empire) has become enmeshed with, and cited as an example of, Graham Allison's notion of a "Thucydides Trap." Named for Thucydides's contention in *The History of the Peloponnesian War* that Sparta's fear of Athens's rapid growth led to a destructive confrontation between the two Greek city-states, it has become a metaphor for the cycle of fear and antagonism that emerges between rising and established powers. It is a trap that can produce grim results: "in 12 of 16 [such] cases over the past 500 years," Allison argues, "the outcome was war."[4] The 2014 centennial of the July Crisis that sparked World War I has further inspired scholars to examine this analogy in greater detail. Some of the most significant contributions to this discussion can be found in *The Next Great War?*—a collection of essays sponsored by Harvard University's Belfer Center for Science and International Affairs, in which prominent thinkers specifically focused on Europe in 1914, U.S.-China relations today, and the applicability of the "Thucydides Trap" to both.[5]

Less often, however, are Chinese voices heard at length in this scholarly discussion; for example, there were no Chinese contributors to *The Next Great War*? Yet, given the intellectual comfort with the use of historical analogies in China, several variants of this conversation are active there. Most prominently, Chinese president Xi Jinping has specifically addressed the "Thucydides Trap" in public remarks.[6] As a result, the phrase is now a staple of official discourse and openly discussed in Chinese Communist Party–supported newspapers such as the *Global Times* [Huanqiu shibao]. Yet these are simply references to, rather than explorations of, this historical analogy; much may be implied by such utterances, but little is explained directly. In this vacuum, overseas analysts have taken to reading between the lines. Sheena Chestnut Greitens, for instance, suggests that the Chinese leadership sees another trap, different from Allison's, in Thucydides: entangling alliances that can allow minor powers to draw great powers into unanticipated and unwanted wars.[7] This "trap" could only ensnare the United States, with its complex web of Asian allies, rather than a mainland China that has a nominal alliance with only a single other nation, North Korea. Similarly, as Andrew Erikson has pointedly suggested, official Chinese use of "Thucydides Trap" rhetoric sometimes carries the insinuation that the "trap" can only be avoided through U.S. restraint and concessions.[8] At the level of authoritative state discourse in China, there is little evident recognition that this historical analogy has anything to teach a rising power like China. Rather, it functions only as a warning to fearful, declining hegemons.

Beneath this official discourse, however, a much richer and more nuanced discussion is taking place. Xu's *Fragile Rise*, though it never directly addresses the "Thucydides Trap" thesis, is one of the most substantive and influential Chinese contributions to the global conversation that the concept has engendered.[9] Xu, though an officer in the People's Liberation Army, ultimately speaks for himself, rather than for his government, in this work; *Fragile Rise* represents only what one very serious, committed scholar thinks about the lessons of history. The wide circulation his book has enjoyed inside China, however, suggests that his interpretation is one worth taking seriously by anyone interested in contemporary Chinese strategic thought. *Fragile Rise* is unique, as well, in its place in the Chinese scholarly landscape. Although he modestly claims not to be a historian, Xu combines primary source research in both English and German with an interpretation of the voluminous existing secondary literature on European diplomatic history. No other scholarly work in mainland China (other than works translated from other languages into Chinese) covers this same ground.

Unlike foreign scholars or Chinese political figures who focus, either implicitly or explicitly, on what the historical analogy between Europe before 1914 and East Asia in the twenty-first century suggests for U.S. policymaking, Xu argues there is much for present-day China to learn from Wilhelmine Germany's historical experiences. His specific interest is German "grand strategy"—the coordination of diplomatic and military power in order to balance national capacity with national interests—from national unification in 1871 to the outbreak of war in 1914. Xu argues that Germany had an effective grand strategy during the chancellorship of Otto von Bismarck, but after Bismarck's 1890 dismissal from office, this grand strategy was abandoned and not replaced. The policy drift that ensued contributed directly to war. Xu, however, refrained from writing a conclusion that extends his thesis beyond August 1914. Neither China nor the twenty-first-century world are mentioned in anything more than a few brief asides.

Yet make no mistake—*Fragile Rise* is profoundly about contemporary China. Xu hints at this on the cover of the Chinese version in the quote that begins this note. He also suggests it in his own preface, and implicitly organizes his book in such a manner that the parallels are inescapable. Read with twenty-first-century China in mind, as his Chinese audience certainly does, the implicitly comparative aspects of Xu's *Fragile Rise* become evident. Examples of this abound. The attention lavished on the "pressures" that rapid economic growth created in German political, social, and intellectual life have a visible counterpart in a China that has experienced over a generation of rapid economic growth. The suggestive discussion of the role of an increasingly nationalistic public opinion in late Wilhelmine Germany, too, seems paralleled by the rising importance of Chinese public opinion on politics, particularly as filtered through new platforms provided by the Internet. The portrayal of a German political system struggling to find a role for sectors of society newly empowered by rapid industrialization seems mirrored in the rise of a substantial middle class and a smaller, but influential, stratum of wealthy entrepreneurs in contemporary China. The focus on the imbalance between Germany's technological capacity to construct a world-class battle fleet and the inability of that navy to improve Germany's security environment invites comparisons with contemporary debates over Chinese military modernization. Xu never directly suggests these linkages, yet carefully and subtly draws the reader's attention to them.

As Xu portrays it, the path that German history followed after 1890 was not foreordained. Poor leadership—characterized by the abandonment of not only grand strategy itself, but even the belief that grand strategy was possible—accounted for its fate. The drift from crisis to crisis and the increasing polarization of the European state system that led to war in August 1914 did not result from a German plan, but the *lack* of one. Although Xu does not characterize it as such, this is a claim that the decades before 1914 were essentially a "lost chance." Better leadership, coupled with strategic planning, could have allowed Wilhelmine Germany to continue its (relatively) peaceful rise well into the twentieth century. The persistence of that Germany—an industrial powerhouse with a territory larger and more populous than the current German Republic, possessed of one of the world's most formidable militaries, and spared the physical and psychological devastation of defeat in two world wars—would surely have changed the course of world history to an incalculable degree.

Following Xu's logic, it stands to reason that if grand strategy could have allowed Germany to sidestep catastrophe in 1914, it will also help China avoid a similar fate in the twenty-first century. The precise elements of such a grand strategy he leaves unstated, but his portrayal of Bismarck's policies suggests several of its foundations. The first of these is psychological. Policymakers should be flexible, dynamic, appreciative of the emotional aspects of interstate diplomacy, and sensitive to the limits of power. Xu's Bismarck grasped the value of such insights; his successors did not. The next foundation is institutional. The policymaking organs of government—particularly those engaged in diplomatic or military affairs—need effective coordination from a central authority. Bismarck, generally, accomplished this; under his successors, intrabureaucratic links (particularly those that bound the military and diplomatic establishments) disintegrated, and agencies pursued independent, and contradictory, policies. The final aspect is philosophical. History, Xu argues, provides "gaps" or opportunities that a skilled leader can use to reshape unfavorable situations. Bismarck sought these out, while Germany's post-Bismarckian leadership overlooked their existence. Instead, his successors fatalistically came to believe that they were helpless pawns buffeted by forces that were both powerful and inevitable. Believing that events were beyond their control, they designed short-term plans that ensured that, one day, a local crisis would snowball into a continental war.

There is an optimistic element in Xu's history: Germany's leaders failed to find a grand strategy for themselves, but China need not fall into this same trap. While this assessment might reflect the sense of relative optimism that pervades Chinese society in the early twenty-first century, it is certainly also an artifact of Xu's exclusive focus on Germany. Recent histories that focus on the broader European scene, epitomized by Christopher Clark's *The Sleepwalkers: How Europe Went to War in 1914*, offer much bleaker appraisals of the continent on the brink of war.[10] Clark portrays a world of complex, contradictory, and poorly understood events navigated by overwhelmed and second-rate national leaders themselves preoccupied with thorny domestic political crises. A more pessimistic observer reading Xu and Clark in tandem might wonder if strategists such as Bismarck are the exceptions, rather than the norm, or if some situations are so thorny that even a Bismarck could not ensure a favorable outcome.

The quotation that begins this note emphasizes the importance of history, "even the history of other people," in shedding light on potential futures. The Belfer Center's decision to have his book translated takes this commitment one step further. Rather than being limited to a Chinese audience, Xu's interpretation of German history can now be analyzed by readers of English interested in contemporary Chinese strategic thought. This, admittedly, may be of limited practical assistance to those tasked with the difficult work of crafting U.S. policy toward China during this moment of transition. At the very least, however, it will hopefully contribute to a trans-Pacific dialogue that takes history seriously both as a field of academic research and as a tool for talking about hopes and fears for the future. Such a conversation may prove to have a value all its own in solidifying lasting intellectual links between China and the United States.

A Final Note on Translation: Citations to English-language originals have been substituted for the original text's citations to Chinese translations of English-language books. When appropriate, citations to German-language texts that the author had translated into Chinese have been replaced by citations to existing English-language translations. In a few instances, source material quoted in the Chinese edition could not be located; similar quotations have been used. Some errors in the Chinese edition were corrected—but, almost certainly, new (and different) errors have been introduced.

Joshua Hill
Changsha, Hunan and Athens, Ohio
September 2015

Preface

Xu Qiyu

I HAVE LONG BEEN interested in using the concept of "grand strategy" to examine pre–World War I Germany's rise as a great power.

As a scholar of contemporary strategic issues, I came to this rather unlikely topic only by chance. Yet, as my research progressed, I found myself increasingly fascinated by it. I also realized that much of what I thought I knew about this topic turned out to be, at best, unreliable and, at worst, wholly inaccurate. Some of my knowledge was based on the "authoritative" assessments of that era's politicians and intellectuals. Such people, reacting to the immediate demands of their times, drew conclusions that later generations have simply accepted as received wisdom. Gradually, these assessments came to be taken as fixed judgments about the past. Likewise, attempts originating in U.S. international relations scholarship to combine greatly simplified theoretical models and contemporary frameworks have provided only unsatisfactory understandings of the past. The process of historical research, I learned, does not result in the confirmation of existing conclusions as often as it leads to the endless overturning of established arguments and conceptual frameworks.

Many aspects of the pre–World War I German Empire, also referred to as Wilhelmine Germany, are worthy of investigation. In contrast to the bottom-up extremist ideology and top-down political restructuring of the Nazi period, social tolerance and political conflict characterized Wilhelmine Germany. It was a rapidly growing power, yet also had to contend with a fragile and extremely complex security environment. Material life improved dramatically, but spiritual life became shallow and uneasy. Intellectuals, stimulated by the growth of national power, embraced irrationality. This ultimately gave rise to a mass irrationality that carried the respectable tint of scientific rationality. Wilhelmine Germany illustrates the notion that nation-states can reflect the flaws of human nature. The experiences of Wilhelmine Germany—a classic example of a rising great power that failed—are worthy of reflection and analysis.

I decided to use the notion of "grand strategy" to examine the rise and fall of Wilhelmine Germany for two particular reasons. First, it gave me a thread to follow through the enormous mass of historical materials. Second, it allowed me to resolve a series of deeper doubts and concerns. One of these concerns is the balance between inevitability and chance as causal factors in international disputes. Are conflicts, particularly direct clashes between great powers, inevitable? Are there deep-rooted elements that "determine" the outbreak of an "inevitable" conflict? This question is ultimately philosophical in nature, as it impinges on humanity's understanding of itself and its place in the world. Most people accept that both chance and inevitability exist, yet the notion of chance often leaves many uncomfortable. As a result, it is often seen as secondary in importance to inevitability, or as some sort of an "exception." In fact, the "laws of history" leave "gaps" that are large enough to allow people to take an active, dynamic role. Chance plays an important part too, but the task of grand strategy is to adapt to these laws of history while, as much as possible, simultaneously exploiting the "gaps" in history.

In Wilhelmine Germany, Chancellor Otto von Bismarck understood this well and, as a result, was always ready to accept imperfect or uncertain results. His successors, however, were the exact opposite. They sought certainty in all things and placed an excessive emphasis on the concept of "inevitability." These philosophical differences were an important element in the quick disintegration of German grand strategy after Bismarck's forced retirement. Ultimately, the emphasis that German leaders placed on "inevitability" developed into an obsession. They became ever more firm in their belief that a major war was "unavoidable." This led them to engage in a series of "inevitable" preparations that, ultimately, did make war truly "unavoidable."

Researching pre–World War I Germany from the perspective of grand strategy also touches upon the issue of rationality and irrationality. While reading the ancient Greek historian Thucydides as a graduate student, I was struck by one of his observations of political culture in wartime Athens: "Prudent hesitation [came to be seen as] specious cowardice...the advocate of extreme measures was always trustworthy; his opponent, a man to be suspected."[1] Later, after I began working at the Institute for Strategic Studies at National Defense University and had the opportunity to interact with many officials and scholars (both Chinese and foreign), I came to recognize that this phenomenon has been replicated in many other times and places. The irrational assault on policymaking and grand strategy that this phenomenon leads to was readily apparent in Wilhelmine Germany.

Arguably, some of Germany's policies might not have been so extreme in the absence of pressure from a bellicose public. World War I itself might even have been avoided. What were the origins of this mass irrationality? What was the connection between it and the rapid growth of the nation and of society? Why did the tide of public opinion always favor hard-line policy positions? Would it have been possible for anyone to control this irrationality? These problems constitute an important aspect of my research. All of the chapters in this book, particularly the analysis of this specific topic presented in Chapter 5, concentrate to a greater or lesser extent on these pivotal "internal factors."

During the course of my research, it was a special pleasure for me, as someone who is not a professional historian, to immerse myself in primary source materials. I particularly enjoyed reading the correspondence between Bismarck and the German ambassadors stationed abroad. Bismarck's instructions and memoranda contained a profound yet flexible grand strategic vision. In these documents, I saw a balance between attention to detail and an understanding of the overall situation. Throughout, Bismarck's writings are characterized by his deep ability to observe the human condition. German diplomatic documents after Bismarck, however, fell far short of the standards he set. Their assessments often flowed from wishful thinking, while their strategic thought and even their style of writing became increasingly formulaic. Sometimes, the obviousness of their errors and the rigidness of their logic frustrates those who read them today.

By contrast, this discrepancy did not exist in British diplomatic documents. While none of Great Britain's senior policymakers were grand masters on the level of a Bismarck, overall they were quite talented. Essentially all of their documents reflected decent strategic analysis, clear appraisals, and a consistent style. Some could even be used today as a model for writing strategic reports. This difference reflected disparities in the grand strategies of the two nations. The question remains, however: How was Great Britain able to train cohort after cohort of highly skilled practitioners, while Germany was not? Nanjing University's Wang Shengzu proposed the concept of "diplomatic properties" as a means of encapsulating the essential character of a nation's diplomacy. Wang argued that the British Empire could best be represented as "a lion and a fox." How was this maintained for generation after generation? Some perhaps will point to institutions, but there are other intangible attributes such as culture and tradition that are deserving of attention too. Such things became part of the accustomed thinking and actions of people through long periods of education and training. These invisible factors, perhaps, were ultimately stronger and more enduring than any tangible institution. An investigation of this issue is not the task of this book, but this idea has informed my research and writing processes.

I would like to express heartfelt thanks to the teachers and friends who have given me their unwavering support. Then-director of National Defense University's strategy teaching division, Major General Zhu Chenghu, provided me with significant support, without which this book might never have been completed. My former supervisors—the former director of the National Defense University's Institute for Strategic Studies, Rear Admiral Yang Yi, and my doctoral dissertation advisor, the former vice director of the Chinese Academy of Social Sciences World History Institute, Professor Zhou Rongyao—gave me great support during the writing process. Mei Zhaorong, former chairman of the Chinese People's Institute of Foreign Affairs and former ambassador to Germany, Wang Jisi, former dean of the School of International Studies, Peking University, and Zheng Yongnian, director of the East Asian Institute, National University of Singapore all provided valuable advice and encouragement. The former rector of Sweden's National Defense College, Major General (ret.) Karlis Neretnieks generously offered source materials and suggestions. Bundeswehr Lieutenant Colonel Olaf Wiedenfeld greatly helped with translations from German, for which I am truly thankful. Finally, I wish to express thanks to the China Foundation for International and Strategic Studies for its support of this book's publication.

I must admit that, as a researcher of strategy who focuses primarily on contemporary issues, I lack a historian's professional training and was somewhat over-ambitious in terms of managing the vast amount of materials. My German-language skills were self-taught in order to research this period of history. I depended on brute force to examine and translate the primary source materials that form the basis of this book. Even with the aid of friends, however, errors are unavoidable. I hope that readers will not hesitate to offer their advice and criticisms.

Xu Qiyu
Beijing
February 2011

Fragile Rise

1

A Low-Posture Rise

"Bismarck had been in politics long enough to know that conspicuous success invites suspicion and hostility."
Gordon A. Craig

On January 18, 1871, a unified German Empire was proclaimed from the halls of France's Versailles Palace. This marked a revolutionary reconfiguration of Europe's geopolitical map—a previously splintered continental heartland had become a unitary, powerful country; what had once been a periphery for great-power conflict was now a powerful core that could exert influence over its neighbors. During the previous two centuries, France had been the contender for continental hegemony, but no longer. To cite a contemporary witticism, "Europe had lost a mistress and gained a master."[1]

From the German perspective, unification was a clear sign of Germany's rise as a great power. At the same time, however, it also marked the point at which Germany had to begin to bear new burdens and responsibilities. Germany soon found that it had fallen into the famous paradox that has confronted rising great powers throughout history: as its power grew, so too did the apprehensions of other great powers, leading to ceaseless increases of diplomatic and security pressures. In order to respond to the dangers brought by its newfound strength, the newly unified Germany initially sought to keep a low profile by adhering to a policy of "hiding strength and biding time."[2] In terms of grand strategy, this was a period of cautious exploration.

A New Empire's Fragility

The 1871 unification of Germany was accomplished by Prussia during the course of three dynastic wars. Historians agree that this Germany was essentially an enlarged Prussian kingdom. The actual strengths of Prussia and the new Germany, however, were quite different: Prussia had been militarily strong, but the unified Germany became a great power that inspired nervousness in its neighbors. After unification, its national territory nearly doubled, and its population increased from 19.3 million to 34.6 million people.[3] More significantly, however, unification prompted dramatic economic expansion. One historian has commented that "after 1871 German industry advanced in such great strides that all the other economies of Europe, including that of Britain, were left behind."[4]

This rapidly growing great power, however, also had problems and weaknesses. Most significantly, these included structural issues that made the development of a German grand strategy, or any other form of comprehensive planning, very difficult. Outstanding manifestations of this could be found in Germany's political, social, and strategic decision-making systems.

The Political System

From the perspective of domestic politics, the establishment of the German Empire was entirely the result of compromise and balance. Such compromise was embodied in the balance between the ideologies of liberalism and monarchism, and between the demands of German nationalism and the tradition of local sovereignty. As a result, the post-unification German state had a constitution, but was far from being a truly modern constitutional state. Its political system was essentially "mixed": it was a combination of a monarchy and a democratic representative system; it was a combination of a federal system and a centralized system.

The Reichstag's position in German political life was an outstanding example of this phenomenon. At the time of the empire's establishment in 1871, a national representative assembly based on universal, equal, and direct elections had been written into the new imperial constitution. This was an important result of the political cooperation between Bismarck and bourgeois liberals. The Reichstag, made up of 397 representatives who would be elected by all German men over the age of 25, had as its principal power the right to approve executive orders, including the military budget. This does not, however, imply that Germany had a modern, representative government. Compared with Britain, France, and other Western European countries, there were notable limits on the power of the German Reichstag. It could pass or reject various executive orders and budgets, but it did not itself possess the power to set law, nor could it make motions of "no confidence" against the government. In theory, the chancellor of the empire was responsible to the Reichstag; in actuality, however, chancellors answered to the kaiser and served at the kaiser's pleasure. Beyond this, representatives of the monarchs of each of the German states made up the Bundesrat, the upper chamber created by the constitution. This body had power over legislation, thus further reducing the authority of the Reichstag.

By contrast, the German Empire preserved the traditional powers of the monarchy to the greatest degree. The monarch and Germany's representative institutions (both at the imperial and state levels) were linked according to the principles of constitutional monarchy. The monarch himself, however, was the sole possessor of sovereignty, wielded vast powers (especially in military and diplomatic affairs), and had the power of arbitrary rule. In terms of military affairs, the kaiser carried on the Prussian tradition of the "soldier king," and military personnel swore loyalty to him, rather than the government, as command of the military was entirely vested in the monarch. In foreign policy, except for issues concerning trade, communications, and customs taxation—all of which required the approval of the Reichstag—international treaties, including those that established alliances with other countries, were concluded at the sole discretion of the monarch. Declarations of war, too, only required the approval of the upper house, rather than the Reichstag. In fact, at the outbreak of World War I, Kaiser Wilhelm II did not even seek the approval of the Bundesrat before issuing his own declaration of war, which was then only retroactively authorized by the upper house.

The relationship between the imperial government and the empire's constituent states was also a mixed system of federalism and centralized rule. On one hand, few factors contributed to the empire's unity, and this fact was expressed in the form of a loose federalism. For example, in terms of sovereign power, the ruling families of the various constituent states jointly shared national sovereignty; the kaiser was the sole representative of German sovereign power only with respect to foreign policy. This can even be discerned from the kaiser's formal title. When the empire was proclaimed in 1871, Wilhelm I planned to use the title "Kaiser of Germany [Kaiser von Deutschland]," but this was rejected by the kings of Bavaria and Württemberg as impinging on the sovereignty of the constituent states. The title finally selected—"Kaiser of the Germans [deutscher Kaiser]"—only signified nationality.[5] The German military system gave primacy to the army, which itself comprised the armies of the various constituent states, yet these armies were ordinarily responsible to the rulers of those states. Only in wartime would they form a united German Army under the command of the kaiser.

A number of important military institutions also belonged to the constituent states. An example of this was the so-called German General Staff; in actuality, this organization was simply the Prussian General Staff. In terms of structure and position, only the Reichstag and the chancellor represented the empire as a whole. Ministries were not established for the empire, and the chancellor's office took responsibility for the administrative functions of the empire. It was only in 1878 that the chancellor's office was expanded and divided into eight imperial offices that were respectively responsible for foreign affairs, finance, internal affairs, the navy, the postal system, railroads, justice, and matters related to Alsace-Lorraine. The heads of these offices were known as "State Secretaries."[6] Thus, the German Empire lacked cabinet secretaries and, in fact, did not have imperial-level ministers other than the chancellor.

On the other hand, however, Germany did not have a truly federal system. The principal reason for this was that Prussia had an outsized role in managing imperial affairs. It constituted two-thirds of the empire's territory and made up 60 percent of its population; additionally, the empire's most important natural resources and industrial bases lay within its borders. Imperial and constituent state tax revenues, moreover, were kept separate; Prussia's tax revenues typically exceeded those of the German Empire itself—as late as 1913, Prussia's annual revenues of 120 million marks were greater than that of the central government.[7] Even more importantly, Prussia held a special position in political decision-making—its king was the German kaiser, and the imperial chancellor (except for brief intervals in 1873 and 1892–1894) concurrently served as the prime minister of Prussia. Prussia also held 17 of the Bundesrat's 58 seats, enough to veto any proposal that it did not agree with. It could truly be said that whoever controlled Prussia also controlled the fate of the entire German Empire.

The Social System

Post-unification German society was rife with tensions and stresses. The most significant of these included the traditional tension between the individual German states and the unified nation as a whole, as well as the strife between social classes, especially the bourgeois and the Junker landlord class.

The first of these conflicts was very apparent during the early years after the 1871 unification. That unification had been accomplished through Prussian force, so the wounds of defeat lingered in those states (Hanover and Saxony among them) that had originally opposed Prussia. Furthermore, separatism based on different royal houses had deep roots in German history, thus loyalty to a particular dynasty had always been a stronger bond than nationalism. As Bismarck himself noted in his memoirs, *Thoughts and Reminiscences*:

> The particular nationalities, which among us have shaped themselves on the bases of dynastic family and possession, include in most cases

> heterogeneous elements, whose cohesion rest neither on identity of stock nor on similarity of historical development, but exclusively on the fact of some (in the most cases questionable) acquisition by the dynasty whether by the right of the strong, or hereditary succession by affinity or compact of inheritance, or by some reversionary grant obtained from the imperial Court as the price of a vote. Whatever may be the origin of this factitious union of particularist elements, its result is that the individual German readily obeys the command of a dynasty to harry with fire and sword, and with his own hands to slaughter his German neighbors and kinsfolk as a result of quarrels unintelligible to himself.[8]

The legacy of this separatism even affected issues relating to Polish and other minorities in the empire. The unified Germany was supposed to be a nation-state, based on a shared sense of ethno-national identification, rather than loyalty to a dynasty. This produced a serious problem, however: what would be the status of non-German minority groups living on German territory, especially the Poles living in the eastern portions of the country? In the past, Poland had been partitioned between Russia, Prussia, and Austria. The Poles in Prussia owed loyalty only to the Hohenzollern ruling house of that state, while still retaining their Polish ethnic identity. Thus, under Prussian rule, the "Polish Question" was not particularly disruptive. The situation changed dramatically with the unification of the German Empire, however. The construction of a state based on German ethnic identity inspired an awareness of Polish ethnicity, too. Many Polish nobles proclaimed that while they could be Prussians, they never could be Germans.[9]

Religious issues were intertwined with the ethnic problem. Following the Protestant Reformation, Germany was split between Catholics and Protestants. The devastating Thirty Years' War, which had been particularly disastrous for Germany, was partially a result of these religious tensions. German unification did not extinguish these tensions; instead, it breathed new life into them (at least to some extent). In Germany—and particularly among the Prussian people—the 1871 victory and subsequent establishment of the empire was understood as a victory of Protestants over Catholics (which included, but were not limited to, the French). Although Protestantism was dominant across Germany as a whole, there were regions of Catholic predominance in the south and the west. Some of these areas, which included the kingdoms of Bavaria and Württemberg, had both political and religious reasons for separatist inclinations toward Prussia and its Protestant majority.

Furthermore, most Poles were Catholic, and this generated endless tensions with the Protestant-based German state. From the perspective of German policymakers and the German government, validating the leading role of Protestantism was vital to maintaining domestic stability and the unity of the empire. In 1906, German Chancellor Bernhard von Bülow worried about the potential repercussions caused by the addition of the Austro-Hungarian Empire's German-speaking regions (which were majority Catholic), in the event of that empire's collapse: "We shall thereby receive an increase of about fifteen million Catholics so that the Protestants would become a minority… the proportion of strength between the Protestants and the Catholics would become similar to that which at the time led to the Thirty Years' War, i.e., a virtual dissolution of the German empire."[10]

The second type of conflict existed primarily between social classes. Traditional German society had been primarily agricultural. Government officials, and especially the army officer corps, tended to hail from the Junker landlord class. This class both controlled the land and held a dominant position in the country's political life. By the time of unification, however, industrialization was already comparatively advanced and agriculture's share of the national economy was rapidly declining. For the period 1850–1854, the agricultural, forestry, and fishing sectors produced 45.2 percent of the country's net economic output, while the industrial and handicraft sectors accounted for only 20.4 percent. By 1870–1874, however, those proportions had shifted to 37.9 percent and 29.7 percent, respectively.[11] Thus, traditional domestic power structures grew increasingly separated from the country's new economic base. The rising industrial and commercial capitalist classes actively began to demand political power consummate with their enhanced economic position. The post-1871 German Empire, however, had been founded and led by Prussia's feudal aristocracy, allowing the Junker landlord class to maintain the pre-existing distribution of political power. The coincidence of Germany's relatively brief experience as a politically unified nation with its era of super-heated industrialization allowed a feudal, militarized elite to form a "hard core" of power at the center of this industrial society. This contrasts with the experiences of Britain and France, whose slower paces of industrial development provided enough time either to sweep away traditional elites or to absorb them into the new social and economic structures.[12] This resulted in a uniquely German social phenomenon: the coexistence of two evenly matched interest groups—industrial capitalists and Junker landlords—each of which could influence the government through its own channels. Social conflict in the newly-unified Germany thus assumed a bipolar nature.

It should be pointed out that as time went on, national unity grew stronger and identity-based domestic conflict abated somewhat. Class-based social conflict, however, grew increasingly prominent. The increasing might of the working class both expanded the nature of this conflict and made it more complex.

The System of Strategic Decision-making

Germany's system of strategic decision-making can be analyzed primarily from two perspectives—foreign policy and military policy. The chancellor, who was directly accountable to the kaiser, managed both ordinary policy-making and diplomacy. Before 1878, the chancellor's office was responsible for determining and managing foreign policy, and the entire diplomatic apparatus (including Germany's diplomats stationed abroad) were directly managed by Bismarck. After the 1878 expansion of the Chancellory, an Office of Foreign Affairs was established, with a State Secretary for Foreign Affairs in charge. This position was similar to the foreign minister of other countries, but with limited power. Incumbents in this position, in fact, merely assisted the chancellor in his management of foreign policy. The general process for enacting foreign policy at the time could be summarized as: embassies gathered diplomatic information, which the Office of Foreign Affairs aggregated with other information from a variety of sources, and the resulting product was reported to the chancellor. The chancellor made decisions and guided policy, with the final prerogative resting in the hands of the kaiser. In the administration of policy, once the chancellor gave concrete orders, either diplomats stationed abroad were tasked with carrying them out or the chancellor himself would personally work directly with foreign ambassadors in Germany.

In practice, this process often broke down. Germany's diplomatic corps was populated by aristocrats. At times, they would use their special connection to the monarchy to report directly to the emperor. This would lead to conflict between the chancellor and the diplomats. Soon after unification, the German ambassador to France, Count Harry von Arnim, disagreed with Bismarck's policies toward France and proposed instead that Germany proactively seek to stabilize France's domestic situation and aid a monarchical restoration. Bismarck, however, believed that an unstable, republican France was in Germany's best interests, because that situation would be an important impediment to any alliance between France and Russia. A stable, monarchical France, by contrast, would be a "possible and appropriate ally" for czarist Russia.[13] Arnim, rather than accepting Bismarck's disapproval of his plan, wrote directly to the kaiser and thus challenged the chancellor's role in managing foreign policy. Bismarck could not accept this. Tensions between the two escalated until, in the end, Arnim was stripped of his position on charges of "improper handling of public documents." After the conclusion of this incident, foreign policy decision-making was completely centralized in Bismarck's hands. Except for instances when the kaiser himself intervened, foreign policy proceeded according to Bismarck's ideas.

In military affairs, however, the chancellor's power was much more restricted. The German military system was essentially the Prussian system writ large. It had formed under an absolute monarchy and was carefully maintained in order to avoid any interference by civil officials or elected representatives. Germany adopted a system in which military administration and military orders were separated, with the Prussian Army primarily responsible for the management of the entire German Army (with the exceptions of Bavaria, Saxony, and Württemberg). The chancellor was limited to a small and symbolic role. Military appropriations, for instance, required his countersignature on the emperor's approval. Military orders, however—including military planning, the organization and training of the army, mobilization, and deployment—were entirely within the kaiser's purview. The Prussian General Staff (which acted as the General Staff of the entire German Army) wielded enormous power; it was responsible for devising war plans during peacetime and implementing the kaiser's orders during wartime. Additionally, a small number of army and navy senior officers formed a military cabinet that made daily reports to the kaiser and deliberated on military issues. This body was, in fact, parallel to the Prussian military command and the General Staff as a group of military officials directly responsible only to the kaiser. These three military command organizations had no substantial linkages among them; Germany's armed forces lacked a single command center other than the kaiser himself. Thus, the army (mainly the Prussian Army) had a special place in German strategic decision-making which even the chancellor, the empire's political leader, could not influence. The German strategic decision-making process was bifurcated between the political and the military systems, and it was only at the very top—in the person of the kaiser himself—that these two systems linked together.

In summary, the institutional preparations of the newly established German Empire were inherently insufficient. Its decision-making system, political structures, and social structures all contained significant flaws. Each of the many interest groups and institutions sought to expand its own power but, in an environment lacking established rules and regulations, this soon degenerated into a war of all against all. This situation was not beneficial to the formation of a balanced grand strategy and made the execution of comprehensive and continuous planning difficult. Arguably, German grand strategy during the Bismarckian era developed only with great difficulty and, to a significant extent, this development relied solely on Bismarck's own wisdom and actions.

Managing Crises Sparked by Germany's New Strength

The Crises

The newly formed German Empire faced substantial external challenges. First, Germany suffered from a distinctly unfavorable geographic position. Located at the center of Europe, it had long and complex land boundaries. It also bordered the ocean as well, and shared the classic characteristics of both land and sea powers. Thus, it was easy for the nation's power to be split between these two different aspects. At the same time, Germany was surrounded by other powerful countries on land: Russia lay to its east, Austria to its south, and France to its west. Only on its northern flank, on the shores of the North and Baltic Seas, did Germany not share a land boundary with a great power. Yet, from this direction, it had to contend with Britain's dominance of the seas. Bismarck himself summarized this situation by noting that Germany was hindered by its "central and exposed position...with its extended frontier which has to be defended on every side, and the ease with which anti-German coalitions are made."[14]

Even more significantly, however, German unification fundamentally changed the European power structure. Moreover, this had happened as a result of German battlefield victories over two of the continent's five great powers. This necessarily attracted the strong reaction of the other countries—and policies that both Britain and Russia adopted toward the new Germany clearly represented the stresses and pressures brought by the country's newfound power. Before unification, both Britain and Russia would, to varying degrees, aid Prussia in its disputes with France or Austria. They were Prussia's natural allies. After unification, by contrast, Germany leaped into the position of the continent's strongest land power, whereas France and Austria were placed on the defensive. Both Britain and Russia adopted the same view of these dramatic changes: Germany's relative power could not be allowed to continue to grow, nor could France's position be allowed to further erode; thus France would be given support to balance Germany.

Britain's reaction was especially swift. Soon after the end of Germany's wars of unification, Britain began to demonstrate its interest in supporting

France and containing Germany. Even while the Franco-Prussian War was still ongoing, Britain sought to use humanitarian pressure to intervene in the Prussian Army's siege of Paris. During the gap between the armistice and the signing of the Treaty of Frankfurt, influential British political figures busied themselves with an attempt to prevent France's cession of Alsace and Lorraine. The leader of Britain's Conservative Party (and later prime minister), Lord Salisbury, had not approved of his country's negative policy of "neutrality" during the war and instead favored the adoption of an activist foreign policy, asking "Is not the crisis worth some risk?"[15] Benjamin Disraeli, another Conservative Party leader, best encapsulated the British view in a February 9, 1871, statement in the House of Commons. He argued that the Franco-Prussian War was:

> No common war.... This war represents the German revolution, a greater political event than the French revolution of the last century. I don't say a greater, or as a great a social event. What its social consequences may be are in the future. Not a single principle in the management of our foreign affairs, accepted by all statesmen for guidance up to six months ago, any longer exists. There is not a diplomatic tradition which has not been swept away. You have a new world, new influences at work, new and unknown objects and dangers with which to cope.... The balance of power has been entirely destroyed, and the country which suffers most, and feels the effects of this great change most, is England.[16]

Great Britain's true fear, however, was the path that the newly unified Germany would follow. Would this newly risen great strength use its growing power to press its advantages even further, until it established hegemony? Many in the British policymaking elite strongly suspected this in the years immediately following 1871, and many believed that Germany would continue to expand. Disraeli himself thought that "Bismarck is really another old Napoleon again, and he must be bridled," and that, as a consequence, "there might be an alliance between Russia and ourself [sic] for this special purpose."[17] Britain's post-1871 ambassador to Germany, Lord Odo Russell, argued that Bismarck's purpose was "the supremacy of Germany in Europe, and of the German race in the world" and that the annexation of Alsace-Lorraine was merely the first step of a plan to rule all German-speaking European territories.[18]

Russia reacted more slowly to the growth of German power. This was in part due to the traditional ties between the dynasties that ruled the two countries. It was also linked to a beneficial opportunity created by German unification—Russia seized the moment of France's defeat to abrogate the 1856 Treaty of Paris's humiliating stipulation on the "neutralization" of the Black Sea, which had restricted Russian naval power on that body of water. This proved short-lived, however, and the deeper effects of German unification would soon be reflected in Russian policy. Just as had been the case in Britain, Russia moved away from its traditional anti-French alliance with Prussia to become a supporter of France. In September 1872, Bismarck tirelessly worked to arrange a meeting in Berlin between the monarchs of Germany, Austria, and Russia in order to demonstrate the "unity of the monarchies," yet the Russian government struck a discordant note during the proceedings. The Russian Foreign Minister, Alexander Gorchakov, signaled to the French ambassador in Berlin that he supported French rearmament, averring that his country desired a strong France.[19] Bismarck himself had an accurate view of the Russian position, arguing that it was hard to believe that "the Russian cabinet clearly foresaw that, when [the Franco-German War] was over, Russia would have as neighbor so strong and consolidated a Germany." He anticipated that Russia would find a new bottom line once the situation became clear: "That for the Russian policy there is a limit beyond which the importance of France in Europe must not be decreased is explicable. That limit was reached, as I believe, at the Peace of Frankfurt."[20]

France and Austria, which had both been defeated by Germany on the battlefield, naturally became increasingly hostile. After the loss of Alsace-Lorraine, French hatred for Germany became deep-rooted and a desire for vengeance dominated French policy toward Germany until 1914. During the forty-four years leading up to the outbreak of World War I, France reached for every opportunity that presented itself to land a blow against Germany; any nation that was unfriendly to Germany became France's potential ally. Austria's problems with Germany, by comparison, could be accommodated. Austria was relatively weak and was beset by internal crises. In 1867, after it reconstituted itself as the Austro-Hungarian dual monarchy, it lost interest in reclaiming leadership of the German people. After the conclusion of the Franco-Prussian War, Austria increasingly felt that had no hope of vengeance, leading to the dismissal of the revanchist minister-president, Count Friedrich Ferdinand von Beust, and accepted German success.[21] Yet, once Germany became entangled in other crises, Austria-Hungary remained vigilant for opportunities to reclaim its lost position.

Bismarck's Early Responses to the Crises

Bismarck had already mentally prepared himself to deal with these pressures. He deeply understood the principle that newly risen great powers would encounter apprehension. In his *Thoughts and Reminiscences*, a memoir which functioned as his political last testament, he again pointed to the dangers brought by national strength, and again reminded his fellow Germans that they should manage their foreign affairs with care.[22]

Recognizing a problem is one thing; solving it is yet another. During the initial phase after unification, Bismarck continued to use the old methods of Prussia to respond to these new pressures. To a certain extent, it was as if he thought that a post-unification German Empire could act like the pre-unification Prussia, "pretending" that it was not a rising power. This, perhaps, was a German version of the "hide and bide" strategy.

For example, Bismarck maintained a low profile in his relations with Great Britain, hoping to use the historical tradition of alliances between Prussia and Britain to ease British apprehensions and pressures. In November 1870, the British ambassador to Germany expressed his country's serious concerns about the recent Russian abrogation of the clauses in the Treaty of Paris that related to the Black Sea. The ambassador also noted that England believed that Germany had secretly supported Russia in this move as a reward for Russian neutrality in the Franco-Prussian War. Bismarck did not respond directly, but used the opportunity to express friendship toward Britain. He claimed that Germany and Russia did not have a secret agreement and that the relations between the two powers were all public. With regard to this kind of relationship with Russia, he "not only does not attempt to deny, but openly declares to be a national and family alliance of friendship and gratitude for past services, which it is his duty to maintain until future events bring about more advantageous alliances." Bismarck also emphasized, however, that Great Britain and Austria were Germany's "natural allies" and that Germany would make sacrifices for such an alliance. This clearly hints that, if Great Britain had been willing to conclude an alliance with Germany similar to the ones that had once existed between it and Prussia, then Germany might abandon its support for Russia.[23] This was an attempt to apply the model of Anglo-Prussian relations to Anglo-German relations. Such a strategy could not succeed. Post-unification Germany was not the old Prussia, and Great Britain's suspicions of this newly risen continental great power were deep-rooted. Bismarck's suggestion, as a consequence, would not be acted on and the issue was left unsettled.

Bismarck's policies toward Austria-Hungary also mirrored the old Prussia-Austria relationship, particularly in an emphasis on the relationship between the monarchs. Due to the growth of the international communist movement at that time, autocratic rulers and the capitalist classes felt threatened. Bismarck took threats and crises as opportunities, as they could both be used to force others to cooperate with him. Or, failing that, they could be used to counter those inside Germany who were opposed to him. Bismarck was an admirer of former Austrian Chancellor Klemens von Metternich, and thus naturally wanted to use international communism (particularly after the 1871 Paris Commune) to frighten monarchs into reviving the "Holy Alliance" and stabilizing the European great powers. Yet this old method proved problematic. The new Germany was immeasurably more powerful than old Prussia. Austria and Russia both worried that a revived Holy Alliance would naturally be centered on Germany. Moreover, Austria and Russia themselves had unresolved conflicts in the Balkans and were unwilling to be drawn into an alliance together.

Austria-Hungary, therefore, hoped that Germany would distance itself from Russia and would support Austria against Russia at the critical moment. Russia's desires were more complex. On the one hand, it was unwilling to acknowledge Germany's enhanced international status and was not interested in acting in accordance with German ideas. On the other hand, Russia believed that it possessed enough "freedom of action" that it could maintain good relations with France or even Austria in order to check Germany, so Russia was not in a hurry to accept Bismarck's notions of a new "Holy Alliance."

Bismarck soon adapted old Prussian strategy to meet this new reality through the addition of tactics from power politics. He first turned his attention to the relatively weak Austro-Hungarian Empire, on the theory that once he had brought the Austrians on board he could bargain with the relatively stronger Russians from a better position. For the subsequent two decades, Bismarck's policies toward Austria and Russia would follow this line of thought. His negotiations with the Austrians clearly revealed that he would not sacrifice Germany's ties with Russia for an improved relationship with Austria-Hungary, and that the Austrians would have no choice but to accept this. The Austrian Emperor Franz Joseph I's formal visit to Berlin in 1872 marked Austria's acceptance of its defeat by Germany. The growing friendship between the two German-speaking powers naturally made Russia nervous.

In order to avoid exclusion by these two countries, Russian Czar Alexander II and Gorchakov also journeyed to Berlin for a "fortuitous" meeting of the three monarchs. This "meeting of three emperors," however, was simply diplomatic posturing and did not result in any new signed agreements. In fact, through this meeting, both Austria and Russia realized that, given that the conflict between the two countries was unlikely to diminish, neither could allow the other to build stronger relations with Germany, and thus a decision by all three countries to be in contact was the optimal choice.

In May 1873, Kaiser Wilhelm I, accompanied by Chancellor Bismarck and Helmuth von Moltke, chief of the Prussian General Staff, paid a return visit to Russia. There, he signed a military alliance with the Russians that obligated the two powers to send an army of 200,000 soldiers if either was attacked by another European power.[24] This agreement revealed that Russia was prepared to, at the very least, maintain neutrality in any resumption of the Franco-Prussian War; this functioned as an indirect guarantee of continued German occupation of Alsace-Lorraine. Bismarck was not primarily interested in this, however. Instead, he attached far more importance to orchestrating the relationship between the three powers. From his perspective, as long as Germany, Austria, and Russia could maintain a basic unanimity on foreign affairs, then France would have no opportunity to act on its revanchist desires. As a consequence, he declared that the agreement would be invalid without Austrian participation. Austria was not willing to join this restrictive guarantee and instead embarked on its own direct negotiations with the Russians. In June 1873, during a state visit to the Schönbrunn Palace, the Russian czar and Austrian emperor inked a very general agreement that provided a broad commitment to "maintaining the peace of Europe." From Germany's perspective, this agreement did not have nearly the value of the German-Russian military agreement, but it did thaw the relationship between Russia and Austria, thus allowing Germany to avoid having to choose between the two. This satisfied Bismarck. In October 1873, Germany joined the Schönbrunn Convention, thus forming the first League of Three Emperors.

While organizing the relationship between these three monarchies, Bismarck also closely followed Britain's reaction. He feared that the league might provoke Britain, pushing it to ally with France; to avoid this, he constantly signaled to Britain that this arrangement would not be detrimental to British interests. Thus, he continued to support a "low posture" in international affairs, but at the same time he took concrete steps to express the purity of Germany's intentions. In the summer of 1873, for example, Germany facilitated the first Anglo-Russian agreement on spheres of influence in Central

Asia, helping to stabilize Anglo-Russian relations. Overall, this "low posture" policy bore results during the years between 1871 and 1875. Germany's entire foreign relations environment was completely changed, and both English and German misgivings about Germany's rise were somewhat ameliorated. Italy, fearing French interference in its own conflicts with the Vatican, proactively sought German support. For some time, all of the structural pressures sparked by Germany's rise seemed to be extinguished.

The 1875 "War in Sight" Crisis

Acting in accordance with the old Prussian model could not mislead others into thinking that Germany was merely Prussia, nor would it change the fact of Germany's rise as a great power. The outbreak of the 1875 "War in Sight" Crisis revealed Germany's seemingly improved diplomatic situation to be nothing more than a mirage. The German version of "hide and bide" would be seriously tested. This crisis originated in the collection of pressures brought about by Germany's rise. Its proximate causes, however, were fairly complex and were inextricably linked to the domestic struggle between politics and religion.

The Kulturkampf *and Franco-German Tensions*

Prussia had been a predominantly Protestant country. In the early nineteenth century, having confirmed the position of Protestantism within the country, Prussia practiced a separation of church and state. At the same time, Catholic forces worked to maintain their own rights as a minority. After 1852, the Prussian legislature included Roman Catholic political groups. These entities sought to protect the rights of Catholics within this Protestant-majority country, but never impeded Prussian national policy.

After the unification of Germany, however, as the concepts of nation and state became ever more tightly intertwined, the relationships between religion and politics—and between Catholics and Protestants—became increasingly tense. This was in step with broader trends across Europe. In the second half of the nineteenth century, the Catholic Church had been increasingly excluded from national political life, and the separation of church and state had become a general trend. The Church decided to strike back against this worrisome situation. Under the leadership of Pope Pius IX, the Catholic Church launched a powerful movement to consolidate its authority. In 1864, the Vatican released a tract titled the "Syllabus of Errors," that opposed the separation of church and state and reaffirmed papal authority over secular affairs. Six years later, the Church issued a statement on papal infallibility that claimed the pope represented God's will. These acts further increased tension between the Catholic Church and state governments.

Bismarck had initially hoped to remain on the sidelines of this international aspects of this conflict between religion and politics. As late as 1870, he instructed the Prussian ambassador to the Vatican to adopt a restrained and neutral response. Soon, however, this conflict reached Germany itself. German liberals and Protestants strongly opposed the actions of the Catholic Church, while German Catholics themselves were split on the issue of papal infallibility. Catholics opposed to this policy experienced persecution at the hands of the German Catholic establishment and sought the protection of the government. Soon afterward, the Catholic political groups began to proactively organize themselves and, in December 1870, formed their own political party, the Catholic Centre Party. In the 1871 imperial Diet elections, the party won 63 of the 382 open seats and earned nearly 20 percent of the ballots cast. They emerged from the election as Germany's second largest party and the largest opposition party to Bismarck's government. Catholic activism also became entangled with the Polish question. The majority of Poles were Catholic; many Catholic churches in Polish areas advocated for the use of Polish, rather than government-mandated German. The German government faced the threat of an alliance between Catholic religious interests and Polish national interests, causing issues of national security to be implicated in this struggle over religious rights.

Bismarck's government soon took action to clarify the connection between church and state and to solidify the unity of the new state. In the summer of 1871, the government slowly moved to exclude Catholic influence from public affairs. Within the nation's borders, the government initiated a movement opposed to clerical power that came to be known as the *Kulturkampf*. State institutions generally have difficulty gaining the upper hand in struggles against popular religious beliefs and, unsurprisingly, the *Kulturkampf* quickly became very complex. Not only did the German government's strong-arm tactics fail to weaken Catholic forces, but they also sparked a widespread sympathy for Catholics. Catholic political power continued to grow in this period and, in the January 1874 imperial elections, the Catholic Centre Party expanded its representation in the Diet from 63 to 91 seats. Furthermore, Catholic forces inside Germany received support from both the Vatican and French Catholics. This highlighted the international aspects of this domestic political dispute, as well as the extent to which it touched upon substantive diplomatic problems, such as sensitive aspects of the Franco-German relationship. In early August 1873, the bishop of Nancy, France, sent an open letter to his diocese, asking them to pray for the return of Alsace and Lorraine to France. A month later, the bishop of Paris issued a similar call. Soon after, five French bishops advocated that Catholics in Alsace and Lorraine work with German Catholics in opposition to that government's repressive measures.

Bismarck suspected that France and the Vatican were secretly plotting against Germany, and these developments inside France only served to deepen that suspicion. In the Treaty of Frankfurt that had concluded the Franco-Prussian War, Germany had demanded 5 billion francs as an indemnity for the French territory it had occupied. The German intention had been to saddle France with a huge financial burden in order to slow its recovery. The French paid these war reparations much more quickly than Germany had expected. By 1873, the payments had been completed and by September 16, Germany evacuated territories occupied by its military. On November 20 of that year, French voters elected Patrice de MacMahon, a former subordinate of Napoleon III, president of the republic. The constitutional crisis that had vexed French politics began to recede and the country began to stabilize. French rearmament had already started after the conclusion of the war, and by 1873 the pace of that process quickened. This rapid French political, economic, and military recovery attracted a high level of attention from German policymakers. The German military led the response. Moltke, the chief of the Prussian General Staff, had already drafted a plan for "preventative war" against the French as early as 1872. On May 1, 1873, he mentioned the possibility of another war with France in discussions with the British ambassador.[25] Tension lay in the atmosphere.

Rumors of war began to circulate, which proved even more effective at stirring up the situation. In December 1874, German newspapers carried the information that a Belgian would attempt to assassinate Bismarck, and that the bishop of Paris had already pledged 60,000 francs to support this endeavor. Bismarck issued a stern rebuke to the Belgian government. In early 1875, the rumor began to circulate that Bismarck intended to partition Belgium.[26] Another rumor that year was started by the Radowitz mission to Russia. Problems had arisen in the Russo-German relationship, and the German ambassador too Russia had resigned due to illness, leaving the office vacant. Gorchakov was meanwhile seeking to distance his country from Germany in order to demonstrate to Germany the value of a relationship with Russia. In February 1875, Bismarck sent Joseph Maria von Radowitz as a special envoy to St. Petersburg on a mission to coordinate the two countries' policies toward Serbia and Montenegro, as well as to mollify Czar Alexander II's displeasure with Germany. The rumor that spread, which Bismarck blamed on Gorchakov, suggested that Radowitz was seeking either Russian support or neutrality in any upcoming second Franco-Prussian War. In return, Germany would support Russian policy in the Balkans.[27] In this way, the possibility of renewed Franco-German conflict came dimly into view.

"War in Sight"?

On March 4, 1875, Germany forbade the export of horses after Bismarck received reports that German horse dealers had received an order from French buyers for the immediate purchase of ten thousand horses.[28] On March 12, the French parliament passed a law expanding the size of each army battalion from three to four companies and each regiment from three to four battalions. According to the calculations of the Prussian General Staff, this law would raise the wartime strength of the French military by 144,000 soldiers, which might be enough to change the balance of power between France and Germany.[29] Suddenly, it seemed that the two sides were taking the first steps down the road to war.

Bismarck's calculations were equally complex. First, he did not agree with the German military's (and particularly the Prussian General Staff's) perception that France was preparing to launch a revanchist war.[30] Instead, he held the opposite view: France would not risk another war with Germany without first securing an ally.[31] Second, Bismarck seemed to really believe that there was an international Catholic conspiracy, centered on France and the Vatican, that opposed Germany. As the *Kulterkampf* slowly lost ground at home, Germany needed a foreign policy victory to restore its prestige and to prove that the new empire would not be split by the *Kulturkampf*. Third, he could use this moment of increasing tensions in order to gain the support of other great powers and to bring greater pressure on France and thus prevent or delay its recovery of military might.[32] He therefore set off alarm bells about a war with France. On April 5, 1875, the German newspaper *Kölnische Zeitung* ran an article headlined "New Alliances" that linked Franco-German tensions to the *Kulturkampf*, stoked fears about the purpose of French rearmament, and pointed to a "Catholic coalition directed against Protestant Germany" comprising France, Austria-Hungary, Italy, and the Vatican.[33] On April 9, the Berlin-based *Die Post* printed the famous article, "Is War in Sight?" This piece forcefully stated that France was preparing for a revanchist war and this had caused the tense atmosphere of imminent war to descend upon

Europe.[34] High German officials also became involved in hinting at war. At a dinner on April 21, 1875, German envoy Radowitz offered a philosophical view on the issue of war and peace to the French ambassador to Germany. He first explained that the present crisis between France and Germany had already been resolved, but added that if France continued to harbor revanchist desires, then why should Germany sit and wait while France rearms and seeks allies? From the "political, philosophical, and even Christian" perspectives, it would be reasonable for Germany to launch a preventive war. On May 2, Moltke, chief of the Prussian General Staff, said in a discussion with the British ambassador that, in the event of a preventive war, responsibility for the conflict lay with the side seeking conflict, not the side that launched the first blow. But, he added, if the great powers of Europe all stood on Germany's side, thus deflating French hopes of revenge, then war could be avoided.[35]

On the whole, Bismarck still relied on a Prussian style of diplomacy, especially as it was practiced during the wars of German unification: proactively aggravate tensions, then use a series of diplomatic maneuvers to force the other side to make concessions. He did not, however, realize that a fundamental change had taken place or that Germany's status within the international system was entirely different from Prussia's old position. Before 1871, Prussia could instigate a small crisis that would force the other great powers to mediate, but post-unification Germany could not act in such a manner. For the other European great powers, this new Germany was too strong. Any threatening behavior on its part required their full attention—and perhaps might even prompt other nations to ally themselves in opposition. Thus, by 1875, it was France that needed to be protected and Germany that needed to be restrained. German calls to protect against the French threat not only failed to generate a sympathetic response, but also turned Germany into a target for criticism. The various powers, particularly Britain and Russia, desired to guarantee against further erosion of France's status and power in order to balance Germany's rise. Thus, Bismarck's failure in the "War in Sight" Crisis was assured.

Furthermore, France's diplomacy during this crisis—unlike its inept handling of the crisis leading up to the Franco-Prussian War—was foresighted. The French Foreign Minister, Louis Decazes, grasped the extent of apprehension about Germany's rise. His diplomatic efforts emphasized the scope of German threats and urged other great powers to intervene. He actively lobbied the governments of Britain, Russia, and Austria, portraying Bismarck as a threat to European peace. Decazes also utilized the power of the international media. He ordered a response to German justifications of preventive war drafted; when published in the *London Times* on May 6, 1875, this response created an impact throughout the continent.

Other Great Powers React

Great Britain took the lead in intervening. As early as February 10, 1874, Queen Victoria had written to Wilhelm I, warning him that a second attack on France would have serious consequences.[36] After the publication of the editorial "Is War in Sight?"in April 1875, British Foreign Secretary Edward Stanley, Earl of Derby, immediately sought a meeting with the German ambassador. He conveyed to the ambassador that France had already assured Britain that its military reorganization was only intended to restore French power and authority in Europe and that none of France's political leaders believed that they could prevail in a second war with Germany.[37] On May 9, the British ambassador in Berlin, Lord Russell, sought an emergency meeting with the German foreign secretary to declare that his country did not believe that France was planning to start a war and did not intend to reclaim its lost territories through military force. Great Britain, furthermore, was deeply disturbed by the current crisis.[38] Britain extended an invitation to Italy, Russia, and Austria-Hungary jointly to pressure Germany in order to "guarantee the peace." Lord Derby addressed the British House of Lords on May 31, proclaiming that France lacked any desire to start a war and suggested that "persons of high position in Germany" were responsible for this crisis.[39] This address was printed by the *London Times* the following day, making the attitude of the British government toward the "War in Sight" Crisis clear to Europe.

The Russian standpoint was similar. On May 5 and 6, 1875, the Russian ambassador in Britain, Peter Shuvalov, stopped in Berlin on a return trip from St. Petersburg to London to convey his government's displeasure with the crisis directly to Bismarck and Wilhelm I. The common view toward this crisis in Great Britain and Russia sparked a partnership between the two countries. After Shuvalov arrived in London, he reported to Lord Derby that Bismarck had been in an extremely poor mental state, full of suspicion that the other European states were uniting against Germany.[40] On May 10, Queen Victoria herself wrote to the czar, proposing that the two countries take joint action. Under this plan, the czar would make a peace proposal during a trip to Berlin, which the British ambassador would be ordered to use all means at his disposal to support. Between May 10 and May 13, the czar and Gorchakov visited Berlin, where they conveyed Russian opposition to a German preventive attack on France and demanded that Bismarck clearly explain his intentions. Bismarck was only able to reply that Germany had no plans for preventive war, whereupon Gorchakov telegraphed Russian embassies around the world, claimed that peace in Europe was now assured.[41]

At this point, German leaders suddenly realized that their country had been completely isolated within Europe: Britain and Russia had united to pressure Germany, Austria-Hungary was sitting on the sidelines, and Italy was attempting to play both sides by accepting the British proposal and passing information to Germany in hopes of profiting itself.[42] Of these, intervention by the British proved to be the most active and effective. This left a deep impression on Bismarck. He remarked, with no little sarcasm, that had Britain devoted even one-tenth as much energy to preventing war in 1870, then France would never have attacked Germany and the Franco-Prussian War would never have begun. At the same time, he was forced to admit that "we must draw the conclusion that England was prepared to raise Europe against us and in France's favor, if at any time we intended—which is now not the case—to make military or diplomatic preparations against the renewal of French attacks."[43] Germany had no choice but to retreat and explain to all that it had no intention of gaining the initiative by striking the first blow. This process extended over a long period of time, causing the German government to fall into a state of reaction on the international and domestic fronts. As late as February 1876, Bismarck spoke before the German Diet to offer an explanation with the hope of disavowing his government's responsibility of the crisis.

Arguably, the "War in Sight" Crisis—which Bismarck had provoked—ended in his complete defeat. Bismarck's own mistaken judgments about Germany's new international status and strategic environment were the primary causes for this defeat. In particular, he failed to fully appreciate the feeling of insecurity that Germany's rise would generate in the other great powers. He continued to use the old tactics of the Prussian era, and as a result ran afoul of an important principle: a rising power must go out of its way to avoid becoming the flashpoint of conflict. This mistaken policy caused Bismarck to lose control over events. Britain, Russia, and other great powers were able to seize the opportunity to make their stance known to Germany, while France obtained what was, in effect, a security guarantee. Lord Derby, not without a level of sarcasm, commented that Bismarck's attempt to test European opinion had now been answered.[44] This "answer" had a deeper implication, too: that a "low posture" was a wholly insufficient response to the stresses brought by Germany's rise. At best, such a policy could only work during moments of calm.

The "War in Sight" Crisis left a deep impact on Bismarck himself. In May 1875, he offered his resignation (which was duly rejected by the kaiser) and then removed himself from Berlin, resting at his country estate in Varzin until November.[45] During these months away, Bismarck placed himself in a form of self-imposed exile. He took this period of extreme isolation as a chance to reflect on Germany's current situation and its future. No one will ever know exactly what Bismarck's thoughts were during this period, nor will we ever know if this experience matches Arnold Toynbee's notion of "withdrawal and return."[46] Historical research is only able to reveal that, after the "War in Sight" Crisis, a readjustment of German-style "hide and bide" policy began. Bismarck started to think more about the new reality of Germany's rise and this thinking culminated in a far-reaching, comprehensive strategic plan.

The Growth of International Responsibilities: The Near East Crisis and Germany's Choice

The "War in Sight" Crisis revealed the pressures a rising Germany placed on other great powers; the subsequent Near East Crisis, by contrast, highlighted ways in which Germany's rise forced it to take on greater international responsibilities and the various risks associated with them. Even during the period of Bismarck's "low posture" foreign policy, Germany had not been able to avoid this completely. Even more critically, the Near East Crisis, which began in 1875, struck at the very heart of Germany's foreign policy—the League of Three Emperors.

As mentioned above, this League of Three Emperors was not an alliance directed at any other power (in present-day terminology, it was not aimed at a third party). Instead, it was an attempt to build an alliance that could paper over the conflicts of interest between the three countries, particularly the tensions between Russia and Austria over the Balkans. From Germany's perspective, this was of prime importance. As long as Germany was part of an alliance system with both Austria and Russia, neither of those two countries would have reason to seek an alliance with France or any other power. France, as a result, would be isolated. This, in turn, would secure Germany's status and security within the European system.

This alliance, however, faced two serious challenges. The first was Great Britain. Historically, Great Britain had never been comfortable with alliances among the great powers of the continent. Bismarck's league reminded many of Metternich's Holy Alliance, and naturally led to British fears of an alliance that could dominate the continent. As a result, Britain would seize every opportunity it could to weaken the league. The second was the Eastern Question. Most of the inhabitants of the Balkan peninsula were Slavs, although this Slavic population had been ruled by the Ottoman Empire since the late fourteenth century. As the Ottoman Empire declined in the ninteenth century, Slavic struggles for independent statehood convulsed the Balkans, creating what contemporaries called the Eastern Question. This question had the potential to overturn the existing balance of power between the great powers. First, disputes over the disposition of former Ottoman lands could create serious conflict (or even war) between the powers. Second, this situation could serve to increase Russian power in the Balkans (or even in the broader Mediterranean region); Russia saw itself as a "liberator" of its "Slavic brothers," and newly independent Slavic states were seen as extensions of Russian power. Third, once the Ottoman Empire collapsed, the Austro-Hungarian Empire would become the next "Sick Man of Europe." That empire was home to a large Slavic population as well, and any further growth of the Slavic national movement could threaten to dissolve Austria-Hungary.[47] In terms of the Eastern Question, Russian and Austrian interests were thus opposed to one another. If tensions in this region became inflamed, Germany might be forced to choose one ally over another. This background structured the Near East Crisis of 1875–1878.

A Basic Chronology of the 1875–1878 Near East Crisis

An anti-Ottoman uprising broke out in Bosnia-Herzegovina in July 1875. Fueled by ethnic sympathies, support for national liberation movements, and a desire to seize Ottoman territory, three countries—Serbia, Montenegro, and Russia—began to use a variety of channels to funnel aid to the rebels.[48] Austria-Hungary grew concerned about this rebellion's growth by the end of the year. On December 30, Austro-Hungarian Chief Minister Count Gyula Andrássy proposed a series of moderate reforms for the Ottomans to implement and asked for the other great powers to join in forcing Ottoman compliance. This, he hoped, would serve to pacify the rebels and the other Balkan territories still under Ottoman rule. Great Britain, however, rejected this approach. British reasoning was two-fold. First, Prime Minister Benjamin Disraeli did not believe that Britain had much at stake in this conflict. Second, and more important, both Disraeli and British Foreign Secretary Derby understood the League of Three Emperors as a diplomatic mechanism for isolating Britain from continental affairs, and hoped that this crisis could be used to drive wedges between Russia, Austria-Hungary, and Germany.

The intensity of this crisis within Ottoman territory only increased in 1876. Early in the year, the uprising spread to Bulgaria, and both the German and the French consuls in Salonica were killed. Disturbances even broke out in Constantinople, the capital, and the entire Ottoman imperial edifice seemed to be on the verge of collapse. Germany, Russia, and Austria-Hungary planned another great power intervention in order to stabilize the situation. Representatives from the three countries gathered in Berlin and proposed a cease-fire, which Great Britain rejected. Britain's policy was commonly understood as a form of encouragement for the rebels. By the end of June, Serbia had declared war on the Ottoman Empire, and Montenegro followed suit on July 2. The crisis had intensified.

Russia and Austria-Hungary, the great powers with the most at stake in the Balkans, each had their own assessment of these trends. The Austrians hoped to maintain the Ottoman Empire in its present boundaries—but, if changes were to be made, then Austria must receive her fair share in order to limit Russian and Serbian expansionism. Within Russia, pan-Slavists took the ethnic uprisings in the Balkans as their own issue and viewed the liberation of Balkan Slavs as a natural expansion of Russian power. Serbian and Montenegrin declarations of war against the Ottoman Empire were greeted with jubilation inside Russia, and over a thousand volunteers rushed to join the Serbian war effort. Significant quantities of weapons were shipped to Serbia and a Russian general even took command of the Serbian Army.[49] The Russian government (particularly the czar and Gorchakov), however, did not approve of nationalism or national liberation, although they saw the situation in the Balkans as evolving favorably to Russian interests. As a consequence, the Russian government saw a need to reach an agreement with the Austrians in response to this developing situation. After negotiations between Gorchakov and Andrássy at Reichstadt, the two sides reached a secret agreement on July 8, 1876. The two sides agreed that, in the event of an Ottoman victory, the Turks would be compelled to accept the *status quo ante*, while in the event of a Serbian victory, Serbia and Montenegro would split the territory of the Sanjak of Novi Pazar, Austria would gain the lion's share of Bosnia, Russia would reclaim territories lost at the end of the Crimean War, and Bulgaria, Romania, and Albania would be granted independence. If the Ottoman Empire collapsed entirely, Constantinople would be made a free city.[50] Two things here are worth nothing: first, as this agreement made clear, Austria-Hungary had already agreed in principle to the partition of Turkey (marking a significant change from its stated policy in the December 30, 1875, Andrássy Note) and second, both sides seemed to expect the Ottomans to be defeated, thus the negotiations focused on how to deal with victorious Serbia and Montenegro.

Events in the field proved that the Ottoman Empire was not as weak as Slav nationalists had imagined. The Turkish Army established a new headquarters and, in September 1876, decisively defeated the armies of Serbia and Montenegro. According to the terms of the Reichstadt Agreement, Russia and Austria should have considered pressuring the Ottomans to return to the *status quo ante*. An enormous change, however, had taken place in Russia, as public opinion had become inflamed and the voices inside the government that advocated for war had gained the upper hand. Russian policy had already begun take steps toward armed intervention. Russian policymakers, however, faced two serious considerations. The first was British intervention, which had the potential to turn the situation into a replay of the devastating Crimean War. The second was Austria-Hungary's stance. If the Austrians took advantage of the Russian Army's deployment against the Ottomans in the central and southern Balkans to send their own army down the Danube River, the Russian Army would be cut off. At that moment, British intervention against Russia seemed unlikely, as British public opinion was fixated on Turkish atrocities against Bulgarian civilians. William Gladstone, leader of the British Liberal Party and former prime minister, was at the forefront of this anti-Ottoman campaign, making it difficult for the Tory government in power to take any action supportive of the Ottomans. Russia initially considered using force, or the threat of force, against Austria-Hungary, and sought to feel out German opinion. In response, Bismarck made it clear that Germany would not allow Austria-Hungary to be routed.[51] The Russian leadership then returned to the thinking that had originally led them to the Reichstadt Agreement and decided to "buy" Austrian support. The two countries inked a new agreement at Budapest on January 15, 1877.[52] They added a supplement to this understanding on March 18. Austria-Hungary promised neutrality in the coming war and to oppose the attempts of other great powers to broker a cease-fire. In return, Russia agreed to support Austria-Hungary's occupation of Bosnia. With these issues resolved, Russia could make war on Turkey without undue worry.

Russia declared war on April 24, 1877, and the Near East Crisis entered a new phase. Russia, however, did not achieve the speedy victory it expected, as its army was checked at Plevin. Russian advances only overcame Turkish resistance in December. By January, they were within striking distance of Constantinople itself, although the Russian military was too exhausted and overextended to launch a final assault against the city. During the months after the Russian declaration of war, British opinion, influenced by the stubborn Turkish resistance, had made an almost comic about-face, as the nation's public sympathies turned toward the Turks.[53] The British government was thus forced to taken actions of its own. In mid-February 1878, ships from the Royal Navy entered the waters near Istanbul. Soon afterwards, on March 3, a Turko-Russian peace agreement, the Treaty of San Stefano, was signed.

For Russia, this treaty turned out to be a serious diplomatic failure. The Russian representative at the negotiations, General Nikolay Ignatyev, was an ardent pan-Slavist intoxicated by military success. He did not see how fragile his country's entire diplomatic situation actually was. He added stipulations to the treaty that went beyond his government's instructions, ignored the interests of the other great powers, and cast a blind eye to the previous treaties between Russia and Austria-Hungary. The territory that he demanded be ceded to Russia—largely lands in the Caucasus on the eastern shore of the Black Sea, though also including some territory in Europe itself—did not unduly alarm European nations. Yet he (perhaps under the influence of pan-Slavic ideology) also planned for a "Greater Bulgaria" that reached from the Black Sea to the Aegean. This state would remain under Russian military occupation for two years. This not only represented a significant expansion of Russian power in the Balkans, it also raised the specter of a Russian outlet on the Mediterranean via its new creation in Bulgaria.[54]

For Austria-Hungary, however, this treaty meant that not only would its own southern route to the Aegean be blocked, but also that the Bosnian territories that Russia had used to buy Austrian acceptance of the war would be transformed into independent states. Austria's only compensation would be a form of nominal oversight of those new countries. All of the pre-war agreements with Russia appeared to have been in vain. For the British, no Russian outlet on the Mediterranean would be acceptable. Britain had already been willing to fight the Crimean War to prevent that outcome in the 1850s; the opening of the Suez Canal during the intervening two decades only raised the strategic significance of the Mediterranean for the British. Both Britain and Austria-Hungary took the lead in opposing the Treaty of San Stefano. Three days after the treaty was signed, Austria-Hungary invited the other great powers to a conference in Berlin, where the issue of treaty revision would be discussed.

The Russians attempted to buy Austrian support again in the weeks before the Berlin Conference met, but the Austrians would not be moved. Left without a choice, the Russians attempted direct negotiations with the British. British Prime Minister Disraeli's intentions were clear—to block any Russian access to the Mediterranean and to widen the divisions within the League of Three Emperors—and thus he was happy to make a deal.[55] An Anglo-Russian agreement was concluded on May 30 that pulled back the Bulgarian border from the Mediterranean and simultaneously divided Bulgaria into two parts. This took care of British opposition to the Treaty of San Stefano. Yet Britain set another scheme into motion, too. Although the British agreed to Russian annexation of Ottoman lands in Asia, they also signed a secret treaty with the Turks on June 4 that guaranteed the territorial integrity of their Asian holdings. This gave the British an excuse to deploy troops to Turkey if needed, and allowed the British to compel the cessation of Cyprus, which then became an important British strategic base in the Mediterranean. On June 6, Britain also inked an accord with Austria-Hungary that supported Austrian claims in Bosnia in exchange for Austrian acquiescence to the June 4 agreement with Russia. This was the background for the famous Berlin Conference.

Germany's Dilemma

The 1875–1878 Near East Crisis placed Germany in a delicate situation. Working in Germany's favor was the fact that it had fewer direct connections with the Balkans than any other great power, giving it the option of taking a detached position on the issues at hand.[56] Working against Germany, however, was that the crux of the crisis was a dispute between Russia and Austria that could result in an armed conflict between the two. This created a dilemma for Germany: without German intervention, one of the two powers might be defeated, thus knocking Germany's security environment out of balance; German intervention on one side, on the other hand, would offend the other power and might result in the offended party joining an anti-German alliance with France, thus degrading Germany's security environment. Even if the crisis did not result in a war between the great powers, and instead was resolved through a conference, the results could place Germany in an unfavorable situation. In such a conference, Russia might be willing to have dealings with France, and Austria might draw close to Britain, again placing Germany in a delicate and dangerous situation: either it would have the thankless job of mediating between the two sides or it would lean toward the British and Austrian position, leaving it open to threats on both its eastern and western fronts from France and Russia. As the crisis developed, doubts about Germany grew. The German diplomat Friedrich von Holstein claimed in his correspondence that some believed that Germany hoped to use the crisis as an opportunity to "attack somebody," but, in fact, "the two or three people who have influence here have not the slightest intention of doing so."[57]

Bismarck was very clear that, in a situation such as this, the more active Germany became, the more dangerous its predicament would become, just like a man struggling to free himself from quicksand. Thus, in his handling of the Near East Crisis, Bismarck's basic principle was to emphasize the point that Germany had the least at stake: "Our reputation and our security will develop all the more permanently, the more, in all conflicts which do not immediately touch us, we hold ourselves in reserve and do not show ourselves sensitive to every attempt to stir up and utilize our vanity...in just the same way in future Eastern negotiations Germany, by holding back, will be able to turn to its advantage the fact that it is the Power which has least interest in Oriental questions."[58] Bismarck opposed demands that Germany act as a mediator and did not support a German-hosted great power conference. From his perspective, such a meeting would only serve to reveal the splits that had developed within his alliance and would expose himself to criticism from all sides.[59] Bismarck had two objectives: preventing the crisis from sparking a general European war, as Germany would inevitably be drawn in to such a war, and preventing both Russia and Austria from feeling completely isolated, which would push them closer to France. Arguably, all of Bismarck's policies during this crisis and during the Berlin Conference were derived from these two objectives.

Not long after the beginning of the Near East Crisis, in December 1875, Bismarck had already expressed to Gorchakov that Germany's primary concerns were to maintain peace in Europe and friendship between Austria and Russia.[60] He also emphasized again that Germany had no concrete interests in the Balkans. During a speech in the Reichstag, he proclaimed that "the whole of the Balkans is not worth the bones of a single Pomeranian grenadier." Bismarck adopted active strategies for managing the crisis, too, such as encouraging the other great powers to partition Ottoman territories in such a way as to create a new pattern of mutually balancing interests and thus reducing the pressure on Germany.[61] On January 2, 1876, Bismarck proposed to the British that they, the Russians, and the Austrians divide up Ottoman territory, with the Austrians receiving Bosnia, the Russians Bessarabia, and the British a more secure foothold in Egypt.[62] On January 5, he sent the same proposal to the Russians. He again suggested partition to the British on February 19, emphasizing that Germany was content within its current borders and that it lacked interest in Ottoman territory.[63] No response from either Britain or Russia was forthcoming. After the Russian declaration of war in April 1877, Bismarck renewed his suggestion that the great powers partition the Ottoman Empire, with Egypt going to Britain.[64] These repeated proposals, however, only had the effect of raising the suspicions of the other powers that Germany was plotting to instigate an Anglo-Russian war so that it could annex Holland.[65] Disraeli, in a fury, exclaimed that "there must finally be an end to this.... I find him everywhere in my way.... The man is a European nuisance. Bismarck, more than Russia, is my problem, and I am firmly resolved to thwart him."[66] Bismarck never again raised the issue of partition.

These methods, however, did not mean that Bismarck was following a policy of avoidance. As Russo-Austrian tensions worsened, and Britain hoped to exploit the fault lines within the League of Three Emperors, events pushed Bismarck to the fore. In the fall of 1876, Gorchakov, working through Bernhard von Werder, Wilhelm I's personal representative in the czar's palace (rather than ordinary diplomatic channels), inquired whether or not Germany would remain neutral in event of a Russo-Austrian War, just as Russia had remained neutral during the wars of German unification.[67] This must have infuriated Bismarck, as there would be no record of this conversation in its diplomatic files. Regardless of whatever promise Germany made, the Russian government could also later announce that that it had no knowledge. Bismarck angrily wrote: "We can never hold the Russians to their word or make them responsible for what they say to us through Werder, because the commissions which Prince Gorchakov gives General von Werder for us reach the latter solely through the medium of verbal confidential conversation between a monarch and his 'adjutant.'"[68]

Even more alarming to Bismarck were the contents of Russia's inquiry. They seemed to be the portent of a greater crisis to come: a final split within the League of Three Emperors, a rupture of relations between Russia and Austria, and Germany forced to choose one over the other. Regardless of which side Germany backed, it would itself emerge as a loser, as the other nation would enter into an anti-German alliance with the French. Alliances became critical for Germany even as German reliance on alliances meant that Germany lost autonomy in foreign affairs, perhaps even leading to situations in which Germany acted on behalf of an ally, rather than its own strategic interests. This truly became the situation by the outbreak of World War I.

Thus, Bismarck worked his hardest to avoid having to make such a choice. At first, he employed delaying tactics and recalled Werder to Germany. Later, when the situation could no longer be avoided, Bismarck directly stated his position to Russia. He emphasized that Germany would do its utmost to preserve the peace in Europe and the balance within the League of Three Emperors. He also elaborated that:

> it cannot correspond to our interests to see the position of Russia seriously and permanently injured by a coalition of the rest of Europe, if fortune is unfavorable to the Russian arms; but it would affect the interests of Germany just as deeply, if the Austrian monarchy was so endangered in its position as European power or in its independence, that one of the factors with which we have to reckon in the European balance of Power, threatened to fall out for the future.[69]

This answer reflected Germany's real bottom line on the Near East Crisis, and also revealed the fundamental basis of Bismarck's foreign policy. As he emphasized in his memoirs: "If, to our sorrow, [peace] was not possible between Russia and Austria, then we could endure indeed that our friends should lose or win battles against each other, but not that one of the two should be so severely wounded and injured that its position as an independent Great Power taking its part in the councils of Europe would be endangered."[70]

The Berlin Conference

As the Near East Crisis grew, German hopes of remaining uninvolved faded. For Prussia and for Germany, the major difference between the 1854 Crimean War and the crisis in 1875 was that during the former events, Prussia had ardently desired to take part in the war and in the peace negotiations, yet was ignored by the other great powers. In the latter, Germany had hoped to pull back from events, yet was ultimately pushed of the center of the stage. This can be seen as one related result of Germany's rise, namely its expanded responsibilities. Regardless of whether it was willing or not, the newly powerful Germany had to take part in the management of the continent's affairs. The burden Germany had to carry increased, while its room for maneuver narrowed.

That was the predicament Bismarck faced. After he revealed Germany's standpoint on the Russo-Austrian tensions to Russia, he worked hard to keep Germany away from the center of contention. In February 1878, as the powers discussed holding a conference to settle these disputes, he decisively rejected the notion that Germany would be roped into hosting the conference. He even opposed locating the conference in Berlin.[71] When he could no longer avoid this, he tried to decline the role of mediator and proposed the French delegate William Waddington as the conference's chair.[72] These efforts came to nothing and, in the end, Bismarck had to call an international conference in Berlin.

Even after he was forced into becoming the mediator, Bismarck's fundamental assessment of the issues did not change: if Germany leaned to one side, the other side would be isolated and seek a friendship with France that might become an anti-German alliance. Bismarck assigned himself, as a consequence, the role of the "honest broker" and strove to maintain an unbiased point of view. On June 13, 1878, the conference opened. Even before this formal opening, however, the two sides had already reached a variety of secret agreements on various issues. For this set of issues, the conference was simply a public announcement of these settlements. This was a typical hallmark of European "conference diplomacy."[73] Remaining differences between the great powers (particularly between Russia and Austria) created large problems for the conference. As the chair, Bismarck had to strive to maintain balance between all of the powers and, using all of the diplomatic methods at his disposal, to push the conference's agenda forward. Bismarck supported Russian claims to territories along the Black Sea while supporting Austrian military occupation of Bosnia. He rejected the claims of smaller states and weaker ethnicities, restricted their ability to "interfere" with deals made between the great powers, and expressed resentment toward British interest in the pretentions of these smaller groups. Bismarck removed a name from a list of nationalities deserving of protection, claiming that he had never heard of such a group before.[74]

The conference concluded successfully on July 13, 1878. Solutions were found to all of the direct problems that had led to the crisis. The Treaty of Berlin, which was signed at the end of the conference, significantly revised the earlier Treaty of San Stefano. The Greater Bulgaria created by that treaty was divided into three pieces: the largest part would fall under Ottoman sovereignty, although it would be temporarily occupied by the Russian Army and would be reorganized under a Russian-chaired committee; the second part, Eastern Rumelia, south of the Balkan mountain range, would be conditionally self-governing but would accept Turkish political and military control under the oversight of a European commission; the third part would remain under direct Turkish military control. The treaty also granted complete independence to Serbia, Montenegro, and Romania; the borders of each of these countries also expanded to various extents. The grants of territory in Ottoman Asia to Russia made at San Stefano were generally reconfirmed by this treaty, although Bayazid and the Alashkerd Valley were returned to Turkish rule. Austria occupied Bosnia and had the right to station troops at Novi Pazar, thus militarily separating Serbia from Montenegro.[75]

A deeper analysis of the terms of this treaty is not relevant to the main purpose of this book. The true meaning of these events, both the conference itself and the treaty that it produced, is symbolic. They indicated that Europe had entered a new era of balance between the great powers, and that the focal point of that balance lay in Berlin. They also meant that Germany's rise to great-power status had reached a certain level: regardless of whether it was willing or not, Germany would now be forced to take center stage in international politics and take greater responsibilities upon itself, even though some of the required tasks might be thankless, burdensome, or even damaging. The immediate aftermath of the Berlin Congress provided an example of this. Bismarck had expended enormous effort to prevent a rift between Austria and Russia, but the price was a deterioration of Russo-German ties. Public opinion inside Russia was angered by the Treaty of Berlin's requirement that Russia return some of its spoils of war. Blame for this was placed squarely on Bismarck himself, and many felt that Germany had "sold out" Russia. A wave of anti-German feeling rose in Russia, and relations between the two countries became icy.

2

"Active Shaping" and the Foundation of a Grand Strategy

"Politics is the art of the possible."
Otto von Bismarck

THE 1878 CONFERENCE of Berlin was Bismarck's diplomatic masterpiece, although Germany paid a significant price for it. This sparked a further realization on Bismarck's part that his nation's rising power had already created a new international situation. Any policy now had to take this as a starting point. He progressively began to drift away from the German-style "hide and bide" policies that had characterized his earlier diplomacy. Instead, he moved toward an active shaping of European politics. Beginning around 1877, the outline of a grand strategy that aimed to preserve Germany's rise slowly became apparent.[1] Two mutually balancing yet self-supporting factors lay at the core of this strategy: diplomacy and the military.

Designing the Basic Thinking: The Kissingen Dictation

The true grand masters of politics, both of the domestic and the international varieties, are always those who have the deepest insights into human nature. Bismarck certainly fit this description.

Bismarck believed that, as a general principle, strength incites the jealousy of others. Thus, from the very beginning, he was intellectually prepared for the dangers and pressures created by Germany's rise. Bismarck had a pragmatic understanding of post-unification Germany as a European land power, perhaps even the continent's potential hegemon. After the 1871 unification, Germany's population, territory, economy, and military power had already begun to solidify this "potential."[2] The common fear in Europe was that if Germany followed the logic of national unification to its conclusion—bringing the sixty million Germans living between the North Sea and the Adriatic into a single state—then the country would be transformed from a potential to an actual hegemon.[3] Bismarck himself was not interested in this outcome. Instead, he pursued a "Little Germany" policy that maintained the preeminence of Prussia and its Hohenzollern ruling house. This policy also avoided the creation of a powerful Greater Germany that might, like Charles V's Habsburg Empire or Louis XIV's France, push the European political system past its breaking point. Arguably, the decision to forgo the creation of a "superpower" German state was a manifestation of Bismarck's wisdom as a grand master of strategy. His conception of Germany as the "potential continental hegemon" can also be seen as an acceptance of a European *status quo* in which Germany's advantaged position was relatively acceptable to the other great powers.

Bismarck's positioning, which included an awareness of Germany's geographical particularities, was both conservative and an objective assessment of the situation. Germany was different from both Great Britain and Russia. Those powers were located on the edges of Europe and thus continental affairs had relatively little impact on them. In the words of A. J. P. Taylor, Great Britain and Russia "asked nothing of Europe other than to be left alone," thus creating the necessary preconditions for the "world policies" they pursued.[4] Germany's geographical position, however, dictated that it would always need to concentrate on Europe; it could only seek to become a world power after becoming the continent's actual hegemon. As long as Germany could not do as it wished in Europe, all of its extra-European interests and objectives would need to take a backseat. It was exactly this point that Bismarck's successors ignored and, as a result, their continental policies and world policies all met with failure.

This positioning, however, was merely a foundation. Being situated in the heart of Europe and surrounded by strong neighbors meant that Germany would never be able to adopt a foreign policy of drift and neglect, lest it find itself the focal point of multinational conflict and dispute.[5] The 1875 "War in Sight" Crisis and the Near East Crisis had swiftly revealed the pressures brought by Germany's rise. Traditional methods and policies proved ineffective; maintaining a low posture would not be enough to prevent Germany from becoming the center of a European struggle for power. Germany had little choice but to reject traditional forms of strategic thought and adopt a new mindset in order to navigate the difficulties created by its own rise.

This new mindset was already being formed by 1877, as is demonstrated by the Kissingen Dictation. Bismarck dictated this memorandum on June 15, 1877, while at Kissingen, a German resort. It represented a rough outline of Bismarck's general vision for German foreign policy and revealed the depth of his strategic thinking. The complete dictation reads:

I desire that we should encourage the English, without making it too obvious, if they have intentions concerning Egypt. I consider that it will suit our interests and be better for our future to promote a compromise between England and Russia, which may establish relations between the two Powers as good as they were at the beginning of this century, and which may be followed by the rapprochement of both to ourselves. Such an aim may never be realized, but one never can tell. If only England and Russia would come to an agreement on the basis of the one controlling Egypt, and the other the Black Sea, both might find it possible to remain content with maintaining the *status quo* for a long period. At the same time, in their chief interests they might be led into a rivalry, which would practically preclude their joining in coalition against us, quite apart from the internal influences urging England against such a combination.

A French paper said of me lately that I suffered from '*le cauchemar des coalitions* [the nightmare of hostile coalitions].' This sort of bogey will for long—perhaps forever— be quite rightly feared by all German Ministers. Coalitions may be formed of the Western Powers, joined by Austria, against us, or, with more danger to us, one based on the union of Russia, Austria and France. A close rapprochement between any two of these may be taken advantage of by the third, to exercise grievous pressure upon us. My anxiety in the face of these possibilities leads me to regard as desirable, not at once, but as time goes on, the following consequences of the Eastern Crisis:— (1) Gravitation of the interests of Russia and Austria, and their mutual rivalries, toward the East; (2) Russia to be impelled to take up a strong defensive position in the East, and on her own shores, and to stand in need of our Alliance; (3) For England and Russia a peaceful *status quo* giving to them the same interest which we have in the maintenance of things as they are; (4) Separation of England from France, ever hostile to us, over the Egyptian and Mediterranean Questions; (5) Relations between Russia and Austria such as may make it difficult for them both to join in carrying on theanti-German conspiracy, which in some measure attracts the clerical and centralizing elements in Austria.

> If my health permitted me to work, I could fill in and develop in greater detail the picture which floats before my mind. It is not one portraying any acquisition of territory, but rather one showing a combined political situation, in which all the Powers, except France, have need of us, and are removed from the possibility of coalescing against us by the nature of their relations toward each other.
>
> England would not consider the occupation of Egypt sufficient to remove the difficulties regarding the Dardanelles. The system of double-guardianship, with the Dardanelles for England and the Bosphorus for Russia, is risky for England, because, all things considered, her forts on the Dardanelles could be easier taken, than defended, by land troops. That fact is probably present in the minds of the Russians, who, moreover, may possibly be not displeased to see the Black Sea closed for a generation. The whole question will be a matter for negotiation, and the combined result, as it appears in my mind, can be thoroughly worked out just as well after as before the decisive battles of the present war. I should regard it as an important asset for us, which would out-weigh the probable injury to our interests in the Black Sea, which it may bring in its train, — quite apart from the possible security for the latter, which the Treaty may contain. Even if a war between England and Russia could not be prevented, our aim should, in my opinion, continue to stand as before, namely, to promote a peace which would satisfy both parties, at Turkey's expense.[6]

Bismarck's statement clearly demonstrated his grasp of the overall situation in Europe and his ability to make judgments based on potential developments. His core insight was to actively influence the interactions between the great powers such that the relationship between any one power and any other power was weaker than the relationship between the first power and Germany. This vision of acting as Europe's "middle man" was undoubtedly influenced by another master of strategy: former Austrian Prime Minister Klemens von Metternich. After the end of the Napoleonic Wars, Metternich's ability to maneuver amid the other great powers allowed Austria, the weakest power, to become the continent's political core and thus able to protect its own interests. Henry Kissinger identified the essence of Metternich's foreign policies:

> Austria's central position had been transformed into a diplomatic asset by seeing to it that the differences of the major powers among each other were greater than their respective differences with Austria, so that in every international crisis Austria emerged as the pivotal state. [British secretary of state for foreign affairs] Castlereagh considered Metternich the most 'reasonable' of Continental statesmen, a little timid perhaps, but still the easiest to deal with, the most moderate, the least abstract. [Russian Czar] Alexander [I] considered Metternich the most ideological of European statesmen, not quite ready, to be sure, to follow him to the heights, but still the only one capable of understanding the exalted flights of his imagination."[7]

Of course, by the time that Bismarck had come into power, it was no longer possible to use ideology to bind the great powers together. Politics in Bismarck's era had already become more practical and more oriented toward issues of power. A rapidly rising Germany did not lack power, so Bismarck adopted a policy of alliance-building in order to "actively shape" his foreign policy environment.

The Beginning of Bismarck's Alliances

German Alliance Objectives and Selection of Alliance Partners

Bismarck's alliance system stands out as the largest, most complicated diplomatic project in the history of modern international relations. Yet, two aspects of this system were fairly simple.

The first of these was the system's objectives. Given Germany's immense power, no single nation could present a threat, yet an anti-German alliance of great powers would place Germany in a disadvantageous geopolitical situation. Moreover, in the wake of the Franco-Prussian War, France had become an implacable opponent; any other enemy of Germany would be its natural ally. As a consequence, Germany's first strategic objective was painfully clear: prevent the emergence of an anti-German alliance. In Bismarck's own words, "everything depended on inducing at least one of the two mighty foes whom we had beaten in the field to renounce the anticipated design of uniting with the other in a war of revenge."[8] This would be the central objective of Bismarck's post-1879 quest to build alliances.

The second was system's "principal line," or direction. Bismarck correctly understood that while the most immediate and direct threat to Germany was the French desire for a revanchist war, the most substantive threat came from Russia.[9] Russia's geographic position and resources meant that any anti-German alliance that included Russia could actually endanger Germany's existence. To state this from another angle: as long as relations between Germany and Russia were friendly and stable, no anti-German combination could threaten Germany, and it would still be able to maintain maximum freedom of action in European affairs. Thus, Bismarckian strategy was firmly focused eastward toward Russia. Bismarck himself claimed that "it has always been my endeavor to promote not merely the security of the country against Russian attacks, but also in Russia itself a peaceful tone, and a belief in the unaggressive character of our policy."[10]

A direct alliance with Russia would, under these conditions, seem to be the simplest and most logical strategy. Bismarck's brilliance lay in the fact, however, that he saw that such a strategy would actually be a giant trap. Instead, he took an indirect, seemingly illogical approach to achieving his objective. After the 1878 Berlin Crisis, Bismarck felt that the unsettled state of great power relations after the dissolution of the first League of Three Emperors might lead to a Russian alliance with France. Once that alliance was established, Austria might seek to join in the hopes of regaining its former preeminence in Germany, thus recreating the Kaunitz League alliance of the Seven Years' War that had nearly defeated Prussia. Germany had no choice but to proactively build alliances of its own to prevent this result.

In his choice of alliance partners, Bismarck made a careful analysis. First, he admitted an alliance with Russia would solve these problems, because he believed that "in point of material force…a union with Russia…[had] the advantage" and that dynastic connections between the countries would further strengthen ties.[11] He feared, however, that if "German policy confined its possibilities to the Russian alliance, and, in accordance with the wishes of Russia, refused all other states, Germany would with regard to Russia be in an unequal position, because the geographical situation and the autocratic constitution of Russia made it easier for her to give up the alliance than it would be for us."[12] Furthermore, dependence on Russia might force Germany to follow Russia's risky policies, thus dragging it into conflicts. There was another piece to Bismarck's analysis, as well: anti-German feelings were on the rise in Russia. An alliance with Russia might be seen as a sign of German fears of Russia. In sum, the costs of a Russian alliance were too great, and such an alliance would place Germany in a subordinate position.

Bismarck's calculations led him to select the Austro-Hungarian Empire as an alliance partner. First, it was the weakest of the so-called Three Eastern

Monarchies and was in a weak geographic position. An alliance with the Austrians would assuage their feelings of insecurity, prevent them from acting on their own, and might allow Germany to influence Austrian policymaking. Second, Austria had been aligned with Britain and France during the Crimean War. If Austria felt that it was losing ground in its struggle with Russia, it might again appeal to Britain and France for aid. This would create an ally for France and might push Germany into dependence on Russia. Cooperation between Britain and Austria continued to be close, and the two powers succeeded in pressuring Russia to evacuate Bulgaria in July 1879. The renowned Russian statesman Shuvalov claimed that Russia's forced withdrawal from Bulgaria was the product of Russia's isolation within Europe.[13] From this perspective, there was a possibility that Austria, Great Britain, and France could reconstitute a "Crimean alliance." Bismarck later told the Russian ambassador to Germany that the purpose of the German alliance with Austria was to "dig a ditch between [Austria] and the western powers."[14] This claim was more than mere pretext. Third, the Austro-Hungarian Empire had once been an importance member of the German federation and had been the empire at the core of the German nation. An alliance with Austria would be a satisfactory substitute for those who hoped that the two states would merge to form a Greater Germany.[15] Fourth, and most important, once the alliance was signed, the configuration of the Three Eastern Monarchies would shift into a two-versus-one formation, with Russia as the disadvantaged party. This would make it easier to bring Russia into a revived League of Three Emperors.

The Austro-German Alliance Takes Shape

Bismarck's negotiations with the Austro-Hungarian Empire proceeded without much difficulty. In mid-August 1879, Bismarck visited the Austrian city of Gastein. There, he learned that Austrian Prime Minister Gyula Andrássy might retire but would be willing to remain in office for several extra weeks in order to build an anti-Russian alliance with Germany. Bismarck immediately replied that his hope was that Austro-German friendship could be used to transform Russian attitudes. After this meeting, diplomats from the two sides began preparing for the negotiations.[16] On September 21, Bismarck himself travelled to Vienna to negotiate the terms of the alliance with Andrássy. The sticking point was that Bismarck hoped that the alliance would be anti-French as well as anti-Russian, but Austrian negotiators were uninterested in this proposal.[17] According to Andrássy, he and Bismarck held long, heated discussions that, at times, became dramatic. This, perhaps, revealed aspects of Bismarck's personality. Bismarck even used threatening tones: "Consider carefully what you are doing. For the last time I advise you to give way." Afterward, he raised his voice, saying "Please accept my proposal…or else I will have to accept yours." In the end, it was Bismarck who backed down.[18]

The real obstacle to the Austro-German alliance came from Bismarck's sovereign, Kaiser Wilhelm I. Wilhelm was already very old by that time and attached great importance to heritage and dynastic blood ties. He did not understand why Germany would want to ally itself with a country it had fought barely more than a decade ago or why that alliance should be directed against Russia, which had never been a traditional threat to Prussia and whose czar, Alexander II, was his nephew. The old kaiser's objections created headaches for Bismarck. Much of the documentary material covering this period focused on Bismarck's attempts to persuade the kaiser. In the end, however, Bismarck was forced to take strong measures. On September 26, he chaired a meeting of the Prussian cabinet and demanded that each of the cabinet officers pledge to resign if the alliance with Austria was not approved. The cabinet agreed and Wilhelm I could do nothing but acquiesce. The treaty was signed in Vienna on October 7.

This treaty was defensive in nature. It contained four important stipulations. First, if either Germany or Austria were attacked by Russia, the other party must send its full military force to assist in repulsing the invasion. Second, if either country were attacked by a third party, the other party could remain neutral as long as Russia remained on the sidelines. Third, the treaty would be in force for five years. Fourth was a secret provision stipulating that, if signs began to point to a Russian attack, the two parties would notify the czar that they believed an attack was imminent and that an attack on one party would be considered an attack on both.[19] In plain words, this meant that if Russia and France jointly attacked Germany, Austria would support Germany; if Russia invaded Austria, Germany would intervene.

The 1879 Austro-German alliance was an important event in modern European history. One historian has called it "the first thread in a network of alliances which was soon to cover all Europe."[20] It needs to be pointed out that, although the alliance on paper was directed against a Russian attack, resisting such an attack was not the ultimate objective of the alliance. Its true value was to "nail down" Austria and prevent it from ever again wandering outside of German influence and control. This greatly-strengthened German position could then be used to force Russia to realistically reassess its relations with Germany and reestablish a stable strategic relationship between Germany, Austria, and Russia.[21]

This strategy was not without risks, of course. The alliance might have the opposite effect—it might push Russia and France closer together. To prevent this, Bismarck had another form of "insurance": negotiations for an alliance with Great Britain. Britain was already locked in a heated struggle with Russia in Afghanistan, so its reaction to a proposed anti-Russian alliance with Germany would be relatively positive. In September 1879, while the Austro-German alliance was still being negotiated, Bismarck inquired of Britain what its policy would be if Germany came into conflict with Russia "due to its friendship with Britain and Austria" rather than any direct threat to its own interests.[22] Prime Minister Disraeli replied that, in event of such a conflict in Eastern Europe, Great Britain would prevail upon France to "remain quiet." This was a logical guarantee for Britain to make. If Bismarck truly wanted to form an anti-Russian alliance with Great Britain, Disraeli had already played the highest card that he could, as this promise meant that Germany and Austria together could defeat Russia without fear of trouble in their rear. Yet Bismarck, in his notes, still asked, "Is that all?"[23] Afterward, Bismarck never raised this question again. Great Britain, at this time, was greatly interested in cooperation with Germany. In October, the German ambassador in London specifically reminded his government of the benefits that Britain could provide.[24] British Foreign Secretary Salisbury, though he held doubts about Bismarck's intentions, pledged to the German ambassador in October that he was "pretty sure [Great Britain] could prevent any French Government from joining Russia against [Germany]; but that [Germany] might rely on [British] goodwill and assistance in the contingency of an attack on Austria and Germany."[25] There was no German response to this. The most reasonable explanation for this silence is that Bismarck never saw a relationship with Great Britain as a goal in and of itself, but used it as a means to improve his negotiating position with Austria and to create an impression on Russia. Once his true objective was achieved, he did not need this method any more.

The Impact of the Austro-German Alliance on Russia and the Formation of the Revived League of Three Emperors

Russia's actions revealed the success of Bismarck's policy. News of the Austro-German alliance and of Bismarck's feelers toward Great Britain were poorly kept secrets, and word soon reached Russia. As a result, anti-German feeling in Russia quieted and Russian policy toward Germany returned to a rational and practical path. At the end of September 1879, the pro-German diplomat Peter Saburov was appointed Russian ambassador to Berlin and soon proposed a new mutual security agreement: if Russia and Great Britain went to war, Germany would promise neutrality; if Germany and France went to war, Russia would do likewise and would implore other nations to do the same. Russia would furthermore respect the territorial integrity of the Austro-Hungarian Empire on the condition that it did not seek further expansion in the Balkans.[26] Bismarck was fully satisfied with this: "Now I have the best receipt for my Vienna policy. I knew that the Russians would come to us, once we nailed down the Austrians."[27]

He was not, however, interested in signing a bilateral agreement with Russia. He already had an alliance with Austria, and now he sought to bring the Russians into that, too, in order to further restrain Austria. Management of these opposing tensions could allow Bismarck to guarantee Germany's leading position within the alliance with Austria. (He thought that if German-Russian relations ever suffered an irreparable split, then Austria would use its alliance with Germany to challenge Russia, and Germany would thus be pulled by its alliance into conflicts in the Balkans.[28]) Bismarck consequently directly told Saburov that any Russo-German agreement must include Austria. Given that a League of Three Emperors was "the only system offering the maximum of stability for the peace of Europe," Germany would be happy to recreate such an alliance.[29] Russia did not raise any objections and essentially accepted Bismarck's idea in its entirety.

The main obstacle to the realization of this plan came from Austria. Austria had originally understood the alliance with Germany to mean automatic German support for Austrian expansion in the Balkans. From the perspective of Austria-Hungary's new prime minister, Heinrich Karl von Haymerle, the ideal would have been to ally with Great Britain. Austria and Great Britain (with additional support from Germany) could then jointly check the Russian threat in the Balkans. This would allow Austria-Hungary to dominate the European portions of the Ottoman Empire, and Great Britain to control its Asian territories. Given Great Britain's longstanding commitment to restraining Russian expansion toward the Mediterranean, Austria had reason to believe that such an alliance was a possibility. These calculations made Austria unenthusiastic about Bismarck's proposed new League of Three Emperors.

From Bismarck's perspective, Austria's vision was completely unacceptable, especially the notion of cooperating with Britain to "contain" Russia. Germany's most effective path to preventing close relations between Russia, Britain, and France was for Russia to continue threatening British (and French) interests in the Black Sea and the Balkans. Bismarck's Kissingen Dictation had been quite clear on that point. He incited Russia's actions and expressed support for them on several occasions. Once, he said to Russian ambassador Saburov that "an empire like Russia cannot let herself be cooped up by England in the Black Sea."[30] When Bismarck was unable to persuade Austria, however, British domestic politics unexpectedly came to his assistance. After the April 1880 general election, the Liberal Party's William Gladstone took the helm as prime minister. The idealistic foreign policy promoted by Gladstone differed greatly from Britain's traditional foreign policy, leaving Bismarck and other old-style political figures uncertain about where things stood.[31] On the Eastern Question, Gladstone's pro-Russian, anti-Austrian policies were the exact opposite of Disraeli's. He advocated Anglo-Russian compromise on all outstanding issues in the Black Sea and the Balkans, while publically and severely criticizing Austria. Bismarck saw Great Britain's new pro-Russian policy as something to be resisted, and said as much to the Austrians: "The essential point is always that between Russia and England no agreement or rapprochement exists; I cannot emphasize too strongly how necessary it is to avoid everything that can facilitate this."[32]

Britain's anti-Austrian policies, however, were something he could use to extinguish Austrian hopes of allying with Great Britain against Russia. They could, moreover, be used to force the Austrians to accept Bismarck's vision of a new League of Three Emperors. After Gladstone came to power, Great Britain promoted a Concert of Europe that included all of the continent's great powers and could resolve the Eastern Question once and for all. Bismarck did not directly oppose this, but covertly used it to realize his own objectives. Among these was his desire to bring Austria and Russia closer together. By late July 1880, Russia had already lost all hope in the Gladstone government and proactively prompted Bismarck to push Austria into discussions for a new League of Three Emperors. Austria had, by this time, seen that there was no hope of forming an anti-Russian alliance with Great Britain, and was willing to enter into negotiations.

Those trilateral negotiations proceeded with great difficulty. Bismarck had to balance two tasks: he had to persuade Austria that the agreement would contain Russia and he had to convince the Russians that the treaty would, in fact, check Austria. He told Russia that the treaty was necessary to restrain Austria, as "the only Power which would not be inclined to keep an engagement is Austria."[33] Just as the three sides neared an agreement, Russian Czar Alexander II was assassinated on March 13, 1881. New factors were now added to the negotiations. Although the new czar, Alexander III, had no special affection for Germany and possessed only a modest intellect, he was uninterested in dramatically changing foreign policy. On June 18, 1881, the treaty creating the second League of Three Emperors was signed in Berlin.

The new league had essentially nothing in common with the earlier one. The older version had been designed to display the unity of traditional monarchies, while the new incarnation had mostly discarded that old ideological apparatus, leaving only practical calculations of power and exchanges of interest. The agreement stipulated three major points. First, if one of the three signatories became involved in a war with a fourth power, the other two would remain neutral (with an exception carved out for war with the Ottoman Empire—in such a war, this clause would only be operable with the previous agreement of the three signatories). Second, the three countries pledged that none would act unilaterally to change the status of the Ottoman Empire's remaining European territories. Third, the three countries guaranteed the closure of the Dardanelles and Bosphorus passages to the Black Sea. Of these, the first point was really an agreement between Germany and Russia that, if a new Franco-German war were to break out, Russia would remain neutral. This was decidedly in Germany's favor. The second point was mostly an arrangement between Austria and Russia that amounted to a mutual recognition of spheres of influence in the Balkans. The third point can be seen as an Austro-German gift to Russia, as Russia naval forces on the Black Sea were virtually non-existent and, if a British fleet could freely transit the straits into the sea, it could threaten Russia's vulnerable underbelly, particularly Ukraine.

The tension between this new league and the pre-existing alliance between Germany and Austria has been noted both by historians and by some German diplomats at the time. If, however, we understand it primarily as a means to draw Russia in, then Bismarck's motives and strategies become evident. The Austro-German alliance had been primarily designed to push the Russians, while the new League of Three Emperors was, by contrast, designed to pull them—together, these two aspects can be seen as constructing a structure built out of the balance of competing forces. For Germany, the league meant not only that Russia would remain neutral in any future conflict with France, but also that Austro-Russian tensions could be brought under control, thus bringing the strategies of the three empires into a relatively balanced, stable state. It can be said that if Austria and Russia had been able maintain this sort of stable relationship—neither too close nor too distant—then Germany could be guaranteed freedom of action, and even leadership, on the European continent. Preventing a Franco-Russian alliance was a nice additional benefit.

The Alliance's Expansion

If the League of Three Emperors had been enough to completely control Austro-Russian tensions, then Bismarck's alliance-building might have ended with that. Instead, events developed in a different way.

Russian Uncertainty and Bismarck's Response

After the creation of the new league, Bismarck felt satisfied. In a letter to Wilhelm I, he claimed that this arrangement had settled the issues between Russia and Austria, solidified the peace between those two countries, and had also banished the threat of a Franco-Russian alliance.[34] But, as was soon to be revealed, relations between Austria and Russia had not improved. Bismarck was particularly unsettled by a return of pan-Slavic sentiment in Russia. Mikhail Skobelev, the Russian general who had led his soldiers to victory in the 1877 war against the Ottomans, was one of the loudest advocates of pan-Slavic sentiment. On an early 1882 trip to Paris, Skobelev publically stated that Germany was the real enemy of Russia and of all the Slavic peoples. On his trip homeward he stopped in Warsaw and promoted pan-Slavic ideas to the Polish people. In the end, he was reprimanded by the czar, and the pro-German Nikolay Giers was appointed Russia's foreign minister. Despite this outcome, the Skobelev incident made a big impact on Bismarck. He began to doubt that the conservative elements within the Russian leadership, who had promoted strong relations with Germany, could really control the political situation inside Russia. At the same time, he began to doubt the effectiveness of the league itself.

Bismarck's immediate response was to apply greater pressure—to push Russia a little more in order to prevent Russian policy from becoming unsettled and to protect German strategic balance. Bismarck's attitude toward the expansion of the Austro-German alliance, particularly its inclusion of Romania and Italy, changed dramatically.

As early as 1880, Romania had pushed for inclusion in the Austro-German alliance. Although Romania had been a Russian ally during the recent war against the Ottomans, its territory in Bessarabia had been ceded to Russia as a result of the Berlin Conference. Romania, consequently, became deeply dissatisfied with Russia. Even more unsettling to the Romanians was the fact that their country lay in between Russia and its protectorate in Bulgaria, leading to worries that Russia would attempt to annex more Romanian territory. Therefore, they turned to Germany and Austria for protection. In theory, the inclusion of Romania in the alliance should have been unproblematic, given that preventing Russia from acquiring a land corridor to Bulgaria was in Germany's and (especially) Austria's interest. Additionally, blood ties existed between the reigning dynasties in Prussia and Romania. Bismarck, however, clung to his opposition to any expansion of the alliance and was only willing to promise that if Romania were threatened by Russia, Germany and Austria would support it.[35] Bismarck's concern was that while an expansion of the Austro-German alliance might be effective at containing Russia, it would be counterproductive for his strategy of pulling Russia into a new set of relationships. After the Skobelev incident, however, his attitude slowly began to change. In 1883, a tripartite German-Austrian-Romanian pact was concluded. The agreement committed Austria and Romania to come to each other's aid in event of a Russian attack; Germany, through its previous agreement with Austria, was also indirectly committed.

The other country that sought inclusion in the alliance was Italy. Italy's situation differed significantly from Romania's. Italy, like Germany, was a newly formed nation-state. It had also played a constructive role in the German unification process. In the 1866 Austro-Prussian War, it had fought Austria in alliance with Prussia. Italy's desire around 1880 to be included in the Austro-German alliance came not from fear of another great power, but from tensions in Italian politics, which leaders hoped could be improved by a foreign policy victory. In foreign policy, Italy had ambitions to seize colonies, but these had been quickly smashed when Tunis, in which Italy had made significant investments, was seized by the French. With the shattering of the Italian dreams of empire, domestic public opinion had turned against the government and the monarchy. Inside Italy, the struggle between secular authorities and the Pope had not yet come to an end. Progressive forces within Italy urged the Pope's expulsion, but this sparked the strong opposition of Catholics across the continent, leaving Italy isolated. Supporters of the Papacy pushed for a restoration of the people's secular authority, thus challenging the power of the ruling house, while republican forces plotted to overturn the monarchy itself.[36] Italy asked both Germany and Austria at the same time for inclusion in their alliance, claiming that it could use its own ties with Great Britain to bring that country into the alliance as well. Bismarck did not respond, leaving the ball entirely in Austria's court. There are four major reasons for this. First, Italy was in a weak geographical position with a long coastline that could easily be invaded. Second, Italy had conflicts (both over territory and over the future of the Papacy) with Austria, and any direct German negotiations with Italy might affect ties with Austria. Third, Italy was a weak country and had little value as an ally. Fourth, Bismarck doubted that Italy's traditions of liberalism and parliamentarianism would allow it to be a dependable ally. In public, however, Bismarck emphasized this fourth point, claiming that Italy's parliamentary system prevented it from maintaining a stable, continuous policy, thus negating the country's value as an ally. When Italy's ambassador to Germany assured Bismarck that the Italian king could rely on the army to implement policies that Bismarck could accept, the German chancellor suggested that "a Monarch who is wearing civilian clothes does not do everything in his power to keep in contact with his army."[37]

In October 1881, this "Monarch who is wearing civilian clothes" visited the Austrian prime minister in Vienna and proposed that the two countries sign a "reinsurance pact" against aggression from other countries (France and Russia in particular). This was a first step to finding a way into the Austro-German alliance itself. Although Austria was interested in the Italian proposal, the new Austrian foreign minister had a low opinion of Italian power. In the end, the Italian king earned nothing from his trip to Vienna. Within two years, however, Germany suggested that negotiations between Italy and Austria be restarted as a direct response to the 1882 Skobelev incident. Cause and effect followed directly: Skobelev's incendiary remarks in Paris were made on February 17 and Bismarck's proposal to restart the Italian talks came on February 28.

The Establishment of the Triple Alliance

The Skobelev incident had highlighted for Bismarck the potential of a future Franco-Russian alliance. This prospect made Italy's political value much clearer. Bismarck understood that Italy had little military value as an ally, but in a putative war between a Franco-Russian alliance and the Austro-German alliance, politically it would be valuable for Italy to join the war against France (rather than joining the war against Austria), even if Italy merely deployed "one Italian corporal with the Italian flag and a drummer at his side."[38] In many ways, Bismarck absorbed Italy into the alliance in order to promote Austrian interests in having a stable rear flank. After the conclusion of this alliance, Austria had to give up its traditional policies toward the Papacy, but this was a sacrifice of prestige more than anything else. Italy, for its part, could no longer make territorial claims to the Italian-speaking portions of the Austrian Empire, which was a real concession.

For these reasons, some in Germany were not enthusiastic about this alliance. Foreign ministry official Friedrich von Holstein (who would soon become influential in the foreign ministry and ultimately replace Bismarck as the steward of German foreign policy) thought that Germany's recent reestablishment of ties with the Vatican that had been severed during the *Kulturkampf* of the 1870s could be threatened by this alliance with Italy. This, he feared, might have a negative impact on German Catholics. The price of the alliance would be paid by Germany, but the benefits would accrue to Austria.[39] Bismarck insisted, however, that aiding Austria in this way would have positive effects for Germany's entire strategic situation. These were far more important than Germany's relationship with the Vatican. Bismarck's son—in what was surely an echo of his father's opinion—explained that: "I entirely share your opinion on the Italian affair. Italy will never attack us directly...for Austria, however, Italy is what France is for us—even though less dangerous because weaker."[40] In 1883, Bismarck discussed this issue with the French ambassador to Germany, saying that the alliance with Italy had been concluded in consideration of Austria's interests and that the Triple Alliance was "the completion of the policy of reparation which I [have] follow[ed] toward Austria since Sadowa."[41]

Negotiations between the three countries concluded in May 1882 and the treaty was formally signed on May 20. The preamble to the treaty declared that its goal was "to increase the guarantees of general peace, to strengthen the monarchical principle, and by that to assure the maintenance of social and political order in their respective states."[42] This gave Italy what it needed the most: support for the country's monarchical system. The treaty's second clause guaranteed Austrian and German assistance to Italy in the event of an unprovoked French attack and mandated Italian assistance in case of an unprovoked attack on Germany. The third clause obligated all of the signatories to go to war in the event that one or two of them were attacked by a coalition of two or more other countries. In practice, this meant that if Austria and Germany ended up in a war with France and Russia, Italy would be duty-bound to join them. The fourth clause of the treaty, however, is also worthy of serious consideration: if any one of the signatories found themselves in a war (unprovoked or otherwise) with a single other country, the other two signatories would be merely required to maintain benevolent neutrality. To translate this into the political landscape of the time, this clause meant that if Germany launched a preemptive war against France, the other two countries must remain neutral. In such a case, if Russia came to France's aid, then Austria and Italy would automatically have to join the war. If the Austro-German alliance was best characterized as a "defensive alliance," then the Triple Alliance needs to be understood, in contrast, as also having an "offensive" character. This would naturally bring an element of uncertainty to the future.[43]

In terms of geography, the Triple Alliance brought all of central Europe together, almost like the Holy Roman Empire of the Middle Ages. When war came in 1914, however, the alliance entered the struggle without one of its members. This makes it easy for many to overlook the importance of the alliance. In reality, the Triple Alliance was always only of secondary importance to Germany's diplomatic plans and its grand strategy. On the whole, the Triple Alliance is best understood as a derivative product of the Austro-German alliance. Its military implications were significantly less than those of the Austro-German alliance and its political value paled in comparison to the League of Three Emperors. A comparison of the processes by which the league and the Triple Alliance were created reveals that Bismarck attached great importance to the establishment of the league: he had promoted it and shaped it deliberately and methodically. The Triple Alliance, for Bismarck, was mostly a means to ameliorate problems within the league that had become evident since its creation. One additional point must be acknowledged, however. Italy's position in the Mediterranean meant that it maintained close, albeit complex, ties with Great Britain and France. The creation of the Triple Alliance meant that Bismarck had also begun to establish indirect connections with those two powers (but particularly with Great Britain), as well. Germany could possibly be able to use these connections to stabilize the weak balance between Germany, Russia, and Austria while also preventing a Franco-Russian alliance.

German Policy and the Anglo-French Split

German Appraisal of Anglo-French Relations

The Triple Alliance acted as a bridge between Germany and Great Britain, although this did not become fully apparent until the late 1880s. In the years around 1882, Germany did not have much of a lever with which it could influence Great Britain and France. The political trends in Britain and France (where liberalism was mainstream) differed considerably from those in Germany, Russia, Austria, and Italy. The conservative principle of monarchical unity had little influence in those two countries and, in fact, served only to highlight the ideological differences between those societies and Germany. Strategic interests also separated the two sides. Irreconcilable disputes existed between Germany and France. Although Great Britain lacked a similarly fundamental conflict with Germany, it also had few interests that intersected with Germany's. Therefore, when Bismarck created an alliance system that embraced all of the other great powers on the continent, the two powers that remained outside of his system became something of a political uncertainty.

Most important, Britain and France stood together on a wide range of issues and, historically, had been allied on several occasions. If Bismarck's League of Three Emperors and Triple Alliance caused them to feel excluded, then they might once again ally themselves and revive the old dream of a liberal alliance. This undoubtedly would constitute a major challenge to Germany. In the Kissingen Dictation, Bismarck raised the possibility of using Egyptian and Mediterranean disputes to drive a wedge between the two countries. This became one of the five major objectives of German foreign policy. Bismarck, however, could not directly incite tensions between Britain and France. Given the level of tension existing between France and Germany, any such move might be spotted immediately and result in German disgrace. Thus, he adopted a very different approach to these two counties, acting cautiously and patiently.

To summarize, there were two main aspects of German policy toward Britain and France: first, to push for a thaw in ties with France and second, to wait for (and then exploit) Anglo-French disputes over Egypt.

Bismarck's behavior while attempting to promote better relations with France proved interesting. On the one hand, he never believed in his heart that reconciliation between France and Germany was possible. In his memoirs, he linked this belief not only to the dispute over territories ceded to Germany after the Franco-Prussian War, but also to France's replacement by Germany as the major power on the continent.[44] On the other hand, he actively pursued a policy of reconciliation and his true thoughts do not appear to have influenced the sincerity of this policy. Perhaps it was simply that Bismarck excelled at politics and diplomacy. In June 1882, Bismarck told the French ambassador to Germany, "I want appeasement, I would like to be reconciled. We have no sensible motive for seeking to do you harm; we are rather in the position of owing you reparation."[45] Germany manifested this concern for France in concrete policies, too—particularly in colonial affairs. In 1877, the British government championed the cause of "reform" in Morocco, in order to allow the government of that country to exercise greater independence, giving it the ability to assist Great Britain in guaranteeing free navigation of the Straits of Gibraltar.[46] France, however, hoped to maintain Morocco in a weakened state in order to one day absorb it into the French Empire. Consequently, it vehemently objected to the British proposal. At Great Britain's suggestion, the European great powers held a conference in Madrid, Spain in 1880 to discuss the Moroccan reforms. At the conference, Germany initially backed away from its early support of reform, then swung its full support to the French position, and—in a coordinated action with Austria-Hungary—finally caused the conference to reject the British proposals. Elsewhere in North Africa, Germany supported France over Italy in the contest for control of Tunisia.

The intent of Bismarck's conciliatory policies seemed blatantly obvious to the French: to lure French attention away from the territories lost to Germany in 1871 and thus prevent French consideration of a war of vengeance. Even though the French saw through Bismarck's designs, they had little recourse. His alliance system had already isolated France in Europe and left it with the potential for free action only in overseas colonial affairs. The result was that France devoted ever more effort to colonial expansion, creating more points of dispute with the world's largest colonial power, Great Britain. Under these conditions, there was little possibility of rekindling a liberal alliance, and Germany could enjoy maximum room for maneuver. Of course, Anglo-French colonial disputes were not caused by German policy. The history of the two countries, combined with their overseas interests and domestic political structures, made that contest unavoidable. Throughout this process, Bismarck was merely a master of waiting for, and making use of, the opportunities that presented themselves. His attitude allowed events to develop in the manner most beneficial to Germany. He himself emphasized that "arbitrary interference in the course of history, on purely subjective grounds, has always resulted in the shaking down of unripe fruit…the gift of waiting while a situation develops is an essential requirement of practical politics."[47] This was to be clearly reflected in the 1882 Egyptian Crisis.

The Egyptian Crisis and German Policy

Anglo-French conflict over Egypt had been latent ever since the Napoleonic Wars. Napoleon had fought the British there, but Great Britain did not control Egypt even after defeating him. By the nineteenth century, particularly after the opening of the Suez Canal in 1869, the strategic value of Egypt rose immensely, and Anglo-French rivalry over Egypt reintensified. For the British, the Suez Canal was the strategic link to India, the most important British colony. They could not allow it to be controlled by another great power. Egypt had economic importance for the French. There were already many French business interests in the country—even the Suez Canal itself had been completed by a French engineer. In November 1875, British Prime Minister Disraeli suddenly bought the Egyptian government's shares in the Suez Canal itself, indicating that Britain had begun to exert control over Egypt. Afterward, during an Egyptian fiscal crisis, British involvement increased. In 1876, it established joint control with the French over the country's financial affairs. Of course, this supposedly cooperative joint control was actually a means for Great Britain and France to monitor each other. As Salisbury explained in a letter, "You may renounce—or monopolize—or share. Renouncing would have been to place the French across our road to India. Monopolizing would have been very near the risk of war. So we resolved to share."[48] As the situation in Egypt worsened, however, joint control became increasingly unable to contain the struggle between Britain and France. In September 1881, a revolt broke out and by February 1882, the rulers of Egypt were forced to assemble a new cabinet comprising nationalists. This cabinet rejected joint control, which lit the fuse of the 1882 Egyptian Crisis.

In the early stages of the crisis, Britain and France maintained a united front. In January 1882, the French proposed joint Anglo-French intervention in Egypt. Germany objected, suggesting instead an intervention of a more general European character, which was accepted by the British and French. In May 1882, the European great powers met at Constantinople to discuss the possibility of Ottoman intervention in Egypt, which was still nominally Ottoman territory. The Ottoman sultan, however, refused to send a delegate to the conference, so nothing came of it. On May 2, Egyptian authorities had lost control of the situation to such an extent that they appealed for Anglo-French assistance. By May 20, both countries dispatched warships to Alexandria as a show of force. Neither, however, had a prearranged plan, nor had they received the authorization of the other great powers, leaving the ships unable to take military action. This Anglo-French invasion, however, sparked resistance from the Egyptian people, and an anti-European nationalistic uprising began in Alexandria on June 11, thus escalating the crisis. In June and July 1882, diplomatic efforts by the great powers to seek Ottoman intervention made little progress, so Great Britain decided on a course of unilateral action. On July 11, the British fleet began to bombard the port of Alexandria; French ships withdrew in protest. The British Army made landfall and, by September 13, had defeated the Egyptian forces and occupied the country. The 1882 Egyptian Crisis had ended.

Germany played an important role in these events. Bismarck himself had long hoped for such a crisis that could, as he stated in the Kissingen Dictation, allow him to use Egyptian and Mediterranean issues to drive a wedge between Britain and France. Out of all the possible outcomes of this crisis, unilateral British occupation of Egypt was the most likely to damage Anglo-French relations. Once this happened, Egypt would become a long-term sore spot in the Anglo-French relationship, leaving Germany plenty of space to maneuver between the two countries. Moreover, the British occupation of Egypt also brought stability to Anglo-Russian relations, as each country was now assured control over its own strategic weak points (for Britain, the sea lanes to India; for Russia, the Black Sea and Ukraine). Both, then, would be interested in the long-term maintenance of the *status quo*. Thus, Germany's position in Egypt was the opposite of its position in the Balkans: it made the gains without taking any of the risk.

Based on this judgment, Bismarck's overall calculation was to prolong, or even intensify, Anglo-French tensions in order to further Germany's European policy. As Bismarck himself emphasized to Germany's diplomats, German policy on Egypt depended entirely on Germany's relationships with other powers in Europe.[49] In sum, Bismarck's handling of the Egyptian Crisis can be reduced to three points that were also continuations of his regular policies.

First, he continued to maintain Germany's low posture in the management of the crisis. Germany had never been particularly active in the Egyptian issue. Only the escalation of the crisis between Anglo-French interests and Egyptian authorities in 1879 caused Germany to pay attention. Its goal, however, was not to resolve the issue, but to placate France in order to forestall closer Franco-Russian ties (especially since Russo-German relations were particularly tense at that point). At the same time, he also hoped to maintain Egypt's role as a latent source of conflict between Britain and France.[50] On January 27, 1882, the German consulate in Alexandria reported that the Egyptian authorities might not be able to maintain order and requested German intervention. Bismarck responded that, although the consul's desire for order was understandable, "These international considerations should not make us forget that the furtherance of this condition is *not* among the higher political tasks of Germany.... The consciousness of being a major great power should not be allowed to seduce us into a policy based on prestige, on the French model. Our actual international or pan-European interests are not sufficiently great to make it desirable for us to take the lead in Egyptian affairs."[51]

The second was to facilitate the appearance of cooperation in order to prevent actual Anglo-French cooperation. Bismarck, perhaps absorbing a lesson from his handling of the 1875 Near East Crisis, did not actively make any suggestions to the countries party to the dispute, in order to dispel any suspicion that he was seeking to use this conflict for his own ends. On the surface, he appeared to promote Anglo-French cooperation and to seek to cool the confrontation, but in actuality, Bismarck paid close attention to the course of events in order to prevent Anglo-French cooperation.[52] When French

Prime Minister Léon Gambetta proposed joint Anglo-French action against the threat of Egyptian nationalism in January 1882, Bismarck was opposed. Instead, he suggested that such joint actions often lead to disagreements among those who undertake them and isolate those countries from the rest of Europe, such as was the case in France's seizure of Tunis. He criticized British policy, saying, "England is at present being governed with a lack of foresight, such as has hardly been equaled in the long history of that country."[53] In fact, Bismarck was worried that if Great Britain and France worked together on this issue, this cooperation would only deepen once those countries learned that the rest of Europe was in opposition. Thus, his counterproposal was a European mediation that would enmesh Anglo-French cooperation in a much larger, much more complicated context. This would also serve to increase German ability to influence events. Bismarck's notion was that the European powers together should demand that the Ottoman Empire, Egypt's nominal sovereign, should restore order in Egypt. This would bring Anglo-French actions in Egypt back into compliance with existing international agreements, and would gain the support of "the Concert of Europe."[54] The Ottoman sultan refused to attend a conference to discuss this, and a Concert of Europe was never able to get off the ground. This proposal, therefore, only served as an obstacle to Anglo-French cooperation and postponed the resolution of the crisis. When the crisis intensified further, the two powers were only able to muster a joint show of force, after which the two country's different actions paced the way for conflict.

Third, Bismarck encouraged British occupation of Egypt. Even before the crisis, he had advocated unilateral British action in Egypt.[55] As early as November 1875, when British Prime Minister Disraeli took the decisive step of purchasing the Suez Canal, Bismarck expressed his strong support. In 1877, the German crown princess wrote to her mother, Queen Victoria, that "all lovers of England are so anxious that this opportunity should not pass by, of gaining a firm footing in Egypt."[56] Disraeli himself thought that "[this letter] might have been dictated by Prince Bismarck. If the Queen of England wishes to undertake the government of Egypt, her Majesty does not require the suggestion, or permission, of P. Bismarck."[57] The queen responded that Britain did not take other country's territory except when necessary, and that "Prince Bismarck would probably like us to seize Egypt, as it would be giving a great slap in the face of France, and be taking a mean advantage of her inability to protest."[58]

As it became apparent that Bismarck's proposed Concert of Europe solution had not advanced, the British government served notice to Herbert von Bismarck on June 24 that the conference had failed, and that Britain would occupy the Suez Canal, either unilaterally or with French cooperation. Even more significantly, Britain had already completed military preparations and could deploy some 8,000 soldiers from Gibraltar and Malta to Port Said within a week. Within two weeks, Britain could send an additional 10,000 men. After learning this, Bismarck realized that Britain was about to throw its cards on the table. He recognized that the failure of the Concert of Europe was mathematically certain.[59] Yet Bismarck felt that Germany should continue to proceed cautiously, as any open hint that Germany hoped to fan the flames of Anglo-French conflict might bring about the opposite. He sent clear orders to his government that once Britain took military action in Egypt, German's main objective was to prevent itself from being associated with any other country's reactions. If, for instance, France asked for German support in opposing the British action, the German answer would be that if Egypt's Ottoman sovereign could accept British operations in Egypt, then Germany had no right or reason to object.[60]

In July 1882, signs of impending British military action were already clear. Bismarck's worry at this point was that Britain might change course and give up the military option. To prevent this, Bismarck restated Germany's policy of non-interference in order to allay British concerns about Germany. That same month, British Foreign Secretary George Granville Leveson-Gower probed German intentions: "I should of course reserve full liberty of action, but the knowledge of what the Chancellor thought was practicable and desirable would be a most useful guide and probably prevent some unnecessary mistakes being made."[61] Bismarck replied that Germany hoped Britain, France, and the Ottoman Empire would reach an understanding over Egypt, but, as long as Germany's own vital interests were not harmed, Germany would not hinder Great Britain from taking any sort of action to protect its own vital interests. Bismarck, too, became extremely annoyed at the German consul in Alexandria's indiscreet public expressions of his own opinion and ordered him to be quiet so as not to affect British calculations. On July 4, after the commander of the British fleet threatened to attack the Egyptian rebels, the German consul in Alexandria, Anton von Saurma, sent an emergency telegraph to Berlin, imploring that "it seems urgently desirable to warn the irresponsible Admiral most earnestly to keep quiet." Bismarck replied, "Our task is not to warn the English Admiral but Saurma to keep quiet. It is not his business to interfere in the conduct of one of the European Powers or put forward petita if German interests do not demand it."[62] On July 9, Saurma received another warning to the effect that he "refrain from any action for which you have not received authorization from Berlin."[63] On July 11, when British ships bombarded Alexandria and the French refused to participate, Bismarck finally relaxed a little bit. Herbert von Bismarck wrote in a letter that, "My father is decidedly pleased about the bombardment."[64]

Diplomacy's Support and Supplement: The Army and Military Strategy

Germany's diplomatic strategy had assumed its fundamental form by the early 1880s. Through its flexible, balanced diplomacy, the foreign pressures that Germany experienced during the early period of its rise had diminished significantly and the defensive attitudes of other nations had noticeably faded. This created a relatively favorable international environment for Germany's rise. This success, however, was not due to Bismarck's diplomacy alone. Instead, the organic combination of diplomatic and military affairs—or, in other words, German grand strategy—played a major role. The German Army and German military strategy played an important role in this process.

Relations between Germany's Army and Government

After unification, Germany had the most powerful army in the world. Its military organizational structures, particularly the Prussian General Staff, became models widely imitated around the globe.[65] This military power was an immense asset to German diplomacy and spurred no small measure of national pride. The Austrian ambassador to Germany wrote that the tone of conversations with Prussian officials changed dramatically after the 1871 unification. When he asked one his thoughts on the future of Europe, the reply was: "We ourselves with a million soldiers are the equilibrium of the future."[66]

Yet there were also problems associated with this. The structure of the German military was extremely complex and its various components often worked at cross-purposes. The Prussian Ministry of War provides an example of this phenomenon. It was tasked with the administration of the whole German Army (with the exception of three states that maintained their own independent ministries), which included personnel issues, mobilization, and oversight of the General Staff, military academies, and logistical departments. The head of the ministry, the Minister of War, swore loyalty as a military officer to the kaiser and thus had a duty to ensure the throne's complete control of the military. As a Prussian minister, however, he also pledged obedience to the constitution and was accountable to the elected Landstag.

These two roles often conflicted. The nature of the Minister of War's position changed in significant ways after Germany's reconstituted as an empire. First, there was no such position as Imperial Minister of War. Second, Bismarck was the only cabinet minister to hold appointment at the imperial, as opposed to state, level, but he did not command the military. Thus, it fell to the Prussian Minister of War to be the representative of the national military and to communicate as such with the Reichstag. Thus, the army—and, particularly, the Minister of War—came to be seen by the Reichstag as representing the military, while in the eyes of the rest of the military (particularly the General Staff), he was seen as a representative of the government and of the Reichstag. These other elements of the military worked to restrict his authority, leading to a precarious set of relationships within the military.[67]

The German Army also had its own extremely distinctive military culture. At the imperial level, the military played a very important role in national life. As William Liebknecht, leader of the German Socialist Party said, "If you want to understand Germany you must grasp the fact that Germany, particularly Prussia, is an inverted pyramid. Its apex, firmly embedded in the ground, is the spike on the top of the Prussian soldiers' helmet. Everything rests on that."[68] The army had at its core an "officer clique." This was an extremely tight, closed group with its own ranks, conventions, and regulations formed among military officers. They saw themselves as loyal to the Prussian king (who was also the German kaiser) and as the imperial guards of the Hohenzollern house. It should be pointed out that this did not reflect an absolute willingness to blindly follow the orders of one man regardless of legal or organizational restrictions, because under normal circumstances, the kaiser could not become overly involved in military issues. This allowed management of military affairs to stay in the hands of a few high-ranking officers—that is to say, in the hands of the officer clique itself. On December 15, 1897, Kaiser Wilhelm II paid a visit to Bismarck, whom he had forced into retirement years before. Bismarck, who was nearing the end of his life, offered a final warning to the young monarch: "So long as you have this present officer corps, you can of course do as you please. But when this is no longer the case, it will be very different for you."[69] Wilhelm proved unable to heed this advice and, in 1918, it would be the leaders of the German officer corps, Paul von Hindenburg and Erich Ludendorff, who toppled him from power.

When relations between the civilian government and the military are rocky, it is easy for tensions to emerge between diplomatic affairs and military policies. Such tensions emerged between Bismarck and the army as early as the wars of German unification. In the 1866 war with Austria, Bismarck and his generals quarreled over whether or not to advance on Vienna after their victory at Sadowa. During the 1870–1871 Franco-Prussian War, the Prussian General Staff (the elder Helmuth von Moltke, in particular) involved themselves in a running series of disputes with Bismarck. The German crown prince, disturbed by this tension, attempted to mediate between the two men, but to no avail. In a letter to his wife, Bismarck angrily wrote, "The military gentlemen make my work terrifically difficult for me! They lay their hands on it and ruin it and I have to bear the responsibility."[70] From the elder Moltke's perspective, however, he was the actual commander on the battlefield—not only did he have to think about issues from a military point of view, but he was also responsible for the lives of those serving under him. Thus, he was unable to understand why political and diplomatic considerations should be allowed to interfere with military planning.

These tensions between Bismarck and the elder Moltke naturally carried over into the post-unification era. The origins did not lie in the personal relationship between the two or in the elder Moltke's view of Bismarck as an individual, but rather in the elder Moltke's worldview. The elder Moltke saw himself as a student of Carl von Clausewitz, the famous German military theorist, and in principle supported the notion of "war as an extension of politics." In his 1869 "Instructions for the Senior Troop Commanders," Moltke specifically emphasized that the "objective of war is to implement the government's policy by force." When it came, however, to the intersection of politics and military strategy during the actual conduct of a war, the elder Moltke's view departed drastically from that of Clausewitz. For Clausewitz, military strategy needed to be subordinate to politics even during wartime; the elder Moltke, by contrast, stressed the independence of military strategy: "the first duty and right of the art of war is to keep policy from demanding things that go against the nature of war, to prevent the possibility that out of ignorance of the way the instrument works, policy might misuse it."[71] In his essay "On Strategy," the elder Moltke went even further, claiming that:

> Politics uses war for the attainment of its ends; it operates decisively at the beginning and the end [of conflict], of course in such manner that it refrains from increasing its demands during the war's duration or from being satisfied with an inadequate success.... Strategy can only direct its efforts toward the highest goal which the means available make attainable. In this way, it aids politics best, working only for its objectives, but in its operations independent of it.[72]

After Bismarck assumed the position of imperial chancellor, his conflicts with the military manifested themselves over the issue of "preventative war." During the 1875 "War in Sight" Crisis, the elder Moltke and the Prussian General Staff contemplated a preemptive war against France, but were stopped by Bismarck. Over a decade later, during the 1887–1888 Bulgaria Crisis, forceful voices in the military again called for preemptive war (this time against Russia). It required tremendous effort for Bismarck, with his unique position in the government and his considerable influence, to ensure even a basic level of coordination between politics and the military. Under the German system, such coordination was not the normal state of affairs. Bismarck himself knew this and wrote in his memoir about his pessimistic view on the potential for military domination of politics: "[The fact that at times] the staff and its leaders have allowed themselves to be led astray and to endanger peace, lies in the very spirit of the institution, which I would not forego. It only becomes dangerous under a monarch whose policy lacks sense of proportion and power to resist one-sided and constitutionally unjustifiable influences."[73]

Compared to his successors, however, the elder Moltke had a strong grasp of the overall picture. During his time as chief of the General Staff, he devoted significant attention to coordination with the political leadership, particularly Bismarck. Although their relationship could be acrimonious, the elder Moltke allowed Bismarck access to the military's plans, thus allowing him to make informed foreign policy decisions. This is something his successors would be unwilling to do.

Changes in German Military Strategy under the Elder Moltke

The true level of cooperation between Bismarck and the elder Moltke can be seen in the realm of German grand strategy, where Bismarck's diplomacy and Moltke's military strategy complemented each other extremely well.

In his role as head of the Prussian General Staff, Moltke proved himself both an exceptional commanding officer and a careful strategic thinker, the likes of which had rarely been seen in German military history. He had a firm grasp of post-unification Germany's security environment. As early as April 1871, he predicted the dangers that a two-front war would present to a future Germany. He anticipated that a firm, friendly relationship between Germany and Russia, based on ties of royal blood such as existed during the Napoleonic Wars, was unlikely to be stable; that Austro-Prussian antagonism would be replaced by Austro-German cooperation; and that Russo-German relations would ultimately grow frosty. Russia, however, would not attack Germany by itself, without an ally in western Europe—and France was just such a potential ally. Thus, a future Germany would likely have to face a two-front war against both France and Russia.

The elder Moltke thought about the possibility of such a war with great clarity. Although he was the field commander for Prussia's quick victories over both Austria and France, he maintained a cautious attitude about whether or not quick victories would be possible in future wars. His experiences during the Franco-Prussian War told him that when a war between great powers was strictly limited to battlefield military operations, quick victory could be gained through superior troops, superior command structures, advanced weaponry, and other such factors. If such a war expanded, however, to become a total war, the quest for quick victory would become a dangerous, uncertain undertaking. In his April 1871 plan for a two-front war, the elder Moltke specified: "Germany cannot hope to rid herself of one enemy by a quick offensive victory in the West in order then to turn against the other. We have just seen how difficult it is to bring even the victorious war against France to an end."[74] Moltke instead proposed a strategy of "offensive defense" on both the eastern and western fronts. In the early phases of the war, the military would attack in order to bring the war to the enemy. Then, it would shift to the defensive and attempt to diminish the enemy's effective strength, with the goal of causing it to lose the will and the ability to continue the fight. The war would then end with a favorable peace treaty.

Germany stationed equal numbers of troops on its eastern and western frontiers. In 1872, France established a German-style system of compulsory conscription and inducted three-quarters of the targeted age group into military training. It also adopted a highly effective general staff and mobilization system, also modeled after Germany's. These innovations considerably eroded Germany's pre-existing superiority in mobilization speed and military organization. Thus, in 1873, Moltke looked to strengthen German defenses in the west, and even proposed that preparations were needed for the eventuality that French troops crossed the Rhine. He planned that, in such a situation, German forces would regroup on the banks of the Rhine. Geography would force the advancing French Army to separate into two groups, one north and one south, allowing Germany to concentrate its military forces and break though the French center, pushing the northern forces back toward Paris and the southern forces back to Lorraine. Once this plan succeeded, Germany would offer France generous terms for a peace treaty.[75]

By 1877, Moltke's vision of strategic equality of the eastern and western fronts underwent further modification. In a February 3 memorandum, he noted the quick growth of French military strength and the increase in speed of its pre-war mobilization capabilities. These led him to finger France as Germany's most important future foe. As a consequence, he retreated from his original notion of equal deployments on Germany's eastern and western frontiers, instead concentrating his forces in the west. He calculated that within three weeks after a mobilization order was given, a decisive battle would be fought with France's main force. After this victory over France, the army would be moved to the eastern front to confront Russia. On the surface, this plan seems similar to the Schlieffen Plan of later years, but two fundamental differences exist. First, the elder Moltke's decisive battle was not the same thing as the battle of annihilation sought by Alfred von Schlieffen. He in fact specifically warned against the notion that France could be completely routed: "It must be left to diplomacy to determine whether it can achieve peace for us on this side, even if it can be done only on the basis of the *status quo ante*."[76] Second, the Schlieffen Plan did not make any allowances for setbacks, but Moltke's plan considered a number of unpleasant possibilities, including what Germany should do if it loses the "decisive battle" with France. If that were to occur, the German Army would shift immediately to the defensive, retreating behind the Rhine if needed. A portion of the army would be diverted to the eastern front in order to strengthen German defenses there and blunt any Russian attack.[77]

Such a strategy did not fully satisfy Moltke. As French military power steadily grew and French defensive works were constructed along the Franco-German border, he came to view the potential results of a western offensive as meager. Conversely, he saw conditions for German defenses in the west as extremely favorable: the Franco-German border, which ran from Belgium to the Alps, was relatively short, well protected by German fortifications, and contained the Rhine as a natural barrier. Moltke's view shifted to the judgment that "it would be a mistake to launch an immediate strategic offensive" on the western front. His strategy for the western front was for limited German forces to defend a region with the Saar at its core, Metz as its forward position, and Strassburg as its southern flank. France, rather than Germany, would be allowed to go on the offensive. Given the strong desire to recover Alsace-Lorraine, it was likely that France would rush to launch an attack. Once French forces had completely left their prepared positions and entered open territory, the German Army, with its strong defensive fortifications, would pounce. Moltke saw this sort of defensive battle as being easily winnable by the German Army. Even so, he considered what would happen if the army's defense failed. His plan for this possibility called for a retreat behind the Rhine and a reconsolidation of the withdrawn armies on the Main River between Mainz and Frankfurt.[78] Moltke's plans should not be understood as negative defense of the western front, but as a form of "offensive defense." As he argued, "even facing superior numbers, we must risk a battle in front of the Rhine before withdrawing behind it."[79]

On the eastern front, by contrast, Moltke envisioned a strategic offensive. He did not think it was practical to effectively defend the 750-kilometer-long Russo-German border. It was, however, a region suitable for a strategic offensive. In particular, he saw East Prussia as a strategic bulge that could be easily encircled and cut off if used defensively or that could be used effectively to surround the main force of the Russian Army in Russian-occupied Poland. Given Russia's vast size, Moltke did not think a strategy of seeking a "battle of annihilation" to be sensible and any German attempt to seek such a confrontation would merely be a futile action. If, however, the German Army were able to inflict a series of serious defeats on major Russian military units and coupled this with a systematic, measured call for nationalist uprisings inside the Russian Empire, then Russian resolve would crumble. The Russian government might then be willing to negotiate peace, particularly if Germany offered reasonable terms. Moltke saw this final point as being possible because "the Russians…have absolutely nothing which one could take from them after the most successful war; they have no gold, and we don't need land."[80] Thus, as long as Germany only sought limited war objectives, it would be possible to fight a relatively short, victorious war against Russia. Once Russia departed the war, an isolated France would lose its motivation for continuing to fight and the war would conclude with negotiations. Moltke himself provided a one-sentence summary of his post-1879 military strategy: "If we must fight two wars 150 miles apart, then, in my opinion, we should exploit in the west the great advantages which the Rhine and our powerful fortifications offer to the defensive and should employ all the fighting forces which are not absolutely indispensable [in the west] for an imposing offensive against the east."[81] German forces were still to be equally deployed on both fronts, but the 300,000 soldiers in the west would be tasked with defense, while the 360,000 troops in the east were to seek opportunities for the offensive against Russian forces in Kovno and Warsaw.[82]

With the signing of the Austrian alliance in 1879, conditions for German offensive operations in the east improved even further. Although the elder Moltke doubted the fighting potential of the Austrian Army, he took on a role as chief of the alliance's general staff and began dialogue with the Austrian military command in 1882. His subordinates and a member of the Austrian

General Staff eventually worked out a plan for a joint offensive against Russia. German forces would move from East Prussia in coordination with Austrian units from Galicia to envelope the Russian Army near Warsaw. This would force the Russians to leave their defensive fortifications and create the conditions for a decisive battle. The offensive's goal would be to push the front back to Brest-Litovsk, the Bug River, and the Austro-Russian border. This would merely drive a wedge into the bulge of Russian-occupied Poland that separated Austria and Germany. This suggests that, like his strategy in the west, Moltke did not seek a battle of annihilation, much less a complete victory. Instead, his goal was a limited victory that would allow diplomats to negotiate peace on favorable terms.

The elder Moltke's military strategy can be reduced to two basic points. First, strategic objectives should be limited, with the aim of achieving favorable terms of peace, rather than complete victory. Second, the best plan was to attack in the East and defend in the West by first placing emphasis on defeating Russia and then focusing on fighting France. These two strands of thought were mutually supporting and both were necessary. The Schlieffen Plan that eventually was put into action discarded both.

Special Characteristics of the Elder Moltke's Strategy

The elder Moltke's military strategy had at least four strong points, based on an analysis of the conditions at the time:

First, it was objective in the sense that it matched the objective conditions of the time. After the Franco-Prussian War, Germany annexed the French territories of Alsace-Lorraine. This was a political mistake, as it transformed France into a permanent enemy and greatly reduced German room for diplomatic maneuver. In military terms, however, it had merit: these two regions, if they remained in French hands, would be important massing points for the French Army and would directly threaten the German industrial center of the Saar. Germany's occupation of these regions gave it control of the two important fortresses on the Franco-German border, Strassburg and Metz, giving it a strong defensive front line. As long as Switzerland and Belgium maintained neutrality, any French attack on Germany could only come in this region, which was, in the words of Engels, "the strongest and biggest quadrangle of fortresses in the world."[83] It could be defended by a relatively small number of German soldiers for a lengthy period, providing some military compensation for the political costs of the original decision to occupy the region.

Second, it allowed for an organic coordination with diplomacy. The elder Moltke's "attack in the East and defend in the West" strategy was, in its basic spirit, harmonious with Germany's overall foreign policies. Bismarck was not seeking to conquer new lands or to obtain hegemony over Europe. Similarly, Moltke did not seek complete victory, but planned to use limited military successes to force Germany's opponents to lose the desire to fight. He emphasized that this would create favorable conditions for diplomacy and political maneuvering. This strategy was also incorporated into the alliance with Austria after 1879. As that alliance was only directed against Russia, and not against France, Germany had a two-to-one advantage in the east, giving his basic strategy an even firmer footing. His far-sightedness must be stressed here. Even though he essentially did not trust the alliance and, as a Prussian military officer, did not respect the Austrian military or its General Staff, his establishment of a joint general staff as an instrument for coordination between the two countries allowed German military strategy at the operational level to work with the foreign policy strategy.

Third, it was controllable. It provided a level of control over the development of events during a crisis, providing policymakers with a safety valve. As the ultimate method for responding to crises and protecting national security, military strategy is always directly linked to a nation's ability to control situations. If a military strategy is entirely rooted in responding to the most extreme situations, then, when faced with a relatively less serious crisis, the only available choices will be to do nothing or to adopt measures meant for extreme cases. This second option would create a self-fulfilling prophecy, as it would escalate the crisis into being that most extreme situation, which would force the nation into choosing between surrender and fighting a devastating total war. This would prove to be the choice provided by the Schlieffen Plan in later decades. Moltke's strategy, by contrast, embodied a high degree of flexibility. Even in a situation that involved fighting on both fronts, it would allow Germany a measure of control over the situation. In the west, German forces would be on the defensive in favorable territory, while in the east, it would have the assistance of an ally, making a defeat of Russia's main forces (or at least the blunting of Russian abilities to go on the offensive) highly likely.[84] This put the initiative in Germany's hands. As long as it did not seek to seize Paris or occupy large amounts of Russian territory, this plan would create favorable military conditions for making peace. French and Russian losses, by contrast, would cause them to lose motivation to fight to the end.

Fourth, it was cost-effective. As the three points above make clear, this strategy was a method for using a limited amount of money to guarantee national security without needing to greatly expand the armed forces. During the Bismarckian era, the German military grew at a relatively stately pace.

The 1880 seven-year budget projected an expansion from 401,000 men to 427,000, while the seven-year budget adopted in 1887 called for a further expansion to 468,000.[85] The lion's share of attention was devoted to the army. In 1870, a sum of £9,600,000 was spent on the German Army. This increased to £18,200,000 in 1880 and £24,200,000 in 1890. Looking at this comparatively, German share of the total army expenditures of the five great powers was 15 percent in 1870, 19.3 percent in 1880, and 22.7 percent in 1890. Its shares of the total naval expenditures for the same period were, respectively, 5.7 percent, 9.3 percent, and 14 percent.[86] Considering that Germany's share of the combined economies of the five great powers was 16 percent in 1870, 20 percent in 1880, and 25 percent in 1890, the pace of military expansion appears rather moderate. It did not increase suspicion in the other great powers, nor did it cause an arms race.[87]

In conclusion, the frameworks of both Bismarck's foreign policy strategy and the elder Moltke's military strategy had been established. At a philosophical level, these strategies were consistent with one another: both sought limited victory and manifested conservative instincts. In the realm of actual practice, the two strategies likewise supplemented and supported one another. Despite the serious defects in German decision-making institutions, these two pillars formed a comprehensive grand strategy with limited objectives, and its indirect path of development fully fit the needs of a rising Germany's complicated foreign affairs environment. Within little more than a decade after unification, Germany's power had increased quickly without provoking foreign push-back. The opposite had, in fact, happened: Germany's leading role had earned acceptance by the other great powers. This "miracle" in international relations history cannot but reflect the success of this grand strategy.

3

Working to Maintain the Grand Strategy

"I think it may be true that fortune is the ruler of half our actions, but that she allows the other half or a little less to be governed by us."
Niccolo Machiavelli

The essence of grand strategy lies in the coordination and balance of various resources, methods, policies, and demands. Often this coordination is both subtle and fragile; it is buffeted by the contest of other interests and changing outside forces. The obligation of strategic decision-makers, however, is to make that coordination as flexible as possible so that it can respond to changes while maintaining its own balance and harmony. Throughout the course of Germany's rise, its grand strategy faced a double assault. First, the rapid development of national power spurred enormous changes in domestic politics and society, which created social forces that substantially affected political leaders' appraisal of costs and benefits. Second, the ever-changing international environment continually confounded pre-existing strategic arrangements, such as in the case of the continued tensions between Austria and Russia. Pressure for continual revision of policies was relentless. Until his forced retirement, Bismarck was locked in combat with these two forces, and he emerged mostly victorious in maintaining the balance and stability of his grand strategy.

Pressure Generated by Social Trends

Grand strategy mainly focuses on foreign policy, yet domestic factors significantly affect it as well. For a rising great power, the rapid increase of national power is always accompanied by radical changes in domestic structures of authority. The accumulated pressures of this process seek release in a variety of ways, some of which will manifest in powerful social trends.

The primary way that social trends influence grand strategy is through transforming both domestic society and the calculation of cost and benefits for decision-makers. This point has been well explained by economists. For example, the study of institutional economics has done much to explain the frequency of irrational behavior. As Douglass C. North has pointed out, interference by ideological factors often produces behaviors that do not align with any clear cost/benefit analysis. A successful ideology does, in fact, change perceptions of cost and benefit, leading to "abnormal" results.[1] Social trends can have the same effect on politics and strategy.

Perhaps we should directly take social trends to be a form of ideology. "Ideology" as a term can be understood in a narrow sense and in a broad sense. In the narrow sense, ideology is primarily a conceptual system for linking class society on the one hand and the economic base and superstructure on the other. In the broad sense, ideology is a factor that can be understood through several disparate disciplines, including political science, sociology, literary studies, and economics.[2] In each of these fields, ideology represents a way of knowing. North further argued that ideology is foremost an "economizing device." Through ideology, people can come to understand the environment in which they live. Under the influence of a "worldview," the process of decision-making is simplified.[3] Louis Althusser further emphasized that ideologies must go through a process of extreme simplification in order to make them easier for the masses to accept: "It is indeed a peculiarity of ideology that it imposes (without appearing to do so, since these are 'obviousnesses') obviousnesses as obviousnesses, which we cannot fail to recognize and before which we have the inevitable and natural reaction of crying out (aloud or in the 'still, small voice of conscience'): 'That's obvious! That's right! That's true!'"[4] Understanding ideology as a mode of cognition that has been simplified for the masses clearly reveals the functions and characteristics of ideology. Thus, this book adopts the term ideology, in the broad sense, as a replacement for the phrase "social forces."

A careful consideration of Germany's situation in the late nineteenth century clearly reveals that its rise wrought profound changes inside the country. The rapid growth of some of these social currents mobilized parts of the population, and different ideologies came to exhibit immense political power. The dominant ideologies in Germany included nationalism, democracy (sometimes called national liberalism), imperialism, and socialism.[5] The first three of these had the greatest impact on diplomacy and security policy. Socialism's impact was largely on domestic politics, so it will not be discussed here.

Nationalism

Nationalism is an ancient phenomenon that developed into its modern form during the French Revolution and the Napoleonic Wars. It manifested itself in the strengthened sense of a common, shared consciousness that grew on the foundations of shared living space, language, and history and understanding of legitimate political authority. This sentiment began to have the power to mobilize the loyalty of the population.[6] By the latter half of the nineteenth century, nationalism in Europe underwent a series of significant changes. First, nationalism shifted from being a relatively tolerant belief into an ideology of competition colored with a strong tint of chauvinism.[7] Second, the phrase "self-determination" came to be used to describe not only countries that demonstrably had the political, economic, and cultural ability to exist, but also for any group that called itself a "nationality." Third, complete independence as a sovereign nation became the only way to satisfy calls for national determination.[8]

The rise of nationalism had a number of serious consequences for Germany. First, German unification itself was a product of nationalism, and Germany's existence as a sovereign nation-state further stimulated the growth of nationalist sentiments. Second, the redirection of popular loyalty from monarchical dynasties to the nation weakened the traditional ties between royal families that had previously been so important in international relations. This made it ever more difficult for Germany to use the principle of monarchical unity to bind Russia and Austria together. Third, the struggle for national independence in the Balkans—the so-called Eastern Question—grew sharper, leading to higher tensions between Russian and Austria and creating a greater danger that Germany would be drawn into the dispute. Fourth, nationalism, especially when accompanied by chauvinism, stressed the competitive side of international relations. By the end of the nineteenth century, an increasing number of Germans saw international relations as being the struggle between various ethnic nationalities, such as Teutons, Anglo-Saxons, and Slavs, among others. For example, when Great Britain went to war against the Boer Republic in South Africa, popular sentiment in Germany was anti-British not for any political or economic reason, but because the Boers were identified, like the Germans, as Teutonic.[9]

Democracy

For the majority of European countries, the period from 1871 to 1914 was an era of democratization. Inside Germany, which was undergoing dramatic economic and social changes, democratic politics were both a result of these changes and an impetus for them. The most direct expression of democratic politics in Germany was the growth of popular participation in national political life. Taking the voter participation rate in Reichstag elections as an example, only 50 percent of enfranchised voters cast ballots in 1871, and that number never exceeded two-thirds of registered voters over the next fourteen years. By 1887, however, the voter participation rate increased to 77.2 percent, and in the 1907 and 1912 elections, it went as high as 84 percent.

Mass popular participation in politics had a variety of consequences. Foremost of these, from the perspective of national strategic decision-making, was that traditional "cabinet diplomacy" and secret diplomacy were ever more restricted. Decision-makers now could not just consider the demands of national interest. They also needed to account for popular acceptance and approval of their policies. The British Foreign Secretary, the Earl of Clarendon, expressed this in 1869, saying, "Governments no more than individuals can afford nowadays to despise public opinion."[10] Second, wider popular participation in politics provides greater opportunities for interest groups to exert influence. As a late-rising power, Germany's rapid economic growth promoted the democratization of domestic politics. Compared to Britain and France, Germany's political processes and institutions (although they were influenced by democratic trends) were imperfect and did not constitute a fully mature political culture. Under these conditions, enthusiastic mass public political participation provided a new route for interest groups to exert pressure on the government: the direct mobilization of people to create or manipulate public opinion. Without the rise of democratic politics, nationalism, imperialism, and other popular ideologies could not have had such a large effect. Thus, democracy played a fundamental role in the development of these other ideologies.

Imperialism

Imperialism, of all of the popular ideologies, had the greatest impact on high-level German policymakers. Late nineteenth-century European imperialism was an admixture of nationalism, racism, Social Darwinism, and other intellectual trends. Beyond simply emphasizing the economic need for overseas expansion and the seizure of colonies, advocates of imperialist expansion appealed to the eternal principles of the "struggle for survival" and "survival of the fittest." In Germany, the forces in favor of overseas expansion included not only a portion of the industrial and mercantile communities, but also some intellectuals. The most famous of these included Heinrich von Treitschke and Friedrich Fabri. They gave a number of reasons for Germany's pressing need for colonies. First, the seizure of new markets was necessary to absorb excess German industrial production and to provide a destination for German capital. Second, colonies could reduce social dissatisfaction by acting as a relief valve for domestic pressures. Cecil Rhodes, the famous British imperialist, made a similar argument in 1895: "In order to save the forty million inhabitants of the United Kingdom from a bloody civil war, our colonial statesmen must acquire new lands for settling the surplus population of this country, to provide new markets.... The Empire, as I have always said, is a bread and butter question." Third, it could protect the national labor force, as German colonies could absorb over a million German migrants, who might otherwise immigrate to the United States, thus strengthening an already frightening economic competitor. Fourth, imperialism could ensure survival amid international competition, as other European powers all already had large colonial empires. According to the natural law of survival of the fittest, German survival depended on copying these countries by seizing colonies.[11] Fifth, taking foreign colonies in order to propagate German culture and national consciousness could re-ignite the German national spirit.[12] These viewpoints were ceaselessly promoted through the repeated propaganda efforts of a number of pro-imperialist organizations, and imperialism became one of the main ideologies in Germany. The pressures this placed on government decision-making were apparent even in Bismarck's era.

To use for a moment the ideas of Ferdinand Braudel, a French historian of the *Annales* school, social ideologies are the "deeper level" of the history written about in books, similar in force and effect to the movement of plates beneath the earth's surface.[13] In the face of this, the space for any political figure to have an impact is limited. But the task of political leaders, especially those who carry the fate of the nation on their shoulders, is always to seek the possible in the midst of the impossible. Bismarck's wisdom lay in his deep understanding of the objective existence of these powerful forces. He did his utmost to use these forces to his own ends, while maintaining the initiative in his own hands and protecting the balance and flexibility of his policies.

Bismarck, unlike the political figures of Wilhelm II's day, did not allow himself to be pushed along by these forces, nor was he locked into rigid opposition to them (with the exception of the socialist movement). Instead, he tried to get ahead of these forces in order to restrain them. In other words, before these forces had fully formulated their political demands, he would decisively grant demands that they might seek, thereby controlling and dominating the process. For example, he controlled demands for nationalism and democracy by completing the process of national unification and implementing full male electoral suffrage. As Friedrich Engels explained, this was an attempt to prove to the German bourgeois that "Bismarck had shown it that he knew better what was good for it than it knew itself…[he] fulfilled its national program with a speed and accuracy that surprised the bourgeoisie itself."[14] British historian Eric Hobsbawm provided this wonderful description of Bismarck's (and British Prime Minister Disraeli's) ability to dominate:

> First, they found themselves in a situation of economic and political change which they could not control, but to which they had to adapt. The only choice—and statesmen recognized this clearly—was whether to sail before the wind or use their skill as sailors to steer their ships into another direction. The wind itself was a fact of nature. Second, they had to determine what concessions to the new forces could be made without threatening the social system, or in special cases the political structures, to whose defense they were committed, and the point beyond which they could not safely go. But thirdly, they were fortunate to be able to make both kinds of decisions under circumstances which permitted them a considerable initiative, scope for manipulation and in some cases actually left them virtually free to control the course of events.[15]

Bismarck relied on timely and flexible policies to successfully avoid conflict with domestic political and social forces, allowing German grand strategy to achieve a measure of stability. The classic example of this is the case of Germany's overseas colonies in the Bismarckian era.

Bismarck's Overseas Colonies

In the second half of the nineteenth century, a wave of imperialist interest in overseas expansion and colonialism swept over Germany.[16] An interest group comprising capitalists engaged in light industry and manufacture, as well as mercantile bourgeois centered in Hamburg and Bremen, lay behind this. Through the promotion efforts of this interest group and some intellectuals, this ideology quickly spread throughout Germany. To a great degree, it came to shape the foreign policy views of ordinary Germans. Traditional German disinterest in colonies was overturned. In its place, German society filled with the hope that overseas colonies could be a "magic pill" that would promote economic, social, and even racial improvement.

Bismarck retained a politician's calmness in facing this new environment. From his pragmatic perspective, colonies would be a useless burden to Germany. First, the acquisition of colonies had political and economic costs. Management of colonies would require additional investments of effort and capital, with unclear prospects of any return. Overall, the losses would outweigh any gains.[17] Second, Germany's domestic situation did not lend itself to the pursuit of colonial acquisitions. Germany had only existed as a unified nation for a short time, and a sense of shared national identity was still not completely in place. The establishment of ties between a mother country and colonies, however, required "a mother country in which national feeling is stronger than the spirit of partisanship."[18] Third, colonies would increase Germany's vulnerabilities. Bismarck once commented to the British ambassador to Germany that colonies would not be a source of strength for Germany, but instead would "only be a cause of weakness, because colonies could only be defended by powerful fleets, and Germany's geographical position did not necessitate her development into a first-class naval power."[19]

Between 1879 and 1882, Bismarck basically adopted a policy of resisting pressures for overseas expansion in order to avoid disrupting Germany's overall foreign policy. He ignored powerful public opinion and interest group pressure in favor of such a policy, refusing requests to send German naval forces to Africa and other distant regions.[20]

As social pressures intensified further, however, Bismarck began to shift strategies to get out in front of this issue. This was an attempt to exceed expectations by going even beyond what advocates hoped for and then reimposing restrictions on them, thus returning them to a controllable, harmless state.

The Origins of Bismarck's Colonial Policy

In the spring of 1883, a German merchant established a factory in Southwest Africa's Angra Pequena (now part of Namibia). In May, he raised a German flag over his factory, inciting friction with local British colonial authorities. Past practice would suggest that the German government would merely lodge a protest with the British, demanding protection for overseas German people and economic interests. This time, however, Bismarck acted differently. In November 1883, he directly inquired of the British whether or not Britain was claiming sovereign control over that territory and the basis for any such claim.[21] On November 21, the British government gave a muddled reply, whereupon Germany renewed its original question in a formal communication on December 31. The British continued to stall. Simultaneously, British colonial authorities in South Africa demanded that the British government declare at once that the entire region from Angra Pequena to Wallis Bay was to be British territory. The British government accepted this suggestion and informed the German government of its new claim. In response, Bismarck took unilateral action: on April 24, 1884, he telegraphed the German consul in Capetown, ordering him to inform the British authorities that Angra Pequena was already under German protection. The British, naturally, were unwilling to surrender this colony. On May 16, the colonial secretary announced in the House of Lords that Great Britain was not prepared to formally make Angra Pequena its own colony, but that it also had the right to prevent other countries from doing so. In early June, British colonial authorities announced that they had already completed preparations to occupy the entire coastline from South Africa to Wallis Bay, including Angra Pequena.

On the whole, Great Britain had taken a firm line on this issue, rather than, as one historian has claimed, engaging in "confused negotiation" or acquiescing by default.[22] Bismarck angrily responded that Britain's policies were "a Monroe Doctrine for Africa."[23] In order to bring sufficient pressure to bear against the British government, he listed all of the liabilities placed on Germany by British actions in Egypt and the Black Sea, and demanded that Britain clearly state "whether England is inclined, in her present situation, in return for our firm offer of greater support than before for British policy, to satisfy our overseas grievances by ceasing to lay hindrances in the way of the legitimate enterprises of German nationals."[24] Bismarck expressed his dissatisfaction with the performance of the German ambassador in London, saying: "You would have been all the more justified in expressing your astonishment, that the right of German subjects to trade there was not unconditionally admitted in the House of Lords speech, and much more so, that the Monroe Doctrine, that monstrosity in International Law, was being applied in favor of England to the coast of Africa."[25] In order to coordinate colonial policy with German strategic support for Britain, Bismarck prohibited his ambassador from further entanglements with the British colonial secretary, instead ordering him only to have direct contacts with the British Foreign Office.[26] By early June, in order to further increase pressure on the British, Bismarck dispatched his son to London to work with the ambassador to clearly articulate the German position on these colonial issues, and also to emphasize the possibility that Germany might "completely change" its original support for British policy in Egypt.[27]

Anglo-German colonial disputes over the Fiji Islands and other locations also erupted at the same time. Germany, in an eye-raising move, inserted itself into Anglo-French colonial disputes in Africa. In the early 1880s, the European struggle for African territory, particularly in the Congo River basin, had become intense. On November 30, 1882, French explorer Pierre Savorgnan de Brazza signed a treaty with local chiefs in the Congo basin. In response, the British announced in December 1882 that Portugal had the right to make the region near the mouth of the Congo its own colony. On February 26, 1884, the British and Portuguese inked a treaty granting this region to Portugal and giving Great Britain special privileges in this new Portuguese colony. This treaty sparked intense opposition from the French, creating the most serious crisis between Britain and France since the 1882 British intervention in Egypt. This time, however, Bismarck's intervention in the crisis was not quiet or behind-the-scenes. Instead, he leaped wholeheartedly into the dispute, giving France his full cooperation, and created a common Franco-German opposition to the British. This was a natural extension of Bismarck's original line of thought when he first encouraged French colonial expansion.

In the face of such strong German pressure, Great Britain had no choice but to consider giving ground. Lord Granville, the British foreign secretary, thought that given British reliance on German assistance in a number of other areas, Britain should "pay the bill" by acquiescing to German colonial expansion.[28] On June 22, 1884, Great Britain formally recognized German occupation of southwestern Africa, and four days later it annulled the treaty with Portugal. Granville further claimed that, as long as German colonies remained open to trade, Britain would be quite satisfied to see Germany establish its own colonies. France typically imposed protective tariffs of up to 50 percent in its colonies; German colonies, by contrast, had much lower tariffs, thus complying with the principles of free trade.[29] Great Britain's attitude allowed German colonial expansion to proceed smoothly. By 1885, Germany had acquired a series of colonies totaling over a million square kilometers and comprising about 90 percent of all the colonial territory that Germany would hold at the outbreak of World War I.

Characteristics of Bismarck's Colonial Policy

Several particular characteristics of Bismarck's colonial policy stand out when compared to the colonial policy Germany would pursue under Wilhelm II. First, Bismarck's colonial policies were part of a larger grand strategy. They were subordinate to the nation's overall foreign policy, particularly its policies toward Europe. For Bismarck, the core mission of German foreign policy was to forestall the creation of an anti-German alliance—or, if that failed, to ensure that Germany ended up in the stronger of whatever groupings of great powers emerged. In 1880, he told the Russian ambassador in Berlin that Germany needed to pay attention to "the importance of being one of three on the European chess-board."[30] The 1882 British occupation of Egypt and consequent worsening of Anglo-French relations presented Bismarck with an opportunity to reconcile with France. This further reduced chances for a Franco-Russian alliance. Colonial policies, too, aided this process. The most suitable path for reconciling with France was to cooperate with it during common arguments over colonial expansion with the British. Bismarck said as much to the French ambassador to Germany in 1884: "I want to persuade you to forgive Sedan as you have forgiven Waterloo."[31] In order to further improve the atmosphere for reconciliation with the French, Bismarck seemingly deliberately made his colonial disputes with the British "noisy." For instance, he had the German ambassador to London query the British foreign secretary, "How can [he] contest our right [to establish colonies] at the very moment when the British Government is granted an unlimited exercise of the same right?"[32] As a result, the Franco-German reconciliation promoted by German colonial policy seemed to provide an inkling of future possibilities, as evidenced by public discussions in the French newspaper *Le Figaro* and the German *Kölnische Zeitung* (a mouthpiece for Bismarck) on the potential for a Franco-German alliance.[33] The course of events, however, would ultimately expose many deep conflicts between Germany and France, and this alliance became increasingly unlikely. Particularly after France's 1885 war with China, coupled with the toppling of the Jules Ferry cabinet in the wake of French battlefield defeats, hopes that colonial policy could create grounds for a true reconciliation became ever dimmer. Bismarck rationally faced this reality and ended his policies of colonial expansion. Bismarck's principle that colonial policy existed in the service of Germany's overall foreign policy, and particularly its policies in Europe, came through most clearly in his words to an advocate of colonial expansion: "My map of Africa lies in Europe. Here lies Russia and here lies France, and we are in the middle. That is my map of Africa."[34]

The second characteristic was that Bismarck had a clear bottom line to his colonial policies: they could not be allowed to harm German national security. From 1883 to 1885, there was a period of complete German security: the Egyptian occupation had shattered the Anglo-French liberal alliance and had pushed Britain into a reliance on German cooperation; the League of

Three Emperors had been successfully renewed; and Russo-Austrian tensions had quieted in the Balkans. Even under these favorable conditions, however, Bismarck proceeded carefully and paid attention to maintaining the appropriate degree. He hoped to use limited colonial tensions to maintain ties of mutual restraint and mutual dependence with Great Britain. This ensured that the narrow colonial concessions made by the British did not exceed what they could tolerate, and prevented any limited short-term troubles from developing into long-term opposition.[35] Overall, the Franco-German reconciliation that Bismarck promoted was far from being an anti-British alliance. Instead, its purpose was to display Germany's space for diplomatic action and to seize the initiative in relations with Great Britain. Bismarck himself explained, "I do not want war with England, but I desire her to understand that if the fleets of other nations unite, they will form a counter balance on the ocean and oblige her to reckon with the interests of others."[36] In another letter, he wrote, "We will only gain England's goodwill—if only a goodwill accompanied by gnashing of teeth—by way of an alliance with France."[37] In his private conversations, he averred, "The friendship of Lord Salisbury is worth more to me than twenty marshy colonies in Africa."[38] Bismarck made choices in colonial policies: he quarreled with Britain over Southwest Africa and worked in unison with France to pressure Great Britain in the Congo. For matters that touched core British interests, such as Egypt, however, he remained behind the scenes and allowed the French to take the lead.[39]

The third characteristic was that Bismarck maintained control and initiative over German colonial policies, even though those policies were created in response to domestic political motives. Domestic political needs were one cause of Germany's colonial expansion in 1884–1885. Bismarck hoped to use special interest groups, particularly the northern capitalists who had been disappointed by the 1879 tariff, to maintain his Reichstag majority in the 1884 elections. He hoped, too, to use their support to block the political ascendancy of any British-style liberal forces inside Germany.[40] The existence of these motives, however, did not mean that Bismarck allowed his colonial policies to be the hostage of domestic political pressures. Bismarck controlled the pace of German colonial expansion from start to finish—unlike his successors during the era of Wilhelm II. When Bismarck came to feel that the foreign policy climate had changed, making the continued pursuit of colonies deleterious to Germany's overall interests, he stopped. Even more interesting, his colonial policies, similar to his policies in other areas, were nimble and flexible. As a result, he was willing to trade away the things that he had just struggled to win, if needed. For example, in 1889, he expressed his belief that colonies were a burden to Germany and his hope that Southwest Africa could be transferred to the British.[41]

A policy based on these characteristics allowed Bismarck to harness domestic political interest groups and public opinion while maintaining a stable foreign policy and balanced grand strategy. If we take the maxim "expansion always provokes reaction" as a principle of international politics, then Bismarck's accomplishment—the creation of overseas colonies in two short years without increasing security pressures on Germany—must be seen as a rare exception. This suggests the value of grand strategy.

The Bulgaria Crisis

Changes in external conditions challenged Bismarck's grand strategy as much as domestic political pressures. This was especially the case when trends in the Balkans brought Russia and Austria into renewed conflict with one another, threatening the dissolution of the League of Three Emperors that Bismarck had struggled so hard to create—as happened in the 1885 Bulgaria Crisis.

The Beginning of the Crisis

Bulgaria was a creation of the 1878 Berlin Conference. At that time, Russia had advocated the creation of a larger Greater Bulgaria, but as a result of British and Austrian opposition, that plan did not reach fruition. In many ways, the division of the region into Bulgaria and Eastern Rumelia symbolized Russia's foreign policy failure at the conference. The situation, however, changed rapidly. The Russians discovered that the monarch they selected for Bulgaria, Prince Alexander of Battenberg, would not accept Russian control. Bulgaria, it turned out, would not simply be an extension of Russian power. Movements for national independence in the Balkans continued to grow. In September 1885, an uprising broke out in Eastern Rumelia; the victorious rebels ejected the Ottoman civil and military commanders and proclaimed union with Bulgaria. This was the result that Russia had struggled to win at Berlin in 1878, but by 1885, it had become something the Russians fought to avoid. This was not only because the rebellion was led by anti-Russian forces, but also because the emergence of a Greater Bulgaria would enhance the position of Prince Alexander and serve to diminish the Russian sphere of influence in the Balkans. Russia thus transformed itself into a defender of the 1878 settlement and strongly opposed the union of Bulgaria and Eastern Rumelia.

The fight initiated by the Eastern Rumelia rebellion spread to Macedonia, which had a substantial Bulgarian population. This stoked fears of Bulgarian aggression in Austria and Serbia. Finding a quick resolution to the Bulgaria Crisis became extremely important for the Austro-Hungarian Empire, leading its opinion to converge with Russia's. In October 1885, the European great powers and the Ottoman government held a conference in Istanbul. Russia proposed Ottoman military intervention in Bulgaria to restore the 1878 settlement. Germany, Austria, France, and Italy all lent their support. Great Britain, however, objected. Instead, it proposed that the Ottoman sultan appoint Prince Alexander as the chief civil officer in Eastern Rumelia. This would create the *de facto* unification of the two territories. Britain's proposal reignited Austro-Russian antagonism in the Balkans. Austria found itself steadily drawn to the British side, causing the tensions with Russia to escalate into a crisis. This was exactly what Bismarck did not want to see.

Initially, Bismarck was able to maintain control over the situation. He tamped down Austrian designs for seizing primacy in the Balkans. He pointed out that Bulgaria was in the Russian sphere of influence and cautioned that Austria should not look to Germany for support if it was drawn into a war with Russia over it.[42] At the same time, he called for Russia to keep its composure, arguing that British policy on this issue was more hard-line than Austrian—and that, in fact, all of Austria's anti-Russian moves had been instigated by Great Britain. He also expressed hope that Russia would not push for Prince Alexander's immediate abdication, which would only complicate the matter further.[43] Bismarck's pressure allowed fragile cooperation to continue between Russia and Austria for a time.

The crisis, however, grew further in November 1885. Serbia, with the support of the Austro-Hungarian Empire, demanded compensation on account of Bulgarian unification. When this was rejected by Bulgaria on November 14, Serbia declared war and sent its army across the border. The whole situation had spun out of control. The war soon moved in unexpected directions. The Bulgarian Army won a decisive victory and counterattacked, advancing toward Belgrade. Austria began preparations for an emergency intervention, warning that if the Bulgarian advance continued, Austria would intervene on Serbia's side. As a first step, Austria demanded an immediate withdrawal of Bulgarian troops from Serbian soil. Under pressure, Bulgaria complied. By this point, however, Austro-Russian competition for spheres of influence in the Balkans had already been ignited, and in Austria, pressures to support Prince Alexander grew. Great Britain, too, pushed Austria to the front line in resisting Russian expansion in the Balkans. Bismarck, however, still sought to maintain pressure on Austria. On December 9, 1885, Germany warned Austrian Foreign Minister Gustav Kálnoky that continuing to incite Russian hostility would only serve to further British schemes. Although Germany spared no effort in attempt to persuade the Russians to remain calm, it was even more explicit in its warnings to Austria-Hungary. In particular, Austria was cautioned not to take unilateral action, so that Germany's efforts would not be in vain. Germany further counseled that, if Austria continued to take hostile actions, then Russian Foreign Minister and supporter of the League of Three Emperors Nikolay Giers would be forced from office and the Russian pan-Slavists would gain the upper hand. This would greatly damage German interests and security.[44]

In 1886, at Britain's urging, the Ottoman Empire and Bulgaria entered into negotiations and concluded an agreement that largely accorded with British desires. It avoided entirely the question of unification and instead appointed Prince Alexander as civil administrator in East Rumelia. The agreement thus avoided breaking the Treaty of Berlin while allowing the two regions to enjoy *de facto* unity. This compromise clearly revealed British foreign policy wisdom: the other great powers could hardly object and Russia could do nothing but accept it in April 1886.

The Intensification of Austro-Russian Tensions and Germany's Response

This agreement did not end the crisis. Instead, the conflict between Russia and Austria, as well as the conflict between Russia and Bulgaria's Prince Alexander, escalated. On August 21, 1886, Russia instigated a coup in Bulgaria during which a group of pro-Russian military officers took the prince hostage. This threw Bulgaria into chaos. On September 7, the prince announced his abdication, and control of the country passed to Russian General Alexander Kaulbars. Anti-Russian forces in Bulgaria strenuously opposed his rule. In late November, Kaulbars and all other Russian officials in Bulgaria were removed. Russia then severed relations with Bulgaria and, for a brief time, it appeared that an armed Russian invasion was imminent. If Russia occupied Bulgaria, the situation in the Balkans would revert to that on the eve of the 1878 Berlin Conference: there would be a Greater Bulgaria within the Russian sphere of influence that neither Austria nor Britain would be willing to accept. Calls for war in the Hungarian portion of the Austro-Hungarian Empire grew louder. The Hungarian prime minister announced that he did not recognize the authority of any power "to undertake single-handed armed intervention or set up a protectorate within the Balkan peninsula." This, essentially, declared that the League of Three Emperors was finished.[45] In November 1886, the Austrian foreign minister asserted that, if Russia intervened militarily in Bulgaria, then his country would be forced to "take action."[46] Germany was forced to consider an old quandary again: which side would it choose in a showdown between Russia and Austria? If Germany supported Austria, the two might be able to intimidate Russia, but it would also inspire Russian hostility—and perhaps push it closer to forming an anti-German alliance with France. If, however, Germany allowed Russia to crush Austria-Hungary, then its own national security environment would become distinctly worse.

Advocates for both options existed within German policymaking circles. An anti-Russian faction, exemplified by Friedrich von Holstein, desired to use this crisis to sever German ties with Russia. This group considered Bismarck's policies too pro-Russian. They saw Bismarck's policies as being guided by his son Herbert, and Herbert, in turn, steered by his own arrogance and Russian influence.[47] The other group, of which Bismarck's son Herbert was a representative, thought that Austria was an unreliable ally and instead pushed for a new alliance system based on an alliance with either Russia or Great Britain.

Bismarck himself opposed both of these notions. For the former, he clearly saw that once ties with Russia were ruptured, Germany would have to shoulder the burden of supporting Austria all on its own. Austria, moreover, could demand even greater support from Germany:

> Suppose, however, that the breach with Russia is an accomplished fact, an irremediable estrangement. Austria would then certainly begin to enlarge her claims on the services of her German confederate, first by insisting on an extension of the *casus foederis*, which so far, according to the published text, provides only for the measures necessary to repel a Russian attack upon Austria; then by requiring the substitution for this *casus foederis* of some provision safeguarding the interests of Austria in the Balkans and the East, an idea to which our press has already succeeded in giving practical shape.[48]

For the latter notion, Bismarck's attitude is best summarized in an October 1886 letter he sent his son Herbert:

> [In event of a Austro-Russian war] we could certainly tolerate Austria's losing a battle but not that it should be destroyed or fatally wounded or made a dependency of Russia. The Russians do not possess the kind of self-restraint that would make it possible for us

> to live alone with them and France on the Continent. If they had eliminated Austria or brought it to their heels, we know from experience that they would become so domineering toward us that peace with them would be untenable." Thus, the Austro-Hungarian Empire must continue to be protected, although German attitudes could not be expressed too clearly, or else "we would then have no guarantee against Austrian provocations [against Russia].[49]

Thus, even as the crisis intensified and the League of Three Emperors demonstrated its weaknesses, Bismarck still refused to choose between Russia and Austria. His reaction, instead, hinged on two points. The first was to continue to push back against Austrian desires to challenge Russia in the Balkans. Several times in October 1886, Bismarck harshly warned his Austrian allies against creating problems for Russia in Bulgaria, to avoid letting the situation spiral out of control.[50] The second was to pull Britain into resisting Russian expansion in the Balkans. In other words, Bismarck still supported Austria and would not allow it to be dominated by Russia, but responsibility for this would fall to Great Britain, not Germany. Great Britain, however, would not lightly undertake this role—it, instead, would demand that Germany do it. Thus, from early 1886, Great Britain and Germany began a game of "passing the buck."

Shifting Responsibility and Anglo-German Competition

Great Britain asserted that the League of Three Emperors could resolve the Eastern Question itself without any British intervention. Bismarck, in turn, claimed that Germany had no interests at stake in the Eastern Question and thus had no reason to manage Russo-Austrian differences in the Balkans. He ordered his ambassador in London to emphasize the need for British initiative.[51] Bismarck further made use of the blood ties between the British and German monarchies (the German crown princess was a daughter of Queen Victoria) to further pressure the British and demand their support for Austria.[52] On August 12, 1886, Great Britain responded that Britain was a naval power, with only limited land forces, and so therefore hoped to work with Austria to jointly ensure the safety and stability of the Balkans. Great Britain had calculated that this nominal Anglo-Austrian alliance would force Germany to support Austria if it got into trouble. Great Britain could then withdraw and maintain its freedom of action. Germany, of course, saw this clearly, too. The German ambassador in London, Paul von Hatzfeldt, expressed his belief that the greatest danger came from France, thus avoiding the entire issue.[53] Bismarck bluntly replied:

> The Chancellor observed that if England has neither troops nor money, the question arises what she can do at all. If she desires support for her policy, she must herself take the risks, and not count on her chestnuts being picked out of the fire by others. Austria might support England, but not represent her. England, if she has no troops, would be forced to create them in the Turkish army with English money. In Turkey money could do anything, even create a fresh Sultan.[54]

In the face of the lack of a positive German response, Britain made another proposal. In September 1886, British Chancellor of the Exchequer Randolph Churchill proposed to Hatzfeldt that, although Britain's ruling Conservative Party could not take the lead on a foreign affairs initiative due to domestic political pressures, it could work with Austria-Hungary on the Bulgarian issue to check Russia. Germany would only need to need to offer support in principle to the two sides.[55] Bismarck, however, felt that Britain was up to its old tricks, hoping to entice German support for Austria—and, once that support was stated openly, Britain could withdraw from the region whenever it wanted. Moreover, Churchill's position in the government did not give him the power to make such guarantees. Churchill, if needed, could always resign from office to allow Britain to escape from any entanglement.[56]

Just as the Anglo-German contest of "passing the buck" seemed to enter into a stalemate, an event in France came to Bismarck's aid—the Boulangist Crisis. Strictly speaking, the Boulangist Crisis was not a real crisis at all, but rather an emotional outburst from the French public. In January 1886, General Georges Ernest Boulanger, who had advocated for a revanchist war against Germany, had entered the French cabinet as the minister of war. A wave of nationalist and revanchist sentiment spread across the country. By the latter half of 1886, pro-war voices in French newspapers grew louder, and Boulanger ordered the construction of new army barracks and massed a portion of the army in eastern France. This created the impression that France could launch an attack at any time.

Bismarck's take on these events was that they happened at exactly the right time. "I couldn't invent Boulanger," he remarked, "but he happened very conveniently for me."[57] Once the crisis began, Bismarck paid close attention to

French politics and made full use of what he learned to serve his own domestic political and foreign policy needs. Within Germany, he greatly played up the French threat, forcing the Reichstag to pass a new army bill that increased the force size from 427,000 to 468,000 troops. His speech in the Reichstag on this topic was masterful: he hyped the French threat while clearly stating his personal desire to avoid any other countries' thinking that Germany hoped to use this as an excuse for preventive war. In his speech, he emphasized that the increase in the German Army was purely in response to a potential French attack. This potential war, from his perspective, had not been the desire of the French government. Instead, ambitious politicians orchestrated it by manipulating public opinion. He said that the French could trust that Germany would never launch a preemptive war against them. Who could, he asked, convince Germans that a France governed by military officers—beholden to the mistaken belief that they had a military advantage, or to the idea that war was necessary to escape from domestic political problems, or to the notion that the sword was the solution to all problems—would not attack?[58] Arguably, his speech played no small role in avoiding a repeat of the 1875 "War in Sight" Crisis. When Bismarck's new army bill was rejected in the Reichstag, he dissolved the chamber and called for new elections. He placed this bill, and the so-called Boulangist threat, out in public for discussion. This led to even more newspapers spreading the threat of Franco-German conflict. On January 21, 1887, the Berlin newspaper *Die Post* (which had run the 1875 "War in Sight?" editorial) printed an editorial entitled "The Razor's Edge." It raised the specter of a Franco-German war, claiming that if the Boulangist fever could not be quieted, then war was unavoidable. Bismarck also dispatched 72,000 soldiers to Alsace-Lorraine for training maneuvers, further increasing the sense of impending war.[59] In the end, Bismarck triumphed in domestic politics: his supporters won a majority in the Reichstag, while his opponents, the German Liberal Party, lost seats. His army bill sailed through to passage. In foreign policy, he could use these events as an excuse to refuse the British, claiming that he could not aid Austria in the Balkans as he needed to prepare against a French threat in the west. Under such circumstances, he could not risk offending Russia and becoming enmeshed in a two-front war. By the end of 1886, Bismarck made a counter-proposal to the British: Russia could be isolated through British support of Austria (which neither Italy nor the Ottoman Empire would object to), while Germany would intimidate France.[60]

Germany maintained a position of relative autonomy during the Bulgaria Crisis through Bismarck's careful observation of trends and flexible responses to events. It cannot be denied, however, that this crisis had a serious impact on Germany's security environment. The core of Bismarck's foreign policy—the League of Three Emperors—was now defunct, even if Bismarck was not yet willing to accept that. Even in the final weeks of 1886, he still maintained his commitment to knitting the league back together.[61] The German Foreign Ministry called for the league's continuation.[62] By early 1887, however, it had become clear that the rift between Russia and Austria could not be healed. Thus, Germany's entire diplomatic and strategic environment began to shift. Bismarck needed to take new measures to ameliorate the situation, to maintain a balanced grand strategy, and to allow Germany to preserve initiative in the face of complicated and changing strategic currents.

The Russo-German Reinsurance Treaty and the Two Mediterranean Agreements

The Bulgaria Crisis had ended by 1887, as had Bismarck's efforts to perpetuate the League of Three Emperors. He could only work on two parallel tracks: attempting to tie down the pre-existing relationship between Germany and Russia while trying to build anti-Russian forces without implicating Germany. The first of these resulted in the Russo-German Reinsurance Treaty; the second produced the two Mediterranean Agreements.

The Creation of the Reinsurance Treaty and its Strategic Meaning

The Bulgaria Crisis not only pushed Austro-Russian relations to the breaking point, but also revealed the first signs of Franco-Russian rapprochement. In the summer of 1886, the French poet Paul Déroulède visited Russia and promoted a Franco-Russian alliance to counter Germany and Austria. This elicited a loud response in Russia. In June, the *Moscow News* printed an essay by the famous journalist Mikhail Katkov that criticized the government's European foreign policy. He argued that the abstract concept of monarchical unity had once rested upon national interest, but now was a historical mistake. This mistake could by repaired only by rejecting the limits of treaties or other traditional concepts and restoring freedom of diplomatic movement. At the end of 1886, conversations in France about the possibility of a Russian alliance had steadily grown, and feelers had been sent to Russia.

This potential threat, of course, would not immediately become an actual threat. Giers, the Russian foreign minister who held to his country's traditional policies, still remained in office, while the popular emotions stirred up by Boulangism in France made autocratic Russia cautious. In January 1887, under pressure from Giers, Czar Alexander III agreed to send Peter Shuvalov to negotiate a new bilateral agreement to replace the league with Bismarck. The two sides signed a draft that would commit Russia to neutrality in a Franco-German war. Germany recognized Russia's special position in Bulgaria and committed itself to benevolent neutrality in event of a Russian occupation of the Bosphorus. There were several additional supplemental clauses that provided Russian guarantees of Austrian territorial integrity and recognition of Austria's sphere of influence in Serbia.[63] The czar refused to sign the treaty, however, believing that Franco-German rivalry would continue to intensify and that Russia could maneuver between them to obtain a more favorable deal. Thus, no further Russian response was forthcoming after the January meeting.

The Russian delay clarified for Bismarck the crisis that had emerged in Russo-German relations—and impelled him to quickly take measures in response. He looked to pull Great Britain into an united anti-Russian front while also continually signaling his interest in negotiations to Russia. In April 1887, Boulangist fever had cooled in France, and by May Boulanger himself was forced out of office. These events led the czar to consent to renewed talks with Germany. On May 11, 1887, Shuvalov presented Bismarck with a Russian draft proposal. Its first clause read, "If either of the contracting parties enters a state of war with another Great Power, the other party shall maintain benevolent neutrality." This, in essence, meant that Russia would abandon France in exchange for Germany abandoning Austria-Hungary. Bismarck was unwilling to contemplate this. He read the Austro-German treaty aloud to Russian ambassador Shuvalov, explaining that the situation in 1879 had forced him to conclude that treaty and that he was bound to its stipulations. In the end, the two sides reached a negative agreement: a German attack on France and a Russian attack on Austria were both excluded from the treaty's promise of neutrality.[64]

The Russo-German Reinsurance Treaty was signed on June 18, 1887. Its first clause read: "In case one of the high contracting parties should find itself at war with a third Great Power, the other would maintain a benevolent neutrality toward it, and would devote its efforts to the localization of the conflict. This provision would not apply to a war against Austria or France in case this war should result from an attack directed against one of these two latter Powers by one of the high contracting parties." The second clause mandated that Germany recognize Russia's sphere of influence in the Balkans (particularly in Bulgaria), and that both countries seek to maintain the territorial *status quo* in that region. The third clause stated that both nations "recognize the European and mutually obligatory character of the principle of the closing of the Straits of the Bosporus and of the Dardanelles" and will "take care in common that Turkey shall make no exception to this rule in favor of the interests of any Government whatsoever, by lending to warlike operations of a belligerent power the portion of its Empire constituted by the Straits." The treaty also contained a secret addendum in which Germany pledged to "lend her assistance to Russia in order to re-establish a regular and legal government in Bulgaria" while refusing to "consent to the restoration of the Prince of Battenberg." Germany further promised neutrality in event of a Russian seizure of the Black Seas Straits.[65]

The text of the treaty appears to be a unilateral expression of German goodwill toward Russia. Nothing in the treaty itself, moreover, prevented the creation of a Franco-Russian alliance. As a result, many historians have judged it to have little real meaning. In fact, the value of the treaty lay outside of its actual content. First, Germany lost nothing; most of what it promised to Russia would, in fact, be negated by the second Mediterranean Agreement. Bismarck showed himself to be a master at playing both sides of the equation. Second, although the Reinsurance Treaty did not provide guarantees against a Franco-Russian alliance, it acted as a replacement for such an alliance. Through this treaty, Germany essentially provided a guarantee to Russia that it would neither ally with Austria to attack Russia, nor would it demand the right to attack France. This obviated the need for a Franco-Russian alliance. Third, the treaty was the last symbol of traditional Russo-German ties and thus could solidify the power base of Russian conservatives, giving them capital to continue to implement the old policies. Otherwise, they might be overthrown by radical pan-Slavists. If that happened, the elements within Russia that prevented an alignment with France would no longer exist.

"Opposing but Complementary" Principles and the Two Mediterranean Agreements

Bismarck's diplomacy was a dialectical process. To achieve his goals, he sought to link similar forces into mutually reinforcing systems, yet he also embraced the dialectical logic that sought to likewise unify opposing forces into complementary wholes.

Even as he was putting the finishing touches on the Reinsurance Treaty, Bismarck was simultaneously pursuing the completely opposite policy: pushing Great Britain to support Austria against Russia. In early 1887, Italy, as a member of the League of Three Emperors, hoped to gain support for its expansion in the Mediterranean. Great Britain, for its part, desired Italy's backing for its policies in Egypt. These objectives began to bring the two countries closer together. On January 17, British Prime Minister Salisbury mentioned his desire for a closer relationship to the Italian ambassador. Germany worked to promote Anglo-Italian cooperation, even threatening that if Britain retained its policies of isolation, then "we should have had no reason for refusing to encourage the French desires in Egypt, or those of the Russians in the East…[our] interests were not endangered by the presence of France in Egypt or of Russia in Constantinople."[66] Bismarck also suggested that he would "reduc[e] his alliance with Austria to its literal engagement to maintain the integrity of the Austrian Empire and allow Russia to take not Constantinople but the Bosphorus and the Dardanelles" in order to cool Russian hostility toward Germany.[67] Propelled by Germany, Great Britain and Italy signed a treaty on February 2, 1887, that promised to maintain the *status quo* in the Mediterranean. Its true purpose, however, was to prevent French expansion in the region. Germany's true interest was Russia, not France, and it saw this treaty as merely an opening move. Its true value would lie in tying the British to the Austrian Empire.[68] On February 19, in a bid for further support in the Mediterranean, Bismarck proposed that Austria indicate its acceptance of the Anglo-Italian arrangement. With German blandishments and threats, Austria quickly agreed to make an agreement with Britain, even accepting as a condition that any agreement would not mention cooperation in the Balkans.[69] On March 24, notes exchanged between Great Britain and Austria committed the two countries to the *status quo* in the Mediterranean. The British note stated, in part, that it would seek to maintain the regional *status quo* and, "should that unhappily cease to be possible, [will seek] the prevention of the growth of any novel domination hostile to the interests of the two countries."[70] The Austrian note explained, "Although the questions of the Mediterranean in general do not primarily affect the interests of Austria-Hungary, my Government has the conviction that England and Austria-Hungary have the same interests so far as concerns the Eastern Question as a whole, and therefore the same need of maintaining the *status quo* in the Orient, so far as possible, of preventing the aggrandizement of one Power to the detriment of others."[71] This completed the first Mediterranean Agreement, which was aimed at preserving the *status quo* in that region.

This agreement, coupled with the Reinsurance Treaty, was still not enough to enable Germany to effectively maintain a balanced foreign policy. More was needed to restrain Russia. In July 1887, the election of Ferdinand of Coburg as Prince of Bulgaria led to a renewed outbreak of the Bulgaria Crisis. Russia objected, seeing Ferdinand as pro-Austrian, and the situation grew tense. Great Britain grew impatient as both Bismarck and Austrian Foreign Minister Count Gustav Kálnoky suggested on separate occasions that, if Great Britain refused to support Austria in the Balkans, then Austria would have no choice but to reach to a unilateral accord with Russia. The British government would then have to confront a Russia that, with Austrian and German consent, operated according to its own wishes.[72] Under pressure, the British ambassador in Constantinople drafted, along with the Austrian and Italian representatives, a ten-point plan to stabilize the region. The prime minister in London signaled his approval of the document. On November 2, Salisbury wrote to the ambassador in Constantinople that "a thorough understanding with Austria and Italy is so important to us that I do not like the idea of breaking it up on account of risks which may turn out to be imaginary."[73] On November 3, the British cabinet discussed strengthening ties with Austria-Hungary, but doubts were expressed about the ten-point proposal and a desire for a clearer German position was enunciated. Salisbury called on Bismarck to assist in persuading the cabinet—a task that Bismarck was more than willing to take on. He sent a copy of the Austro-German treaty of alliance to Salisbury, and added a letter explaining that if Austrian independence were threatened by Russian invasion, or if Britain or Italy became targets of a French invasion, then Germany would need to enter the war.[74] The British cabinet then agreed to negotiate a new agreement with Austria and Italy on the basis of the ten-point draft.

Great Britain submitted a revised draft agreement on November 25, 1887; Austria and Italy replied on December 5 with a united response. Diplomatic notes were exchanged on December 12, thus constituting the Second Mediterranean Agreement. Great Britain accepted greater responsibility in this newest agreement. The three nations agreed to maintain the peace and the *status quo* in the Balkans, particularly the right of free passage through the Black Sea Straits and Ottoman sovereignty in Asia Minor and Bulgaria. If the Ottoman state resisted "illegal enterprises" by any other nation in those areas, the three states would "immediately come to an agreement as to the measures to be taken" to protect the Ottomans. If the Ottomans consented to these "illegal enterprises," then the three powers had reason to occupy "such points of Ottoman territory as they may agree to consider it necessary to occupy in order to secure the objects determined by previous Treaties."[75] The Second Mediterranean Agreement was a particularly interesting document. First, although Germany, Austria, and Italy had a formal treaty alliance, Germany placed itself out of the system on Russian issues and brought Great Britain in to support its allies. Second, this agreement came only six months after the Reinsurance Treaty, but the two agreements contradicted one another. The tension between the two was particularly apparent on the approaches to the Black Sea: the Second Mediterranean Agreement called for open access to the straits, while the Reinsurance Treaty presumed the opposite. On the Bulgarian issue, the two documents also stood in contrast to one another. Yet, in the late 1880s, these two contradictory diplomatic agreements offset the demise of the League of Three Emperors and allowed Germany to reestablish its grand strategy by drawing mutually contradictory forces into a complementary dynamic.

Coordinating Diplomatic and Military Affairs

At the end of 1887, Bismarck made what would be his last great effort to maintain Germany's grand strategy: a rebalancing of the relationship between diplomatic and military policy. In December 1887, as the Bulgaria Crisis intensified, the pressure for war against Russia grew in Austria-Hungary, particularly within the Hungarian parliament. The German military, believing that Russia was preparing for a spring 1888 invasion, planned a preemptive attack of its own that winter. At the behest of the elder Moltke, chief of General Staff, the head of military logistics Alfred von Waldersee, the chief of the Army Cabinet Emil von Albedyll and other high-ranking officers, German military calls grew for a preventive war against Russia, and discussions on the issue were opened with Austria. Several rounds of secret consultation were held between the representative of the German military in Vienna and the chief of the Austrian general staff. The German representative was "completely controlled by militaristic emotions" at these meetings, suggesting that the Austrian Army be dispatched to the eastern frontier and raising the possibility of removing the restrictive clauses of the 1879 treaty.[76] His moves left Austria with the impression that Germany hoped to ally with Austria to attack Russia.

These moves infuriated Bismarck. He believed that a divorce between the needs of the military and those of diplomacy could produce an existential crisis for Germany. To remedy this, he first took measures to hold Austria back. In December 1887, Bismarck used his ambassador in Vienna to tell the Austrians that the 1879 treaty of alliance was purely defensive in nature—Germany was not obligated to come to Austria's aid if it invaded Russia.[77] He repeated the same message in mid-December, saying, "So long as I am minister, I shall not give my consent to a prophylactic attack upon Russia."[78] He further demanded that German officials in Vienna refrain from offering political suggestions to the Austrian throne without first receiving his approval. In late December, he instructed his ambassador in Vienna to demand that the Austrians abandon their illusionary hopes: "I cannot avoid the impression that it is the aim of certain military circles in Vienna to distort our defensive alliance…we must both take care that the privilege of giving political advice to our monarch does not in fact slip out of our hands and pass over to the General Staffs."[79] Germany, moreover, had no intention of promising to support an Austrian attack on Russia.

Second, Bismarck resolutely opposed the interference of military officers in German policymaking. He directly wrote to Waldersee on December 7, threatening that if there were further interference from the General Staff or if influence were brought to bear on diplomats or the cabinet outside of official channels, he would no longer be able to take responsibility for German policy. On December 17, Waldersee and other high-ranking officers brought Prince Wilhelm (later Kaiser Wilhelm II) to help persuade the ruling Kaiser Wilhelm I to support a preemptive attack, but were blocked by Bismarck.[80] Bismarck harshly criticized Waldersee's interference in foreign policy and schemed to have him removed from office, but failed after encountering resistance from the elder Moltke. Through these heated political disputes, Bismarck began to pull military and diplomatic policy back into accord with one another and squashed army notions of a preemptive war. At the end of December, the elder Moltke and other army leaders gave Bismarck their assurances that military interference had been unintentional.[81] In March 1888, the Bulgaria Crisis was peacefully resolved.

A Brief Critical Appraisal of Bismarck-Era German Grand Strategy

From 1871 until his forced retirement in 1890, Bismarck dominated German domestic and foreign policy. During this period, the string of effective, mutually coordinated military and diplomatic polices he adopted formed a highly integrated grand strategy. This grand strategy not only managed to master the conflicts engendered by Germany's rise, but it also enhanced Germany's international status. Bismarck's rule coincided with the era of rapid German growth. Taking three important industrial measures—the production of coal, iron, and steel—as an example, the pace of this growth becomes clear. Coal production rose from 34 million to 89 million tons, pig iron production from 1.3 million to 4.1 million tons, and steel production from 300,000 to 2.3 million tons. Even more important than the absolute increase in German power was its relative increase compared to other nations.

In 1871, the German share of the total coal production of the European great powers was 20 percent. By 1891, it was 26 percent. Pig iron rose from a 13 percent to a 26 percent share, and steel from a 23 percent to a 30 percent share, of the great powers' total during the same period. Put in another way, German production in 1871 was equivalent to France's, but by 1891 Germany produced more of these three items than France, Russia, and Austria combined. Only Britain produced more.[82] This rapid growth, however, did not prompt any obvious foreign resistance. Even Germany's rapid colonial expansion did not lead to significant international tensions. The fears and defensiveness sparked by German unification in 1871 greatly diminished after the 1878 Berlin Conference. Germany, which once might have become the destroyer of the established order, instead became its defender. It had become the guarantor of European stability.

The importance of grand strategy to Germany's rise is unmistakable. Given Bismarck's central role in the formulation of this grand strategy, any evaluation of that grand strategy is, to a certain extent, a judgment on Bismarck and his policies. Bismarck was, without a doubt, the most brilliant diplomat of the nineteenth century. The success of his foreign policies rested on his insightfulness, his ability to see the whole situation, his flexibility, and, even more important, two aspects of his personal character—patience and self-control. Bismarck knew clearly that Germany's rise had made it the focal point of European politics. Overly active policies would thus cause harm, while waiting for, and seizing, the right opportunities was the key to success. As he once said, "The gift of waiting while a situation develops is an essential requirement of practical politics."[83] His self-control reflected his correct appraisal of Germany's long-term interests, as well as his precise understanding of the relationship between giving and taking. He was generous in giving (although he often gave away other people's things), while he was extremely careful in terms of taking. This was critical to Germany's assumption of a pivotal role in European politics, and greatly eased the path for Germany's smooth and stable rise.

Bismarck was the consummate pragmatist. British Prime Minister Lord Palmerston's famous saying—"No permanent friends, no permanent enemies"—could also have been applied to Bismarck. He not only remained true to his vision of Germany's interests when devising policy, but also he held a flexible, practical notion of "friends" and "enemies." He clearly understood the threats emanating from France and Russia, yet expended enormous energy to managing relations with Russia and exerted himself to create an atmosphere of Franco-German reconciliation. He remained cautious of Austria-Hungary,

Germany's critical ally, in order to forestall a situation in which "the weak lead the strong." According to Bismarck, "We shall not avoid the dangers which lie in the bosom of the future by amiability and commercial *pourboires* to friendly Powers. We should only increase the greed of our former friends and teach them to reckon on our anxieties and necessities."[84]

Posterity has criticized him for complexity—in particular, the establishment of an alliance system that was too intricate for any successor to understand, much less properly manage. The difficulty of the situation facing Germany, however, dictated the complexity of Bismarck's response. His policies, ultimately, were suited to Germany's objective situation. Historian Gordon Craig correctly observed that:

> If there had been a simpler way to attain his objectives, the Chancellor would certainly have taken it, for he was no admirer of complexity for its own sake. But all the simple routes were dangerous and self-defeating, and Bismarck found it necessary to go the twisted way at the cost of bewildering not only posterity but even some of his closet collaborators—his son, the political counsellor Holstein, and such leading members of his Diplomatic Service as Ruess in Vienna and Radowitz in Constantinople.[85]

A number of historians claim that Bismarck's polices failed, as they did not fundamentally prevent a Franco-Russian alliance. This thesis is not a particularly valid one. Generally speaking, policy (especially foreign policy) does not seek to fundamentally achieve a particular objective. Instead, the task of policy is to grab hold of various kinds of possibilities and to try to realize them. Henry Kissinger, in his evaluation of the other master of nineteenth-century diplomacy, Klemens von Metternich, noted that, "Metternich's policy thus depended on its ability to avoid major crises which would force an unequivocal commitment and on its capacity to create the illusion of intimacy with all major powers. It was finely spun, with sensitive feelers in all directions and so intricate that it obscured the fact that none of the fundamental problems had really been settled."[86] Bismarck's policies, too, were intricate and subtle. His successors could not understand such things, and so abandoned them.

Bismarck's true failings lay in three specific realms. First, he did not take any measures to improve Germany's domestic policymaking system or power structure. He excuse was national security: "My aim was the strengthening of our national safety; the nation would have time enough for its internal development when once its unity, and with it its outward security, was consolidated."[87] In truth, Bismarck did not care much about these issues. For Bismarck, institutions and systems were tools of power and supplements to his own wisdom and authority, rather than goals in and of themselves. Thus he did not think to devote himself to reforming Germany's policymaking system or power structure when he was at the height of his power. He was even willing to use such systems and structures as bargaining chips in the pursuit of short-term political interest. During the 1883 reorganization of the German Army, for instance, Bismarck sided with army logistics chief Waldersee and other high-ranking officers in allowing the General Staff, the Army Ministry, and the Army Cabinet to become three separate and independent entities. Rivalry between the three dramatically increased. The unified military system created in Prussia by the army reforms of Gerhard von Scharnhorst was destroyed, damaging Germany's mechanisms for strategic decision-making.[88]

Second, he ignored the training of other policymakers. While in power, Bismarck held tenuously to the notion that he alone was the government. Under Germany's existing system, this aided in the unity of decision-making power, the stability of policies, and the formulation of a grand strategy. For the others who worked in Germany's foreign ministry, however, it meant that Bismarck was too strong. He essentially blocked them from participating in policymaking and did not explain his plans to them. Over the long term, Germany's diplomats became little more than Bismarck's tools to execute policy. Under these circumstances, Bismarck could not train a strong corps of diplomats—nor could he even produce a single official who could truly understand the policies he was supposed to promote. Once Bismarck was out of power, the precision mechanics of his diplomatic system had basically reached its limits, too.

Third, he did not seek to educate the German people. Bismarck was a grand master of politics and understood well the influence of public opinion, but he never invested time or energy in instilling any sort of "correct worldview" in the German people. Instead, he used public opinion for his own political purposes. If the use (and misuse) of public sentiment was a longstanding habit of Germany's leaders from 1871 to 1945, then Bismarck cannot escape part of the blame for this. When his successors proved able only to inflame, but not control, public opinion, the government became a hostage of public opinion.

Thus, when Bismarck was forced into retirement in 1890, the keystone to Germany's grand strategy disappeared. He left behind a country that was swiftly growing in power, a political system full of problems, a team of "able mediocrities," and an easily aroused public.

4

Entering the Post-Bismarckian Era

"Unfortunately, after Bismarck's departure, moderation was the quality Germany lacked most."
Henry Kissinger

Bismarck's forced departure in 1890 was a watershed moment for German diplomacy. The Second Reich would never again have a strong leader able to grasp the whole picture. His carefully crafted strategic framework and his carefully balanced strategic vision would be discarded amid the excitement created by newfound national power. German grand strategy slowly disintegrated after 1890, with results that would soon become apparent. The nations of Europe would find that, just as the German ship of state was gaining speed, its helmsman had stepped off onto the shore.[1] Both the direction and the fate of that ship became marked by extreme uncertainty.

A New Diplomatic Path

In March 1888, Kaiser Wilhelm I passed away—and with his passing, Bismarck's strongest source of political support vanished. In June, his son and successor, Frederick III, died, leaving Wilhelm I's grandson, Wilhelm II, as the country's monarch. Bismarck and the new kaiser did not get along. On March 20, 1890, Bismarck was forced out of office. This set into motion dramatic changes in Germany's foreign policy.

A New Foreign Policy Team

The kaiser formed the crucial element of Germany's political system. Yet at this critical phase in Germany's rise, that extraordinarily powerful position was held by the likes of Wilhelm II. Both his contemporaries and later historians have been unanimous in their assessment of him: he was vain, shallow, impatient, and capricious. His uncle, British King Edward VII, called him "the most brilliant failure in history."[2]

Wilhelm II fervently desired not just to reign, but also to rule. Yet he lacked the spirit of perseverance and the ability to view things comprehensively. He had only a glancing interest in politics beyond army and navy affairs. What little interest he did have was mostly focused on bringing glory to himself. In fact, even in army and navy affairs—in which he meddled incessantly—he proved fickle and inconstant. During his reign, particularly in the first few years after Bismarck's departure, a few high officials dominated German foreign policy. Thus, it is necessary to briefly introduce several of the key diplomatic and military figures from this era.

The first is Bismarck's successor as imperial chancellor, Leo von Caprivi. Born in 1831, he entered the Prussian Army in 1849 and fought in both the Austro-Prussian and Franco-Prussian Wars. He served as chief of the Imperial Admiralty from 1883 to 1888. Afterward, he commanded the Tenth Army Group, stationed at Hanover, before assuming Bismarck's vacated post. Caprivi was, without a doubt, an excellent military officer, but he had essentially no grounding in politics and even less in foreign policy. Likewise, Herbert von Bismarck's successor as state secretary for foreign affairs, Adolf von Marschall, had no foreign policy experience. During his chancellorship, German foreign policy depended on single advisor in the foreign ministry, Friedrich von Holstein.

Holstein was a key player in the post-Bismarckian era. He had deep diplomatic experience, having worked in foreign policy since 1860 and maintained close professional and personal ties with Bismarck. Beginning in 1875, he served as a high-ranking advisor within the foreign ministry. Yet he did not approve of Bismarck's policies. The self-contradicting treaty system, in particular, stoked his ire. He saw the ambiguity that Bismarck had so painstakingly worked to build as irresponsible and unprofessional. He did not understand why Bismarck devoted so much energy to the relationship with Russia, and he considered Germany's Russia policy to conflict with other aspects of its foreign policy. Holstein proposed instead to clarify Germany's foreign policy. The most important element of this was strengthening the alliance with Austria-Hungary so that it could function as the basis of an anti-Russian coalition. From Bismarck's perspective, Holstein's flaws were the flaws of German national character: "the inability to wait upon events and the insistence upon prejudging situations."[3] These flaws might also be seen to include excessive demands for precision and an overreliance on logic. For an individual, demanding clarity and an adherence to logic in every matter is not entirely a good thing. For a country, particularly a rising great power that is attempting to set foreign policy strategy, it could easily be a disaster. After a series of political struggles (not least of which were with ambassadors that Bismarck had appointed), Holstein essentially secured actual power over

German foreign policy. His flaws would thus become the flaws of German foreign policy.

The Abandonment of the Russo-German Reinsurance Treaty and its Strategic Significance

The new foreign policy team radically revised Germany's foreign policy after Bismarck left the stage. This began the period of Germany's new course, and its first mark would be the abandonment of the Reinsurance Treaty with Russia.

The original 1887 agreement had specified that the treaty would remain in effect for three years. This term ended on June 18, 1890. The Russian czar expressed interest in renewing the treaty late in 1889, although he also conveyed his worry over the difficult relationship between Bismarck and Wilhelm II. At that time, Bismarck promised the Russian ambassador that the kaiser would approve of such an extension. After Bismarck's fall from power in March 1890, his son Herbert encountered the Russian ambassador to Berlin. In what was perhaps a bid to aid his father, he reported to the kaiser that the czar had changed his mind about the treaty after learning of Bismarck's ouster, feeling that such issues could not be discussed with the new chancellor. Wilhelm II's attitude at that moment was still positive, and he merely penciled "Why?" in the margins of the younger Bismarck's report.[4] On March 21, the kaiser personally asked the Russian ambassador to enquire about the czar's view on the treaty. He also indicated Germany's willingness to begin immediate negotiations with the Russians, as well as his hope that the younger Bismarck would continue to work at the foreign ministry in order to facilitate discussion of the treaty. Afterward, Wilhelm II worked to persuade Herbert von Bismarck to remain in his position and complete the negotiations with Russia. At his father's insistence, however, the younger Bismarck offered his resignation on March 21. Wilhelm II had no choice but to direct Caprivi, the new chancellor, to take the lead on the renewal negotiations.[5]

After receiving his orders, Caprivi proceeded to the German Foreign Ministry on the morning of March 22, asking to see all of the documents relevant to the Russo-German relationship (especially those relating to the Reinsurance Treaty) and seeking advice from foreign ministry experts. It happened to be Holstein who received him there. Caprivi's requests completely surprised him, and he immediately advised the chancellor not to rush into matters without first hearing the advice of foreign ministry experts. On March 23, Holstein convened a meeting of foreign ministry officials who shared his views. He collected opinions from those opposed to the treaty and shared them with Caprivi. These collected opinions advanced three major arguments. First, the treaty provided enormous benefits to Russia without offering Germany anything in return: it would not prevent a French revanchist war against Germany and did not exclude the possibility of a Franco-Russian alliance. Second, German promises in the treaty directly contradicted German treaty agreements with Austria-Hungary, Italy, and (especially) Romania. Third, the treaty gave Russia the advantage of being able to weaken the ties between Germany and its allies through the threat of publicly announcing the contents of this secret treaty. The meeting concluded that a renewal of the Reinsurance Treaty was unnecessary and that a new, simpler, and more respectable "new course" in foreign policy was needed.[6]

The March 23 meeting made a deep impression on Caprivi, but he refrained from making a decision. Instead, he hoped also to hear from the foreign policy experts that Holstein had not invited, such as the German military attaché in Russia, Lothar von Schweinitz, and the ambassador to Constantinople, Joseph Maria von Radowitz, who had once been ambassador to Russia and had long experience in Eastern Europe. Four days later, Caprivi had a chance to speak with Schweinitz and presented him with copies of Bismarck's treaties. Schweinitz responded that the Reinsurance Treaty significantly conflicted with the other treaties, particularly the treaty with Romania. Furthermore, he thought the treaty gave too much to the Russians, especially with regard to the Black Sea Straits, and that the Russians would never give the Germans a concession of comparable value. Thus, he advised against any extension of the treaty—or, if the czar was insistent on its renewal, demanded the deletion of the clauses regarding the Black Sea Straits.[7] Radowitz also opposed a continuation of this treaty, instead advocating that Germany "hold fast to the Triple Alliance...and avoid everything that could arouse mistrust against it, especially in Vienna."[8] This was a sad situation: essentially all of the high-ranking officials who had served under Bismarck opposed his policy. Even sadder, his policy was actually correct, yet the opposition of his former subordinates was sincere. This was the rotten fruit that grew from Bismarck's failure to develop a team and his insistence on concealing his motives and strategies.

In the end, the German government decided not to renew the treaty. The motivating concern was that the treaty conflicted with the obligations of the Triple Alliance and the principle of friendly relations with Great Britain. In Caprivi's analysis, "Leakage of the Treaty, whether through a calculated or through an accidental indiscretion, would endanger the Triple Alliance and tend to alienate England from us."[9] After learning of this rejection, Russian Foreign Minister Nikolay Giers attempted to resuscitate his traditional foreign policy course by offering to drop both the secrecy clause and the Black Sea Straits clause from the renewed treaty. The German government had already made it up its mind, however, and refused the Russian proposal. When the kaiser and the czar met in person two months after the June expiration of the treaty, Giers proposed another written agreement to demonstrate Russo-German friendship. This, too, was rejected by the Germans. German government documents indicate that both of these rejections resulted from fears that close ties with Russia would impact the Anglo-German relationship.[10]

Beyond severing the traditional relationship with Russia, Germany's new policymakers also sought radical readjustments in their country's Balkan policies. They perceived events in the Balkans, particularly those involving Russia, as critical to Germany's national interests. This line of thought ran counter to Bismarck's belief that the Eastern Question was not Germany's concern. As Balkan policy changed, so too did policy toward Austria. Bismarck had seen the alliance with Austria as a tool for restraining Austria and Russia while ensuring a strategic balance favorable to Germany. He had always emphasized the defensive nature of the alliance and schemed to force Britain to bear the burden of Austria's Balkan interests. Germany's new policymakers, however, saw the alliance with Austria as an end in and of itself. In order to strengthen it, they informed Austria of the now-defunct Reinsurance Treaty with Russia in August 1890. Caprivi and Austrian Foreign Minister Kálnoky came to an oral agreement that the Black Sea Straits issue could not be settled using the methods Russia demanded, and that no territorial concessions in the Balkans would be granted to Russia without Austrian approval.[11]

The internal contradictions in Germany's foreign policy were thus resolved, Germany's alliances were placed on a logical basis, and a clarified strategy adopted. The price of this strategic clarity, however, was the destruction of Bismarck's complex, yet carefully maintained, balance. Germany's grand strategy had begun to disintegrate. In concrete terms, there were two direct results from this. First, Russia was left feeling completely isolated and was forced to chart a new course. Bismarck had always followed two parallel policies with Russia: as a threat to defend against and as a partner for alliance. The former led Germany to the alliance with Austria, the Triple Alliance, and the two Mediterranean Agreements; the latter led to the League of Three Emperors and the Reinsurance Treaty. Together, these policies created equilibrium. After Bismarck's successors destroyed this balance, Russia discovered that it was isolated in Europe, in the Balkans, and in the Mediterranean. Breaking out of this isolation would require an alliance with another isolated great power: France. This made a Franco-Russian alliance inevitable. Second, Germany directly took on the full burden of supporting the Austro-Hungarian Empire. At the same time, the leadership of that alliance underwent a subtle alteration. Germany's new policymakers not only transformed the alliance, they also made clear Germany's total support for its ally. Thus ended Bismarck's twenty-year game of attempting to foist responsibility off on the British. Once Austria-Hungary became certain of German support, Germany lost the ability to use the alliance to restrict Austrian behavior. Over the next two decades, the manner in which "the weak lead the strong" in this alliance would become manifest.

Seeking British Friendship

The rejection of the Reinsurance Treaty was only one part of Germany's new course in foreign policy. Another major point of emphasis became the readjustment of policy toward Great Britain. After Bismarck's retirement, the new policymakers sought to promote closer ties with that country. Wilhelm II, ever since becoming crown prince, had disliked the autocratic Russia and greatly envied the liberal Great Britain. These monarchical preferences coincided with the majority political view inside Germany at the time. Liberals and Social Democrats naturally welcomed it, while even the Catholic Centre Party supported it, as it implied enhanced support for Austria-Hungary. Even more interesting, German colonial activities had pushed Germany toward a greater reliance on Great Britain (the simplistic argument that the colonial struggle had worsened ties with Great Britain had validity only for one particular period of time). As early as 1888, Holstein had written, "Our colonial crises lie upon us like a nightmare, and we need England in all places. Our relations with the English government are being most carefully cultivated."[12]

The ongoing Anglo-German colonial negotiations seemed to provide an opportunity for this. In 1890, the two countries had begun to discuss African colonies. On the table was a British proposal to exchange the island of Heligoland in the North Sea for two German colonies in East Africa. Prime Minister Salisbury had difficulty making progress in these negotiations while Bismarck was in office. At the time of Bismarck's dismissal, the negotiations were essentially deadlocked. For the new policymakers, however, this was an excellent chance to demonstrate friendship toward Britain and to pull the two countries closer together. As a result, they quickly violated two taboos of great power diplomacy. The first is never to reach a hasty agreement on a non-emergency issue or fail to fully exploit the negotiation process in pursuit of benefits. The second is never, under non-emergency conditions, to surrender to another great power or even proactively consider the domestic political needs of the other country. Caprivi held that "the position of the English government was not an easy one in view of the excited public opinion…Germany had to keep in mind the need to lighten Lord Salisbury's task and to make possible his retention in office." The kaiser even admitted to the British ambassador in Berlin that "he had said to General Caprivi that it was of the highest importance that [Salisbury's] position in Parliament should not be weakened, and has asked [Caprivi] to bear this in mind as a first condition in the negotiations. Africa…was not worth a quarrel between England and Germany."[13] Violating these taboos greatly strengthened Great Britain's negotiating position, and an agreement was quickly reached. The Heligoland-Zanzibar Treaty was signed between the two powers on July 1, 1890. Germany acquired Heligoland; Great Britain received protectorates in Zanzibar, Uganda, and Kenya. The two country's spheres of influence in East Africa were thus delineated.

The treaty did not work to Germany's benefit, as the text of the agreement itself reveals. In the eyes of late nineteenth-century Europeans, it was foolish to exchange two rich and populous East African colonies for a single North Sea island. The negative impact of this treaty on Germany was also evident in its implications for the strategic relationship between the two countries. It proved to be yet another step in destroying the balance of strategic needs that had previously existed. The British Empire's strategic focus was on India and on the four regions—Central Asia, Egypt, the Black Sea Straits, and South Africa—that directly impinged on it. Of these, Central Asia most directly impacted India, but serious Russian expansion into Afghanistan was still only on the horizon in the early 1890s. South Africa was likewise relatively stable. British concern, as well as British need for German support, was thus focused on the other two regions, Egypt and the Black Sea Straits. The shift in German policy in 1890 toward greater and more substantial support for Austria meant that Great Britain no longer needed to pay a price for German support on Black Sea issues. The balance of Anglo-German strategic needs had become lopsided. The situation in Egypt was more complicated. Great Britain still needed German support for its policies—but the absence of such support would not force Britain to leave. Instead, Britain feared that another European power (probably France) would seize control of the headwaters of Egypt's economic heart, the Nile River, and then leverage this control to force a British withdrawal.[14] Ever since the Mahdi's army had driven the British from the Sudan, rumors circulated in Great Britain that one European power or another power plotted to control the source of the Nile.[15] Arguably, closure of the Nile's entire course in order to protect Egypt was the emphasis of British policy in Africa in the 1880s and early 1890s. Domestic political considerations prevented British governments from allocating money for a second invasion of the Sudan, leaving the government to rely solely upon diplomacy to close off the various routes to the Nile. Some of the routes ran through the interior of Germany's East African colonies. If Germany controlled these routes, then Great Britain would have no choice but to depend on Germany. Bismarck, understanding this, had always refused to precisely delineate the two country's spheres of influence in the region.[16] The Heligoland-Zanzibar Treaty, however, removed this strategic option. This further disturbed the balance of strategic needs between the two countries, thus weakening their ties.[17]

In conclusion, the Anglo-German rapprochement sought by Germany's new policymakers was a case of "unrequited love." Structural conflicts naturally existed between Germany, with its status as a rising power, and Great Britain, in its position as the world's established hegemonic power. Close cooperation, much less shared governance, might be applicable in some concrete policy areas, but was unlikely as a comprehensive policy. A complex stability in the relationship between a rising power and an established hegemon can generally only be maintained by mutual reliance, mutual fear, and mutual restraint. Thus, while Germany blindly expressed friendship toward Great Britain, Britain's attitude toward Germany did not change. Prime Minister Salisbury, a classic example of a British politician, possessed a keen appreciation for power politics. He had seen Germany as a potential threat to Great Britain since the 1870s, given the comparative weakness of both France and Russia. His concerns about Bismarck diminished after the 1878 Berlin Conference, but he never entirely abandoned his original judgment.[18] Salisbury's cooperation with Germany in the 1880s had been the result of Bismarck's maneuvering—or, stated more precisely, as a result of Bismarck's ability to maintain a balance between the two countries' strategic needs. Bismarck's successors after 1890 visibly did not impress Salisbury. In a letter to the British ambassador in Rome, he commented: "I do not like to disregard the plain anxiety of my German friends. But it is not wise to be guided too much by their advice now. Their Achitophel is gone. They are much pleasanter and easier to deal with; but one misses the extraordinary penetration of the old man."[19] The British undoubtedly made full use of this opportunity to extract themselves from promises made to Bismarck's government and to reclaim their own freedom of action.

The Results of the New Course

The Establishment of the Franco-German Alliance

The most detrimental result of Germany's new course in foreign policy was that it spurred the creation of a Franco-Russian alliance. After Germany's refusal to extend the Reinsurance Treaty, the political fortunes of Giers and other Russian conservatives was gravely weakened; Germany's policy of reconciliation with Great Britain only served to deepen Russian doubts. Schweinitz, the German military attaché in Russia, warned that a Russian leader would look in other places for "the support he did not get from us."[20] The Heligoland-Zanzibar Treaty caused seismic shockwaves in both Russia and France. Leaders in those two countries assumed that some sort of deeper consideration must be at work for Germany to sign such a disadvantageous agreement. French Foreign Minister Alexandre Ribot assumed that the agreement contained secret clauses, while Russia believed it reflected a commitment to further Anglo-German cooperation. The Russian ambassador in London remarked:

> The principal importance of this transaction seems to me to reside in the rapprochement effected between England and Germany, a rapprochement of which the present arrangement gives palpable witness. When one is united by numerous interests and positive engagements on one point of the globe, one is almost certain to proceed in concert in all the great questions that may arise in the international field...virtually the entente with Germany has been accomplished. It cannot help but react upon the relations of England with the other powers of the Triple Alliance.[21]

Both Russia and France felt isolated; forming closer ties, or even an alliance, was a instinctual reaction. To a great extent, therefore, German policy pushed the two countries together. One month after the Heligoland-Zanzibar Treaty, Deputy Chief of the French General Staff General Raoul Le Mouton de Boisdeffre sent feelers to the Russians, and the pace of events began to pick up. In February 1891, as part of a German effort to improve relations with France, the German empress dowager visited. While in Paris, however, she unwisely visited a symbol of the 1870 Prussian invasion, resulting in large-scale protests. Wilhelm II's subsequent criticism of the French government further inflamed the situation. This minor incident provided yet another impetus for Franco-Russian reconciliation. The Russians delighted in the worsening relationship between France and Germany. Foreign minister Giers hastened to affirm the correctness of the French actions. On March 26, the Russian government extended an invitation for a port visit by a portion of the French fleet that summer. Hoping to create a fundamental breakthrough in the relationship, the French government then instructed its ambassador to Russia to inquire about where that country's sympathies would lie in the event of a new Franco-Prussian war. The Russian government, feeling that the time had not yet come for it to make a decisive choice between Germany and France, avoided the question. This slowed the pace of events for a time.

Two factors prompted the Russian government to change its mind quickly. First, the French government decided to shift from small-scale expressions of mutual friendship to the application of economic pressure. Under the direction of the French Foreign Ministry, the Rothschild banking conglomerate refused to extend a 500-million-ruble loan to the Russian government. The given pretext was the Russian treatment of Jews. Second was an increase in activity between Great Britain and the Triple Alliance. In early 1891, Great Britain had rejected a Triple Alliance proposal for augmented cooperation in the Mediterranean. Britain did, however, offer a consolation prize in the form of frequent expressions of friendship toward the alliance: in late June, a British fleet visited both Italy and Austria, where it was greeted by the monarchs of both countries; on July 4, the kaiser visited Great Britain, where he received a grand reception. These superficial phenomena may have comforted German policymakers, but they generated extreme anxiety in France and Russia. The two came to feel that Great Britain was drawing ever closer to the Triple Alliance and that, in the absence of any action on their part, they would soon be completely isolated. On July 17, Giers invited the French ambassador to begin formal negotiations on an alliance. A week later, a French fleet received a warm reception when it made its scheduled visit to Kronstadt. In August, a political agreement was cemented through the formal exchange of notes, and a critical step was taken in the creation of an alliance.

This August agreement was not yet a true alliance. The military obligations of the two nations, for instance, were left extremely vague. Moreover, Giers, who had long advocated a traditional policy of close ties with Germany, may have had reservations about joining France in opposition to Germany. Under his influence, the promises of mutual support made between the two countries had a marked anti-British flavor. Objectively speaking, if Germany had responded to this situation in a timely manner, it might have been able to postpone or even prevent a true Franco-Russian alliance from emerging. Yet, German policymakers directed their gaze solely to Great Britain. Not only did they fail to see the seriousness of a Franco-Russian alliance, they assumed that the emergence of such an alliance would increase pressure on Britain. This might push Britain into the Triple Alliance, thus enhancing Germany's position.[22] Germany likewise continued to make errors in its policies toward Russia. In the winter of 1891, Russia experienced a serious famine. Giers, hoping that Germany might provide aid and that this might lead to improved relations, made two suggestions. First, that German banks join in the purchase of Russian government bonds. Second, he hoped to pave the way for a Russo-German customs treaty. These met with German indifference, thus increasing Russia's (and the czar's own personal) doubts about German intentions. Additionally, Germany's conciliatory policies toward Poles living within its borders alarmed Russia, as it was taken to be a step toward ensuring Polish support for a war with Russia.[23] This seemed even more significant because the joint repression of the Polish people had been one important foundation of the traditional friendship between Russia and Prussia. This policy change seemed, to the Russians, to be the equivalent of a complete rejection of that relationship. Pro-French forces within the Russian government, represented best by Russian ambassador to France Arthur Pavlovich Morenheim, thus became able to push back against Giers and other traditionalists, allowing Russia to conclude a formal anti-German alliance with France. Czar Alexander III declared that, if war broke out between France and Germany, the Russians "must immediately hurl ourselves upon the Germans."[24] On August 18, 1892, the two countries signed a military treaty, thus completing the alliance. This accord was entirely directed at Germany and stipulated that if France were attacked by Germany or by Italy with German support, the Russian Army would attack Germany. If Russia were to be attacked by Germany or by Austria with German assistance, then France would attack Germany. The two countries would coordinate their mobilizations and entry into the conflict in order to force Germany to fight a two-front war.[25]

Anglo-German Estrangement

The formal establishment of a Franco-Russian alliance was a serious blow for Germany. Germany's international security environment had essentially become hopeless. Not only did it no longer have a lever to exert power, but also it now faced the threat of a two-front war. Germany, however, did not yet understand the seriousness of these problems, and instead placed its hopes on Great Britain's entry into the Triple Alliance. In fact, the Franco-Russian alliance had already essentially negated the power of the Triple Alliance, as the formation of two alliance systems on the continent created a balance-of-power situation favorable to Great Britain. Britain thus was visibly delighted at the new treaty arrangement. On the eve of the French fleet's visit to Russia in 1891, Georges Clemenceau, who opposed the French alliance with the autocratic Russia, visited Great Britain. In a long conversation with Joseph Chamberlain, leader of the British Liberal Party, he asked for Britain to support an Anglo-French understanding that would obviate the need for an alliance with Russia. In return, he promised to push the French government to allow Britain freedom of action in Egypt. Salisbury rejected the idea.[26]

In fact, the expiration of the Reinsurance Treaty and the signing of the Heligoland-Zanzibar Treaty had completely smashed the balance of Anglo-German strategic needs. Great Britain had already begun to distance itself from Germany. As early as August 1890, Salisbury warned the German ambassador in Britain that "we have, besides, plenty of opponents who are anxious to raise the cry that the German Emperor has too much influence over us."[27] This was only a small signal, but Germany had dimly begun to grasp that Anglo-German "close cooperation" would not be easy. In 1891, just before the renewal of the Triple Alliance, Great Britain impolitely brushed aside suggestions from Italy about strengthening British connections to the alliance. Even on the Morocco issue, which had originally created the foundation for British ties to the alliance, British policy and alliance policy had begun to drift apart. First, Salisbury refused to join the agreement of May 4, 1891, which had been brokered by Spain and Italy, to maintain the Moroccan *status quo*. In a move to block French infiltration into Morocco, he also refused to provide any foreign policy support for Spain or Italy. In June 1891, France made territorial claims to the Tuat region along the Algeria-Morocco border, thus causing anxiety in Italy. From the perspective of Germany and Italy, Britain had the most at stake in Morocco, and thus should cooperate with Italy and Spain to exert pressure on the Moroccan sultan and on France. Salisbury responded that Italy and Spain, in fact, had the closest ties with Morocco, and that Britain would not interfere with this French action.[28] This displeased Germany, causing Holstein to complain that in settling international disputes, "England will first try to get British interests looked after by other Powers without herself co-operating."[29]

In July 1892, the Conservative Party government in Great Britain was replaced by William Gladstone's Liberal Party. Given Gladstone's dislike for Germany's imperial system and his inclinations toward liberal France, Anglo-German estrangement took on a quickened pace. It was important for

Germany to ensure that the change in British government did not impact the Anglo-Italian strategic partnership, and to maintain Britain's ties to the Triple Alliance. The new British Foreign Secretary, Archibald Primrose, the Earl of Rosebery, was a Francophobe who planned to retain Salisbury's foreign policies. Germany, as a consequence, had high hopes for him. The Franco-Russian alliance, however, had already begun to change the overall strategic picture. Great Britain no longer needed to shoulder any responsibilities for the Triple Alliance. This was clear to Rosebery. In a meeting with German ambassador Hatzfeldt, he explained that he wished "to re-assure the Italians to the utmost," but that he could not provide any written guarantees.[30] Under repeated German entreaties, he expressed a "personal view," which he emphasized did not represent the view of the British government, to the effect that:

> In the event of France groundlessly attacking Italy, the interests of England as a Mediterranean and Indian Power would bring her naturally to the rescue of Italy.... That was my personal conviction, but beyond that I could say nothing, and in any case I could not make an authoritative communication as from the British Cabinet to the Italian Government. My belief was simply this, that in the eventuality that was dreaded and contemplated the natural force of things would bring about the defensive co-operation they desired.[31]

Two years of relentless expressions of goodwill had not brought Great Britain closer to the Triple Alliance. Instead, they had slowly begun to drift apart. German disappointment can only be imagined. Further events turned this disappointment into unease, as German officials learned that Great Britain was seeking conciliation with France on a variety of issues. Britain's new Liberal cabinet had essentially already reached consensus on the need for good ties with the French and an end to any reliance on the Triple Alliance.[32] The outbreak of the Siam Crisis in Southeast Asia, however, caused a moment of British hesitation—and Anglo-German relations seemed to be at the threshold of a breakthrough. France had been working to solidify its control over colonies in Indochina, and came into conflict with Siam. The British government strongly hoped to maintain Siam's current status as the last buffer zone between British-held India and Burma on the one hand and French-controlled Indochina on the other. On July 20, 1893, the French delivered a final ultimatum to Siam and, upon its refusal, blockaded the Siamese coast. Great Britain had not been prepared for such a forceful French action and, in this crisis situation, had to rely on the Triple Alliance. Rosebery sent a complaint about France to the German ambassador on July 27, which obliquely implied that Germany would be the beneficiary of an Anglo-French war in that it could cause the Triple Alliance to become a Quadruple Alliance.[33] At the same time, the British press hinted at the possibility of Britain's entry into the alliance. German hopes for an expanded alliance were thus reignited. A report received in Britain on July 30 claimed that France had ordered British warships to leave Siamese territorial waters and retreat behind the French blockade line. Rosebery, believing that an Anglo-French war was about to break out, persuaded the queen to send her secretary to meet with the kaiser in Cowes (Wilhelm II was in Britain at the time for a boat race). The secretary conveyed the following telegram from Rosebery: "French Government demands withdrawal of our gun-boat from before Bangkok. I have refused this. Desire to see Count Hatzfeldt [the German ambassador] in London immediately."[34] This appeared, to Germany, as a request for German support on the eve of an Anglo-French war. The kaiser immediately declared that France was deliberately seeking war and that he desired to stand with the British in the fight against the French. Caprivi wrote on Hatzfeldt's report, "For us the best beginning for the next Great War would be for the first shot to be fired from a British ship. Then we are sure of being able to convert the Triple Alliance into a Quadruple one."[35] When the German delegation's first secretary (Hatzfeldt himself being confined to a sickbed) arrived in London the next day, however, he learned that the previous day's news had been inaccurate. The war scare had passed and the recently reignited hopes for closer Anglo-German ties were thus extinguished. This event had a great impact on Germany's new policymakers: they decided that Britain was untrustworthy and their attitudes toward the country began to shift.

Great Britain would once again feel a momentary need for Germany in the final half of 1893. In October, the French people enthusiastically greeted a Russian fleet visiting Toulon. The British discovered that, although the Franco-Russian alliance was directed against Germany, it was they who were the first to feel its impact. The British ambassador to France, Frederick Hamilton-Temple-Blackwood, Marquess of Dufferin and Ava, wrote, "In view, therefore, of the strong feelings of hostility toward England which prevail in this country…if war were inevitable, a war with England would be as popular, and would be considered less dangerous, than a single-handed encounter with Germany."[36] Rumors, too, circulated that France had granted the Russian Navy use of the port in Bizerta, that Russia had itself prepared to lease an eastern Mediterranean island as another naval facility, and that the entire Black Sea fleet's passage through the straits and into the Mediterranean was imminent.[37]

The British government decided to strengthen its fleet in light of the Franco-Russian threat; Rosebery, now prime minister, immediately allocated additional funds to the navy. This process would take time, however, and Britain needed to search for a partner to share the burden of countering French and Russian pressure. Germany's Triple Alliance was the natural choice.

Rosebery expressed his desire to strengthen cooperation with the Triple Alliance against the Franco-Russian combination, particularly in the Black Sea region, in January 1894. He told the Austro-Hungarian ambassador to London, "I assure you that I am absolutely determined to maintain the status quo in the Straits question and that I would not recoil from the danger of involving England in a war with Russia." He also indicated that, if the French entered the war, the British fleet would be insufficient to defend Istanbul, and "in such a case we should require the assistance of the Triple Alliance to hold France in check."[38] Germany was the intended recipient of these comments, as it was the only member of the Triple Alliance capable of "checking" France. German calculations at this time, however, had become much more complex. First, the Franco-Russian alliance was already a reality, so Germany had to consider the price of tying itself to Great Britain. In order to accomplish the deterrence sought by the British, Germany would have to be prepared to fight a two-front war. Great Britain would only be risking its fleet in such a war; Germany would be risking its national existence. Second, if Germany agreed to "check" France without Great Britain committing to any specific obligations of its own, then Britain would retain the power to decide its actions independently. In other words, Great Britain would dominate the Triple Alliance. Third, without the limitations imposed by a treaty, Great Britain might again act as it did in the Siam Crisis: a hawk one moment, and a dove the next. This could cause the Triple Alliance to be left suddenly exposed on the frontlines of conflict with France and Russia. Thus, Germany refused to "force the French to remain neutral" without first inking a treaty with the British: "If England wanted our help, let her enter into a definite engagement with the Triple Alliance in which our mutual obligations would be securely established, not only for Lord Rosebery's tenure of office, but for that of any other Government; we should then be able to attempt to prevent England concluding an isolated peace prematurely."[39] If that proved unobtainable, Germany preferred to maintain its own freedom of action. By this time, Germany moreover began once to again to appreciate the value of a relationship with Russia. It was unwilling to abandon the opportunity to pry Russia and France apart in exchange for unenforceable British promises.

Anglo-German Frictions Intensify

As relations between Great Britain and Germany cooled down, a series of colonial disputes between the two powers flared up. First, British authorities in Singapore had restricted the ability of German companies in New Guinea to recruit Chinese laborers. Second, a conflict had broken out between the German colonial government in Southwest Africa and a local chief. Handling the conflict as a war, the British colonial government in the Cape refused German military shipping access to Wallis Bay. It also offered protection to the chief who had antagonized the Germans. This enraged the German government, which threatened that, unless Britain changed its stance on German colonial interests, Germany would be forced to reconsider its support for British policies.[40] Third, the two countries also argued about the status of the Pacific island of Samoa. An 1889 agreement assigned the island group to the joint management of Britain, the United States, and Germany, but Germany had always hoped to become the sole ruler. During the first half of 1894, the U.S. government expressed an interest in withdrawing from the joint management consortium and was looking to make a deal of some sort. Germany saw this as an excellent opportunity to establish rule over the whole island group and began negotiations with the British. Great Britain, however, proved unwilling to consider this. A difficult sticking point in Anglo-German colonial disputes had become clear: Germany's colonial holdings were limited, so it had little to trade with Great Britain. Therefore, Britain was unwilling to make any concessions in colonial disputes. If Germany wanted Britain to satisfy its colonial demands, it would have to depend on pressure rather than horse-trading.

Great Britain and Belgian King Albert II's Congo Free State signed an agreement in May 1894 that incited intense French displeasure. Germany saw this as an opportunity to pressure the British.[41] Great Britain had assumed Germany was pleased with the support it had given Austria-Hungary and Italy in the Mediterranean; it did not anticipate that Germany would work with France against Great Britain on Congolese issues. On June 13, British Prime Minister Rosebery threatened that if Germany continued to side with France in these colonial disputes, then Great Britain would need to reassess its overall policies in Europe, particularly in the Mediterranean and the Balkans.[42] This did not frighten Germany. Foreign Ministry Secretary

Marschall took it as a bluff, as Rosebery had never done anything substantial on behalf of the Triple Alliance.[43] Germany, moreover, was simply uninterested in Rosebery's January suggestions.[44] Rosebery attempted to use Italy to pressure Germany, but Germany insisted that Italy stood with Germany on France's side and demanded that Great Britain respect the agreement reached at the 1885 Berlin Conference concerning the Congo Free State.[45] The reasons for Germany's later retreat are complex. Although Germany did not fear Rosebery's threats, they realized that their actions had already drifted far from their original objective, and that it was even less likely that Britain would agree to concessions in Samoa. French attitudes, too, raised German doubts. On June 17, Marschall received a formal diplomatic communication from the French ambassador in Germany, from which he concluded that "my impression is that the French Government intends, by enlarging the original suggestion, to let the matter sink away into the sand, so as to be able later to refuse joint action."[46] Such an assessment, combined with Germany's inability to achieve its initial objective, forced Germany to reconsider its actions and to pull away from the French position. Britain proposed compromise measures at this moment, too, which Germany accepted on June 18 in order to prevent Anglo-German relations from deteriorating further.

The Congo dispute had pushed Germany and Great Britain further apart. It was the first dispute since Bismarck's departure in which Britain found Germany and France jointly opposing its wishes. Half a month later, Rosebery received a response from Austria that entirely avoided his January proposals. He would no longer hold any illusions about the Triple Alliance.[47] Germany's attitude toward Great Britain shifted simultaneously. The heart of the "new course"—building a closer relationship with Great Britain—had been exposed as wishful thinking. As the illusion of an alliance with Great Britain evaporated, Germany realized that its own security environment had deteriorated. The Franco-Russian alliance had already made Germany's foreign policy strategy a dead letter; Germany would no longer be able to maneuver between the various powers. Germany had no choice but to rely increasingly on two pillars for its security. The first of these were its alliances. Germany would have to increasingly accommodate itself to its two allies, Austria-Hungary and Italy. Over time, this would lead to its slow loss of strategic leadership and autonomy, until the weak led the strong within the alliance. The second pillar was an expanded military. In November 1892, Caprivi had presented the Reichstag with an enormous army bill that called for an additional 77,000 soldiers and an additional 60 million marks.[48] This expansion eclipsed the combined total of all previous expansions between 1871 and 1890. Germany, moreover, had already strengthened its artillery forces before this. After the Reichstag rejected this proposal, Caprivi dissolved the legislature and called for elections. The newly elected Reichstag approved an expansion of 66,000 troops in 1893, making it the largest single expansion of the army since German unification.[49] Reliance on these two pillars further revealed the antagonistic relationship between the two alliances. Germany had slowly entered into a vicious cycle of military expansion breeding insecurity, which in turn supplied justification for further military expansion.

The End of the New Course and the Illusion of a Continental Alliance

Faced with the disasters wrought by the new course, Germany's policymakers began to seek opportunities to escape their predicament. Their policy adjustments, however, bore the traits that marked all of the diplomatic initiatives of Wilhelm II's reign: hastiness, wishful thinking, a lack of comprehensiveness, and a lack of continuity.

Germany Abandons the New Course

The new course had not lasted even three years before Germany began considering a change. Faced with continual rebuffs from Great Britain and a formal Franco-Russian alliance, the German government hoped to improve ties with Russia—and perhaps even imagined it might pull Russia back into a relationship. Czar Nicholas II, heir to the Russian throne, visited Berlin in January 1893. Wilhelm II assured him that the Triple Alliance was purely defensive in nature and that it was directed against socialist revolution and U.S. economic competition. Germany, moreover, hoped to maintain "monarchical unity."[50] Holstein, too, underwent a surprising transformation. He had always opposed Bismarck's pro-Russian policies, but now moved to the opposite extreme of favoring Russian freedom of action in Bulgaria, Romania, and Ottoman Turkey. Even a treaty, if Russia wanted one, was possible, regardless of Austrian objections. Bismarck, by comparison, had promised treaties to the Russians only after closing off their paths for expansion.[51] Wilhelm II told the Austrian foreign minister that September that Germany would not fight a war with Russia over the Balkans. If the Russians occupied Istanbul, then the Austrians could occupy Salonika as compensation.[52] This had essentially been Bismarck's policy; Germany foreign policy had apparently reverted to what it was before the start of the new course.

Domestic political forces inside Germany also added fuel to the fire. The liberal forces which had supported Caprivi had splintered. Some of these liberal groupings began to see Great Britain as a commercial and colonial competitor. Closer relations thus no longer seemed as attractive. Industrialists began seeking markets in Russia and demanded improved relations with that country, particularly strengthened commercial ties. Although Junker landlords, seeking to protect their agricultural interests, opposed this policy, they were in a weak position from the beginning. By the end of 1893, political consideration of improved ties with Russia became more obvious, and Junker opposition was steadily repressed. Wilhelm II even claimed, "I have no desire to wage war with Russia on account of a hundred crazy Junkers."[53] The Reichstag approved a commercial treaty advantageous to Russia in March 1894. On October 29, Caprivi resigned and was replaced by the conservative Chlodwig zu Hohenlohe-Schillingsfürst as chancellor. This personnel change marked the final end of the already nearly defunct new course.

The Failure of a Continental League

Germany's ideal was to return to the situation before the implementation of the new course. This was exactly the role that Holstein and others hoped the new commercial treaty with Russia would begin to fulfill. In international relations (particularly when great powers are involved), however, direct economic interests can never substitute for deeper strategic interest. The Russo-German trade agreement absolutely would not be able to replicate the effect of the Reinsurance Treaty. Even more important, Germany's foreign policy environment had undergone a revolutionary change. First, the establishment of the Franco-Russian alliance created a balance of power in Europe. This was a deadlocked situation in which it was difficult for any great continental power to achieve a strategic breakthrough. Second, Britain's strategic need for Germany had greatly diminished, and its so-called era of splendid isolation had begun. Third, the strategic stalemate on the continent coupled with the intensification of imperialist expansion caused the European powers to let their European conflicts lie in abeyance while shifting the focus of their conflict to other regions, particularly East Asia and Africa.

Germany did not entirely understand this new situation. When it realized that it was impossible to return to the *status quo ante*, Germany could only place its hopes in making use of tensions between Great Britain and the Franco-Russian alliance. German policymakers plotted a Continental League with two purposes. The first of these was to build closer ties with France and

Russia. The second was to frighten the British into making colonial concessions. Germany vacillated between these two objectives, or pursued both at once.

Germany soon found an opportunity to demonstrate its Continental League in East Asia. On July 25, 1894, the Japanese Army launched a surprise attack on Qing forces, thus starting the First Sino-Japanese War. Soon after hostilities began, the failure of the corrupt Qing government became apparent, and Great Britain and Russia began to coordinate to protect their interests in China. Germany had two considerations at this point: first, to prevent other great powers from partitioning China before Germany was ready; and second, to prevent Great Britain and Russia from using this opportunity to improve their overall relationship. Germany actively inserted itself into these events. At the beginning, Germany had supported Japan. German-Japanese relations had always been close: most of Japan's military advisors were German, Krupp provided a significant amount of armaments for the Japanese Army, and the two countries had close economic ties. German policy noticeably shifted by 1895, however. On March 8, Germany warned Japan that any seizure of any Chinese territory on the continent might invite British, French, and Russian interference, but the warning was ignored.[54] Germany was left with no choice but to take action itself in concert with Russia in order to prevent Anglo-Russian coordination. On March 20, 1895, negotiations opened between China and Japan. During the talks, Japan's demand for a treaty clause endorsing its occupation of the Liaodong peninsula became public. On April 8, Russian Foreign Minister Alexey Lobanov proposed a joint action by the great powers, noting that "the occupation of Port Arthur was…an obstacle to good relations between China and Japan and…a lasting threat to peace in Eastern Asia." Britain refused such action, but Germany vigorously supported it. Wilhelm II wrote to his ambassador in Japan that "we must do it even without the British."[55] France, too, lent its support. On April 17, the day that the Treaty of Shimonoseki was signed, Lobanov invited Germany and France to jointly intervene. The two countries immediately accepted. The ambassadors to Japan from the three countries visited the Japanese Foreign Ministry on April 23, bringing with them strongly worded letters protesting the occupation of Liaodong. On May 5, the Japanese government was pressured to accept the three nations' "advice," and abandoned their occupation of the peninsula.

This so-called Triple Intervention seemed on the surface to reflect a Continental League, yet Russia was its political beneficiary and France its economic beneficiary (the Qing indemnity to Japan was paid by loans issued from French banks). Germany did not gain any advantage from it. This result undoubtedly left Germany disappointed.

Failure to Build Closer Ties with Great Britain

Salisbury returned as Britain's prime minister in June 1895. Germany, believing that a Conservative government in power would be beneficial to the improvement of bilateral relations, began a half-hearted attempt to draw close to Great Britain. The first consideration of the Salisbury government, however, was the partition of the Ottoman Empire. On July 9, Salisbury held a long conversation with German ambassador Hatzfeldt in which he claimed that unless the Ottoman sultan made concessions on domestic political reform, "the time may always come…when Russia and England may again come to an agreement…and that would mean the end of the Turkish domination." He further hinted that this agreement would allow for the Russian annexation of Armenia.[56] While discussing Italian hopes for British assistance in Abyssinia on July 30, Salisbury further remarked that Italian policy in Africa had been a complete failure, and claimed that Britain could help Italy receive two Ottoman provinces, Albania and Tripoli, in compensation. Hatzfeldt concluded from this that Great Britain had already begun to consider the partition of the Ottoman Empire.[57]

Germany originally held great hopes for British foreign policy after Salisbury's return to power. It had even increased its support for Britain in the Middle East. Yet Salisbury's suggestions raised immediate doubts in Germany. Neither the kaiser nor the chancellor were in Berlin at the moment, so foreign policy was left in Holstein's hands. After Salisbury's July 9 hints of British concessions to Russia in Asia Minor, Holstein wrote in a letter that Britain desired to postpone conflict with Russia and perhaps hoped that "in the meanwhile…the Franco-Russian storm may break on the Continent."[58] German doubts deepened after learning of Italy's potential colonial gains. Since the 1885 Berlin Conference, Britain had opposed Austria-Hungary's acquisition of Salonika on the grounds of trade. Yet Italian possession (with British support) of Albania would necessarily increase mutual suspicion between Austria and Italy, thus threatening the Triple Alliance. Disposition of lands along the Mediterranean, particularly allowing the Italian occupation of Tripoli, might even lead to a war in which Britain, as it had in the early days of the Napoleonic War, could content itself with observing from the sidelines.[59] Once Salisbury learned of the German anxieties, he immediately changed his tune, suggesting Italian compensation in Morocco and Austrian gains in "the direction of Salonika." Finally he announced that he had no definitive plan, and suggested that Germany draft a proposal for discussion.[60] Holstein, however, rejected this idea. Germany's interests in Mediterranean and Middle Eastern affairs were limited, but if the partitioning of the Ottoman Empire led to European disputes, it would have to bear the brunt of it. If word leaked that Germany proposed a division of Ottoman and Moroccan territory, relations with France would sour. Holstein also suspected that Salisbury's move was intended to create trouble in Asia Minor and the Balkans that would draw the attention of the great powers and reduce Franco-Russian pressure on Britain in Egypt.[61]

Objectively speaking, Germany's doubts were reasonable. At the beginning, Salisbury's partition plans were worth considering. In the public documentary records, only German accounts make any mention of Salisbury's plan, and even these do so only vaguely. Some historians have pieced together a relatively complete plan from these documents. This plan assigned the Black Sea Straits and Constantinople to Russia, freedom of action in the western Balkans to Austria-Hungary, Tripoli or Morocco to Italy, and either Morocco or Syria to France. Great Britain would acquire Egypt and Mesopotamia.[62] The German documents, in fact, did not clearly delineate how the territories that would be distributed after the partition, except for those allocated to Italy and Great Britain. This puzzle was, to a great degree, created by the guesswork of Hatzfeldt or his successors. The territory to be awarded Russia, for instance, appears to be deduced from the July 30, 1895, conversation between Hatzfeldt and Salisbury. In that talk, Salisbury referred to the British rejection of Czar Nicholas I's 1853 proposal to partition the Ottoman Empire as a "mistake." He went on to say that he would not have made that same mistake. Hatzfeldt commented that the plan failed because Napoleon III was only willing to make concessions on Constantinople and not the Dardanelles. In response, Salisbury indicated that Great Britain, too, could not concede the Dardanelles to Russia.

Salisbury's implied plan of partition gave Italy's needs a high priority while discussing Austria's only in broad strokes, seemingly as if Britain placed great emphasis on winning Italian support in the Mediterranean. In fact, however, Salisbury had typically favored Austria over Italy, although at that moment he had little faith in either country, claiming that Britain had "backed the wrong horse."[63] Under these circumstances, his pro-Italy, anti-Austrian plan looked suspiciously like a challenge to the internal unity of the Triple Alliance.

Additionally, if Salisbury truly hoped to solve the Balkan problems through a partition of the Ottoman Empire, he would have made at least some contact with Russia. Yet there is no documentary record that indicates Salisbury discussed this plan with any country other than Germany. After the kaiser's rejection of the idea on August 5, Salisbury never raised it again. Taken together, these points suggest, at a minimum, that Salisbury was being insincere, that it was correct for Germany to avoid becoming involved, and that scholars who argue that it was a "missed opportunity for Anglo-German cooperation" cannot substantiate their claim.[64]

A Second Plan for a Continental League

After rejecting Great Britain's suggestion, Germany decided to move closer to Russia. In the middle of October 1895, Russian Foreign Minister Lobanov visited Berlin to express his concerns that the British might attempt to end the Armenian problem though a surprise attack and occupation of the Dardanelles. The Germans replied that they would not aid Great Britain, but would instead provide Russia with moral support. Soon afterward, the kaiser expressed the same sentiments to the British military attaché: "In the interests of my country it would not do to follow all the moods of British policy and to react to the vague hints and obscure utterances of British statesmen. This attitude of England's was forcing me to make common cause with France and Russia."[65] The kaiser telegraphed the czar on November 8, noting the seriousness of the situation in the Balkans and inquiring about Russia's response. Germany soon found itself reversing course, however. Russia offered only a cold reply to the kaiser's inquiry, making Germany think that Russia did not place great value on the relationship between the two countries.[66] Another factor forced German reconsideration of their planned approach to Russia. The new Austro-Hungarian Foreign Minister, Agenor Maria Adam Gołuchowski, was Polish and liked Russia even less than his predecessors. Austria, too, thus helped pull Germany back from that policy path. On November 14, Germany suddenly informed Austria-Hungary that, if it felt its vital interests were threatened, it could rely on German support.[67]

Even in the midst of messy policy correction, Germany did not abandon its quest for a Continental League. Germany thought that, even with the existence of the Franco-Russian alliance, it was still possible to unite all of the continental great powers together in a display of strength against Great Britain. Wilhelm II wrote to his chancellor on December 20, 1895, that "England's plan to play off the continental powers will not succeed; instead she will find the continent against her as a solid block."[68] Germany's aim was to force Great Britain into renewing its support for the Triple Alliance, rather than to set themselves up in true opposition to the British. The Italian predicament in Abyssinia simply strengthened German motives.

France, engaged in its own colonial competition with Italy in Africa, aided the Abyssinian people in their fight, thus hastening Italian failure. On December 7, 1895, an army of 30,000 Abyssinians defeated the Italians at Amba Alagi. British assistance was late in coming; the Italian government expressed its extreme displeasure at this in early November and threatened to defect to the Franco-Russian alliance.[69] Germany had two options for preserving the Triple Alliance: to effect a conciliation with the Franco-Russian alliance through the Italians, and thus form the faint outlines of a Continental League, or to seek firmer ties with Great Britain in order to push that country to increase its support for the Italians. Germany's final decision was to attempt both of these. First it would reconcile with the French and Russians in order to stabilize the alliance with Italy and then use the prospect of a Continental League to frighten the British and force them to rely on the Triple Alliance. Holstein sketched the framework for this Continental League in a memorandum: France would receive the Congo Free State, Russia would be granted Korea. In exchange, France would make concessions to Italy by ending its support for the Abyssinians, and Russia would guarantee the *status quo* in the Balkans. Germany itself would acquire a naval and coaling station in China (perhaps the island of Zhoushan). Areas connected to Britain's core strategic interests, such as India, Persia, and Egypt, would not be touched. In order to maintain its hold over these regions, Great Britain would ultimately be brought closer to the Triple Alliance.[70]

On the surface, the German plan appeared brilliant. In reality, however, it suffered from three serious problems. First, it mistook the trends of the times. France and Britain did not have any serious colonial disputes at the moment (although they would in 1898) and Russian interest in the Balkans had already diminished. Instead, as the construction of the Trans-Siberian Railroad reached completion, Russian attention shifted to East Asia. It had no desire for friction with Great Britain in Europe. This made it difficult for Germany to find partners for its Continental League and risked turning the whole enterprise into a single-handed challenge to Great Britain. Second, the benefits it dangled as leverage were too small. Holstein's designs were fundamentally different from Bismarck's daring and farsighted concept of "giving in order to take." The support Germany offered France and Russia was insufficient, and they would thus naturally be unwilling to start a conflict with

Great Britain to satisfy Germany. Third, it was not workable. Germany, in order to demonstrate its "reconciliation" and "partnership" with France and Russia, would have to hope for a conflict with Britain, during which it could demonstrate its sincere intentions—but such a situation could easily result in embarrassment instead. These mistakes became clear though the course of events, and left German diplomacy with a defeat.

The Kruger Telegram

Germany's hoped-for dispute with Great Britain soon arrived. On December 29, 1895, a subordinate of Cecil Rhodes and manager of Britain's South Africa Company named Leander Starr Jameson led a small band of armed men in an invasion of the Transvaal, one of the two Boer Republics in South Africa. They exchanged fire with the Transvaal Army; the resulting incident became known as the Jameson Raid. News reached Berlin on December 31, and Germany immediately invoked an 1884 treaty to demand British respect for Transvaal's independence.

Germany's Reasons for Issuing the Kruger Telegram

Some scholars ascribe Germany's move to consideration of its economic interests in South Africa, take this dispute to reveal the intensification of colonial conflict between Britain and Germany, and see an increase in mutual distrust as a necessary consequence.[71] Some of this is beyond doubt—Germany did have significant economic interests in South Africa.[72] Disputes did exist between Britain and Germany. Yet, except for a mention of Germany's economic interests in a protest from German Secretary of State for Foreign Affairs Marschall to Great Britain, there is no evidence that Germany's actions were based on economic considerations. Moreover, even in Marschall's complaint, the emphasis was placed on European issues, while economic interests merely were the preface. He stressed that Great Britain overestimated the antagonism between the Triple Alliance and the Franco-German alliance, and complained that Great Britain "assumed that [this antagonism] was strong enough to allow British policy a free hand to look after its own interests at the expense of other States."[73] German economic interests in the Transvaal did not have much connection to Germany's policy. Thus, this dispute was not the necessary result of an intensified colonial struggle. Instead, it was to a great degree instigated by Germany, largely to demonstrate a Continental League and force the British to rely on the Triple Alliance. Hohenlohe, the German chancellor, directed his ambassador in France to make full use of the opportunity provided by the Jameson Raid and to propose joint Franco-German action. He wrote:

> The basic idea of this plan for a continental understanding for certain definite objects, is that the Triple Alliance has now no prospect of dealing with England, as it used to do, by attracting her to combine in the defense of the interests of the Triple Alliance and England.... Not until England learns by experience that the chasm between the two great continental groups is not unbridgeable, and that these groups, once they are at one in a definite case, are strong enough calmly to ignore England's opposing interests and carry on.... After this realization England may be content to abandon her present system of driving the two Continental groups against each other, and may join that one who would help her in protecting her road to India.[74]

But: how to demonstrate this Continental League to the British?

Germany's leaders initially only wished to teach Great Britain a lesson, but they did not fully consider exactly how to go about doing this. Marschall, after presenting his protest to the new British ambassador, Frank Lascelles, immediately hastened to Potsdam to report the news to the kaiser. Just before this, the German consulate in Pretoria had sent a telegram claiming that Transvaal President Paul Kruger had called for Germany to send marines to protect German nationals.[75] On December 31, the kaiser consented. That same day, the German Foreign Ministry contacted Governor Hermann Wissmann in Dar es Salaam to learn "whether he could send 400–600 men by way of Delagoa Bay to protect German interests in the Transvaal, without risking the security of German East Africa." After Wissmann agreed, the German government began seeking the consent of Portuguese colonial authorities at Delagoa Bay.[76] Germany's actions thus slid toward armed intervention. Yet events did not move in that direction. In order to avoid trouble, Kruger withdrew his request for German soldiers. Germany had to search for another way. On January 2, 1896, Germany transmitted a strongly worded note to Great Britain saying that it would not permit any changes to Transvaal's status. By that time, word that Jameson's small band had surrendered reached Berlin, and the German Foreign Ministry needed to send a response quickly. After changing their minds twice, Germany's leaders finally decided at a meeting on January 3 that Germany would "teach Great Britain a lesson" by sending President Kruger a congratulatory telegram. The telegram was not sent until almost noon. It read: "I express my sincere congratulations that, supported by your people, without appealing for the help of friendly Powers, you have succeeded by your own energetic action against armed bands which invaded your country as disturbers of the peace, and have thus been enabled to restore peace and safeguard the independence of the country against attacks from the outside."[77]

Germany still held to its original notion of organizing a Continental League. They presumed that, once Germany displayed a hard-line attitude toward Great Britain, France, and Russia would fall into line. On January 1, Marschall held talks with the French ambassador to Germany to urge joint action. In accordance with Holstein's design, however, Egypt would not fall within the scope of any such cooperative action. The kaiser wrote the czar on the following day, inviting Russia to work with Germany to preserve the sanctity of international treaties.[78] At the same time, Germany told Great Britain that it would face a united continent in isolation unless it consented to sign a secret alliance with Germany.[79]

At this moment, all of Germany's mistaken judgments became evident. France told Germany clearly that, if Egypt was going to be off limits, then it would not take any joint action with Germany.[80] Russia also reacted with indifference. In response to the kaiser's call, Russia simply responded that it commended the German position and left it at that. Even Germany's allies, Austria-Hungary and Italy, did not support its policy of seeking conflict with Great Britain. The Austrian prime minister announced that widening the Anglo-German split was not in accord with his country's own policies.

Anglo-German Antagonism Appears

Very quickly, the German government discovered that it would face British wrath all on its own. Just as it had overestimated the support it would receive from other continental powers, Germany had underestimated the response of the British people to the Kruger Telegram. All of Britain's papers published strident denunciations of the German government, calling its actions a "humiliation" and a "challenge" for Britain. The hatred of the British people for Germany burst forth like a flood. Dockworkers in East London attacked German workers and sailors, the windows of German stores were smashed, German mercantile activity boycotted, and the German ambassador received numerous threatening letters.[81] Even more embarrassingly, the German notion of frightening Britain into dependence on the Triple Alliance was openly and summarily rejected in the British press. The January 11, 1896, edition of the *Spectator* mocked this as being extremely stupid, because "kicking a Briton into submission is a possible expenditure of energy, but even a man like the

German Emperor, who seldom judges men aright, would hardly dream of kicking him into friendship."[82] Commercial competition between the two countries became grounds on which to criticize Germany. Some politicians took up this call; former Prime Minister Rosebery, for instance, claimed in a public speech on July 24, 1896, that "one very formidable rival…is encroaching on us as the sea encroaches on the weak parts of the coast—I mean Germany." In the summer of 1896, concerns about a "German threat" plotting against British commerce reached a fever pitch. Furthermore, Germany began to be described as Britain's most dangerous enemy. Competition between the two countries for trade and colonies, and even the *similarities* between the two countries (which had once been seen as evidence that the two were "natural allies"), were used as proof. The *Saturday Review* ran an essay by an author only identified as "a Biologist" that read:

> Germany is most alike to England. In racial characters, in religious and scientific thought, in sentiments and aptitudes, the Germans, by their resemblances to the English, are marked out as our natural rivals. In all parts of the earth, in every pursuit, in commerce, in manufacturing, in exploiting other races, the English and Germans jostle each other.… Were every German to be wiped out tomorrow, there is no English trade, no English pursuit that would not immediately expand. Were every Englishman to be wiped out tomorrow, the Germans would gain in proportion. Here is the first great racial struggle of the future: here are two growing nations pressing against each other, man to man all over the world. One or the other has to go; one or the other will go.[83]

Here it is worth analyzing these emotions in Britain. In all fairness, the Kruger Telegram was not as provocative as British newspapers described it. Instead, it can be seen entirely as piece of routine diplomatic business. Even the calm, unemotional Bismarck had agreed with the idea of sending a congratulatory telegram. Half a month before the telegram was sent, Great Britain had received a different challenge, in the form of U.S. President Grover Cleveland's intervention in a boundary dispute between British Guyana and Venezuela. In the message he sent to Congress, Cleveland invoked the Monroe Doctrine, claiming that it would "be the duty of the United States to resist by every means in its power as a willful aggression upon its rights and interests, the appropriation by Great Britain of any lands or the exercise of governmental jurisdiction over any territory which, after investigation, we have determined of right belongs to Venezuela."[84] The tone of the Kruger Telegram was significantly more moderate than Cleveland's statement. Even British newspapers acceded to that point. Yet Great Britain's reaction to Cleveland was entirely calm. What accounts for the difference?

Historians have deduced several reasons for this. First, the British paid much more attention to South Africa, where they had large investments, than to Venezuela. Second, pre-existing Anglo-German trade tensions had already created emotions ready to combust in Britain. Third, South Africa was of critical strategic importance to the British: without the Cape of Good Hope as a maritime base, the British Empire could not exist.[85] The first of these reasons is clearly true on its face, but the second and third deserve closer attention. The existence of Anglo-German trade tensions is indisputable, and British attacks on Germany at this time focused specifically on this. Yet most of essays and pamphlets that promoted the notion of trade competition appeared *after* the Kruger Telegram. Previously, British public opinion had not taken much note of the competition—so it is, at the very least, insufficient to see this as a cause for popular anger. The third of these proposed reasons is factually correct, but it cannot function as a reason *per se*. If it were a reason, the violent reaction would have come from the British government rather than the British people. In fact, however, the response of the British government was much calmer than that of the population at large. It was only on January 8 that Salisbury ordered a "flying squadron" comprising two battleships, two first-class cruisers, and two second-class cruisers. This fleet was not directed at Germany, but was meant as an emergency response force for the British Empire that could be sent anywhere in the world. Thus, we need to look elsewhere for reasons.

British foreign relations had been rocky ever since the 1893 Siam Crisis. A general sense of discontent over this existed throughout British society. President Cleveland's statement greatly intensified this sense of injury. The common cultural origins of the two countries, however, played a role in allowing the British to tolerate U.S. behavior. On a deeper level, U.S. industrial production had already exceeded that of the British by 1890, making expressions of British anger seem unwise. Yet these feelings still needed expression—and the Kruger Telegram provided the perfect opportunity. Joseph Chamberlain understood this, and wrote in a January 4, 1896, letter to Salisbury that "it does not much matter which of our numerous foes we defy, but we ought to defy someone."[86] Moreover, Germany's naval strength at that moment was even weaker than France's or Russia's, so it was the safest, and most appropriate, target for British hostility.

Now it was time for Germany to bear the results of its mistaken judgments and methods. The Continental League that Germany had imagined had completely vanished, leaving Germany itself isolated and locked in a worsening relationship with Great Britain. Germany began to backtrack. On January 8, the same day Salisbury announced the creation of a "flying squadron," the kaiser wrote a letter of apology to his grandmother, Queen Victoria. He claimed that Germany felt no hostility toward Great Britain and that the motives for sending the Kruger Telegram stemmed entirely from a desire to maintain the peace and protect German investors.[87] A week after the Kruger Telegram was sent, Holstein, the would-be architect of the Continental League, also hoped to bring this incident to a conclusion: "Let us be happy therefore, if the affair ends as it seems to be doing—with a small diplomatic success for Germany and a little lesson in politics for England."[88] On February 13, Marschall, who had been the most active proponent throughout the whole process, claimed to the Reichstag that "Germany's relations with England had never for one moment ceased to be good, normal and friendly."[89]

Nothing came of these efforts. Once feelings of enmity are expressed between two great powers, the situation is no longer one which policymakers can control. British Prime Minister Salisbury maintained his calm throughout, understanding that this was merely a German ploy to scare the British into an alliance. This incident, however, fully exposed a deeper level of conflict between the two nations. Previously, the two countries were unable to reduce the distance between them because of differences in strategic interests or unbalanced strategic needs; now, however, the element of emotion had been added. This hostility existed between the peoples and the societies, rather than between the governments. British domestic society was filled with the notion of Germany's challenge to Great Britain, while German society's aversion to Great Britain increased. Many Germans began to believe that Great Britain was trying to block Germany's rise as a great power. The main result of the Kruger Telegram was that it brought this dynamic—the competition between a hegemonic state and a revisionist state—into the open. It became part of the public consciousness in both societies. All future tensions between the countries would be automatically placed within this framework. British actions would be seen by the German public as reflecting jealousy or a desire to encircle Germany; German moves would be understood by the British public as challenges or threats. This vicious circle would limit the ability of their governments to improve relations between the two countries.

British Policies and their Effect on Anglo-German Relations

The outbreak of Anglo-German antagonism pushed Great Britain to take two additional measures that would be disadvantageous to Germany. First, it stepped up measures to negotiate solutions to conflicts with France and Russia. Second, it adopted hard-line techniques to resolve the Egyptian problem. In its negotiations with France and Russia, the British government received a strong impetus from domestic political opinion. The Anglo-French agreement on Siam was published on January 15, 1896. Britain had abandoned its hope of retaining a "buffer zone" in the upper reaches of the Mekong River (in 1893, both the government and public opinion demanded such a zone in strong terms). A series of mutual contacts and explorations began between the British and French governments. Salisbury admitted to Germany that he desired to come to an understanding with France.[90] The British simultaneously attempted to build closer ties with the Russians. Joseph Chamberlain told the Russian ambassador on February 19 that no unbridgeable conflicts existed between the two countries and an understanding between the two countries would be a guarantee for peace and civilization. A few days later, Conservative Party leader Arthur Balfour repeated the sentiments.[91] British efforts in this direction, however, were not fully successful.

In its attempts to resolve the Egyptian problem, however, Great Britain created serious consequences for itself. On March 1, 1896, the Italians were decisively defeated by the Abyssinians at Adowa. Intelligence reached the British on March 10 that nearly 10,000 armed Mahdi fighters had attacked the Egyptian-Abyssinian border town of Kassala. The British had the opportunity to reconquer the upper reaches of the Nile on the pretense of aiding the Italians. As Salisbury explained in a March 13 letter to Egyptian consul-general Lord Cromer, actions of the British cabinet were primarily designed "to prevent dervishes from taking Kassala" and "the safest way of doing so was to authorize an advance of Egyptian troops as far as Dongola."[92] The route of the British Army exposed British intentions. The army set off from Egypt and, if it had meant to help the Italians, it would have marched to Kassala by the shortest route. Instead it ignored Kassala and began a long march down the Nile to begin a military reconquest of Sudan.

The German government did not clearly recognize the true meaning of these events. Conversely, as it was busy trying to repair the damage done by the Kruger Telegram, it even welcomed Britain's action. Even more important, the Germans understood Britain's move as assistance to Italy (which was also indirect help to Germany), and so offered the British critical support.[93] Yet the British move, in fact, represented a revolutionary change of strategic forces in the Mediterranean. Originally, Britain hoped to restrain the Russians at the Black Sea Straits and thus worked with the Triple Alliance (which essentially meant Germany, as Britain had little hope that Austria-Hungary or Italy could provide much assistance) to force the French to maintain neutrality. At the same time, Great Britain needed Germany's support in Egypt to resist French pressure. Great Britain began to move away from a close deterrence to a distant deterrence of Russia. On October 28, 1896, the chief of British naval intelligence warned in a memorandum: "Do not imagine that any lasting check can be put upon Russia by action connected with the Dardanelles... the only way is by holding Egypt against all comers and making Alexandria a naval base."[94] And thus the 20,000-man Anglo-Egyptian Army began its march up the Nile in order to complete the actual occupation of the region.

This seemingly small military action's impact on great power relations was, in fact, revolutionary. As the British occupied the upper Nile, French dreams of forcing a British withdrawal from Egypt by entering the Nile Valley itself were smashed. In the end, this would force France to abandon its colonial contest with Great Britain in Africa; conversely, however, this would also remove a major obstacle to later Anglo-French cooperation and entente. Britain found its position in the Mediterranean stabilized, and it no longer needed any assistance. The balance between German and British strategic needs fell further out of equilibrium, and one of the major strategic cards played by Germany ever since unification in 1871 became worthless. Nothing was left that could function as a stabilization device between Germany and Great Britain. Further efforts to improve relations would soon reach their limits, while frictions and conflicts would be intensified.

5

Institutions, Society, Popular Opinion, and Grand Strategy

"We have been teaching the nation a taste for politics without satisfying its appetite, and it has to seek its nourishment in the sewers."
Otto von Bismarck

SIMILAR TO ITS foreign policies, Germany's domestic politics underwent a profound transformation after Bismarck's fall from power. The multitude of problems and conflicts created by rapid economic growth drove some aspects of this transformation, while others originated from human factors, particularly Kaiser Wilhelm II's reorganization of Germany's decision-making processes. As a consequence of this transformation, Germany was increasingly unable to meld its policymaking systems, society, public opinion, and other elements into an effective grand strategy. Comprehensive planning and coordination became impossible at any level. These domestic changes combined with increasing foreign pressures into a form of "resonance" that forced Germany to follow an increasingly hard-line policy in military and diplomatic affairs. In the end, this degenerated into diplomatic recklessness and military risk-taking.

Restricting Decision-making Institutions

Bismarck had designed the German Empire's decision-making systems. His primary consideration had been to maintain a balance between the Prussian people, nobility, and monarchy, while preserving the leading role of the Prussian royal house. He had allowed a separation between the political and military decision-making systems, thus protecting the role of the monarch as the only individual able to coordinate these two systems. The kaiser was the center of authority. This extreme concentration of power naturally had its uses. It also had costs. Among those was the extreme difficulty in coordinating the various parts of the government. In addition, the coordinating and mediating role of the kaiser turned out to be difficult to realize in practice. While Bismarck was in office, his own personal authority, status, and reputation had allowed him to function as the coordinator between the two systems. After he left office, however, no one else was able to take up this role. The separation between the two systems suddenly became very serious, and the fissures extended down into all of the departments of government. In the words of one German historian, "after Bismarck's dismissal, the Prusso-German pyramid of power no longer had a peak."[1] More significantly, not only did Wilhelm II lack the ability to bridge the gap between the systems, but also his attempts to change the policymaking structure to institute his own "personal rule" intensified the pre-existing separation. Policymaking authority became increasingly dispersed, and comprehensive coordination became even less likely.

Systems of Political and Foreign Policy Decision-making

Wilhelm II's own political inclinations were deeply contradictory. On the one hand, he hoped to be seen both within and without Germany as an enlightened, modern monarch. On the other hand, he revered the divine authority of kings, and he wished to highlight the political importance of the monarchy. As Bismarck himself commented, Wilhelm II's policies were "rooted in the conception that the king, and he alone, is more closely acquainted with the will of God than other men, governs in accordance with the same, and therefore confidently demands obedience."[2] Bismarck's forced departure in 1890 allowed Wilhelm II to tighten his grasp on the reins of power and freed him to seek personal rule. Wilhelm II may have desired power, but he lacked the skill to wield it. Under the constitution in effect at the time, he could only change the decision-making system and process. This, in reality, meant an increase in the separation between different parts of the government in order to stress the centrality of the monarch.

Wilhelm II transformed the policymaking process to a much greater extent than he changed the policymaking institutions themselves. These changes underscored his own importance; he frequently intervened directly in government operations. A prime example of this was his decision to eliminate a cabinet order of the Bismarck era that had required Prussian ministers to submit their reports first to the minister president, who would then transmit them to the king (who, of course, was also the kaiser of the entire empire). This system allowed Bismarck (as he concurrently served as imperial chancellor and Prussian minister president) to act as a coordinator. Bismarck thus strongly supported this rule when he was in power. Wilhelm II, however, rescinded it soon after ascending to the throne, allowing Prussian ministers to bypass the minister president and have direct contact with the kaiser. The minister president's coordinating functions vanished.

Wilhelm II's policymaking process relied largely on a small group of personal advisors. In order to demonstrate the absoluteness of imperial authority, he tended to work with a small group of individuals with whom he had tight personal connections, rather than going through official channels, in order to make policy. In many cases, the functional organs of government had little idea what was going on. Philipp, Prince of Eulenburg-Hertefeld, provides an example. He never held the highest official posts in government (in 1890, he was Prussian ambassador to Württemberg, in 1891 Prussian ambassador to Bavaria, and from 1893 to 1902 German ambassador to Austria-Hungary), but he had a close personal relationship with Wilhelm II that predated the latter's coronation. Thus, he exerted noticeable influence over his monarch. The appointment of Bernhard von Bülow as secretary of state for foreign affairs in 1897 and his later selection as chancellor were both based on the prince's recommendations. Holstein also gained direct access to the kaiser through the prince's political protection.[3] When Germany began a naval rivalry with Great Britain in the early twentieth century, Wilhelm II's actions typified this aspect of his rule. He did not work through the foreign ministry, but instead directly reached out to his personal friends and Albert Ballin, the head of the Hamburg-America Line, to send feelers to the British. The foreign ministry was essentially left in the dark about these communications. On the whole, key government agencies of Wilhelm II's Germany often manifested a form of systemic breakdown as standard policy practices were abandoned. They were replaced by methods that were largely informal and casual in nature. Given the already existing fractures within the German policymaking system, this over-reliance on personal friends simply made communication and coordination between the various agencies of government even more problematic. It merely intensified the problem of each agency doing its own thing in its own way.

Additionally, Wilhelm II was often unwilling to play the role of final arbiter in many concrete policy areas. This increased his direct interference in the operational units of government, particularly the foreign ministry. He enjoyed jotting orders and observations on the margins of diplomatic documents and telegrams. Not only were these excessive in number, they were also often highly emotional, strongly worded, and struck others as superfluous. Beyond this, he often interfered in the actual management of affairs. As the final decision-maker, he often made rash decisions that left the high officials under him uncertain about what to do. Adolf von Marschall, secretary of state for foreign affairs for much of the 1890s, once complained, "He interferes persistently in foreign policy. A monarch ought to have the last word, but H[is] M[ajesty] always wants to have the first, and this is a cardinal error."[4] Even more significantly, Wilhelm II simply did not possess the ability to coordinate or to understand things as a comprehensive whole. Intuition and emotion guided most of his interference in the operations of government. Continuity of policy was completely missing. As he rashly cast his influence through the various departments of government, he aided the growth of competition and contention between those departments and allowed the splits in the power structure to grow wider. This trend conversely served to weaken the kaiser's coordinating abilities. Thus, the personal rule that Wilhelm II sought was actually only "limited to occasional, incoherent interference with ministry-level work."[5] Wilhelm II's function in German policymaking was never the decisive one during his reign. After the 1908 *Daily Telegraph* incident, his direct interventions in the functioning of the government noticeably diminished, and a number of important decisions were made without his initiative.[6]

Military Policymaking Systems

Military policymaking was the area most impacted during the era of Wilhelm II's rule. He believed in the divine right of monarchs and strongly clung to the traditions of the Prussian royal house, which held that the king had absolute power over the military. Bismarck, upon his retirement, warned Wilhelm II that "so long as you have this present officer corps, you can of course do as you please. But when this is no longer the case, it will be very different for you." The kaiser, however, lacked any concept of how to wield his control of the military effectively. He understood his command authority to mean that he could use his power at any time. For instance, he believed that all appointments of military officers should come from him. He thought that the competition and the separation between the various parts of the military were advantageous to strengthening his position as the final arbiter. He completely failed to understand the deleterious effects of his personal rule on the functioning of the entire system, or that in the end it would simply serve to weaken his own power.

Within the German Army, the fragmentation of different systems and agencies had already been a serious problem. After 1883, the General Staff operated completely independently of the War Ministry, while the power to appoint and dismiss army officers had devolved from the War Ministry to the Army Cabinet. These three equally-ranked entities—the General Staff, the War Ministry, and the Army Cabinet—competed with one another and were closed to each other. Germany never had a high-ranking, effective organization equivalent to the British Committee of Imperial Defence (founded in 1902 with the prime minister as chair and a membership included high-ranking army and navy officers, as well as representatives from other ministries) that could coordinate common policymaking.[7] Instead it had a Commission of National Defense comprising only army and navy officers, which coordinated army-navy war planning. Wilhelm II, however, abolished the committee in 1897 in order to concentrate power in royal hands. Germany thereby lost the one mechanism that coordinated army and navy affairs, and the compartmentalization of the military worsened. The kaiser consistently opposed the creation of any similar coordinating institution. After the 1904 Anglo-French Entente, for instance, some naval officers advocated for a Strategy Committee to be made up of the kaiser, important army and navy officers, and the chancellor. This committee would coordinate plans for war against Britain and France. Wilhelm II vetoed the idea.[8]

Simultaneously, Wilhelm II moved to strengthen his coterie in the military. After taking the throne, he enhanced and reorganized the military advisors attached to the royal house (maison militarie) and renamed it the Royal Headquarters (in the past, this name had only been used in wartime). In practice, this was an imperial retinue that included officers from the Army Cabinet and the Navy Cabinet. They often accompanied him on journeys and were responsible for recording and transmitting his military orders. The responsibilities of this organization were completely amorphous. Given the close relationship between the kaiser and members of this retinue, it acted as an important tool for his interference in military policy and operations.[9] Wilhelm II sought to tighten his connection to military leaders and to demonstrate his authority to the army by granting the right of imperial audiences to large numbers of high-ranking officers. During the time of Bismarck and Wilhelm I, this number had been tightly controlled. Even the Chief of General Staff had not received this right until the 1883 military reforms. Under Wilhelm II, the leaders of the various military institutions as well as close to fifty army and navy officers were granted direct access to the kaiser. This served to intensify conflict within the Germany military and to make high-level coordination even more difficult.[10]

Wilhelm's meddling with the navy eclipsed his interference with all other parts of the German military establishment. The Germany Navy's history was much shorter than the German Army's. The competition between and mutual restraint of its internal subdivisions was also much less than that of the German Army. Its decision-making and operational systems were also comparatively well-functioning. After his coronation, Wilhelm II took a great interest in naval construction and thus quickly reorganized the navy's structure. First, he copied the army and established a Navy Cabinet in March 1889 that would be responsible for personnel issues. Its chief would also be tasked with transmitting the kaiser's orders to all of the relevant agencies and units. That same month, he also split the Imperial Admiralty, which had been the highest naval command center, into two separate units: the Imperial Naval High Command and the Imperial Navy Office. The High Command was primarily tasked with strategic orders and deployments, while the Navy Office was responsible for the construction and maintenance of the fleet. This latter agency in theory did not have the power to order deployments, but in fact it was quite powerful. This bureaucratic reorganization did not fully satisfy Wilhelm II, however. The concentrated power of the High Command over orders and planning proved to be great enough to restrict the monarch's absolute control over the navy. After Alfred von Tirpitz's appointment as head of the Navy Office and state secretary of the navy in 1897, Wilhelm II (with Tirpitz's support) engaged in yet another naval reorganization. The Navy High Command was abolished in 1899, and a Navy General Staff was established. Tirpitz, in order to prevent the emergence of an independent, powerful General Staff along the lines of the Prussian General Staff and preserve the status of the Navy Office, implemented a series of restrictions on this new entity.

As a result, the Navy General Staff had only thirty-five officers serving under it. Its functions were sharply restricted. In peacetime it was responsible for strategic planning, training staff officers, conducting naval intelligence, and drafting orders for the routes to be taken by deployed naval vessels. In wartime, it would be responsible for all naval operations, subject to the kaiser's approval. In fact, however, during wartime, command authority would not rest with the Navy General Staff, but with the fleet commander. Wilhelm II himself took the title Supreme Admiral of the German Imperial Navy, and in theory had oversight over all naval affairs. The combined effects of the 1889 and 1899 reorganizations seriously damaged the principle of command unity that had been established in 1871. These reorganizations created fissures between the various parts of the naval bureaucracy. On the surface, it appeared to strengthen the throne, as only the kaiser had the power to oversee all aspects of the navy. After the 1899 reorganization, Tirpitz promised the kaiser, "Your Majesty can now be your own admiral."[11] In practice, however, the German Navy—just like the army and the government as a whole—had fallen into a state of serious fragmentation.

Thus, ironically, the ancient power of the Prussian royal house to absolute control over the military that Wilhelm II wholeheartedly sought to protect through this process of bureaucratic fragmentation became increasingly impossible to wield. Inside the Germany military establishment, each of the major agencies constituted its own power center—and there was no organizational coordination between them. In theory, this fractured environment could have allowed power to concentrate in the hands of the kaiser, who could function as the final arbiter. In practice, however, it would require powerful abilities and a strong political foundation to dominate such an environment. In the absence of these, the kaiser was downgraded to one of many centers of power. In the end, this exacerbated the disorder within the decision-making system, making grand strategy—or even the realization of the most basic forms of coordination—increasingly impossible.

Societal Change and Cartelized Structures

If the influence of decision-making structures on grand strategy can be seen as direct and visible, then the impact of social power structures (defined as the distribution of power between the various major domestic interest groups) should be understood as indirect and subtle. This distribution of power could be manifested in explicit ways, such as the balance of power between political parties in a representative assembly, or in implicit ways, such as using covert activities to influence national politics. The distribution of power determines the outcome of compromise and competition between the various interest groups and, to a great extent, delineates the boundaries within which national policy choices operate. The changes in German social power structures between 1890 and 1914 is thus also a necessary angle from which to analyze changes in German grand strategy.

Cartelization

Many scholars of international politics have explored the relationship between social structures and grand strategy. Political scientist Jack Snyder has noted that at times, countries embrace irrational, self-defeating strategies of over-expansion. This trend is most easily manifested in countries with "cartelized" social systems.[12] "Cartelization" refers to the division of domestic society into several large, evenly matched interest groups. No single interest group, in this type of society, is able to effectively dominate the other groups. Interest groups thus must participate in a process of "log-rolling," in which they accept the policies of other groups in exchange for the unfettered right to pursue their own goals. As a result, there are no natural barriers to expansion; the risks associated with this, even if initially small, can accumulate over time. In the end, this can lead to "strategic over-commitment and self-encirclement."[13] From the perspective of grand strategy, cartelized structures encourage each interest group to go its own way, thus preventing effective, comprehensive coordination, and ultimately making it more difficult to devise or maintain a grand strategy.

Cartelized social structures are not only marked by the existence of evenly matched large interest groups, but are also characterized by the lack of a powerful center of authority. As Thucydides pointed out in his analysis of Athenian overreach during the Peloponnesian War, Periclean Athens had a power center, "what was nominally a democracy become in his hands government by the first citizen." After Pericles's death, however, this center vanished: "More on a level with one another, and each grasping at supremacy, [his successors] ended by committing even the conduct of state affairs to the whims of the multitude."[14] Thucydides's ancient analysis criticized the harms caused by a cartelized society—namely, that it lacks an effective power center that could coordinate between major interest groups. This lack allowed the balance between the interest groups to degenerate into political instability as each group engaged in unrestrained political log-rolling.

A third characteristic of cartelized societies is imperfect domestic political processes. Under a comparatively well-functioning political system, the existence of the previous two characteristics might result in interest groups holding each other in check throughout the policymaking process, resulting in paralysis. With imperfect political institutions, however, the lack of commonly accepted political procedures, combined with the significance of public opinion for policymaking, can result in extremely negative consequences. Samuel Huntington noted this in his discussion of "praetorian" societies:

> The phrase "praetorian society" is used to refer to such a politicized society with the understanding that this refers to the participation not only of the military but of other social forces as well.... In all societies specialized social groups engage in politics. What makes such groups seem more 'politicized' in a praetorian society is the absence of effective political institutions capable of mediating,

> refining, and moderating group political action. In a praetorian system social forces confront each other nakedly; no political institutions, no corps of professional political leaders are recognized or accepted as legitimate intermediaries to moderate social group conflict. Equally important, no agreement exists among the groups as to the legitimate and authoritative methods for resolving conflicts.... In a praetorian society, however, not only are the actors varied, but so are the methods used to decide upon office and policy. Each group employs means which reflect its peculiar nature and capabilities. The wealthy bribe; students riot; workers strike; mobs demonstrate; and the military coup. In the absence of accepted procedures, all these forms of direct action are found on the political scene.[15]

In a certain sense, a praetorian society can be seen as an extreme example of cartelization that has expanded throughout all aspects of society. Its results are basically similar, namely that all kinds of forces and interest groups appeal directly to popular opinion and directly engage in social mobilization in order to exert pressure on the government. As a result, the nation is unable to fashion a coherent, stable policy. It is this flaw in political decision-making institutions that allows negative effects of the balance of power between interest groups and the absence of a political center to fully emerge.

Social Economic Development and the Cartelization of German Social Structures

The social structures of Wilhelm II's Germany are a classic case of the type of cartelized society defined above. As argued in Chapter 1, German development, and particularly German industrial development, occurred in an extremely short timeframe. Thus Germany differed from countries such as Great Britain and France that industrialized slowly over a long period of time. These countries had ample time to eliminate their traditional ruling elites or to absorb that strata into new socioeconomic structures. Germany, instead, preserved its feudal-military elite in its entirety, and this group occupied the "hard core" of stable political power. As the power of the commercial and industrial capitalist classes grew, they began to demand greater political power. This formed the struggle between two major interest groups at the time of German unification. After unification, economic development and industrial growth accelerated, and the superiority of industry and commerce over traditional agriculture became ever more apparent. During the period from 1870 to 1874, agriculture, forestry, and fishing accounted for 37.9 percent of the nation's economic output, while industry provided only 29.7 percent. By the period from 1900 to 1904, the respective amounts were 29 percent and 36.6 percent. Industry had surpassed agriculture and its related occupations.[16] These changes objectively strengthened the position of the capitalist class and intensified the struggle for social and political power between the Junker landlords and the industrialists.

This polarization between the Junkers and the industrialists, however, cannot be called cartelization. In 1879, German domestic politics and social structures experienced a significant change that could even be seen as a watershed moment. That year Bismarck, in a bid to solidify the government's position, broke with his previous allies, the German liberals. Domestic politics shifted toward conservatism, and economic policy from free trade toward protectionism. Bismarck imposed high protective tariffs to satisfy the demands of agriculture and industry (particularly heavy industry). Politically, this caused the two interest groups that supported the tariff—the Junkers and the industrial capitalists—to unite in the so-called marriage of iron and rye. This alliance strengthened Bismarck as the representative of conservative forces in domestic politics. Simultaneously, it dismantled the bipolar structure that had existed between the Junkers and the industrialists.

This transformation, however, was only temporary. From the perspective of the entire structure of society, this marriage of iron and rye only ameliorated tensions with German society, and this alliance held a leading role in German politics only briefly. As the economy continued to develop, a new change occurred in German structures of social authority, and new interest groups began collecting strength and exerting their own political influence. After the marriage of iron and rye, the political and economic demands of industrial workers increased, the workers' movement expanded, and the Social Democratic Party grew powerful. These became important elements of German political life. At the same time, differences within the industrial capitalist class emerged. The interests of the manufacturing industry, the textile industry, and the chemical industry diverged from those of the heavy industries that demanded tariff protection. The former industries had greater dependence on export markets for their products and desired to import raw materials at a cheaper price. The conflict with the heavy industries over the tariff continued to grow until they formed their own interest group in opposition to the marriage of iron and rye. German Catholics, living in a nation with a Protestant majority and a state-supported Protestant church, formed their own interest group and their own political party, the Centre Party. By the later part of the Bismarckian era, several large interest groups (or perhaps a stalemate between several large political forces) had been formed. These included conservatives (representing heavy industrialists and the Junker class), the Social Democratic Party (representing industrial workers), the Catholic Centre Party, and the liberals (based in the bourgeois class and supported by commercial capitalists).

Yet, during Bismarck's rule, this balance of power between interest groups did not cause a cartelization of German social structures. Bismarck's own status and abilities allowed him to be the strong center of authority and the effective coordinator that could stand in the middle of these forces and prevent cartelization. Most important, he was able to organize and rank the demands of these interest groups such that their long-term interests and those of the nation-state were one and the same. Thus, the domestic political structure did not fundamentally influence German foreign policy or grand strategy. It should be pointed out, however, that Bismarck's abilities had their limits, such as his ineffective carrot-and-stick response to the workers' movement, which relied on providing social insurance and implementing an anti-socialist law. In the Reichstag, he likewise had to resort to a variety of tactics to maintain majority support for the government, such as the 1879 protective tariff, organizing a "cartel" out of conservatives and right-wing liberals, and others.

By the era of Wilhelm II, the cartelization of German social structures had already reached an advanced state. First, Bismarck's retirement removed the pre-existing center of authority. Neither Wilhelm II himself nor any of his chancellors were able to direct or coordinate the various interest groups. The Reichstag provides an example. All of the chancellors who followed Bismarck had difficulty earning majority support within the legislature. The Caprivi chancellorship (1890–1894), seeking to change Bismarck's repressive policies toward the Social Democratic Party and the communist movement, promoted social policies, abolished the anti-socialist law, and legalized the Social Democratic Party. The goal was to gain the support of leftists and the Social Democratic Party. This policy incited the opposition of conservatives (with the marriage of iron and rye at the center). The split between the Caprivi government and the conservatives led to its fall from power. During the Hohenlohe era (1894–1900), the government enacted a policy of rallying together, aimed at uniting capitalists to resist the Social Democratic Party. The Catholic Centre Party ultimately split with the other pro-capitalist groups, bringing the policy to a crashing end. Bülow's chancellorship (1900–1909) also saw the construction of a fragile alliance between liberals and conservatives, the so-called Bülow Bloc, which followed a policy of oppressing leftists at home and a "strong policy" overseas. Early on, this alliance had a level of stability, but later the appetites of the relevant interest groups proved greater than Bülow's ability to satisfy them, leading to a slow dissolution.[17] After the *Daily Telegraph* incident, the Bülow Bloc disintegrated. Liberals split into several groups, with the left wing forming its own political party, the Progressives, that immediately allied with the Social Democrats. During Theobald von Bethmann-Hollweg's time in office (1909–1917), party politics and legislative politics became even more unmanageable. In the 1912 Reichstag elections, conservatives won 57 seats, right-wing liberals (the National Liberal Party) 45, the Centre Party 91, left-wing liberals 42, and the Social Democrats 110.[18] None of the realistic combinations could form a majority in a house of 397. The Reichstag was thus deadlocked, and the government could not depend on majority support in the Reichstag. As a result, social legislation stopped.[19]

Parliamentary deadlock was only one of the manifestations of the entire social power structure. In fact, after Wilhelm II ascended to the throne, the balance of power between the various large interest groups became even more deadlocked. This received its impetus from the continued development of the German economy and society, particularly industrialization and urbanization. Between 1890 and 1913, German industrialization continued its quick pace of development, and the importance of industry compared to agriculture only increased. The ratio of capital invested in the two sectors illustrates this. In 1890, 34 billion marks were invested in industry, as opposed to 11.5 billion in agriculture, making a ratio of 2.95:1. By 1910, investments were 43 billion marks and 10 billion marks respectively, for a ratio of 4.3:1. Urbanization followed industrialization at a similarly rapid pace. In 1890, 57.5 percent of the German population lived in the countryside and 42.5 percent in towns and cities. By 1900, the urbanized population had eclipsed the rural population, with 45.5 percent of the population in the countryside and 54.4 percent in the urban areas. By 1910, only 40 percent of the population remained in the countryside, while 21.3 percent of the population lived in large cities and another 27.4 percent in medium-sized cities.[20]

Generally speaking, such rapid industrialization and urbanization are major forces promoting the transformation of social structures. These processes benefit newly emergent classes and accelerate the decline of old classes. In Germany, however, these developments were limited to the economy and society, while politics remained distorted by the imperial political system. Although the economic and social position of the Junker landlord class had been eroded, its traditional political position and authority had been, in great measure, preserved. The capitalist and working classes had grown strong, but a glass ceiling that prevented the rise in their social status existed. Working-class political parties were, in particular, seen as alien, enemy forces. As industrialization and urbanization advanced, these political distortions became ever more pronounced and the pressures inside German society became ever more intense. In the final era of Wilhelm II's reign, the various interest groups were squeezed into a deadlocked balance-of-power situation created by their own strong pressures. This stasis persisted for a relatively long period that created not only the political problems of the Wilhelmine era, but also contributed to the collapse of the Weimar Republic and the rise of Nazism in the 1930s.

Imperfect Political Processes and the Cartelization of German Social Structures

Domestic German political processes and institutions were imperfect in comparison to those of early industrializing nations such as Great Britain. Particularly, as industrialization and urbanization created significant wealth and capabilities in society, the political system proved unable to control or direct these new forces. Although the state tolerated the political demands of ordinary people, it lacked rational processes and pathways to guide them. Universal suffrage and the legislative system were far from sufficient. The foundations for interaction between the people and the government were irregular. This ultimately produced a variety of extra-institutional methods and pathways, thus further degrading the political process. As Bismarck wrote ruefully, "We have been teaching the nation a taste for politics without satisfying its appetite, and it has to seek its nourishment in the sewers."[21]

The collective manifestation of these extra-institutional methods was the large number of political, nongovernmental organizations. The limited powers of the Reichstag meant that political parties could not play a truly significant role in the political life of the German Empire. This led the interest groups to directly construct popular organizations to engage in social mobilization (which consisted of using propaganda and agitation to create popular opinion for a particular political or economic purpose) and exert political pressure on their behalf. These political forces directly originating from society have been called Germany's "secondary system of social power."[22] These organizations had already emerged in large numbers during Bismarck's time. Examples of this include two organizations founding in 1876, the Central Union of German Industrialists, established by manufacturers, and the Association of Tax and Economic Reformers, organized by farmers east of the Elbe River. These two groups can be seen as the concrete social manifestation of the marriage of iron and rye. The publicity, organizational, and social mobilization efforts of these two groups played a profoundly important role in the enactment of the 1879 protective tariff. Beyond groups such as these, which reflected major interest groups, smaller, more complex groups also appeared in the Bismarckian era. These groups typically promoted specific issues. In 1882, for example, pro-colonial intellectuals and merchants established the Colonial Union. Within two years, it had over 9,000 members, had branches in 43 locations, and had received financial support from banking and heavy industrial interests. Leaders from the academic world, such as Adolf Wagner, did publicity work for them.[23] A Society for German Colonization was founded in 1884 and the two pro-colonial societies merged in 1887 to form the German Colonial Society, which created a more unified, influential voice for the promotion of overseas expansion and the seizure of colonies. Each group's mobilization of public opinion caused Germany's originally conflict-laden political system to take on even greater pressures. During Bismarck's chancellorship, however, this was controllable. During his 1884–1885 foray into colonial expansion, for example, Bismarck kept these groups on a tight leash, using them at times and repressing them at others, leaving his policy basically free from their interference.

This situation changed greatly during Wilhelm II's rule. First, the number and scale of the interest groups increased dramatically. Examples of influential groups with large memberships included the 1893 German Agrarian League, the Industrial League (which broke away from the Central Union of German Industrialists in 1895), the 1900 Trade Treaty Organization, and others. Second, organizations became even less scrupulous in their social mobilization efforts and built stronger bonds with the political parties. This allowed the interest groups to become organic combinations of socioeconomic foundations, social organizations, and political parties, thus strengthening their ability to act in domestic politics. The German government was fundamentally unable to control these organizations and was often forced into a reactive mode. Taking conservative forces as an example, when Chancellor Leo von Caprivi attempted to lower German tariffs in order to build a Central European trade zone that would integrate the German, Austrian, and other continental economies, large farmers in the East were virulently opposed and formed the 1893 Agrarian League. This group came to wield ever more influence over the leadership of conservative political parties, causing the social foundation of the conservatives and their political parties to form a tight, compact systemic whole. In this end, this caused Caprivi's policy to be abandoned. Thus, "Prussian conservatism in the age of Frederick Wilhelm IV had been a political worldview and even in the Bismarckian era it still embodied an intellectual tradition, but by the Caprivi period it was purely an interest group."[24]

During Wilhelm II's reign, another sort of social organization with definite political objectives also developed. The interest groups representative of this kind of organization had common political agendas but lacked common socioeconomic bases and thus could encompass different social classes. The rapid development of this kind of group was an important characteristic of domestic politics during the era of Wilhelm II. In 1891, the Pan-German League was founded. This was a right-wing extremist organization that had noticeable influence on domestic public opinion and foreign policy. The philosophy of its founder, Ernst Hasse, essentially represented the organization's political program. His views were: First, that the human ethnic groups are not equal and the German people should be in the leading role. Second, all people of German descent should form a single nation-state, which the current German Empire was not, as over a million people not of German descent lived inside Germany and over a million Germans lived outside of Germany's borders. Third, global competition was not between states but between ethnicities, thus Germany need to strengthen itself, otherwise, "How can the 53 million Germans in the German Empire hope to compete with more than one hundred million Anglo-Saxons, Yankees, and Russians?"[25] This extreme nationalistic perspective propelled the Pan-German League to the forefront of those advocating German colonial expansion and hard-line policies. The league significantly influenced domestic public opinion on a number of international disputes. In the First Morocco Crisis, for instance, the chairman of the league, Heinrich Class, wrote a pamphlet entitled, "Is Morocco Lost?" that emphasized the importance of Morocco for Germany and stirred up popular emotions. During the Second Morocco Crisis, the league advocated annexing a portion of Morocco and was able to bring strong political pressure to bear on the government. Thus, although the league's membership was never very large, it played an important role in German politics. As one leader of the Social Democrats pointed out, it set the direction for many other social groups.[26]

Other examples of this type of organization included the Navy League and the Army League. The Navy League, founded in 1898, had deep connections to government and industrial concerns. It was created singlehandedly by Alfred von Tirpitz, state secretary of the Imperial Navy Office, with the sole objective of gaining greater popular support for the construction of a large blue-water navy. Soon after its establishment, this organization boasted more than 80,000 members. Krupp, the arms manufacturer, provided over a million marks per year in funding.[27] Through the publication of pamphlets, holding of mass meetings, and collecting opinions or writings from famous people, the Navy League successfully mobilized German society, thus transforming the German people, who lacked a sea-going tradition, into enthusiasts for the ocean and the navy. It also transformed the construction of a large fleet into a popular movement. Nothing similar existed for the army. Several retired army generals, seeking to change this situation, formed the Army League in 1912. In structure and activities, it modeled itself on the Navy League. It adopted forceful slogans pointing to German "encirclement" and claiming that "war is imminent" in order to increase public support for the army and to gain a greater share of military expenditures for the army. By the outbreak of World War I, the Army League had grown to 36,000 members.

In conclusion, German social structures during the age of Wilhelm II displayed all of the characteristics of cartelization. Faced with this state of affairs, the comparatively weak government had no ability to plan comprehensively or to coordinate the large interest groups and political forces. Domestic politics descended into stasis, under which it became impossible to form an overarching grand strategy, Foreign policy vacillated directionless under the influence of various interest groups and political forces. Most critically, these various social organizations would simultaneously pursue contradictory interests. Not only did this result in policies that worked at cross-purposes, but it also served to displease other countries that were in a position to take offense. For example, naval construction was aimed at Great Britain, and thus the interest groups associated with it hoped to reconcile with France and Russia in order to concentrate on Great Britain; liberals and Social Democrats hated Russia and tended to seek an accommodation with Great Britain; finance capitalists hoped for a strong relationship with France, while pro-colonial forces advocated the containment of France; and so on. These factions combined together to form the worst possible outcome: each group exerted itself in pursuit of its own interest, leading to all attempts to reconcile with any one foreign power to be vetoed by parties opposed to that power. The end result was "excessive expansion" in all directions. The British historian A. J. P. Taylor's analysis of the interconnection between Germany's foreign policy problems and its domestic problems points to this squarely:

> Each group in Germany had a single enemy and would have liked to make peace with the others. But Germany lacked a directing hand to insist on priorities. It was easier to acquiesce in all the aggressive

> impulses and to drift with events. Germany lay in the center of Europe. She could use this position to play off her neighbors against each other, as Bismarck had done and as Hitler was to do; or she could abuse her position to unite her neighbors against her, not from policy, but by having none...German policy, or rather lack of it, made the Triple Entente a reality.[28]

The Impact of Public Opinion

The late nineteenth and early twentieth centuries were a period of enormous social and economic change and development in Germany. Due to the increases in material wealth and technology, ordinary Germans felt more powerful and had high expectations for the future. Many Germans truly believed that the skills, intelligence, and hard work of the German people would allow Germany to become a world power. Large numbers of people hoped to contribute to this process. In other words, Germany was in an era of fervent passion. The feelings of many Germans could be represented by the words of the wife of a famous German writer who recalled in a letter to a friend, fifty years later, "My thoughts always wander back to that time when you and my husband co-operated in that fine effort: work for the *Grössere Deutschland*, peaceful expansion and cultural activities in the Near East... Vienna the gateway for these policies. Hamburg the portal to the seas and other continents.... A peaceful Germany, great, honored, respected...Our methodical thought should be translated into technology and enterprise."[29]

Eras of passion, however, are also often eras in which the temptations of irrationality loom large. A particularly prominent manifestation of this was the increasing power of the German people to voice opinions about foreign policy. As a result, the German government's strategic policymaking could only accede to the demands of the people and follow a hard-line policy.

Why did this happen? There were several important causes. First, politics had been democratized. Democratic politics had become a powerful tide sweeping across the Western world by this time, and Germany was no exception. Yet Germany's political system, unlike those of other Western countries, could only provide a few limited outlets for this pressure. Thus, popular enthusiasm for political participation and deliberative politics could only exist within an irregular framework. Second, the use of public opinion became an effective political tactic. It became a useful political tool for all kinds of political forces. As argued above, German society presented a classic case of cartelization in which various powerful interest groups were balanced against one another. It was only through the direct mobilization of public opinion to pressure the government that these groups could achieve their goals. These methods of deliberately influencing, organizing, and promoting public opinion and popular sentiments quickly became ordinary in domestic politics, thus magnifying the impact of public opinion. Third, German public opinion preferred hard-line stances. If it had just been a case of public opinion influencing policymaking, the problem probably would not have been that significant. The situation in late nineteenth and early twentieth-century Germany, however, was that the influence of public opinion pushed in the direction of a preference for expansion and support for expansionist and hard-line policies. Any retreat or sign of weakness in foreign policy became increasingly unacceptable. Public influence of this sort undoubtedly removed flexibility from policymaking, making Germany, as a rising power, increasingly unable to respond to its complex security environment. The first two of these factors have already been discussed elsewhere, so the following discussion will primarily focus on analyzing the preference within popular opinion for expansion and hard-lines.

Social Ideologies and Popular Opinion

The preference of German public opinion for expansionism and hard-line policies is tightly linked to prevailing social ideologies. In Chapter 3, this book analyzed the three major social ideologies of the Bismarckian era: nationalism, democracy (also called liberalism), and imperialism. By Wilhelm II's reign, democracy as an ideology had experienced little change, but nationalism and imperialism had developed substantially. Both had become deeply intertwined with notions of Social Darwinism and filled with an aggressive spirit. Nationalism and imperialism themselves became fused into a single ideological system that began to manifest extremist tendencies. The 1891 Pan-German League, an extreme nationalist group that advocated a Greater Germany comprising all people of German descent, provides an example. This group pointed to the 1871 unification as merely a temporary stop on the road to building this larger state, and advocated the use of war to resolve the "living space" problem of the German people. The 1911 book *Germany and the Next War*, by General Friedrich von Bernhardi, serves as a typical example of this marriage of extreme nationalism with extreme imperialism. This book argued that a healthy people needed to continually engage in territorial expansion in order to settle its excess population. Conquest was the only means for accomplishing this; it was a law of necessity. Germany had only one option: "we must fight it out, cost what it may."[30] Ernst Basserman, leader of the National Liberal Party, approvingly commented that the "twentieth century is dominated by the imperialist idea…the concept of international brotherhood and the idea of disarmament are increasingly forced in the background by harsh reality."[31]

In addition to these extremists, radical nationalist and imperialist calls emanated from intellectuals and university professors. A large number of famous scholars favoring "pan-Germanism" entered these ranks, allowing these extreme social ideologies to be cloaked in terms like "science" and "rationality." The effect on Germans from all walks of life was profound. This may look like an extremely strange phenomenon: intellectuals, a group that should help society become more rational, instead became the forerunners of mass irrationality. The irrationality of the intelligentsia allowed the irrationality of the masses to also be cloaked in the term "science" and allowed it to be "rationalized." In the end, this forced the few clear-sighted, rational people in functional government departments into retreat.

Even scholars as influential as Max Weber held pan-Germanist beliefs. Weber, along with pan-German historian Heinrich von Treitschke, served as important spokespeople for nationalism and imperialism. They proposed that German history had three different evolutionary stages: the eighteenth-century expansion of Brandenburg into Prussia, the nineteenth-century expansion of Prussia into the German Empire, and the (just beginning) twentieth-century expansion of the German Empire into a world power. In an 1895 lecture at the University of Freiburg, Weber told his audience, "We have to grasp that the unification of Germany was a youthful prank which the nation committed in its olden days and which would have been better dispensed with because of its cost, if it were the end and not the beginning of a German 'Weltmacht-politik.'"[32] Other famous intellectuals who advocated nationalism and imperialism included the liberal Friedrich Naumann and the moderate conservative historian Hans Delbrück. Essentially all of the Second Reich's major scholars were involved in nationalist and imperialist propaganda. The more than 270 so-called fleet professors who supported expanded naval construction (itself associated with imperialism) were essentially a "Who's Who?" of German intellectuals.

This propaganda deeply affected people's minds because it matched the predominant attitude of the times. It had taken less than forty years after unification for Germany to become the strongest, most technologically advanced power on the European continent. The gap remaining between Germany and Great Britain, the reigning hegemon, narrowed daily. Germans, including the lowest class of factory workers, strongly embraced the concept of "German" ethnic identity and felt pride in their country's rapid rise. Yet post-Bismarckian Germany had experienced real setbacks in international politics. The contrast between these two realities caused Germans to desperately prove their strength to the world and made them ever more willing to accept Social Darwinistic notions of "survival of the fittest." Thus, at least in Wilhelm II's Germany, imperialism as a social ideology that promoted external expansion was not what we might think that term would imply—a trend promoted by monopoly capitalists and groups with overseas interests. Instead, it was a social ideology tightly intermeshed with nationalism that included the government and interest groups, intellectuals and the general public, those with direct interests at stake and those without. Some historians term this "social imperialism."[33]

Once this societal environment is formed, it produces a strong selection effect: political programs that complement it succeed, while those that do not (or that oppose it) are repressed. When the final expression of imperialism and nationalism becomes "patriotism," this selection effect becomes even more pronounced. As a leader of the pan-German movement said, the desire "'to co-operate for the honor and greatness of the fatherland" should animate the entire political spectrum: "the Conservative and the Left Liberal, the National Liberal and the Centre-man." [34] Once patriotism had become a political trend that directly appealed to public opinion and demanded that all take a public stance, support for a hard-line in foreign policy and foreign expansion increased. Advocacy work by the Pan-German League and other extremist organizations only contributed to this trend. Any person or group who openly proposed either compromise with foreign countries (particularly with Great Britain) or the slowing of overseas expansion could be labeled as a "traitor" or as "soft." Any political force that did not wish to commit political suicide had to accommodate itself to this reality.

After the beginning of the twentieth century, the major political parties that had opposed the *Weltpolitik* and objected to the naval armaments race slowly began to revise their positions. When the Catholic Centre Party, for example, began to move closer to the government in 1907, the party newspaper, party leaders, and various bishops argued that "we Catholics are not second-class citizens, but first-class patriots." The left wing of the German liberals (which would later become the Progressive People's Party) had encountered the same issues. This party's stance on the issues was similar to that of the Social Democrats: they opposed the naval arms race and favored repairing relations with Great Britain. In an era of overflowing patriotic sentiment, however, the party assumed that it would be politically dangerous to be open about its true beliefs. As a result, the party newspaper and public speeches became suffused with a "patriotic" tint. The largest socialist party in the Western world, the German Social Democratic Party, came under increasing pressure as well, although it maintained its opposition to war and foreign expansion. The national consciousness of the working class, the party's very base, had grown in tandem with its class consciousness. The appeal of patriotism to the working class thus continued to expand. August Bebel, leader of the Social Democrats, was forced to explain on numerous occasions that the party was not unpatriotic and that it would support the nation in a crisis.[35] With the outbreak of World War I, the words of one working-class leader in the party demonstrated the pressure that so-called patriotism sweeping the nation had brought to bear on the German workers' movement:

> The conflict of two souls in one breast was probably easy for none of us. [It had lasted] until suddenly—I shall never forget the day and hour—the terrible tension was resolved; until one dared to be what one was; until—despite all principles and wooden theories—one could, for the first time in almost a quarter century, join with a full heart, a clean conscience and without a sense of treason in the sweeping, stormy song: *Deustschland, Deustschland über Alles.*[36]

The Post-Great Man Effect and Popular Opinion

Great men and powerful politicians often leave voids in their wake. These voids exist not just in the structures of political authority, but in thoughts and concepts as well. For a great power during its rise, the departure of a leader who led the country to strength and prosperity will lead not only to an increased admiration for that figure, but also to idealization. The policies implemented by that leader, particularly the hard-line elements of his foreign policy, will often be retained, while the accommodating and compromising aspects of the policy will be dropped. These policies become part of the people's spiritual support and the foundation for expressing dissatisfaction with the current government.

In Wilhelm II's Germany, the post-Great Man effect was fully evident in the national psychology. Bismarck had acquired many political enemies during his long time in office and thus was not met with much popular support at the moment Wilhelm II forced him into retirement. Conversely, the power struggle between the two men made the new kaiser appear strong and decisive. With the passage of time, however, the aged former chancellor, due to his immense contributions to German unification, became a hero of the German nation and a symbol of Germany's rise. The ineffective foreign and domestic policies of the new kaiser and his new chancellors soon provided a contrast with this image and served to enhance the deification of Bismarck. As one of Bismarck's biographers commented,

> At first, hundreds of thousands of Germans had regarded the dismissal of Bismarck as a somewhat harsh but salutary action, indicative of the emperor's genius and tact. Now it was plain to everyone that [Wilhelm II] had neither the one nor the other. Consequently, the last feelings of hostility toward Bismarck in the country were dispelled by an outburst of popular acclamation, such as had never before greeted, in Germany, any man who wore neither a crown nor a uniform.[37]

Adulation of Bismarck and lack of confidence in the kaiser and his government were brought together by the 1896 "Bismarck revelations." After Bismarck's departure, German diplomacy had experienced numerous setbacks: Russo-German estrangement, the Franco-Russian alliance, and the worsening of relations with Great Britain caused by the Kruger Telegram. Together, these had combined to isolate Germany within Europe. In September 1896, the new Russian czar, Nicholas II, visited Germany and met with the kaiser at Breslau. The kaiser and the German Foreign Ministry were excited about these developments and imagined that they could use the occasion to restore ties with Russia and break the Franco-Russian alliance. This would redeem their foreign policy. The czar, for his part, deliberatedly concealed his next destination from his German hosts. Thus, when he was warmly greeted in Paris the next month, the German government's illusions were shattered. Moreover, as French, German, and Russian newspapers pointed out, the czar's trip to Paris represented a significant change in European diplomacy. German newspapers in particular pointed out that this change should be seen as a victory for France and a defeat for Germany. Media criticism soon directed itself at the government. At this moment, the retired Bismarck began using the media to attack the government, revealing the origin of the whole slew of post-1890 foreign policy failures: the split with Russia.

The *Hamburg News*, perhaps under Bismarck's influence, was the first to print an editorial critical of the current situation. It claimed that Germany's international isolation and encirclement by two hostile powers was a "consequence of the fact…that during the first year of his administration Count Caprivi had given up the well cultivated relations with Russia and Austria-Hungary of the old course as being 'too complicated.'" On October 24, 1896, Bismarck himself announced in the *Hamburg News* that he had negotiated a Reinsurance Treaty with Russia that his successors had failed to renew—and thus fault for the worsening relationship between the two countries lay with Germany, not Russia. Before this statement, the existence of the Reinsurance Treaty (as well as its annulment) had been government secrets. Once this secret was disclosed, it created a controversy in Germany and a heated debate began in the print media. The majority of newspapers, including right-wing and moderate papers, criticized the government. Only those Social Democratic Party and other left-wing papers that saw czarist Russia as a reactionary force expressed support for the government.[38] This controversy had a powerful impact. By linking for the first time veneration of Bismarck with concerns about the government and the royal house, the monarchy's authority sustained a blow. In a letter to Prince Eulenburg, Holstein wrote, "People no longer take the sovereign seriously. This is a great peril. For when the hour of danger comes, when the question arises: 'Is the Emperor a man who can be depended upon?'—how will that question be answered, in Germany and outside it?"[39]

When Bismarck passed away in 1898, the post–Great Man effect intensified. By this point, it was no longer expressed solely in popular feelings and actions—the German government involved itself, too. The government hoped to change Bismarck's image through active publicity efforts. In particular, it hoped to redeem itself from the impressions left by the "Bismarck revelations" two years earlier. At the same time, authorities wanted to create momentum behind their *Weltpolitik*. In the words of one historian:

> Official initiatives naturally succeeded best where they exploited and manipulated spontaneous and undefined grassroots emotion, or integrated themes from unofficial mass politics.… The German government, countless tons of marble and masonry to the contrary, failed to establish the Emperor [Wilhelm] I as father of the nation, but cashed in on the unofficial nationalist enthusiasm which erected

> "Bismarck columns" by the hundred after the death of the great statesman.[40]

These activities did little to repair the government's image, but they did much to simplify Bismarck's image. All of Bismarck's immense efforts during the period of unification were reduced to his determination during three dynastic wars and his post-unification foreign policy was reduced to the pursuit of a hard-line policy. His numerous compromises, his patience, and his detailed, flexible planning were all completely forgotten.

Even the publication of Bismarck's political last will and testament, his *Thoughts and Reminiscences*, did not change this. In these memoirs, Bismarck spared no effort in reminding Germans to pay attention to the hidden dangers created by German power and in emphasizing the need for action. Yet the German people and government did not seem to notice. During his life, Bismarck made countless public speeches and many famous utterances, yet after he was gone it seems that only three were frequently repeated by the German people and organizations such as the Pan-German League: "We shall have to serve as the anvil if we do nothing to become the hammer,"[41] "Not by speeches and votes of the majority, are the great questions of the time decided—that was the error of 1848 and 1849—but by iron and blood,"[42] and "We Germans fear God, but nothing else in the world."[43] The last of these three quotes illustrates the problem clearly, as many Germans only knew that particular sentence but did not know the sentence that Bismarck had uttered after it: "and it is the fear of God, which lets us love and foster peace." Bismarck's political legacy became ever more divorced from his original intent, even as the German people expressed their admiration and nostalgia for him. His name became synonymous with hard-line policies and the willingness to use force. He became an important source for the preference for the hard-line in German public opinion and a weapon for the political parties, the interest groups, and the general public to attack the government.

Public Opinion and the Government

During the era of Wilhelm II, public opinion exerted a significant influence on the government. In general, German policymakers were extremely sensitive to public opinion. Compared with the relatively mature political structures of other Western capitalist countries such as Great Britain and France, the German political system was a mixed one that lacked effected pathways or procedures for making use of popular political power or responding to the political demands of the masses. As the scope of popular participation in government increased (by 1910, eleven million people casts votes in the election), Germany's weakness in this area became increasingly evident.[44] As a result, the ability of the German government to handle the pressure of public opinion was significantly less than was the case in older capitalist countries such as Britain and France. Even more important, during the age of Wilhelm II, domestic conflicts continued to accumulate, yet the prestige of the kaiser and the government remained low; collectively, these trends increased popular criticisms of government policy and image and reduced the ability of the government to handle public opinion.

This process, of course, was not unidirectional. In fact, the influence of so-called public opinion on the government developed slowly and was the product of mutual interactions between the government and public opinion. In the years around 1895, German public opinion had yet to settle into a concrete form, and its impact on government policy was naturally still indistinct. The Kruger Telegram provides a good example of this. At first, German newspapers praised it, and the German Colonial Society and the Pan-German League passed motions in support of it. Once its drawbacks became evident, however, public opinion shifted and the image of the government dropped sharply among the people.[45]

This situation began to change after 1897. This is the year that Germany began a high-profile implementation of a so-called world policy (*Weltpolitik)* that emphasized overseas colonial expansion and the construction of a High Seas Fleet. A major goal of this policy was to use diplomatic achievements to revive the images of the monarchy and the government, thus consolidating the power of the Hohenzollern ruling house by "rallying the 'loyal' elements around the Kaiser."[46] The German government was, in fact, the leading partner in its interactions with public opinion during the early phases of the *Weltpolitik*. It shifted popular attention from domestic issues to foreign policy, highlighted the government's image of strength and power, and held forth on the fruits of the *Weltpolitik* in order to please the masses and earn popular support.

Newspapers published congratulatory telegrams and celebratory propaganda for each new colonial acquisition (including Jiaozhou Bay in China, Samoa, and the Caroline Islands). All foreign policy victories, real or imaginary (such as the resignation of French Foreign Minister Delcassé), were reported in great detail. The purpose of this was to guide public attention to "the world-shaking and decisive problems of foreign policy."[47] To better achieve this goal, the German government exerted powerful influence over the media, particularly during Bernhard von Bülow's tenure as chancellor. Every day that he was in Berlin, Bülow met with the director of the foreign ministry's news office (while away from Berlin, he would send brief written instructions), suggesting which newspapers should make what kinds of reports, or demanding that Prussian administrative officials or the court system interject themselves into a particular newspaper's business, demanding punishment of reporters whose work had "negative diplomatic repercussions." As a result of Bülow's efforts, some newspapers (such as the *Kölnische Zeitung*) wrote foreign policy articles and editorials entirely in accord with government orders, precisely reflecting the minute changes in Bülow's foreign policy.[48]

Beyond simply publicizing its diplomatic achievements, the German government also intentionally made use of the rising tide of nationalism. As Bülow himself clearly pointed out, "the way to win popular support for the monarchy was to revive the 'national idea.'"[49] This was particularly manifested in the use of national anti-British sentiment to build support for construction of the High Seas Fleet. After Tirpitz took control of the Imperial Naval Office in 1897, he immediately began propaganda efforts designed to strengthen popular awareness of oceanic and naval issues. The most truly effective method was to make the public feel that Germany faced humiliation and bullying at the hands of Great Britain, the world's dominant naval power, and then use this to excite popular enthusiasm for naval construction. The German government—Tirpitz and Bülow in particular—frequently and skillfully used this tactic. During the Boer War, for example, Great Britain searched and seized a German ocean liner heading toward Southwest Africa based on suspicion alone. Germany's protests proved ineffective, and it was forced to threaten a reconsideration of its neutrality until finally the British government, more than two weeks after the incident began, releasing the impounded ship and admitted that no contraband had been found onboard.[50] Great Britain's blatant disregard for international law provided an impetus for German anti-British sentiment, which is a natural and normal response when a people have been treated unfairly. The German government, hoping to use this opportunity to gain greater support for naval construction, sought to utilize these nationalistic feelings. Chancellor Bülow, for instance, immediately rushed to the press office after learning of the incident and issued an order to use the occasion to promote naval construction, specifically noting that "my latest speech for the fleet…can also be alluded to."[51]

The German government's manipulation of public opinion undoubtedly contributed to its preferences for expansion and for hard-line policies. Given Germany's existing social structures, however, this was playing with fire. As events proved, once this kind of expansionistic and hard-line public opinion developed, the government's ability to control events quickly dissipated. In this early period, the government was still able to use its hard-line attitude and the results of expansion in order to satisfy public opinion, but soon popular demands eclipse what the government can provide. Even more important, compromise and setbacks are normal in international relations. The German government's hard-line attitude could not continue to bring the fruits of expansion forever. Public opinion would not be able to accept this; displeasure with, and criticism of, the government would rise dramatically. After the 1908 *Daily Telegraph* incident, popular confidence in the throne and the government plummeted. Pressure from public opinion on foreign policy increased and the government was criticized for being weak. During the Second Morocco Crisis in 1911, popular pressure on the government reached unprecedented heights. The German retreat at the end of the crisis brought heated complaints of governmental and royal softness from not only extremist organizations such as the Pan-German League or the German Colonial Society, but also from organizations and newspapers that had traditionally supported the royal house. *Die Post*, the same newspaper that ran the "War in Sight?" editorial in 1875, complained, "Oh! Would that we had been spared this moment of unspeakable shame, of deep ignominy, far deeper than that of Olmutz! What has happened to the Hohenzollerns?"[52] Ernst Bassermann of the National Liberal Party accused the government of fearing and avoiding war, and claimed that the German people were ready to fight but that the cowardice of the government and the kaiser made the people lose heart.[53] Some began calling the kaiser "Wilhelm the Peaceful." Historical documents reveal that this strong popular pressure had an impact on Germany policy-makers. They would not dare again engage in activities that could be criticized as soft and were determined to maintain a hard-line in the next crisis, even if that meant running the risk of war. Thus the psychological stage was set for outbreak of war in 1914.

A turbulent and overflowing public opinion characterized German society in the age of Wilhelm II. The increasingly powerful pressure created by public opinion squeezed the government's room for maneuver in foreign policy into a narrow space. Hard-line policies became the only option. The German system's multiple semi-autonomous policymaking entities and cartelized social organizations made the situation even worse. Anything that resembled a grand strategy became impossible. To a great extent, Germany's rise had now become dependent on luck.

6

From Weltpolitik *to Encirclement*

"We are supposed to pursue a World Policy. If one only knew what that is supposed to be."
Alfred von Waldersee

AFTER THE PRECEDING discussion of domestic society, we can again return to the topic of German grand strategy itself. Two years after the Kruger Telegram, Germany again engaged in a major strategic reorientation and began to implement its so-called world policy (*Weltpolitik*). This reorientation was not a deeply considered, sophisticated strategic shift. Instead, to a great extent, it was a political risk taken against the backdrop of a security situation and domestic political environment that could not be changed. The implementation of this policy took German grand strategy one step closer to disintegration and degraded Germany's foreign policy environment.

Origins of the *Weltpolitik*

Generally, 1897 is seen as the starting point of the *Weltpolitik*. It should be pointed out, however, that this policy change had its origins in 1894. During Leo von Caprivi's chancellorship, Germany had embarked on a new course in foreign policy that focused on continental Europe. This policy aimed to solidify Germany's leading role on the continent by strengthening the army and consolidating trade relationships with other European powers. During the period from 1891 to 1894, Germany signed twelve-year mutual-tariff limitation agreements with Austria-Hungary, Italy, Bulgaria, Romania, Serbia, Sweden, and Russia.[1] By the final years of Caprivi's tenure, however, Germany's energies had already slowly begun to shift in the direction of overseas expansion. Tensions emerged with Great Britain over Samoa, the Congo, Morocco, and other places. Germany's 1895 participation in the Triple Intervention, which forced Japan to retrocede the Liaodong peninsula to China, and the 1896 Kruger Telegram represented this shift.

Secretary of State for Foreign Affairs Bernhard von Bülow openly claimed during an 1897 Reichstag debate that Germany needed to seize its "place in the sun." This statement was directly pointed at Great Britain, the reigning hegemon and ruler of the world's largest colonial empire. In November of the same year, Germany, using the death of two missionaries as a pretext, occupied the Jiaozhou Bay in Shandong, China. This constituted an unusually public announcement of the new *Weltpolitik*. Germany's traditional position as a continental nation was turned on its head, and distant overseas colonies suddenly became a core national interest closely bound up with Germany's status as a great power. The immediate threat of the Franco-Russian alliance seemed at the same time to evaporate into almost nothing. Beginning in 1897, Germany busied itself with abandoning the traditional policies that had gained it an advantaged position in Europe and diverted its energies outside of the continent.

The Motives behind the Weltpolitik

Typically, analysis of Germany's transition from a continental strategy to a world strategy begins with considerations of economic factors. During Germany's rapid economic growth in the 1890s, its overseas interests expanded. Thus, it was a natural choice for Germany to attempt some sort of policy focused on its overseas interests. Germany's *Weltpolitik*, however, was not only a foreign policy that sought overseas interests. A close examination of the *Weltpolitik* reveals that the only clear idea at its core was the Tirpitz Plan for the construction of a High Seas Fleet. The foreign policies associated with the *Weltpolitik* were complicated and vacillating for both European issues and colonial issues, without an overarching or unifying theme. To a certain extent, the *Weltpolitik* was political posturing that lacked substantive content or purpose. Field Marshal Alfred von Waldersee, who succeeded the elder Moltke as chief of the Prussian General Staff, complained that, "We are supposed to pursue a World Policy. If one only knew what that is supposed to be."[2]

Vladimir Lenin's later conception of overseas colonial expansion notwithstanding, German actions between 1897 and 1914 are better understood as a political performance: when a crisis arose overseas out of tensions with Great Britain or France, it became an issue for the whole society at home and became an important release for popular political sentiments. Yet in terms of its actual contents, it is hard to argue that German policymakers cared about it deeply. Many times, German policy on colonial issues vacillated or even reversed itself. In the dispute with Great Britain over Samoa, for example, the German government first instructed its ambassador in London, Paul von Hatzfeldt, that the acquisition of the islands was of utmost importance and that it must be accomplished. Two months later, however, Hatzfeldt learned that the issue had already "been completely forgotten in Berlin."[3] Moreover, there were few concrete achievements to point to. A popular topic in Germany at the time was that Germany was a fast-growing giant that acutely needed "indispensable" colonies acquired through a *Weltpolitik* in order to absorb its excess products, capital, and people.[4] In fact, however, the colonies held by Germany on the eve of World War I had largely been acquired by Bismarck in the 1880s. The widely trumpeted *Weltpolitik* had not led to the acquisition of many new colonies. Even more important, the notion of the indispensability of colonies seems to be profoundly mistaken—a kind of myth—from today's perspective. In reality, Germany's colonies had little productive value. In 1913, only 7.6 percent of all German exports ended up in all of Asia and Africa (including German colonies). Investments in the colonies were even smaller, given German industry's substantial need for investments at home.[5] In terms of absorbing excess population, as Eric Hobsbawm points out, "the idea that emigration to colonies would provide a safety-valve for overpopulated countries was little more than a demagogic fantasy. (In fact, never was it easier to find somewhere to emigrate to than between 1880 and 1914, and only a tiny minority of emigrants went to anyone's colonies—or needed to.)"[6] In 1910, 30,000 Germans resided in Africa and only 4,000 in Asia, totaling 0.8 percent of all Germans overseas.[7]

Thus, the primary motive for the *Weltpolitik* must be sought elsewhere. Existing documentation suggests that domestic politics played the leading role. As economic and industrial development proceeded, the original bipolar conflict (tensions between the two ruling classes—industrial capitalists and Junker landlords—as well as the tensions between those ruling classes and the working class) deepened. To face this challenge, German policymakers felt the need to unite the ruling classes in order to stabilize political authority. The best route for this would be a forceful foreign policy that could earn the support of domestic society. This could be used to tame and conquer leftist forces, as represented by the Social Democratic Party. Johannes von Miquel, appointed assistant minister president of Prussia in 1897 and tasked with managing domestic politics, claimed that he wanted to focus domestic public opinion on colonial issues and to pull foreign policy into Reichstag debates. Thus foreign policy victories could be used to heal divisions in domestic society, and the socialist movement could be countered.[8] Chancellor and State Secretary for Foreign Affairs Bülow also believed that promotion of a forceful foreign policy could act as a cohesive force for domestic society: "I am putting the main emphasis on foreign policy…only a successful foreign policy can help to reconcile, pacify, rally, unite."[9] These men were important political leaders when the *Weltpolitik* was introduced. Their opinions, therefore, are relatively representative.

The *Weltpolitik* did also contain a level of diplomatic calculation. In the seven years following Bismarck's forced departure from office, German foreign policy experienced a number of serious setbacks. Although Germany's policymakers feigned composure (the documents they composed betrayed little discussion of the situation's seriousness), the series of events from the failure of the new course to facilitate a reconciliation with Great Britain, the establishment of the Franco-Russian alliance, and the damage inflicted by the Kruger Telegram on Anglo-German relations was clear for all to see. German foreign policy in Europe had already fallen on hard times, making it difficult to achieve anything in a short period of time. At the same time, Germany hoped to claim a global status befitting its power. Thus, Germany simply decided not to concentrate on European affairs but instead to push its way on to the world stage. In the words of one historian, "the anxiety which was felt about the direction of German foreign policy in the world was accompanied by a growing fear about the problems created by urbanization and industrialization."[10]

In conclusion, the logic that produced the *Weltpolitik* was an extremely strange one: domestic political needs required it; it would be difficult to forge foreign policy achievements inside Europe, so a *Weltpolitik* that could go beyond Europe was necessary. By this time, German foreign policy was no longer a tool for achieving any long-term national objective or core national interest. Instead, it was something to be used in pursuit of short-term interests and to be subordinate to sentiment. It was nothing more than a form of political risk-taking. The unemotional calculations of national objectives and careful strategic planning of the Bismarckian era had been abandoned, as had (even more important) the concept that Europe and the immediate security environment were Germany's top strategic priorities. Germany's new leaders only had eyes for their own power and their own short-term interests; they could not discern dangers in the distance. For a rapidly rising great power, such dangers might prove to be existential issues.

Implementing the Weltpolitik

The content of the *Weltpolitik* was even stranger than the motives that led to the policy. As argued above, other than the acquisition of colonies, the only long-term consideration to receive concrete instantiation in the policy was the construction of a High Seas Fleet. After 1897, German naval construction gradually increased to unprecedented levels. Naval expansion was no longer a part of national grand strategy or a means to achieve specific objectives; it had become a strategic goal in and of itself. German foreign policy, essentially, had been made to serve the needs of German naval expansion. Bülow, the secretary of state and chancellor, admitted that his primary task was to pave a path for the construction of a large fleet without sparking a confrontation with Great Britain: "the creation of a German fleet without a collision with England, who we were in no way a match for."[11] This backward prioritization not only greatly reduced the strategic space available to German foreign policy, but it also revealed serious problems in Germany's ability to coordinate its goals and its means. Arguably, Germany no longer had anything that could truly be called a grand strategy once the *Weltpolitik* began. From another perspective, this position gave German foreign policy an impossible mission: on the one hand, it must have an anti-British inflection, in order to provide reason to construct a fleet; on the other hand, it cannot go so far in that direction that it incites British "preemptive actions" against a still-weak German fleet. The fundamentals of German foreign policy thus contradicted one another, making setbacks and failures inevitable.

The personalities of individual policymakers associated with the *Weltpolitik* also played a role in destabilizing German grand strategy, causing diplomatic and military predicaments that were difficult to escape. Caprivi's successor as chancellor in 1894, Hohenlohe, had once been German ambassador to France and had been an administrator in Alsace-Lorraine. He was 75 years old when he assumed office (several years older than Bismarck himself had been) and had a cautious personality. As one contemporary pointedly put it, Hohenlohe's motto might as well as be that, although he was weak, at least he wasn't a bully. Wilhelm II had appointed him with the hope that he would command respect yet still be easy to control, and secretly doubled his salary.[12] Yet Hohenlohe proved able to resist some of Wilhelm II's more extreme ideas. Two aspects of his personality helped with this: stubbornness and a talent for evasion. A colleague from his time in Paris recalled, "It is quite impossible to make him do anything of which he disapproves. He flutters away like a little bird when you try to catch him."[13] Thus, although he may not have been entirely suitable for the chancellorship, Hohenlohe was at least able to block some of Wilhelm II's riskier plans.

His successor, Bülow, was very different. His record indicated ample foreign policy experience: he became a diplomat in 1873; in 1878 he was secretary at the Berlin Conference where he assisted Bismarck; from 1888 to 1893 he was an envoy to Bucharest, Romania; from 1893 to 1897 ambassador to Rome, after which he replaced Adolf von Marschall as secretary of state for foreign affairs. In 1900 he assumed office as chancellor. Bülow had more foreign policy experience than all of the others who had served as chancellor, Bismarck excepted. This advantage, however, was offset by his sycophantic political personality. He was able, but also unctuous; he blindly catered to and accommodated Wilhelm II's notions in order to stay in his good graces. As early as 1895, the kaiser had considered replacing Hohenlohe, complaining that he "is too old, and he can no longer handle both foreign affairs and the Ministry of State, and the present Vice-Chancellor [Bötticher] is a cowardly washrag. Bülow shall become my Bismarck, and as he and my grandfather pounded Germany together externally, so we two will clean up the filth of parliamentary and party machinery internally."[14] After Bülow entered the highest circles of policymakers, Wilhelm II's flaws and fleeting but strong notions not only were no longer controlled or opposed, but were welcomed, encouraged, and thoroughly implemented by Bülow. The kaiser thus came to have an even higher view of himself. Wilhelm II's personal friend Albert Ballin, director of the Hamburg-America Line, regretfully commented, "Bülow is a misfortune for us and is destroying the [Kaiser] completely."[15] For the whole country as well, Bülow's methods would prove even more disastrous.

Another important person was Alfred von Tirpitz. Unlike many other military and political leaders, Tirpitz was not born into the nobility. He father was a lawyer and his mother the daughter of a doctor; both belonged to Germany's middle class. Tirpitz joined the navy in 1865 at the age of 16. After graduating from the naval academy, he struggled up the ladder step by step, quickly revealing outstanding talent based on his abilities and vigorous spirit. In 1892, he was appointed chief of the Navy General Staff. By this time, his views on the development of the German Navy had already been formed. He believed that Germany should build a large fleet, centered on battleships, in order to achieve command of the seas. At this time he also developed another talent—the ability to promote his ideas to others. Soon after he took office, he quickly moved his colleagues from their traditional support for "cruisers above all else" to "battleships above all else." This was a complete remaking of the navy. Admiral Senden, a member of the Navy Cabinet, commented, "Tirpitz is a very energetic character…he has too big a head of steam not to be a leader. He is ambitious, not choosy about his means, of a sanguine disposition…he has been very spoiled in his naval career and with the exception of the Chief of Admiralty [Stosch] never had a superior who could match him.... I believe that Tirpitz is the right man to push the Navy onwards in these difficult days."[16] In fact, Tirpitz was the heart and soul of the construction of the German Empire's High Seas Fleet. After taking command as secretary of the Imperial Navy Office, he played pivotal role in whipping up popular enthusiasm for the navy and in planning a massive expansion of the fleet.

The Middle Road, 1897–1904

Naval construction was the main thread of German foreign policy during the era of the *Weltpolitik*. Foreign policy during this period can be divided into two segments: before 1904, a self-confident Germany followed a middle road; after the Anglo-French Entente in 1904, however, Germany became more impatient and, under pressure at home and abroad, veered toward highly risky policies.

During the first period, German foreign policy was based on the flawed assessment that insoluble conflicts existed between Great Britain and the Franco-Russian alliance. Thus Germany could follow a "middle road" that would maintain distance from both sides but could also allow Germany to draw close to one side or the other, if the right price was offered. In the words of one German diplomat, "The task of the German government in the future is to maintain good relations with both Great Britain and Russia and, with the possession of a powerful navy, to keep cool and calm while awaiting the development of events."[17]

Maintaining Distance from the Franco-Russian Alliance

Given the international situation at the time, the preceding assessment was not entirely unreasonable. After 1897, Germany was not at the center of international conflict. Conversely, it was Great Britain (which would prove to be the country most sensitive to the *Weltpolitik*) and the Franco-Russian alliance (which had been directed at Germany) that were locked in heated conflict over territories in Africa and East Asia. These tensions escalated, and both powers sought German help. Suddenly, Germany seemed to be in an advantageous position. Germany's problems, however, arose from the shortsightedness of its policymakers: they failed to recognize that Germany's own tensions with all of these countries would be even more difficult to reconcile. Rising great powers often find themselves at the center of conflict; it is rare for such nations to be able to remain aloof. The pendulum of international conflict will inevitably swing back. Germany's problems secondarily came from the inability of German policymakers to maintain a Bismarck-like control over the various tensions. They could not conceptualize how to create an advantage for themselves between two opposing forces, as Bismarck had been able to do between

Austria-Hungary and Russia. Thus, Germany's middle road policy between 1897 and 1904 was little more than policy drift. Its refusal to draw closer to either combination (as neither side had yet offered the right price) ended up bringing the two sides themselves together, foreshadowing Germany's later isolation.

Maintaining distance from the Franco-Russian alliance was a comparatively simple process for Germany. After the Kruger Telegram incident, Germany had schemed to build a Continental League with those two powers to bring pressure on Great Britain, but nothing came of it. A change began in Franco-German relations in 1898. Its origins lay in the continuing French desire to wrest control of the Upper Nile from Great Britain and thus resolve the Egyptian Question in France's favor. Great Britain's reconquest of Sudan, however, had dashed these hopes. In September 1898, a French exploration team lead by Jean-Baptiste Marchand made an extraordinary trek from West Africa to the upper reaches of the Nile Valley and occupied the town of Fashoda. The French government strongly supported this action. By this time, the British Army had already completed its reconquest and the French exploration team in Fashoda was immediately placed under surveillance by a superior British force. A stand-off ensued and the Fashoda Crisis began.

Given the large gap between the two sides' forces, along with Russian unwillingness to damage relations with Great Britain over Egypt, the isolated French had no choice but to retreat. In November 1898, Marchand's exploration team withdrew from Fashoda. An Anglo-French agreement reached in March 1899 excluded the French from the Nile Valley. For the French, this crisis not only ended any possibility of ejecting Britain from Egypt, it also became a significant political crisis that substantially influenced French popular sentiment. France, as a result, naturally desired better relations with Germany. In 1900, the German ambassador in Paris reported that passionately anti-British sentiment existed in France, while anti-German revanchism had abated. Thus the possibility for improved ties existed. Yet Germany did not attach much significance to this. On June 13, 1901, Holstein and Bülow instructed the new ambassador to Paris, Prince Radolin, "If the new French government decides that rapprochement with Germany will not offend the instinct of the masses there will easily be found areas in which cooperation promises advantages to both sides. Nevertheless, any premature attempts of this type could result in mutual suspicion and shyness." They suggested cooperation in the cultural and social realms. The French government reacted positively and soon produced concrete proposals for cooperation. Germany, however, quickly backed away, claiming that true cooperation with France would be difficult until "both parties announced their intention to guarantee each other's possession." This was essentially a demand for France to publicly renounce claims to Alsace and Lorraine, which it could never consent to.[18]

Germany would similarly reject Russia. After the outbreak of the Boer War in 1899, it appeared that Germany, France, and Russia had found a common objective: forcing Great Britain to end the war. In January 1900, Germany proposed to Russia that the two countries exert pressure on Great Britain. Furthermore, Germany asked Russia to solicit France's opinion. This proposal, however, was only a tool to threaten Great Britain. After France expressed willingness to participate in this mediation, Russian Foreign Minister Mikhail Muravyov made a formal proposal to Germany that the three countries work together to exert "friendly pressure" on Great Britain to end the Boer War. Germany, however, changed its tune. Chancellor Bülow instead suggested that the three countries first mutually guarantee each other's European territories. This, too, was a demand for a renunciation of French claims to the lost provinces. It brought negotiations to an immediate end.[19] When Wilhelm II heard of Muravyov's proposal, he directly said, "If Russia desired to mediate, then let Muravyov go do it on his own, or with France."[20]

Negotiations for an Anglo-German Alliance and German Drift

A complicated relationship developed between Germany and Great Britain. One would expect that the country most impacted by Germany's 1897 adoption of the *Weltpolitik* would be Great Britain, with its extensive overseas interests and immense naval strength—and that relations between the two countries would soon sour. The logic of history, however, does not always work so directly. During the first few years of the *Weltpolitik*, British diplomacy was at a crossroads. Some form of alliance with Germany was one potential policy choice open to the British. Between 1898 and 1902, the deterioration of relations caused by the Kruger Telegram was largely reversed. The two countries sporadically toyed with the notion of an alliance.

Great Britain's interest in an alliance sprang from its lack of other choices. After 1895, British defense spending increased dramatically in the face of threats of war with France, Russia, and Germany. Its fiscal situation had grown desperate. More important, despite this fiscal crunch, defense spending still did not satisfy all defense needs. This was manifested most clearly in the Royal Navy, the mainstay of British power. In the 1895–1896 fiscal year, Great Britain constructed 12 battleships and 37 cruisers, while France and Russia together built 19 battleships and 20 cruisers. In 1901, Britain possessed 45 battleships, compared to 43 for the combined Franco-Russian fleet, 14 for

Germany, 7 for the United States, and 5 for Japan. If Britain maintained its current rate of growth, by 1906 both the Royal Navy and the Franco-Russian combined fleet would have the same number of battleships, 53.[21] Great Britain would then be unable to resist a naval challenge from those two countries. Yet fiscal constraints meant that Great Britain could not afford to spend more. An end to isolation was the only viable policy choice. Germany, a powerful country in its own right, was a natural choice for a partner. Once the British Admiralty's plan for naval expansion was rejected by the cabinet, consideration of an alignment with Germany became possible. First Sea Lord Selborne explained that: "I can see only one possible alternative and that is a formal alliance with Germany. I do not pretend to have examined this possibility in all its bearings—it may not be feasible or the price we should have to pay might be too high; all I can say now is that it seems to me the only alternative to an ever-increasing Navy and ever-increasing Navy estimates."[22]

Even more significantly, the German occupation of Jiaozhou Bay in 1897 had increased the likelihood that China would be partitioned by the great powers. Great Britain's position in China faced challenges from the other powers, particularly Russia. Great Britain's original policy had been to maintain China's nominal territorial integrity, so that China could serve as a single open market. Britain, relying on its industrial and commercial strengths, would claim an advantaged position. Once Germany seized Jiaozhou Bay, however, other powers began clamoring for Chinese territory as compensation (such as the Russian occupation of Port Arthur) and China appeared to be on the verge of dismemberment. If this were to happen, Russia's geographic position would allow it an enormous advantage over Great Britain. To counter this, Great Britain took two steps. First, it sought a direct agreement with Russia. Great Britain's calculation was that it could accede to Russian demands for compensation in exchange for Russian recognition of existing treaty arrangements and the opening of the Russian sphere of influence to British commerce. Russia saw through these designs, however; the czar later wrote to Wilhelm II that these British promises had merely "showed us clearly that England needed our friendship at that time, to be able to check our development, in a masked way, in the Far East."[23] Russia had no inclination to negotiate these issues with Great Britain and, on March 3, 1898, presented the Qing government with a proposal to lease Port Arthur. Second, Britain ended its isolation and sought to work with other countries to resist Russian expansion in China. The prime advocate of this policy within the British government was the powerful Liberal Party politician and colonial minister, Joseph Chamberlain. In 1898, he pointed out that "if the policy of isolation, which has hitherto been the policy of this country, is to be maintained in the future, then the fate of the Chinese Empire may be, probably will be, hereafter divided without reference to our wishes and in defiance of our interests."[24] Initially, Great Britain sought the United States and Japan, rather than Germany, as partners. The United States, however, was unwilling to become involved, as it was just then gathering its forces for a war with Spain and it was still unwilling to surrender its freedom of maneuver by forming alliances that could draw it in to European conflicts. Japan, too, proved unresponsive. Its considerations primarily focused on the fear that, once allied with Great Britain against Russia, it would feel the brunt of Russian pressure—and Japan was not yet ready for that. Germany thus became Great Britain's only viable alternative.

Beginning in the fall of 1897, Great Britain began systematic attempts to draw Germany closer. First, Queen Victoria exerted influence on the print media to dampen its anti-German tone. Next, the British government recognized the occupation of Jiaozhou Bay. Once the relationship improved, Conservative Party leader and Chancellor of the Exchequer Arthur Balfour held talks on March 25 with the German ambassador, Hatzfeldt, in which he hinted that an alliance might be feasible. Four days later, Chamberlain himself sought out Hatzfeldt and directly proposed the notion of an alliance. On May 1, Chamberlain held further discussions with Hatzfeldt, suggesting that Germany act as the protector of Shandong and the surrounding region. This was, in practice, a proposal for Russia, Great Britain, and Germany to divide China into three spheres of influence—and that the German sphere should act as a buffer zone between the Russian and British spheres.[25] Chamberlain also proposed British concessions in Africa in exchange for German concessions in Samoa, to mitigate against colonial tensions between the two countries. The German response, however, was negative. From the perspective of the German Foreign Ministry, British hostility toward Germany ran too deep for an alliance to be possible in the near term, as no such proposal could pass the House of Commons. If a treaty were drafted and then rejected, then Germany would be left, embarrassingly, to face Russian and French hostility directly.[26] As for Chamberlain's notions of resolving colonial disputes between the two countries, Tirpitz understood these colonial struggles, by contrast, as beneficial to building domestic support for German naval construction, and thus forcefully advocated their rejection. This would be the policy taken by the German government. This saddened Hatzfeldt, who wrote in a telegram to Holstein that "if our foreign policy depends on the views of Herr Tirpitz, we will not go far in the world."[27]

Results of the Second Anglo-German Alliance Negotiations—the Yangzi Convention

Even though the first attempt to ally with Germany bore no results, the pro-German groups within the British government, represented by Chamberlain, did not abandon the idea. Chamberlain himself declared in 1899 that "the natural alliance is between us and the great German Empire."[28] After the outbreak of war between Great Britain and the Boer Republics, British military strength was diverted to South Africa, and the need to find an exit from the country's "splendid isolation" became increasingly acute. As one high-ranking official in the Indian colonial government, George Hamilton, explained in 1901,

> I am gradually coming round to the opinion that we must alter our foreign policy, and throw our lot in, for good or bad, with some other Power.... As we now stand, we are an object of envy and of greed to all the other Powers. Our interests are so vast and ramified that we touch, in some shape or other, the interests of almost every great country in every continent. Our interests being so extended makes it almost impossible for us to concentrate sufficiently, in any one direction, the pressure and power of the Empire so as to deter foreign nations from trying to encroach upon our interests in that particular quarter.[29]

The 1900 Boxer Rebellion, and the frenzy to partition China that it sparked among the great powers, caused Britain to again face the prospect of powerful Russian threats to its interests in China. These considerations impelled the British to again seek an arrangement with Germany. In a September 1900 memorandum, Chamberlain advocated cooperation with Germany in China:

> Both in China and elsewhere it is our interest that Germany should throw herself across the path of Russia. An alliance between Germany and Russia, entailing as it would the cooperation of France, is the one thing we have to dread, and the clash of German and Russian interests whether in China or Asia Minor would be a guarantee of our safety. I think then our policy clearly is to encourage good relations between ourselves and Germany, as well as between ourselves and Japan and the United States, and we should endeavor to make use of the present opportunity to emphasize the breach between Russia and Germany and Russia and Japan. We should then, without urging it, let it be

> known that we shall put no obstacle in the way of German expansion in [Shandong], nor in the way of Japan's ambitions in Korea. But, in return, we should obtain written assurances recognizing our claim to predominant interest and influence in the [Yangzi] Valley.[30]

Some within the British government, however, opposed an alliance with Germany, Prime Minister Salisbury among them. From his perspective, Great Britain did not need to fear that France and Russia would work together against British interests in China. These two alliance partners had little in the way of shared interests outside of Europe. Moreover, he had a fairly accurate assessment of Germany's security predicament and did not think a German alliance against Russia to be practical. In a letter to the British Viceroy George Curzon in India, he wrote, "As to Germany, I have less confidence in her than you. She is in mortal terror on account of that long undefended frontier of hers on the Russian side. She will therefore never stand by us against Russia; but is always rather inclined to curry favor with Russia by throwing us over. I have no wish to quarrel with her; but my faith in her is infinitesimal."[31] This opinion did not command a majority, however, and negotiations for an alliance continued apace.

Germany's negotiating posture, too, became somewhat more positive around this time. Germany had hoped to use the opportunities presented by the Boxer Rebellion to demonstrate its status as a global power. The kaiser, through the intervention of the czar, had already secured command of the allied armies in China for the long-retired former Chief of Staff Alfred von Waldersee. These armies, however, had already occupied Beijing before Waldersee arrived in China. Russia had even already proposed the army's disbandment. The kaiser felt humiliated by this and began to harbor doubts about Russian intentions. Thus, he began to seek cooperation from Great Britain. On August 22, 1900, Wilhelm II, during a meeting with the Prince of Wales, suggested that, if the British government would continue its "open door" policies in China, then Germany would offer its support for Great Britain.[32] Negotiations progressed and, on October 16, the Anglo-German Yangzi Agreement was signed. This agreement, however, was not the anti-Russian alliance that Britain had sought. Instead, it was vague and failed to mention the two Chinese regions (Manchuria and Zhili province) in which Britain hoped for German support. Thus, Salisbury sarcastically remarked, this agreement was "unnecessary but innocuous."[33]

After the conclusion of the Anglo-German Yangzi Agreement, Russian expansion in China intensified. On November 8, 1900, the Russian Army commander forced Zeng-qi, the Qing general in Mukden (now called Shenyang), to sign a secret treaty. Under this agreement, Qing troops in Fengtian would disarm, withdraw, and allow Russian occupation of Mukden and other points. Russia would set up an "independent administration" in land earmarked for railway construction, while Qing military deployments in the area would only be "determined by agreement with the Russian government" at some point in the future.[34] In practical terms, this treaty implied complete legalization of Russian occupation of Qing territory. On January 3, 1901, the *London Times* printed the text of this treaty, causing a furious reaction. The Japanese, who had their own ambitions in Manchuria, claimed that Japan and Britain together could have brought pressure on Russia. Britain, however, had opted to work with Germany, which was unwilling to take any measures except for an agreement to warn the Qing government not to accept this agreement. By March 1901, the Japanese government had already decided to oppose Russia. Fearing that France would enter any war on Russia's side, Japan asked Great Britain to ensure French neutrality. Great Britain sought German assistance with this request, but was turned down by Bülow, who declared in the Reichstag on March 15 that the Anglo-German Yangzi Agreement was "in no sense concerned with Manchuria." British illusions of an anti-Russian alliance with Germany were dispelled. Even more important, the German chancellor's public rejection of Great Britain damaged the reputation of pro-German British political figures such as Chamberlain and Lansdowne. Arguably, the unnecessary injury done to these leaders undermined their ability to strengthen the Anglo-German relationship.[35]

The Failure of the Third Attempt at an Anglo-German Alliance and the Worsening of Anglo-German Relations

Attempts to form an alliance still continued. Chamberlain, in January 1901 talks with Hermann von Eckardstein, the first secretary in the German embassy, stated his complete willingness to support an Anglo-German alliance or British entry into the Triple Alliance. He suggested that a secret agreement on Morocco could begin that process. If that proved unsuccessful, then Great Britain would have no choice but to seek reconciliation with France and Russia, regardless of the concessions that might entail.[36] German policymakers, however, clung to the belief that no understanding was possible between Great Britain and the Franco-Russian alliance. Time, they thought, was on Germany's side; they could afford to wait. On January 21, 1901, Bülow wrote a letter to the kaiser that fully reflected this flawed assessment: "Your Majesty is absolutely correct in the belief that the English must now come to us.... Now everything depends on neither discouraging the English nor allowing ourselves to be committed prematurely. England's troubles will increase in the coming months, and with them will rise the price we shall be able to demand."[37]

It is worth noting that Bülow's letter clearly revealed Germany's continuing hopes for Great Britain during this time. This differed from Germany's attitude toward France and Russia. What did Germany hope to gain from Great Britain in exchange for an alliance? Diplomatic documents reveal that Germany's preconditions were extremely high. First, the alliance must be comprehensive, rather than limited to Africa, Asia, or other places that Europeans consider "overseas." Europe had to be included. In other words, Great Britain would need to provide a complete security guarantee in order to prevent the danger of a Russian attack. Second, Great Britain would need to make a series of colonial concessions to the Germans. To convince the British to accept such conditions, the German government believed that it needed to make the British feel a sense of urgency. Germany needed to hold fast to its "middle course" without angering either the British or the Russians in the meanwhile.[38] With these calculations in mind, Germany began to respond to Britain's 1901 proposal.

The role of the German embassy's first secretary, Eckardstein, is worth examining in the context of this process. He was a German nobleman married to an Englishwoman, and a strong supporter of an Anglo-German alliance. On March 18, 1901, perhaps in order to promote such an alliance, he proposed a comprehensive defensive alliance between the two powers to the British government. At the same time, however, he reported to his own government that this idea had been suggested by British Foreign Secretary Lord Lansdowne. This served to confirm the German government's mistaken impression that the British government would seek an alliance at any cost.[39] On the British side, although Lansdowne was anxious for an alliance, he did not believe that Great Britain was yet at the point where it needed to surrender its diplomatic autonomy: "I also said that it seemed to me to follow from any such arrangements that each of the allies would have a right to claim a voice in guiding and controlling the external policy of the others. I was afraid that in this country there would be a great reluctance to allow our liberty of action in regard to questions of foreign policy to be restricted in this manner."[40] Thus, he declined the proposed alliance. On April 23, German ambassador Hatzfeldt expressed his hope that Great Britain would join the Triple Alliance; Lansdowne demurred, too, for the same reason. Yet he continued to search for substitutes and, at the end of May, Lansdowne ordered the foreign ministry to prepare a draft treaty for some form of alliance limited to Great Britain and Germany.[41] This met with Salisbury's firm opposition. In a May 29 memorandum he pointedly explained that, "The fatal circumstance is that neither we nor the Germans are competent to make the suggested promises." Great Britain required domestic approval before the declaration of war; without such approval, "the promise would be repudiated, and the Government would be turned out." Likewise, in Germany, "a promise of defensive alliance with England would excite bitter murmurs in every rank of German society."[42] In the end, Salisbury's opinion carried the day and talk of an Anglo-German alliance was set aside.

Despite this, Lansdowne continued to hope that cooperation with Germany was possible on a number of concrete issues. The Morocco issue had intensified, and conflict between French colonial expansion in North Africa and the Moroccan sultan had sharpened, to the point where British interests in Morocco were threatened. On two separate occasions in January and March 1901, the French government proposed a partition of Morocco into spheres of influence, but the British rejected both offers. Great Britain hoped to use this crisis to work with Germany against the French. Ambassador Hatzfeldt attached great importance to the British suggestion. As early as 1899, he had warned his government that unless Germany supported Great Britain on this issue, any Anglo-French compromise that might result could lead to improved relations between those countries, to the detriment of German diplomacy.[43] Bülow, however, did not see things that way. He believed Anglo-French tensions to be so deeply rooted as to preclude any reconciliation. The cards were all in Germany's hand. He continued to insist that Germany strictly follow a middle course between Great Britain and the Franco-Russian alliance, and had little interest in reaching agreements with Great Britain on particular concrete issues. Instead, Bülow supposed that if there was to be any alliance between Germany and Great Britain, it must be a comprehensive one.[44] He further insisted that not only would Great Britain need to agree to aid in Germany's defense, it would also have to extend that same guarantee to Austria-Hungary and Italy. This clearly would be unacceptable to the British. Even Holstein criticized this notion, saying "one has the impression…that Bülow clung to all the obstacles which stood in the way of the alliance."[45] Bülow likewise had little interest in cooperating with Great Britain on the Morocco issue, claiming Germany "must behave like the Sphinx."[46] By August, the German position was unequivocal. In response to British requests for support, the Germans replied: "The Morocco question by itself is not sufficiently important for us to justify a policy by which Germany might incur the risk of serious international complications."[47]

After this, Great Britain essentially abandoned the fantasy of gaining German support and, in a policy shift, looked toward an alliance with Japan in East Asia and cutting a deal with France over Morocco. Significant progress was made in negotiations with Japan in October 1901, and an alliance was concluded in January 1902. This proved to be of critical importance for Anglo-German ties, and its influence on European diplomacy was arguably second only to the Franco-Russian alliance of 1894. After the alliance with Japan, Great Britain had no strategic reason to rely on Germany again. Yet another limiting factor that had prevented the worsening of Anglo-German ties had been removed. German officials at the time, however, held the exact opposite understanding: they thought the Anglo-Japanese alliance was a welcome development that would help Germany's middle course. Wilhelm II himself conveyed his great "interest and satisfaction," and moreover "he expressed some surprise that the agreement had not been concluded earlier."[48]

After their failure to conclude an alliance, relations between Germany and Great Britain deteriorated. The German government, although it had appeared to consider British requests for an alliance with great care, made unscrupulous use of domestic anti-British sentiments. On October 25, 1901, Chamberlain gave his famous speech in Edinburgh, in which he defended the actions of the British Army in South Africa. Chamberlain argued that the armies of other countries acted similarly (or worse) during wartime. He raised the Prussian Army's behavior during the 1870 Franco-Prussian War as an example. This naturally provoked an enraged response in Germany. The criticism of Chamberlain in German newspapers quickly blossomed into an Anglo-German media war. Officials in both Great Britain and Germany who favored close relations between the two countries hoped that Chancellor Bülow would intervene to tamp down this intense anti-British sentiment. His response to Chamberlain's speech, issued on January 8, 1902, simply encouraged it, however. He quoted Frederick the Great, saying, "Let the man be and don't get excited, he's biting on granite." Afterward, the phrase "biting on granite" spread throughout Germany and became a means for counter-attacking Great Britain. Bülow's actions surprised even Holstein, who found them difficult to understand.[49]

German anti-British sentiment immediately touched off an anti-German press war in Great Britain. British papers defended Chamberlain and demanded that the British public take note of anti-British emotions in Germany:

> It denotes the rancor pent up for years, which has been gradually growing throughout the country, which has become intensified by the war, and which has at last found an outlet in the spontaneous national demonstrations aimed at Mr. Chamberlain directly, but indirectly against the British nation and the policy of Great Britain. No greater mistake could be made than to regard these demonstrations as artificial or to think they are not genuine. They reflect the feeling of the Germans toward the British, a feeling of growing in power and capable of becoming one day a serious menace to peace between the two peoples.... The storm of vituperation...represents no passing emotion, but a deep-seated and apparently incurable popular disease of animosity toward the British Empire.[50]

British advocates of strong ties with Germany were the true victims of this assault. George Hamilton, one of those advocates, said, "we have treated them extraordinarily well...they seem to be more hostile to us even than Frenchmen or Russians." The most influential, and most consequential, result was the change in Chamberlain's own attitude. He transformed overnight from being a leading advocate of ties with Germany to being a chief foe of such connections. From January 1902 on, he engaged in extreme anti-German rhetoric.[51] These changes pushed the entire British government in an anti-German direction. When one British noble arrived in London in January 1902, he found that the official attitude toward Germany had shifted to a shocking degree: "Everyone in the [foreign] office and out talks as if we had but one enemy in the world, and that Germany."[52]

Another critical element made its appearance at this time, too: the naval question. Naval expansion after the passage of Germany's second naval bill put Great Britain on alert. In a November 16, 1901, memorandum, First Lord of the Admiralty Selborne noted to the cabinet that "the [Kaiser] seems determined that the power of Germany shall be used all over the world to push German commerce, possessions, and interests."[53] By August 1902, he claimed:

> I am convinced that the great new German navy is being carefully built up from the point of view of a war with us.... It cannot be designed for the purpose of playing a leading part in a future war

> between Germany and France and Russia.... Sir F. Lascelles [British ambassador to Germany] does not believe that the German [Kaiser] or Government are really unfriendly to this country and he is convinced that the true interests of Germany lie in maintaining friendly relations with us, but he is equally convinced that in deciding on a naval policy we cannot safely ignore the malignant hatred of the German people or the manifest designs of the German Navy.[54]

In other areas, German competition encroached upon vital British interests; naval expansion, however, touched the heart of the British Empire itself. It was a direct threat to British hegemony and an existential challenge. It transformed Germany into Great Britain's principal enemy, and the disputes between the two powers grew ever more difficult to resolve.

From the Anglo-French Entente to the Algeciras Conference

The 1904 Anglo-French Entente

Great Britain's position in East Asia improved after concluding an alliance with Japan. The deterioration of relations with Germany pushed Great Britain closer to France. The Morocco Question played a significant role in that latter process. The colonial secretary, Chamberlain, had been the main obstacle preventing negotiations on that issue with France. When France had offered a partition of Morocco in 1901, for example, Chamberlain had instead hoped to unite with Germany against the French designs. Thus, he warned Foreign Minister Lansdowne, "If we are to discuss such a large question as Morocco please bear in mind that the Germans will have something to say—and both they and we will want compensation."[55] By early 1902, however, Chamberlain had become an advocate of working with France against Germany and pushed for Great Britain to enter negotiations with France over Morocco. In December 1902, Chamberlain (now out of office) told the French government that he now believed that his country must abandon its policy of isolation and that he was pushing the cabinet to reach an accord with Paris. Of course, Anglo-French negotiations over Morocco were not merely fixated on that particular colonial question. Instead, they used this opportunity to discuss a broader array of diplomatic cooperation between the countries. Germany was a particular topic of conversation. Moreover, once an entente was reached, the existing treaty arrangements between France and Russia implied that the odds of an Anglo-Russian rapprochement had increased dramatically: as

British statesman Evelyn Baring discerned, "one of the main attractions in the whole business to the authorities of the Quai d'Orsay is the hope of leading up to an Anglo-Russian arrangement, and thus isolating Germany."[56]

Germany, however, paid no attention to this. German policymakers stubbornly believed that hostility between Great Britain and France was so deeply rooted that the possibility of an agreement was remote. On January 30, 1902, Paul Wolff Metternich, the German ambassador in London, reported that Chamberlain had met with the French ambassador in order to discuss the resolution of outstanding colonial disputes.[57] By September, Richard von Kuhlmann, the German representative in Tangier, informed his government that Morocco was the main topic of the Anglo-French negotiations.[58] Yet Bülow, Holstein, and other senior German decision-makers still refused to believe that an accord was possible. Bülow insisted that Anglo-French conflict remained deeply entrenched and compromise would be difficult. Even more important, Anglo-Russian differences were vast. Any agreement between Great Britain and France would shatter the Franco-Russian alliance, and thus would not be in France's national interest.[59] An agreement between Great Britain and Russia would be simply impossible in his estimate: "An agreement of England with Russia would always be tantamount to England's declaration of bankruptcy in Asia and Europe. Time runs for Russia, and any English paying court to Russia only accelerates the decline of English prestige in Asia and Europe."[60] By May 1903, after Anglo-French efforts to reach an understanding had become apparent, the German embassy in Great Britain reported that a colonial arrangement between the British and the French was taking form. Rather than resulting in a dissolution of the Franco-Russian alliance, the report stated, it would lead to the creation of an entente between the three states.[61] Bülow shared this report and solicited views from Holstein and the German ambassadors in Great Britain, France, and Russia; on May 20, he reported to the kaiser that the collective opinion of senior officials in the foreign ministry disagreed with the conclusions drawn by the report's author, Eckardstein. An Anglo-French agreement would be extremely difficult; an Anglo-Russian one even less likely.[62]

Thus, Germany greeted the April 8, 1904, announcement of the Anglo-French Entente with deep shock. Holstein understood at once that the entente signaled the failure of Germany's *Weltpolitik*, as "no overseas policy is possible against England and France." The entente also opened up a split in the Triple Alliance, as Italy's economy was virtually dependent on Great Britain (95 percent of its coal imports came from there) and its security was deeply influenced by Great Britain and France. Once Britain and France had joined hands,

Italo-German estrangement was unavoidable. Other foreign ministry officials shared similar views. Many held the view that the entente represented "one of the worst defeats for German policy since the creation of the Dual Alliance," and some suggested that a "diplomatic victory" was urgently needed to calm domestic public opinion.[63] Chancellor Bülow, however, did not fully agree. He still thought the entente provided little cause for concern. One reason for this was that Great Britain would never truly support a French revanchist war against Germany; it would only provide rhetorical aid to such an endeavor. Another was that he saw the Anglo-French agreement to cooperate on Morocco as unstable. Great Britain could never really follow through on its duty to support France there.[64] Above all else, however, he persisted in thinking that the entente and the Franco-Russian alliance contradicted one another, thus Germany could find an occasion to split Russia from France and then establish an alliance with it.

The Two Main Themes of the German Diplomatic Counterattack

Disagreements among Germany's policymakers did not affect their unanimous conclusion that Germany needed to take measures to strike back. After the entente was announced, two mutually interacting themes emerged in Germany's policy measures: pursuit of an alliance with Russia and engagement with the Morocco Question.

For Germany, there were two issues implicated in allying with Russia. First: was Russia even willing? Second: would such an alliance have value? The mainstream answer for the latter question, as expressed by Holstein, was initially negative. An alliance with Russia had its uses when Germany had pursued a continental policy, but it would have no use under the *Weltpolitik*. The reasoning behind this was that, as a land power, Russia would only be able to assist Germany on land. It would be absolutely unable to help Germany to confront "the jealousy of Great Britain and the United States."[65] The value of such an alliance, however, dramatically changed upon the announcement of the entente. Many German policymakers correctly predicted that France would exert every possible effort to construct links between Great Britain and Russia in order to form a Triple Entente. Concluding an alliance with Russia would be the best method for Germany to thwart France's scheme. Bülow agreed, claiming that a Russo-German alliance would "destroy the possibility of a Russian-French-British alliance."[66]

Russia was, at that moment, caught in a predicament that seemed favorable to the achievement of Germany's objective. After the outbreak of the Russo-Japanese War on February 8, 1904, the Russian military situation had slowly deteriorated. Russia urgently needed stable relations with Germany; Germany, moreover, provided munitions and support. For a time, Russian's diplomatic environment manifested a curious transformation: France, an alliance partner, acted as an indifferent observer, and Germany, a potential foe, played the role of an ally. This led Germany to think that it could approach Russia about an alliance. The kaiser telegraphed the czar on October 27, 1904, claiming that Germany was facing pressure from Great Britain over its supply of coal to the Russian fleet. The two countries thus needed to strengthen their cooperative efforts and remind France of its duties as Russia's ally.[67] Nicholas II quickly agreed, and proposed that the three countries work together. He asked Germany to draft a treaty to that effect. According the draft developed by the German Foreign Ministry, if either Germany or Russia found itself under attack in Europe, the other country would be mandated to provide assistance. An appendix obligated both countries to remind France of its commitment to Russia. The Russian government understood clearly the implications of these German proposals. On November 7, Russia responded with its own revisions to the draft: first, it would be Russia alone that would remind France of its duties as an ally; and second, Germany should cooperate with Russia as it negotiated an end to the Russo-Japanese War. Thus, not only did Germany not achieve its objective, it possibly might be pulled by Russia into a conflict with the Anglo-Japanese alliance. It could not, of course, agree to this. Thereupon Russia informed Germany on November 23 that the French would have to see any Russo-German treaty before it could be signed. This, in essence, constituted a rejection of the alliance proposal. Overall, this attempt revealed the impossibility of an alliance between the two powers. The purpose of such an alliance for Germany would be to strengthen its own position in Europe while avoiding any commitment that would damage relations with Japan or Great Britain.[68] For Russia, however, the goal was to gain desperately needed wartime assistance while maintaining the alliance with France. This pushed both France and Germany to seek better relations with Russia, even as they remained suspicious of one another.

The Moroccan Question also played a role in this context. Germany did not act in pusuit of a specific, concrete objective. In June 1904, Holstein wrote in a memorandum that "not only for material reasons, but also to protect her prestige, Germany must protest against France's intention to acquire Morocco."[69] Many British and U.S. historians criticize and mock this German motive, but objectively speaking its actions were excusable. Between 1903 and 1904, British hostility and wariness toward Germany had become difficult to control. British Foreign Secretary Lansdowne even admitted,

"The anti-German feeling here has been furious and unreasoning and has I think produced a profound impression on the German mind. It has, however, been allowed to go much too far."[70] The French Foreign Minister at the time, Théophile Delcassé, was a leader of the anti-German faction in French politics. Thus, not only did the entente have a profound anti-German strategic orientation, but also its concrete actions directly served to suppress Germany. For example, Germany demanded compensation for the arrangements developed by the entente for Morocco and Egypt (which Germany, and all of the other great powers, had interests in). According to the accepted international practice of the time, Germany's demand was reasonable. Germany's specific requests were not at all excessive, and included things such as compensation for losses sustained by German citizens during the Boer War and a restoration of trade links between Germany and Canada. Yet the British rejected them all. Germany then filed a claim for a mere £70,000 in compensation. This also met with refusal. The British and French had, by contrast, prepared to offer compensation to Russia, Austria-Hungary, and Italy. It is easy to conclude that Britain and France (but Britain in particular) had set out to deliberately humiliate Germany.[71] Therefore the German desire to use the Moroccan Question to regain face or recover prestige is understandable.

The problem for Germany lay in the fact that the pursuit of prestige is an amorphous goal. The situation in Morocco was complex, and the price and consequences of this quest were unpredictable. Thus Germany rashly leapt into muddy waters, its judgments and plans repeatedly failed, thus dooming the enterprise.

The Outbreak of the First Moroccan Crisis and Germany's Misjudgments

For the first six months after the April 1904 announcement of the entente, Germany did not push for progress on the Moroccan Question. By November, however, the combined total of Russia's rejection of an alliance, the Anglo-French rejection of compensation claims, and the unwillingness of Russia, Austria-Hungary, and Italy to take the lead in opposing Anglo-French colonial deals had left Germany in a precarious diplomatic position. German public opinion mercilessly criticized the government's impotent policies. The pressure of this forced the German government to summon up the courage to take active measures. Kuhlmann, the German diplomatic representative in Tangier, proposed that the kaiser, who was then on a cruise in the Mediterranean, land in Tangier and openly recognize the independent sovereignty of the Moroccan sultan. Wilhelm II personally preferred to use more conciliatory methods to entice France into a Continental League and was unwilling to take such a hard-line action. Yet in January 1905, a French military group was sent to Fez, demonstrating that French Foreign Minister Delcassé would no longer ask for Germany's opinion, but would instead direct active measures to exert control.[72] As a result, Wilhelm II was forced to accept the suggestion of his chancellor and foreign ministry. On March 31, 1905, he landed at Tangier and made a forceful speech that acknowledged the sultan's sovereignty and argued for the necessity of an open-door policy. This visit instigated the First Moroccan Crisis.

Germany's timing was impeccable. In early 1905, approximately two-thirds of the Russian Army was engaged in an East Asian war with Japan. It lacked the strength to fight even a defensive war on its western frontier, leaving the Franco-Russian alliance paralyzed. Delcassé's haste in forming the entente with Great Britain and launching a diplomatic assault against Germany had been rash mistakes, leaving France in a fragile state, both diplomatically and militarily. The initial results of the crisis revealed that the kaiser's trip had caught the French unprepared; Delcassé was forced to seek negotiations with Germany. Great Britain feared that it would pay the price for any Franco-German deal, leading Lansdowne to claim that "the French Government might be induced to purchase the acquiescence of Germany by concessions of a kind which we were not likely to regard with favor, in other parts of the world."[73] To prevent this, Great Britain expressed strong support for France, yet avoided making any precise commitment. Thus, at this point in the crisis, Germany could easily have scored a diplomatic victory and have created cracks in the new Anglo-French Entente, had it only devised an appropriate strategy. German policymakers, however, assessed the situation incorrectly yet again.

During the Bismarckian period, Germany had an unwritten principle for managing crises: engage in bilateral talks when Germany itself is a principal party to the dispute, in order to make the most of Germany's power; seek multi-party solutions when Germany is not central to the dispute, thus dispersing responsibility and pressure while preserving initiative. During the First Morocco Crisis, Germany's policymakers completely forgot this maxim. Holstein supported the need for an international conference that could resolve the Moroccan Question and rejected bilateral talks with France. On April 3, Chancellor Bülow accepted this, and eight days later he called for an international conference of all the signatories on the 1880 Treaty of Madrid. There were two major reasons for Germany's decision. First, Germany's opposition to French annexation of Morocco was an action in defense of an international treaty and, as such, would be supported by the majority of nations.

Calling a conference would allow it to make fullest use of this advantage. Although Morocco was, in name, governed by the local sultan, its politics and economics were controlled by the European powers and the United States. In 1880, these countries with rights and interests in Morocco had met at Madrid to enshrine their "most favored nation status" by treaty. Looking at the issue purely from the perspective of international law, French designs to annex Morocco violated the treaty, while Germany's behavior was firmly grounded in it. Holstein calculated that a German proposal for an open-door policy in Morocco would definitely win U.S. support. Given the British fear of U.S. President Theodore Roosevelt, they, too, would be forced to support it. Although Spain already had an accord with France on Morocco, it still feared that French expansion there would ultimately harm its interests, and thus would also support the German position. Italy and Austria-Hungary were German allies, so their support was assured.[74] Second, the conference would be a blow to France, but not so much that it would damage French dignity, and thus it would not prevent a Franco-German reconciliation once all was said and done. Holstein saw international conferences as a form of collective action. Of all the forms that a defeat for France could take, a conference would be the least damaging. France's defeat in 1814 at the hands of a coalition, for instance, had felt less humiliating than its 1870 defeat by Prussia.[75] Moreover, Germany hoped to use the conference to attack French Foreign Minister Delcassé himself: criticisms were to be directed at Delcassé's policies alone, while respecting French national feelings.[76]

Just as in the past, German strategic judgments contained a significant dose of wishful thinking, particularly the assessment of the United States. The Germans had assumed that the "open door" the United States sought in China would translate into support for a similar policy in North Africa. In fact, President Roosevelt turned the Germans down. He claimed that it had already proved difficult to garner popular support for the open-door policy in China. A similar policy in North Africa had no hope of being understood. On April 20, 1905, Roosevelt repeated his lack of interest in a North African open-door policy, claiming that U.S. interests in Morocco "are not sufficiently great to make me feel justified in entangling our Government in this matter."[77] This did not attract much attention in Germany, however. Germany had already made up its mind; it was determined to call a conference for the resolution of the Moroccan Question and rejected all offers for bilateral negotiations with France. Holstein even directed the German ambassador in France to avoid all formal contact with the French Foreign Ministry.[78]

A German Diplomatic Defeat

In the face of strong diplomatic pressure from Germany, splits developed inside the French government. Delcassé had been the principal advocate of the entente with Great Britain, and he sought British support even as he offered to negotiate with the Germans. French President Émile Loubet saw his policies as risky and potentially leading to war with Germany. Once Germany learned of these tensions within the French government, it pushed even harder. French divisions ultimately burst asunder. On June 6, 1905, Delcassé resigned and Loubet, who had supported cooperation with Germany, added the foreign ministry to his brief. He hoped that this could lead to direct negotiations with Germany over Morocco. Loubet represented French financial capitalists, who themselves favored improved ties with Germany and had little interest in the entente with Great Britain. Thus Germany was confronted with a favorable opportunity to resolve the crisis: if Germany had accepted the French proposal, it would have aided the political position of the pro-German French financial community and helped split the Anglo-French Entente. Curiously, at this point German policymakers (except for Wilhelm II, who wanted to end the matter and improve ties with France after Delcassé resigned) all seemed to forget the original purpose of provoking the crisis in Morocco. In their minds, Germany had already supported an international conference and it could not back away from that. German policy began to be driven by a simple desire to maintain face. Holstein himself admitted that Germany, at that moment, no longer sought to "achieve anything in particular" but wanted to display "that things can't be done without us."[79] By late June 1905, Franco-German disputes over whether or not to call a conference intensified. Germany twisted the screws on Loubet's government, forcing it to accept the conference. In a letter to the German ambassador in France, Holstein claimed to be unable to understand French insistence on direct bilateral talks, as an international conference could resolve the issue while preserving face for everyone involved. The only loser could be Great Britain, because it wanted Germany and France to bicker over Morocco.[80]

In the end, France had to accept Germany's demand, and the two sides reached an agreement on July 8, 1905, to hold an international conference on the Moroccan Question. This result was, on the surface, a German victory, but it in fact planted the seeds for an eventual German defeat. As the British historian A. J. P. Taylor concluded, Germany

> could go from success to success so long as they negotiated with France alone…by agreeing to a genuine conference they exposed

> themselves to the risk of a diplomatic coalition. Their mistake was in large part that of all those who appeal to international conferences: they imagined that somewhere there was an impartial 'world opinion,' which would be voiced by the supposedly neutral powers.[81]

In July 1905, Germany still held an advantageous position. Great Britain only supported the French diplomatically, while the Russian naval defeat at Tsushima forced them to seek peace with Japan. If Germany could ensure that the conference agenda entirely reflected its own proposals, there was still a great possibility it could pull off a diplomatic victory. The improvement of Russo-German ties, however, influenced the solution of the Moroccan Question.

After the Russian defeat at Tsushima, revolutionary fervor grew inside Russia while peace negotiations with Japan proceeded only slowly. Seeing Russia's predicament, Wilhelm II plotted a clever gambit: using his upcoming meeting with the czar to try again for an alliance between the two countries. In July 1905, the two monarchs met onboard naval vessels moored near Björkö in the Gulf of Finland. Unexpectedly, on July 24, the kaiser persuaded the czar to sign a treaty of alliance. This unanticipated course of events completely changed German plans. The kaiser thought that now that a treaty existed between Germany and Russia, the Franco-Russian alliance no longer existed, and that France would be forced to exit the entente with Great Britain and join the new German alliance system.[82] Thus, Germany's objectives in Morocco were to maintain its own prestige, damage the Anglo-French Entente, and improve ties with France in order for it to be easier for France to join the new Russo-German alliance.

From Chancellor Bülow's perspective, Germany needed to extricate itself quickly from Moroccan affairs, thereby reducing Franco-German frictions and demonstrating German magnanimity. He even considered allowing France complete freedom of action in Morocco.[83] As a result, Germany hastily made concessions, particularly by making significant changes (in accord with French opinion) to the structure of the planned international conference. Unthinkingly, Germany paved the path to its own defeat at the conference. Germany had violated a great taboo of international conflict: demonstrating one's own generosity before one's opponent is truly defeated. In fact, the Russo-German alliance inked at Björkö soon ran into problems. Many inside Russia disliked the treaty. Foreign Minister Vladimir Lambsdorff, former Finance Minister Sergey Witte, and other important officials opposed it and pressured the czar accordingly. On October 7, 1905, the czar informed the kaiser that he would need to consult France before the treaty could take effect. The position of the French government was perfectly clear: it rejected the alliance. The czar formally notified the kaiser of this fact on November 23, claiming that it would be difficult to persuade France to join anything like the original treaty. This effectively cancelled the agreement the two monarchs had reached in July. Any dream of an alliance between the three countries vanished into thin air.

None of these facts could be changed by Germany's overly early concessions to France over Morocco. On January 16, 1906, the conference opened in the Spanish coastal city of Algeciras. The entire conference agenda favored France. France and Great Britain had both prepared themselves fully for the conference. Germany, by contrast, assumed that naturally it had the support of other countries and so did little work in advance of the meeting. It failed even to discuss Morocco with the other countries. Therefore, Germany suddenly found itself isolated once the conference began: Germany wanted to maintain Moroccan independence for the general benefit of the great powers, while France wanted to strengthen its own control over the region—and of the thirteen other powers represented at the conference, only Austria-Hungary backed Germany while the rest, including Germany's Triple Alliance partner, Italy, essentially supported France. The conference could only result in German concessions. In the final agreement issued at the end of the conference, the key issue (control of the police in Morocco) was decided in France's favor. The agreement stipulated joint Franco-Spanish management of police and maintenance of order, but this in fact meant French control. The First Morocco Crisis ended in a German defeat.

Anglo-Russian Entente and German Encirclement

The Effects of the First Morocco Crisis on Germany

The First Morocco Crisis had profound and wide-ranging repercussions. For Europe as a whole, this was the first time since German unification that anyone had seriously considered the possibility and prospect of a general war. Thus "it was a true 'crisis,' a turning-point in European history. It shattered the long Bismarckian peace."[84] There were two major repercussions for Germany. First, some in Germany policymaking circles regretted that they had not made use of Germany's temporary military advantage, particularly that Germany had not risked war. A tendency for hard lines and risk-taking reared its head. Russia's defeat at Japan's hands had placed Germany in a position more advantageous than any since the 1894 Franco-Russian alliance was formed. Due to poor application of strategy, however, Germany was unable to transform that moment of military superiority into a political triumph. Some policymakers began to regret that Germany had missed this opportunity. One proponent of using this window of opportunity, Alfred von Schlieffen, has been paraphrased by another as believing that "in 1905, therefore, it was necessary either to utilize the favorable military situation or to push through a complete understanding with France over Alsace-Lorraine." Wilhelm II himself vetoed this idea, to Schlieffen's deep regret. Karl von Einem, the army minister, blamed the kaiser for how events turned out: "having in the years 1905–06—to our misfortune—prevented a collision with France."[85] These feelings caused future policymakers to use ever more hard-line measures in international affairs, particularly during crises, even to the point where they gladly ran the risk of war.

The second repercussion was that German military superiority and diplomatic aggressiveness stimulated Great Britain and France to upgrade their own military cooperation. In late June 1905, when the dispute between France and Germany over Morocco was at its most acute, some in the British government feared that Germany would attack France. The issue of aid to France, if such a situation arose, fell under consideration. John "Jackie" Fisher, first sea lord of the Admiralty, wrote in a late June memorandum that a second French defeat would allow Germany to dominate the continent, "and it might therefore be necessary for Great Britain in her own interests to lend France her active support."[86] On January 10, 1906, British Foreign Secretary Edward Grey informed the French ambassador to London that Great Britain would not stand aside in event of a Franco-German war.[87] Four days later. British Secretary of State for War Richard Haldane ordered the British General Staff and the French military attaché in Great Britain to meet. The result of this discussion was a January 22 promise that, if needed, Britain could mobilize and deploy 105,000 soldiers to France within fifteen days.[88] These measures had extremely important strategic significance. As Winston Churchill recalled in his memoirs, at the Anglo-French military talks:

> The minds of our military men were definitely turned into a particular channel. Mutual trust grew continually in one set of military relationships, mutual precautions in the other. However explicitly the two Governments might agree and affirm to each other that no national or political engagement was involved in these technical discussions, the fact remained that they constituted an exceedingly potent tie.[89]

In other words, this level of tactical coordination demonstrated the treaty-less alliance that had developed between the two countries.

These two repercussions interacted with each other in a volatile manner. This posed a special risk to Germany as a rising power. In 1906 and 1907, it had come to be seen as a security threat. Other great powers had begun to unite to block Germany. Germany's responses had also grown ever more intense and extreme. After the 1906 Algeciras Conference, German policymakers and German society understood that they were diplomatically isolated. A narrative of German encirclement became popular. On November 14, 1906, Chancellor Bülow used this term for the first time in an open session of the Reichstag: "A policy aiming at the encirclement of Germany and seeking to form a ring of Powers in order to isolate and paralyze it would be disastrous to the peace of Europe. The forming of such a ring would not be possible without exerting some pressure. Pressure provokes counter-pressure. And out of pressure and counter-pressure finally explosions may arise."[90] Afterwards, encirclement became a fixed phrase for policymakers and the media alike in discussing German foreign relations. It became deeply implanted in popular consciousness. As a result, Germany became ever less tolerant of external pressure and the use of strong measures to break out of encirclement seemingly became the only viable strategic choice.

The first result of German feelings of encirclement was a reappraisal of the alliance with Austria. The *Weltpolitik* had directed attention outside of Europe; ties with Austria were merely an important part of the continental policy. After the beginning of the *Weltpolitik* in 1897, Austria-Hungary's significance for German diplomacy had declined. Particularly during the period in which Germany thought that it could maintain freedom of action between the Franco-Russian alliance and Great Britain, Germany had essentially ignored Austria-Hungary. Austria-Hungary had, for example, once warned Germany about the likelihood of conflict with Great Britain arising from its naval expansion, but Germany disregarded this.[91] Once the Algeciras Conference revealed that only Austria-Hungary would support Germany, the German attitude suddenly changed. In a 1906 report to the kaiser, Bülow argued that Germany's relationship with Austria had become more important than ever, as it was Germany's only "reliable ally."[92] At the same time, Germany was forced to reconsider the domestic political elements of the alliance with Austria-Hungary. A 1906 constitutional crisis in the Austro-Hungarian Empire had raised the specter of imperial dissolution. Germany feared that if Austria-Hungary fell apart, then its German-majority areas might be absorbed into Germany, creating enormous stresses on German society: "We shall thereby receive an increase of about fifteen million Catholics so that the Protestants would become a minority…the proportion of strength between the Protestants and the Catholics would become similar to that which at the time led to the Thirty Years' War, i.e., a virtual dissolution of the German Empire."[93] Germany's heavy reliance on Austria-Hungary resulted in an inability to refuse Austrian demands. Thus, Austria-Hungary could confidently ask Germany to foot the bill for its expansionist policies. The phenomenon of the weak leading the strong within the alliance, which Bismarck had struggled so hard against, had now come into being. This was accompanied by risky changes in Austrian policy. In fall 1906, there was a major change of personnel within the Austro-Hungarian government: Franz Conrad von Hötzendorf became the chief of the General Staff and Alois Lexa von Aehrenthal the foreign minister. Both of these men were aggressive risk-takers and strongly hoped to manufacture a foreign policy victory in order to restore their country's prestige. Their sights were set primarily on the sensitive Balkan region, which intensified disputes with Russia and harmed Russo-German relations. At this point, considerations of solidifying the alliance with Austria-Hungary pushed other concerns off the German agenda. In May 1907, Germany offered full support for Austro-Hungarian resistance to possible Russian expansion in the Balkans. This greatly increased Germany's own latent conflict with Russia.

The Anglo-Russian Entente and the Intensification of German Encirclement

Simultaneously, an anti-German alliance continued to come into being. British Foreign Secretary Grey had proposed the notion of a three-way entente between Great Britain, France, and Russia during the Algeciras Conference: "The door is being kept open by us for a rapprochement with Russia; there is at least a prospect that when Russia is re-established we shall find ourselves on good terms with her. An entente between Russia, France and ourselves would be absolutely secure. If it is necessary to check Germany it could then be done."[94] The British War Office's opinion was even more positive. On March 20, 1906, a memorandum from the army clearly pointed out:

> By detaching her [Russia] from Germany we should have her on our side if and when Germany reaches the Persian Gulf[95]—a contingency which is far less to be desired than Russia's presence there. It would also tend to weaken Germany's military position in Europe and therefore strengthen our own as well as that of France, the ally of Russia.... This course would, however, probably mean that Germany's enmity toward us would be increased, but her enmity is almost certain to be increased (there is no just reason why it should) if we succeed in coming to an agreement with Russia on any terms.

> Further, Germany's avowed aims and ambitions are such that they seem bound, if persisted in, to bring her into armed collision with us sooner or later, and therefore a little more or less enmity on her part is not a matter of great importance.[96]

Russia's need to restrain Germany was not as pressing as Britain's, but the defeat by Japan had spurred a reorientation of foreign policy. The strategic focus was brought back to Europe, and improved relations with Great Britain were sought. The Russian Foreign Minister, Alexander Izvolsky, who took office in May 1906, pointed out that "the foreign policy of Russia must continue to rest upon the unchangeable base of her alliance with France, but that this alliance must itself be fortified and enlarged by agreements with England and Japan."[97] Arthur Nicolson, the new British ambassador to Russia, arrived in St. Petersburg on May 28, and visited Izvolsky the next day to propose formal negotiations for an alliance. More than a year of seesaw negotiations followed, but an agreement on Persia, Afghanistan, and Tibet was signed on August 31, 1907. Those three regions were divided into clearly delimited spheres of influence and buffer zones. Through this convention, the two countries rid themselves of their most concentrated set of disputes. Although there was no hint of anti-German coloring to this arrangement, objectively it was a blow to Germany's diplomatic and security environments.

The changing mindset of the British government during the course of the negotiations with Russia, particularly its assessment of Germany as a threat, is worthy of notice. Anglo-German relations had been openly decaying since 1895, and by 1902, Great Britain already conceived of Germany as a competitor. Yet, as the world hegemonic power, Great Britain faced a broad array of threats. Germany's rank within those threats was still not settled; assessments of German threats underwent continuous refinement. In November 1903, the Committee on Imperial Defence, Great Britain's core national defense advisory committee, concluded that India was the empire's primary defense problem and thus Russia, not Germany, constituted the greatest threat to Great Britain.[98] The rise of Anglo-German naval tensions and Japan's victory over Russia, however, forced a methodical reassessment of these threats. In 1906, the British government carried out a new estimate of its position and interests in the Middle East and India. It concluded that Anglo-Russian tensions had been reduced to the point where reconciliation was possible; requests from the British military command in India to augment its forces in response to a threat from Russia were denied.[99]

In January 1907, British diplomat Eyre Crowe penned a 24-page "Memorandum on the Present State of British Relations with France and Germany." This document played an extremely important role in British foreign policy, particularly toward Germany. It can even be seen as a milestone. Crowe offered a comprehensive assessment of British foreign policy principles, German behavior and intentions, an analysis of British's current situation, and policy suggestions for the future. Both the document's writing style and analysis represent the wisdom and the traditions of British diplomacy. To a certain extent, Crowe's memorandum was comparable to George Kennan's famous "long telegram" of 1947. His core premise was that Germany had become accustomed to adopting aggressive policies. Regardless of what the concrete objectives of these policies were, Germany's goal was to be a global power. Germany's quest for command of the seas, in particular, had created irreconcilable conflicts between the two countries, because "a German maritime supremacy must be acknowledged to be incompatible with the existence of the British Empire."[100] This memorandum had far-reaching effects on British policies. The document itself leaped beyond the fields of policy analysis and advice to touch upon issues of history and philosophy, making it a useful guide. Foreign Secretary Grey passed the document on to the prime minister, the secretary of state for war, and other important members of the cabinet, calling it "most valuable," a "guide for policy, and something that should be 'carefully studied.'"[101] Beginning with this memorandum, the British policy of containing Germany began to be systematized, clarified, and solidified.

German policymakers naturally recognized the seriousness of these changes. After the First Morocco Crisis, Germany realized that not only had it failed to loosen the Anglo-French Entente, but also the entente had become closer and its role as an anti-German military alliance became more apparent by the day. In early 1907, German ambassador to London Metternich suspected that Great Britain and France already had some sort of military arrangement between them. He reminded Bülow that if Germany attacked France over Morocco, then Great Britain would aid France.[102] The August 31, 1907, signing of the Anglo-Russian Convention was yet another serious blow to Germany. In order to avoid the incitement of domestic sentiment, Chancellor Bülow ordered all major German newspapers to treat the issue impartially, to frame the agreement as the delineation of spheres of influence and not a military alliance nor a threat to Germany. German policymakers themselves, however, were in fact very clear about the agreement's meaning. Wilhelm II himself noted that the European situation had become less favorable to

Germany.[103] The same year, Anglo-German naval competition accelerated into a full-blown arms race. After Britain's launch of the first *Dreadnought*-class battleship in 1906, Germany revealed its second supplemental plan and decided to begin constructing its own dreadnoughts, launching a competition for construction of those ships between the two countries. Germany's move helped form a public consensus within Great Britain. German naval expansion was now understood as Great Britain's greatest threat since the Napoleonic Wars. The country, of course, needed to respond with all of its might.[104] As the hostility between Great Britain and Germany deepened, the Anglo-French anti-German relationship strengthened. In May 1908, French President Armand Fallières's visit to London was enthusiastically received by British society. Metternich, the German ambassador in London, believed that if Germany became involved in a war with France, it would spur the immediate creation of a true Anglo-French alliance. Great Britain, France, and Russia were already united against Germany and its Triple Alliance partners, although the former group did not have a desire to attack.[105] Still, this increased the level of anxiety among German policymakers and made their assessments even more pessimistic. On June 17, 1908, Chancellor Bülow wrote:

> There are, unmistakably, conspiracies against us everywhere now. I continue to believe that for economic and financial reasons England would only very reluctantly take the decision to go to war. I believe that Russia needs and wants peace. And finally I believe that even France, although she has not yet got over Alsace-Lorraine and the loss of her 250-year-old *prépondérance légitime* on the continent and has not given up the idea of revenge, has doubts about running the unpredictable risks of a war. But at the same time I believe that it is in the interest of these Powers to make us appear on edge and restless. That is our enemies' tactic if only because every real or apparent threat from our side induces the French to fortify their Eastern border even more, the English to build more Dreadnoughts, the Russians to move even more troops to their Western border.... We must work as quietly as possible to make our Army swift to strike and ready for war, but outwardly we must avoid anything that draws attention unnecessarily to our work and to us and exposes us to fresh suspicions and intrigues.[106]

Overall, the results of the *Weltpolitik* were apparent for all to see by the policy's tenth anniversary in 1908. Tremendous changes had occurred in Germany's diplomatic environment; the notion of strategic encirclement had already become widely shared among the policymaking class. The *Weltpolitik* had led to public defeats, and Germany's security environment had seriously deteriorated. Splits emerged within German policymaking circles about the continued viability of the policy, particularly the naval plans associated with it. Some proposed returning the focus to the European continent and the army. In an August 16, 1908, letter to Holstein, Bülow first pointed out that once German fiscal reforms were complete, the pace of fleet constriction would drop: "If I am still Chancellor then, I will not permit any such Icarus flight. Not only for reasons of foreign policy, but for domestic policy as well. We cannot have both the greatest army and the biggest navy. We cannot weaken the army, for our destiny will be decided on land."[107] These disagreements between policymakers would not be resolved before the outbreak of war in 1914. One point, however, remained unchallenged: both those who favored strengthening the navy and those who favored strengthening the army agreed that forceful measures were needed to break out of encirclement. This tendency became increasingly evident in each successive crisis after 1908. German diplomacy came to resemble a game of chicken. Both the Tirpitz Plan's advocacy of a High Seas Fleet and the Schlieffen Plan's vision of complete victory on the western front served to transform German military strategy into nothing more than a large-scale gamble.

7

An Obsession with Command of the Seas

"In the case of such commercial and industrial development, points of contract and conflict with other nations increase. Naval power is essential if Germany does not want to go under."
Alfred von Tirpitz

THE CONSTRUCTION OF a High Seas Fleet lay at the core of Germany's *Weltpolitik*. Taken on its own terms, the spate of naval construction that began in the late 1890s was successful. Rooted in an obsession with command of the seas, this program made use of Germany's powerful industry, advanced technology, and organizational ability. It stimulated a powerful wave of public interest in naval construction in a country that had essentially no naval tradition. As a result, within twenty years, this program transformed an inconsequential navy into the second most powerful in the world. Yet this partial triumph was disastrous when viewed from a more comprehensive perspective. Germany's "headlong advance" style of naval construction represented a significant step in the dissolution of German grand strategy. To a certain extent, naval strategy usurped the role of grand strategy. From 1897 to 1914, naval strategy became Germany's only systematic, continuous strategy. This abnormal situation not only led to the misallocation of national resources, it also definitively worsened Germany's security environment. The massive scale of naval construction directly challenged the basis for British hegemony and security—the Royal Navy's command of the seas. Strategically, this placed Germany and Great Britain directly at odds with one another. The two countries slipped into a pernicious, inescapable security conflict. History provides many examples of war between rising powers and established powers becoming unavoidable once the situation reaches this stage.

The Origins of Germany's High Seas Fleet

Changing German Understandings of the Navy

Traditionally, neither Prussia nor Germany had attached much importance to sea power. Given that it was ringed on land by powerful countries, Prussia had always prioritized its army. Before unification, moreover, the German coastline belonged to numerous different states; this divided coastline and the consequent separation of ports made the creation of a powerful navy impossible. After German unification, the rise of German overseas trade and the growth of colonial interests pushed issues of naval expansion to the top of the agenda. Even so, Germany remained uninterested in a navy during Bismarck's tenure in office. This was in part due to the policymaker's deep-rooted recognition that land power must precede ocean power. A letter written by General Edwin Manteuffel to Chief of the Military Cabinet General Emil von Albedyll in 1883 reflected this widespread attitude: "I, too, belong to the uncultured supporters of the policies of King F[riedrich] W[ilhelm] I, who sold his last warship in order to create one more battalion."[1] This attitude was also due in part to Bismarck's own predilections. In keeping with his overarching belief that Germany should not seek to maximize its power, Bismarck held that since Germany already had the most powerful army in the world, naval expansion would inspire nervousness in Great Britain, France, and Russia, and might rouse them to form an anti-German alliance. The notion that Germany needed to assure its own absolute security through the development of a navy capable of protecting Germany's overseas interests did not carry much weight.

In response to calls for a strong navy that could prevent British threats to German overseas interests, Bismarck argued that a more effective method of restraining Britain's naval power would be to join with another second-tier naval power in an armed neutrality pact. Given that the 1856 Paris Declaration Respecting Maritime Law had expressed the right of countries to protect their freedom of navigation on the oceans, it was entirely possible for Germany to organize such an alliance. Bismarck believed this type of guarantee was relatively safe, but he also warned that there was no absolute security for German commercial and colonial interests, as any attempt to rival British naval strength would be negated by an Anglo-French naval alliance.[2] Under the influence of these two factors, the German Navy developed only slowly during the Bismarckian era. Strategically, the fleet of this era focused on the defense of coastal waters.

A mammoth change occurred in German attitudes toward the navy in the 1890s. The construction of a powerful blue-water High Seas Fleet became a strategic objective. Even more surprisingly, Germany discarded its historical indifference to naval force and energetically invested itself in the command and control of the seas and the massive project of fleet construction. Support for the High Seas Fleet became a popular national obsession. In many ways, this was a moment of historical rupture rather than continuity. Behind this change lay a complex but powerful series of motives.[3]

The first was the prevalence of navalism as an ideology. At the end of the nineteenth century, the importance of naval power seemed paramount as overseas imperialist expansion reached its high-water mark. Navalism, much like Social Darwinism and other ideological currents, was widespread in all of the great powers. The writings of strategist Alfred Mahan marked the true starting point of the trend. Beginning in 1890, he successively published *The Influence of Sea Power upon History, 1660–1783* (1890), *The Influence of Sea Power upon the French Revolution and Empire, 1793–1812* (1892), and *Sea Power in Relation to the War of 1812* (1905). Collectively, his works not only pointed to a theory of naval strategy based on battleships and seizure of command of the sea, but they also raised the development of sea power to the level of historical philosophy. Mahan pointed to the tight connection between sea power and the rise and fall of nations, thus creating an abstract, universally applicable model. British naval hegemony and the U.S. conquest of its western territories provided strong examples for this principle.[4] Under Mahan's influence, all of the great powers—including Great Britain, France, Russia, and the United States—experienced a wave of enthusiasm for naval construction. Even some of the middle powers, such as Portugal, Mexico, the Netherlands, and Spain, participated as well, making navalism a powerful international trend.[5] These highly simplified theories and their promised direct linkage to world power held an even greater attraction for a rapidly growing great power like Germany. A large number of Germans saw a powerful navy as a quick, and necessary, road that would take Germany to its future status as a world power. In late 1897, Chancellor Hohenlohe claimed in a speech to the Reichstag that: "Precisely because we want to carry out a peaceful policy, we must make an effort to build our fleet into a power factor which carries the necessary weight in the eyes of friend and foe alike.... In maritime questions, Germany must be able to speak a modest but, above all, a wholly German word."[6]

The second was the need to respond to societal demands. Post-unification German social structures were full of contradictions and tensions. By the 1890s, the development of the German industrial and commercial capitalist classes had advanced to the point that a large middle class had formed.

Actual power inside the country, however, was wielded by the Junker landlord class (although after the 1870s, heavy industrial capitalists won a spot at the table), and the social status of the middle class proved difficult to change. This was readily apparent inside the military. In countries like Germany, where the military enjoyed special status, enlisting and (especially) serving as an officer was a major route for middle-class men to enhance their social standing. The army (and particularly the Prussian Army), however, continued to see the traditional Junker class as its main source of officers and was unwilling to open up to the middle class. Between 1890 and 1914, the percentage of army officers with aristocratic backgrounds declined, but still numbered some 30 percent in 1913. The percentage was higher in the upper reaches of the officer corps. In 1900, 60 percent of colonels and above were aristocrats; in 1913, the number was 53 percent.[7] The navy, by contrast, did not take social status into account for entry into the officer corps and was essentially completely open to the middle class. In 1898, only 5 of the 32 officers in the Imperial Navy Office were aristocrats. Between 1899 and 1918, only one of the 10 chiefs of the Navy General Staff were titled aristocrats; during the same period, of the 48 officers who managed departments within the Navy General Staff, only 5 had aristocratic backgrounds and a mere two were titled aristocrats.[8] Thus naval expansion fulfilled the demands of lower classes to improve their social status.[9] This formed a powerful social foundation of support for such expansion.

The third was a changing security environment. In the late 1890s, Germany's overseas interests had expanded. From 1873 until 1895, German shipping tonnage increased by 150 percent and overseas exports by 200 percent. Even more significantly, Germany had begun to rely partially on overseas food supplies.[10] This coincided with a worsening of the relationship between Germany and the oceanic hegemon, Great Britain, leading many Germans to worry that Great Britain would sever German shipping lines. Spain's defeat by the United States in 1898 had a sobering effect in Germany. Chancellor Hohenlohe concluded that: "We must not expose ourselves to the danger of suffering the fate from England that Spain suffered from the United States. That the English are merely waiting for a chance to fall upon us is clear."[11] Great Britain's hard-line attitude toward Germany also hastened these changes in Germany's security assessments. After the 1896 Kruger Telegram incident led to Anglo-German tensions, the British domestic press called for the use of Britain's naval superiority to teach Germany a lesson. On September 11, 1897, the British *Saturday Review* ran a famous anti-German essay that, after discussing the commercial competition between the two countries, opined that:

> If Germany were extinguished tomorrow, the day after tomorrow there is not an Englishman in the world who would not be richer. Nations have fought for years over a city or a right of succession; must they not fight for two hundred and fifty million pounds of yearly commerce?... England is the only great power that could fight Germany "without tremendous risk and without doubt of the issue."... The growth of Germany's fleet has done no more than to make the blow of England fall on her more heavily. The ships would soon be at the bottom of the sea or in convoy to English powers; Hamburg and Bremen, the Kiel Canal and the Baltic ports would like under the guns of England, waiting, until the indemnity were settled.... [afterwards, we could] say to France and Russia, "Seek some compensation. Take inside Germany whatever you like; you can have it."[12]

Actual British behavior, too, could be extremely overbearing. In 1900, the Royal Navy implemented a blockade of the Boer Republics and arbitrarily seized German ocean liners, claiming that they contained contraband. After searches revealed this to be false, the ocean liners were released. These actions greatly offended German public opinion and provided another powerful motive for naval expansion.

Fourth was the influence of individual policymakers. The kaiser himself was a naval enthusiast. Even early in his youth, Wilhelm II had envied British naval dominance. After reading Mahan's *The Influence of Sea Power upon History* in 1894, his interest in the navy and in command of the oceans deepened. He would claim that he was "not reading, but devouring Captain Mahan's book."[13] His obsession with the navy also manifested itself in a fondness for naval titles and uniforms. In addition to his title as Supreme Admiral of the German Imperial Navy, he also held rank in the Russian, British, Swedish, Norwegian, and Danish Navies, as well as an honorary position in the Greek Navy. He enjoyed wearing his navy uniforms on public occasions. He did not permit other members of the royal house to wear such uniforms, however; this was his own special perquisite. His rank of captain in the British Royal Navy had been granted in 1889 by his grandmother, Queen Victoria, and thus was a particular favorite of his. He even at times wore his

British naval uniform when meeting with the British ambassador. Wilhelm II's passion for the navy seems to have allowed him to find a sense of mission as a monarch. On January 1, 1900, he declared in a New Year's message to officers in the Berlin garrison that: "As My grandfather [did] for the Army, so I will, for My Navy, carry on unerringly and in a similar manner the work of reorganization so that it may stand on an equal footing with My armed forces on land and so that through it the German Empire may also be in a position abroad to attain that place which it has not yet reached."[14]

Even more critically, as Wilhelm II's attention became ever more focused on naval power, his understanding of foreign relations became reduced to an extremely simplistic model: power counted above all. If Germany couldn't accomplish a task, it was due to a lack of power; given that naval power was the most important component of national power, it followed that if Germany couldn't accomplish a task, it was due to a lack of sea power. For example, in March 1897, Wilhelm II blamed Germany's inability to exert pressure on Greece, Germany's limited share of the Chinese market, and the failure of Anglo-German negotiations over a commercial treaty all on Germany's insufficient naval power. In November 1897, he expressed his desire to use the navy in response to British "egotism":

> In the face of such egotism finally nothing avails but the actual might that stands behind one's claims. All skill of diplomacy is of no avail if it cannot threaten and induce fright through this threatening. And this automatically leads to the *ceterum censeo* of the strengthening of the German fleet—not only for the direct protection of German transoceanic trade—although it is also essential for that—but also much more effectively for the concentrated action of an armored battle fleet which, protected by the North-Baltic Sea canal and leaning on Heligoland—whose strategic value is still not recognized—can any moment break out of this strong position against the English Channel and threaten the English coastal cities, when the English naval power was occupied in the Mediterranean against the French or in the East Asian waters against the Russian fleet, perhaps simultaneously.… Only if the armored fist is thus held before his face will the British Lion hide his tail as he recently did in the face of American threats.[15]

Tirpitz's Vision

Alfred von Tirpitz, secretary of state of the Imperial Navy Office, proved himself a master of manipulating the four motives discussed above. He was the person who led Germany's rush toward being a global naval power and served as the actual architect of German naval expansion.[16] He had immense organizational abilities and a profound understanding of domestic politics; he could reasonably be called the soul of German naval expansion. He transformed Wilhelm II's naval enthusiasm into a practical, carefully designed long-term plan and gained support for it from the nation's various political forces. In 1896, the kaiser had hoped to significantly increase the navy's budget, but such notions were unrealizable given Germany's domestic political situation at the time. He contemplated simply dissolving the Reichstag, which could have led to a major domestic political crisis.[17] Tirpitz's methods were completely different. After taking his position in the Navy Office, he resolutely refused to be in opposition to the Reichstag. Instead, he indirectly influenced and pressured the Reichstag through popular mobilization. Tirpitz was a skilled publicist: he transformed naval publications from specialist, technical magazines to popular magazines, so that the German public could have a broad understanding of the navy. Inside the Navy Office, he established a news division, responsible for influencing newspapers and magazines. He also organized a team to translate Mahan's *The Influence of Sea Power on History* and distributed over 8,000 copies free of charge, as well as arranging for the serial publication of this text in German periodicals. Tirpitz even sought the support of famous scholars; nearly 270 university professors would provide support for the navy's propaganda, including Hans Delbrück, Max Weber, and other world-class scholars. In the words of one historian, a list of these fleet professors could function as a "Who's Who?" of the German intelligentsia.[18] He also lavished attention on political and business circles; many influential figures in both were invited to visit the navy. In addition, he strengthened connections with the news media and the publishing world. In 1898, the Navy League was founded as a mass organization with his support. Its mission was to "emancipate large sections of the community from the spell of the political parties by arousing their enthusiasm for this one great national issue." The league's publication, *Die Flotte*, quickly reached a circulation of 750,000. Membership in the league grew from 78,652 in 1898 to 1,108,106 in 1914.[19]

This organization played an important role in spreading publicity about the High Seas Fleet.

The claim that German naval construction was intertwined with Germany's overseas interests formed the core of Tirpitz's propaganda efforts. He expounded upon this at length in a speech to the Reichstag, emphasizing the extraordinary growth of Germany's overseas interests since 1871. These interests had already become a life-or-death issue for Germany; any harm to them would damage the German economic and political situation. Defense of such critical interests could only be ensured by a navy.[20] He would continue to make the connection between overseas interests and great power status:

> Germany sinks in the next century quickly from her position as great power, unless she now systematically and without waste of time advances [her] general sea interests.... Both because a sea power has to be established in the narrowest sense (fleet) and preserved as such and because power is important in itself, Germany must keep her population German. The development of Germany into an industrial and commercial power is irresistible like a law of nature…in the case of such commercial and industrial development, points of contact and conflict with other nations increase. Naval power is essential if Germany does not want to go under.[21]

Very quickly, the simplistic formula of "High Seas Fleet = overseas interests = being a global power" proved to be a very effective piece of popular propaganda. The people realized that no thinking was required to grasp this truth, which could help the nation grow more powerful. This sparked a nationwide fervor for naval construction.

In additional to his organizing skills, Tirpitz was also noted for his planning abilities. He had a complete, long-term concept for building Germany's High Seas Fleet. Arguably, both the German Empire's naval expansion and naval strategy followed his concept from 1897 until 1914. The most noteworthy are the objectives he set for naval development. Under Tirpitz's guidance, German naval expansion from the very beginning was oriented toward Great Britain, the oceanic hegemon. In 1897, just before Tirpitz assumed his position at the Navy Office, the impatient kaiser ordered Tirpitz's predecessor to direct his focus to the Franco-Russian alliance. Once Tirpitz took office, however, he immediately overturned that order. In June 1897, he responded to the kaiser with what would become known as the famous "Tirpitz memorandum." This document stated: "For Germany the most dangerous naval enemy at the present time is England. It is also the enemy against which we most urgently require a certain measure of naval force as a political power factor."[22] He saw Great Britain as the primary opponent because Germany was Great Britain's biggest commercial competitor, which made conflict inevitable: "We must undoubtedly in the next century get into a conflict with England at some point on the globe, be it from economic rivalry or as a result of colonial friction."[23]

Tirpitz advocated seizing command of the oceans through a decisive battle at sea. As a consequence, he emphasized the development of battleships. He attached little importance to other classes of ships and harshly attacked navy officers who emphasized the development and use of cruisers (these were faster and had longer ranges than battleships, but had less armor and firepower). He saw cruisers as useful for resolving colonial disputes or repressing colonial rebellions, yet fundamentally useless in giving Germany command of the seas. His view of submarines was even more negative. In 1904, he called them "second class weapons" that could only be used in certain locations; the navy's submarine fleet was merely "a museum of experiments" and submarines could only be used in localized conflicts.[24]

Yet his concept of using a battleship-based fleet to challenge British naval hegemony raised two issues: (1) Could Germany actually catch up with British naval power? and (2) How could Germany respond to the fact that its naval expansion (which was directed at Great Britain) raised the likelihood that Britain might launch a preemptive attack?

Tirpitz had a series of responses to these questions. First, he argued that German naval strength did not need to equal British naval strength. Once German naval power reached a certain level, the Royal Navy—even though it could still defeat the German fleet—would suffer such losses in any battle with Germany that it could no longer respond to the naval challenge from Russia and France, and thus lose command of the seas.[25] This risk would be so high that it would prevent Great Britain from launching a preemptive attack. Tirpitz's notion became known as his famous "risk theory." Second, Germany enjoyed the advantage of concentrated forces. From the very beginning, Tirpitz rejected the notion of seizing complete command of the ocean from Great Britain. In an 1897 memorandum, he proposed that German naval strength be concentrated between "Heligoland (the German naval base in the North Sea) and the River Thames." His reasoning was that, although Great Britain had the largest fleet in the world, that fleet was dispersed throughout the various oceans. Its naval strength in its home waters, particularly in the North Sea, was limited; a German concentration of naval forces in that region could result in a local superiority that would threaten the British isles themselves: "The lever of our [World Policy] was the North Sea; it influenced the entire globe without us needing to be directly engaged in any other place."[26] Third, tactics could also help Germany cut into British naval superiority. Historically, the British tended to adopt close shore blockades as a strategy—naval commanders such as Sir Francis Drake and Admiral Horatio Nelson had used such tactics in the past. Naval weapons, particularly torpedoes and mines, had advanced greatly by the late nineteenth century, however. Tirpitz believed that these technological improvements would allow the German Navy to wear away at the superiority of the British fleet in coastal waters. The geography of the North Sea, moreover, was favorable to the German fleet's launching a counterattack against a British blockade in a future conflict. This would quickly change the balance of forces on the ocean. Fourth, it was completely possible for German naval power to exceed that of Great Britain. General opinion inside Germany was that Great Britain would never cede command of the ocean and thus, once an arms race between the two countries began, British naval power would continue to exceed Germany's. Tirpitz disagreed with this assessment. His reasoning was that although Great Britain could lead Germany in ship-building, its lack of military conscription would mean that eventually it would not have enough sailors for these new ships. Tirpitz explained: "However many ships [Great Britain] built, crews for them would be absent. We, on the other hand, could with the annual draft of 20,000 recruits into the navy build up a strong reserve in trained crews and finally man the same number of ships as the English."[27]

Of course, Tirpitz also recognized that before the Germany Navy became truly strong, there would be a "danger zone." During that period, the German Navy would have grown to the point that it provoked Great Britain, but would not be strong enough to actually resist a British attack. Britain, in order to protect its command of the ocean, might launch a preemptive strike, thus killing the German Navy in its cradle. Tirpitz estimated that the German fleet would be in danger of a "Copenhagen-style" strike until 1914–1915, with the period of greatest danger coming between 1905 and 1906.[28] As a consequence, he proposed that Germany maintain a low posture while building the navy, do its best not to alarm Great Britain, and keep the fleet's scale and mission a secret: it was something about which "one can certainly think, at times must [think], but which really cannot be written down."[29] Moreover, the navy would require the assistance of German diplomacy to maintain good relations with Great Britain until Germany had safely passed out of the danger zone. At that point, Germany would have an effective deterrent or even a fleet that equaled the Royal Navy. Bernhard von Bülow, the secretary of state for foreign affairs and future chancellor, fully grasped this: "In view of our naval inferiority, we must operate so carefully, like the caterpillar before it has grown into the butterfly."[30]

The Flaws of Tirpitz's Theory and the Innate Insufficiency of the German Navy

As related above, Tirpitz's theories and his plans appear tightly interwoven and interlocked. Yet, assessed carefully, mistakes and strategic flaws become apparent. Several are worthy of note. First, the entire plan is permeated with notions of "absolute security." Bismarck, as mentioned above, was absolutely opposed to this concept. For a rising great power, the pursuit of "absolute security" necessarily results in absolute insecurity. Germany already had the world's foremost army, thus its quest for a powerful navy would definitely cause worries in Great Britain, France, and Russia. It would stimulate these countries to take countermeasures, resulting ultimately in a powerful anti-German coalition.

Second, his plans overlooked the particular characteristics of Germany's geography. Germany is located in the center of Europe, and shared land boundaries with three great powers: France, Russia, and Austria-Hungary. On the north it faced the ocean. This configuration of boundaries meant that Germany would simultaneously face threats from the land and the sea, thus it would be difficult to concentrate enough power to seize command of the ocean. Moreover, the ocean on Germany's border was not open sea; instead, there were straits, island chains, and other natural obstructions to naval movements. During wartime, this would be easy for an enemy navy to blockade. Mahan himself pointed out that "if a nation be so situated that it is neither forced to defend itself by land nor induced to seek extension of its territory by way of the land, it has, by the very unity of its aim directed upon the sea, an advantage as compared with a people one of whose boundaries is continental."[31] The German Navy's opponent, Great Britain, was just such a country. Mahan once compared Great Britain and Germany's oceanic potential, and pointed specifically to Germany's disadvantageous geographical position:

> The dilemma of Great Britain is that she cannot help commanding the approaches to Germany by the mere possession of the very means essential to her own existence as a state of the first order.... Sea defense for Germany [cannot] be considered complete unless extended through the Channel and as far as Great Britain will have to project hers into the Atlantic. This is Germany's initial disad-

> vantage of position, to be overcome only by adequate superiority of numbers.[32]

Tirpitz and his allies may have promoted Mahan's theories, but consciously or not, they ignored the limiting factors on Mahan's notions of command of the sea. Thus, to a great extent, they used Mahan as little more than a propaganda tool.[33]

Third, his assessment of the situation was overly optimistic. Strategy is a multi-player game where everyone moves at the same time; it requires a grasp of complex interactions. Tirpitz, however, saw it as a simple, static-sum operation. He did not even think that Great Britain would quickly enter into a naval arms race with Germany. He completely underestimated Great Britain's determination and sensitivity regarding control of the seas. He thought that some tactical sleight of hand would be enough to keep from alarming Great Britain, thus allowing Germany to pass safely through its danger zone. Moreover, Tirpitz always assumed that Germany could maintain good relations with Russia and might even rebuild ties with France. To a certain extent, he believed as Wilhelm II did: that it was possible to construct a Russian-German-French Continental League. These opinions formed the preconditions for his so-called risk theory. Chancellor Bülow later described Tirpitz as lacking political vision and an understanding of the finer points of international relations, thus leading "him to entertain occasional illusions about Russia and even about France, countries in which he sought support against England, the land he especially hated."[34]

These innate errors essentially sealed the fate of the Tirpitz Plan. In a certain sense, the path of Germany's rise as a great power was determined by them, too. Regardless of whether German policymakers were willing or not, the Tirpitz Plan propelled Germany to play a role in the reenactment of the historical conflict between a rising power and an established hegemon. The more successful German naval expansion proved to be, the greater the danger that this game entailed.

The First and Second Naval Laws and Their Impact

The First Naval Law

For the development of the modern German Navy, 1897 and 1898 were two critical years. During the former, Tirpitz was promoted to command the Imperial Navy Office; during the latter, under Tirpitz's influence, the same Reichstag that had rejected the 1896 navy budget passed a much larger bill, later called the First Naval Law. This bill clearly reflected Tirpitz's vision of naval expansion centered on building battleships. It called for Germany to build 19 battleships, 8 armored cruisers, 12 heavy cruisers, and 30 light cruisers by April 1, 1904. The heavy cruisers would be automatically replaced every 25 years and the light cruisers every 15. Construction costs could not exceed 408,900,000 marks. The totals mandated in the bill included the 12 pre-existing battleships and other ships already built, so the final mandate for new construction in the years 1898–1904 were 7 battleships, 2 heavy cruisers, and 7 light cruisers.

Comparatively speaking, a fleet of this power would be enough to defend against the navies of France and Russia, but would not threaten British naval dominance. Tirpitz had been foresighted on this issue. He understood clearly that even though the German people supported naval expansion, it would create a domestic and international backlash if the first step was too large. Moreover, Germany's existing shipbuilding and military production capabilities would have difficulty supporting the construction of a larger fleet, and the capacity of the ports was limited. Thus, the pace of expansion in the First Naval Law was not huge, but provided a foundation for a long-term plan. Tirpitz wrote as much in a letter to the Chief of the Navy Cabinet, Admiral Senden: "If it is possible to get the bill passed, then in the year 1905 very good ground will have been gained to undertake the further rounding out of the navy."[35] More important, the First Naval Law could become a legal precedent for the planned expansion of the German Navy, particularly by mandating the lifespan of particular classes of ships. This would transform naval expansion from being haphazard, as it had been in the past, to being the result of methodical, planned policy. Chancellor Bülow's comments hit this point on the mark:

> The first fleet law switched the naval policy to an entirely new track. Previously new constructions had been ordered from time to time and in part approved, but the navy lacked the firm foundation that the army possessed in the required strength of its formations. Only by determining the useful life of ships and its effective strength in serviceable ships did the navy become a firm part of our national fighting forces.[36]

This bill was not without its opponents, however. At the foreign ministry, Friedrich von Holstein, even with his narrow vision of the world and inability to understand Bismarck's subtlety, could clearly see the drawbacks of the Tirpitz Plan. Holstein fundamentally opposed naval expansion and Wilhelm

II's single-minded devotion to a large navy. He complained that "the Kaiser wants a fleet like that of England…and wants to direct his entire domestic policy to that end."[37] He considered Tirpitz's notion of expanding the navy while avoiding conflict with Great Britain to be impossible. In a letter to the German ambassador in London, he argued that naval expansion, moreover, would remove one of Germany's most effective tools for dealing with Russia—namely, the threat of Anglo-German reconciliation.[38] Holstein's opinions were quashed, however, as both Tirpitz and Bülow had the kaiser's support. He was left to complain in his private correspondence.

Dissent from Tirpitz's ideas existed even within the navy. A retired naval officer, Viktor Valois, penned a book-length criticism of Tirpitz's strategic concept of a battleship-centered fleet. Valois argued that Tirpitz's theory was actually a call for seizing command of the ocean through naval combat, even though Germany would continue to have a weaker navy than Great Britain for a long time. He thought that the objective of the German fleet should not be to seize command of the sea, but instead to exist on the sea as "a fleet in being" that could attack the enemy's weakest point when needed: the large number of inadequately protected merchant vessels. According to his point of view, this strategy could inflict maximum losses on Great Britain, thus leading the British to seek peace. Tirpitz took strong measures against dissent from within the navy and banned the publication of Valois's book. In 1899, Tirpitz received the right to censor materials from Wilhelm II and used it to increase pressure on alternative views from within the navy officer corps. Arguably, by 1900, there was no longer any force within Germany that could stop Tirpitz's plans.

The Second Naval Law and Great Britain's Reaction

As early as the summer of 1898, just a few months after the first bill had passed, Tirpitz began to mull proposals for increased naval production before the first bill ended in 1905. In November 1898, he suggested to the kaiser an increased pace of naval construction in 1902. In September 1899, he presented a new plan for naval construction to the kaiser that he planned to submit to the Reichstag in 1901 or 1902. This new plan called for Germany to possess a navy of 45 battleships, 11–12 heavy cruisers, and 24 light cruisers when the plan was complete in 1920. The effectiveness of Tirpitz's propaganda and organizational work, however, outstripped even his own expectations. After the First Naval Law was passed, popular enthusiasm for the navy increased, and this new plan received strong support from the public. Moreover, the international situation was also favorable to further naval expansion. The 1898 Spanish-American

War had attracted great popular interest in Germany. As a European country, German opinion naturally inclined toward Spain, but Spain's poor performance provided a great stimulus for German naval advocates. Many thought that Spain was humiliated by the United States precisely because it had a weak navy. In January 1900, the Royal Navy impounded a German ocean liner near South Africa on suspicion that it was carrying contraband. This high-handed act caused a loud outcry in Germany, and some who had originally opposed naval expansion began to change their minds. Chancellor Hohenlohe, for instance, had opposed passage of a Second Naval Law in 1899 but began to support it in January 1900, claiming, "we cannot subject ourselves to the danger of experiencing at the hands of England the fate of Spain at the hands of North America, and it is clear that the English only wait to jump on us."[39]

Under these circumstances, Tirpitz's plan for naval expansion was naturally put forward earlier than planned. On June 14, 1900, the Reichstag passed the Second Naval Law during a moment of intense anti-British sentiment nationwide. This plan was smaller than the one Tirpitz had considered in 1899, but was still nearly twice as large as the increase represented by the First Naval Law. Under it, the number of battleships would increase to 38. According to the law, 2 of these 38 battleships would be designated flagships, 4 would be for a reserve fleet, and the remaining 32 would be divided into 4 squadrons. Unlike the First Naval Law, the Second Naval Law did not impose any financial limits on the construction. The preface of the law itself explained that it was directed at Great Britain and even mentioned the risk theory:

> It is not necessary that the battle fleet at home is equal to that of the greatest naval power. In general this naval power would not be in a position to concentrate its entire naval forces against us. Even if it succeeds in encountering us with a superior force, the destruction of the German fleet would so much damage the enemy that his own position as a world power would be brought into question.[40]

If the First Naval Law was a signal that Germany was sprinting toward status as a world naval power, the Second Naval Law represented an all-out charge for naval expansion. This naturally attracted British attention.

In December 1900, British naval intelligence estimated that the Second Naval Law would allow Germany to outstrip Russian naval power by 1906. Thus the Royal Navy's standard of being as powerful as the next two navies combined would now need to be based on the size of the French and German

Navies. Naval defense of Great Britain itself needed to be beefed up as well, in order to counter the German fleet.[41] Tirpitz's hope of expanding Germany's navy without alarming Great Britain had already proved a failure. In November 1901, Lord Selborne, the First Lord of the Admiralty, drafted a memo for the cabinet that, while continuing to use the standard of measuring the Royal Navy against the combined fleets of France and Russia, pointed to the threat arising from Germany: "[Germany would be] in a commanding position if ever we find ourselves at war with France and Russia."[42] Five months later, Selborne admitted to Chancellor of the Exchequer Arthur Balfour that when he submitted his memorandum, he had "not then realized the intensity of the hatred of the German nation to this country" and that he tended to favor a reevaluation of the Royal Navy's plans for Germany.[43]

Selborne presented the British ambassador in Germany with four questions on April 22, 1902: Is it safe for Great Britain to take only France and Russia into account (and thus disregard Germany) when formulating plans for British naval construction? Is German naval expansion directed at Great Britain? How would the German government and people respond if Great Britain were engaged in a war with France and Russia? What are German policies toward Holland and the Dutch Navy? The ambassador, Frank Lascelles, responded to each of the four queries: The Royal Navy should be at least as strong as the combined navies of the next two strongest naval powers, regardless of whether Germany is one of those powers or not; in a war between Great Britain and the Franco-Russian alliance, Germany would observe and hope for both sides to injure the other, but would not permit the French and the Russians to gain an excessive advantage; although Dutch independence could be assured, a portion of the German population did hope to annex Holland and its overseas colonies. The response to the second question, however, was more complex. In the text of his reply, Lascelles stated that German naval expansion was not directed against Great Britain, but in a supplemental reply claimed that, after a discussion with the naval attaché, Arthur Ewart, he believed that "the German Navy is professedly aimed at that of the greatest naval Power—us."[44] In August 1902, the British Parliamentary Secretary at the Admiralty, H. O. Arnold-Forster, toured Germany, where he was shocked by the pace of naval construction. He quickly reported this back to Great Britain. On this basis, the Admiralty began a reassessment of the objectives and effects of Germany naval construction. Selborne presented the cabinet with a memorandum on the 1903–1904 navy budget on October 17, 1902, which incorporated an assessment of Germany's new navy:

> I am convinced that the great new German navy is being carefully built up from the point of view of a war with us.... It cannot be designed for the purpose of playing a leading part in a future war between Germany and France and Russia.... Lascelles...is equally convinced that in deciding on a naval policy we cannot safely ignore the malignant hatred of the German people or the manifest design of the German Navy.[45]

This conclusion did not lead to an immediate, concrete British response. At the end of 1902, Great Britain was not anxious to revise its naval policies radically, as disputes with Russia had reached a crescendo and half-hearted negotiations with Germany were still underway. The "two-power standard" thus continued to reference the French and Russian Navies.[46] Yet preparations directed against the German Navy were also begun. In March 1903, Great Britain established a North Sea Fleet, to be based on Scotland's eastern coast. Enormous changes took place in 1904, as Japan's victory over Russia freed Great Britain's hand to respond to German naval expansion. First, the Admiralty officially changed the two-power standard to France and Germany in February 1904. In the summer of that year, the Admiralty drafted the first set of plans for war with Germany. Next, Great Britain began to contemplate the possibility of a preemptive strike against Germany. In November 1904, articles advocating a Copenhagen-style preemptive strike on Germany before it became a naval power ran in several British newspapers. The idea circulated within British policymaking circles, too; new First Lord of the Admiralty and Navy Chief of Staff Jackie Fisher proposed this notion to the king himself.[47] Fisher even took concrete actions in support of his suggestion. At the end of 1904, he redeployed the Royal Navy, moving forces from the Mediterranean to the home islands until the British enjoyed decisive naval superiority over the Germans in the North Sea. Other naval officers, such as Admiral C. C. P. Fitzgerald, echoed his call for a preemptive attack on German naval facilities. In 1905, Admiralty Civil Lord Arthur Lee indirectly warned Germany that in event of a war, "the Royal Navy would get its blow in first, before the other side had time even to read in the papers that war had been declared."[48] Third, Great Britain expressed sensitivity about, and attention to, German naval expansion, in hopes of influencing German policy. In 1905, British papers printed an essay (perhaps inspired by First Sea Lord Fisher) suggesting that "the frontier of the British Empire [in the North Sea] has been threatened by the growth of the German Navy, and it is as natural that Great Britain should safeguard her interests in this direction as that France, Russia, and Germany should patrol their land frontiers with troops." Selborne offered a similar assessment to one of Wilhelm II's associates: "What would the German War Office say if there were suddenly created on the German land frontier a new Army, first class in quality, which bore the same proportionate strength to the German Army as the German Navy does to the British Navy?"[49]

Tirpitz's hope of expanding the German Navy without alarming Great Britain thus proved entirely untenable. Great Britain was not only extremely sensitive to German naval construction, but also the moment the international situation permitted, it sent clear signals to Germany. Great Britain was even heavy-handedly prepared to settle the issue through force, this stoking fears within Germany of a Copenhagen-style attack.

German Fears of a Copenhagen-style Attack

British actions in 1904, particularly Fisher's redeployment of the Royal Navy, made Germany nervous. The international situation—the formation of the Anglo-French Entente and the diminishment of the Russian Navy at Japan's hands—provided an ideal opportunity for Great Britain to launch a preemptive strike against the German Navy. Within Great Britain, anti-German feeling ran high both among the populace and within government. A war with Germany that entailed little risk might receive robust support. Thus, Germany had reason to fear a Copenhagen-style attack.

Even more important, once the Russo-Japanese War began, Great Britain, as Japan's ally, began close surveillance of Russian naval activity. Germany, in a bid to build better relations with Russia, actively supported Russia and provided supplies to the Russian Navy. Germany and Great Britain thus were already potential adversaries on the sea. In the latter half of 1904, Russia's position in East Asia reached a state of crisis; in October, the Russian Baltic Fleet set sail to aid the Russian Army in East Asia. Fear of Japan ran rampant in the Russian military, and rumors circulated that a secret Japanese fleet was already operating near the North Sea. On the night of October 21, a Russian fleet near the Dogger Bank in the North Sea mistook several British fishing vessels for Japanese warships. In its confusion, the Russian warships sank a number of the fishing vessels, creating an international crisis. Under these circumstances, Germany naturally felt significant British pressure, and relations between the two countries grew tense. On October 1, 1904, the German ambassador in London reported that British domestic opinion saw Germany as the principal enemy and that a Dogger Bank–like incident between German and British ships might unleash popular passions that the British government could not control.[50] On November 17, the German naval attaché in Great Britain reported that the British fleet was preparing for war. German policymakers thus worried about the potential for a British preemptive strike. On November 20, Wilhelm II ordered the navy to make preparations to repel a British attack in the spring of 1905. On December 5, Holstein, a firm opponent of the naval expansion program, wrote that he now feared the possibility of an Anglo-German war that begins with a British attack.[51] In early December, the Royal Navy detained a German collier from the Hamburg-America Line that supplied coal to the Russian Navy. At the same time, the Royal Navy recalled its fleet from East Asia and cancelled all leaves. Fears of a "Copenhagen" deepened in Germany, where many thought these moves presaged a British attack. The commander of one German naval base sent a secret report to Tirpitz, predicting that a British attack might be imminent, and claiming that "England's war aim is to destroy the German merchant and battle fleets…the moment is favorable for carrying these aims out." In 1907, rumors that Lord Fisher would lead a sneak attack abounded. Reports of "Fisher is coming!" spread throughout German port cities, particularly Kiel, and created a widespread panic. Some people even kept their children out of school for two days.[52]

Fears of becoming another Copenhagen stimulated the further expansion of the German fleet. On December 21, 1904, the kaiser called a meeting with Chancellor Bülow, ambassador to Great Britain Paul Wolff Metternich, Admiral Tirpitz, and Army Chief of Staff Schlieffen. Tirpitz proposed a new Naval Law; none of the other participants, except Metternich, opposed this idea. This time, however, Tirpitz acted with greater care in order to avoid inciting the British. For example, he proposed increasing the quality, rather than quantity, of German ships, thus the budget would increase without the number of ships increasing. In his own words, "The bill is deliberately set up so that it does not look like much, but requests more money than the fleet law of 1900."[53] Tirpitz, however, opposed the kaiser's and the chancellor's insistence on speeding up the pace of construction. One of his most important reasons for this was to avoid obviously challenging Great Britain:

> The fact that Germany would in the next four years start building sixteen ships of 18,000 tons and, further, the realization that England would in the future have to reckon with the presence of 50–60 first-class German ships of the line would effect such a shift in the actual power factors that even a calm and understanding English policy *must* come to the realization that such an opponent must be knocked

> down before he has achieved a military strength so dangerous for England as a world power. The prospect of war in the next four years before a single one of the new ships of the line is ready would be greatly increased.[54]

By 1906, however, Tirpitz could no longer remain patient. He believed that German naval expansion needed to be speeded up and the production of battleships increased from 3 to 4 a year. By December 1906, he had already decided that German production needed to outpace Britain's, regardless of the effects of this on relations between the two countries. In other words, Tirpitz had decided to openly challenge Britain's command of the seas and to engage in an open arms race. He began to transform himself from a long-term, systematic planner of naval expansion into a supporter of an arms race. He became ever more single-minded and ever more heedless of the cost. Victory in the arms race became an end in itself, rather than a means to achieve other objectives.

One primary cause for this transformation was that the British began building dreadnoughts.

The Dreadnought Race and the Beginnings of Comprehensive Anglo-German Naval Competition

On December 3, 1906, the first "all-big-gun" battleship entered the service in the Royal Navy as the dreadnought. This vessel would lend its name to an entire class of similar warships. The dreadnought marked a significant milestone in naval history. It also elevated Anglo-German naval competition to a higher level.

The Origin of Anglo-German Dreadnought Competition

After World War I, Tirpitz claimed that First Sea Lord Fisher's decision to begin building dreadnoughts in 1905–1906 was unwise, as it negated Britain's advantage in traditional warships and gave other great powers the opportunity to catch up.[55]

This, however, is not an accurate assessment of the situation. Realistically, Great Britain did not have many options when it came to choices about whether or not to build a new type of super-battleship. First, the Japanese victory over the Russian fleet at Tsushima had been clearly linked to the greater speed of its fleet, its use of new high-explosive gunpowder, its fire control, and its guns, particularly its 30.5-centimeter cannon. These had already become trends in naval warfare development. Second, many other naval powers had the desire to build "super-battleships." After the Russo-Japanese War, the Japanese government, based on its wartime experience, began work on two 20-thousand-ton battleships. The United States made similar plans in 1904. In March 1904, Germany designed an all-big-gun battleship, Type 10-A, that would displace 14 thousand tons of water; in October 1905, a Type 10-C that displaced 17 thousand tons of water and was armed with 8 same-caliber guns was proposed. This would the embryonic form of Germany's first dreadnought, the SMS *Nassau*.

Thus, Great Britain's decision to move first to construct super-battleships was a natural choice that would allow it to retain its command of the seas. In October 1904, First Sea Lord Fisher established a design committee charged with planning this new kind of ship. In January 1905, Plan H was developed for a ship that would displace 17 thousand tons of water, have a maximum speed of 24 knots, and carry 12 standard-size (30.5 centimeter) guns. The construction of this ship occurred under strict secrecy and efficiency. Work on the keel began on October 2, 1905; the ship was completed by October 3 of the next year, and entered service on December 3. The speed of construction was record-breaking. Arguably, the construction process alone would have had a shocking effect. The dreadnought's performance, however, proved even more stunning. It displaced 17,900 tons of water and was the first turbine-powered large warship. Its most revolutionary aspect, however, was its weaponry. The dreadnought marked a complete departure from the old style of mixing guns of different calibers. Its ten main guns (divided into 5 pairs of 2) were all 30.5-centimeter, while the remaining 22 smaller bore guns were 7.6-centimeter. The placement of these guns was also revolutionary: one of the main pairs of guns sat at the fore, two others at the aft, and the two remaining on either side of the ship. Although the dreadnought had two fewer main guns than earlier classes of battleships, when firing from the side it could bring four pairs of main guns to bear, equaling twice the firepower of earlier ships. In addition to this battleship, Great Britain also built a super-cruiser. In 1906, the design committee proposed Type E, which became the *Invincible* class of cruisers. Construction on the first of this class, the HMS *Invincible*, began in April 1906 and was completed by March 1908. It displaced 17 thousand tons of water and was armed with 8 30.5-centimeter guns divided into 4 pairs of two (one on the bow, one on the stern, and one on each side). This type of cruiser was also called a battle cruiser. In 1909, these ships were grouped with battleships in the category of "capital ships"; by 1912, this new name enjoyed wide acceptance in the Royal Navy.[56]

The construction of the dreadnought was absolutely not the opportunity that Tirpitz later claimed; it was a challenge. Strategically, if Germany followed Great Britain and began constructing dreadnoughts, then its intention of challenging Great Britain for command of the seas would be completely revealed. Further dissimulation or excuses would be useless: Great Britain and Germany would be engaged in an open arms race. The technical demands of dreadnought construction required a complete, and extremely expensive, overhaul of existing German canals, ports, and shipbuilding facilities. Yet at this time, construction of Germany's High Seas Fleet was already well underway. According to the German Navy Office, if the pace of German and British construction did not change, then Britain's lead in the balance of naval forces, which had been 3:1 in 1903, would be reduced to 1.8:1, or perhaps 1.7:1, by 1930. This would fulfill the requirements of Tirpitz's risk theory: "this is not adequate superiority to deliver a successful blow against Germany and to set up an effective blockade.... England can hardly think of concentrating her entire fleet in the German Bight of the North Sea without running the danger of risking her power position."[57] From the perspective of Tirpitz, if Germany did not respond to this challenge now, then all of the work invested in developing its navy since 1897 would have been wasted.

Through the efforts of Tirpitz and others, the Reichstag passed a naval amendment in May 1906 that began a new round of naval construction. In addition to authorizing 6 cruisers, the amendment also earmarked 9.4 billion marks for construction of dreadnoughts and the modification of canals, ports, and dry docks. In total, this amendment allocated 35 percent more in funding than the Second Naval Law of 1900, and mandated the construction of two dreadnoughts and one battle cruiser a year.

The first class of German dreadnoughts, the *Nassau*, comprised 4 ships: the *Nassau*, *Posen*, *Rheinland*, and *Westfalen*. Their keels were laid between June and August 1907, and by 1908 the boats had been launched, with final construction complete by 1909–1910. Each vessel cost 37.4 million marks and displaced 18,870 tons of water. These German ships had thicker armor than their British equivalents (300 millimeters as opposed to 279 millimeters) and used a better watertight compartment design. In terms of firepower, however, a vast gap remained: German dreadnoughts fielded 28-centimeter main guns, smaller than the 30.5-centimeter guns mounted on British dreadnoughts. Moreover, due to unresolved technical problems, the arrangement of the German dreadnought's six turrets was one on the bow, one on the stern, and two on each side. Thus, German ships could only fire four pairs of guns in a side volley broadside and could not conduct a British-style "super" salvo. Moreover, the first class of German dreadnoughts did not use turbine engines for propulsion (Tirpitz considered them usable only on cruisers, and until 1905 the Navy Office's construction department thought they were not appropriate for battleships). This, combined with their thicker armor, made German ships slower than British ones, with a maximum speed of 20 (as opposed to 22) knots.[58]

Germany's Second Naval Amendment of 1908 and the British Naval Scare

The Anglo-German dreadnought competition entered a particularly heated phase in 1908. Great Britain still maintained its technological lead. In 1908, Germany began construction of its second-generation dreadnoughts, the *Heligoland* class, which displaced 22,800 tons of water, had a maximum speed of 21 knots, and carried six turrets with 30.5-centimeter guns (one on the bow, one on the stern, and two on each side). The placement of the guns, however, had been inherited from the *Nassau* class and thus only four turrets could fire a broadside. By 1909, Great Britain began construction of a new class of dreadnoughts, the *Orion* class, with 34.3-centimeter guns, once again seizing the lead from Germany. These guns were arranged in a completely new "center line" configuration, in which five turrets were arranged along the midline of the deck, two in the bow, two in the stern, and a middle turret in a raised location. This allowed all of the guns to fire a broadside at the same time, maximizing firepower and thus beginning the age of super-dreadnoughts. In response, Germany released a third generation of dreadnoughts, the *Kaiser* class, whose turbine engines could reach a maximum speed of 22 knots and whose main guns were arranged in a new order. Although Germans were not able to mimic the British "center line configuration," this type of dreadnought displayed an arrangement of five turrets, with one on the bow, two on the stern, and one on each side. The placement of the side guns was such that each could shoot on the other side, too.[59] Yet, on the whole, this class, too, lagged behind Great Britain's newest design.

Despite this, German dreadnought production generated feelings of intense pressure in Great Britain. In the second half of 1907, Germany released a draft of a second naval amendment that indicated Germany planned to quicken the pace of dreadnought construction. This aroused a high level of alarm in Great Britain. The German ambassador to London reported in January 1908 that it was commonly held belief in Great Britain that German naval expansion was Britain's "greatest crisis since the Napoleonic Wars."[60] The Reichstag passed the Second Naval Amendment in March, mandating an increase in dreadnought production from three to four a year (as a temporary measure—the law also stipulated that the rate would drop to two a year between 1912 and 1917). Three of these vessels would be battleships and the other a battle cruiser. The amendment also reduced the service lifespan of battleships and cruisers from 25 to 20 years in order to speed the pace at which new ships replaced older models. In Great Britain, this law inspired a famous "naval panic." The pace of construction mandated by this law—three battleships and one battle cruiser a year—meant that in four years Germany would have 16 dreadnought battleships. British plans called for two dreadnoughts in 1908, eight in 1909, and five each year in 1910 and 1911, for a total of 20. This would leave Great Britain with only a narrow advantage of 5:4 in dreadnoughts. Tirpitz furthermore ordered German shipyards to stockpile large supplies of metal, particularly nickel. At the same time, he signed contracts for the construction of a battleship and a battle cruiser before receiving authorization from the Reichstag. This raised fears in Great Britain that German construction might proceed quicker than the publically announced pace. One historian noted that "henceforth, the British admiralty had to base their plans on Germany's potential shipbuilding capacity, not on her published program."[61] This undoubtedly intensified Britain's naval scare. At this point, the Anglo-German naval competition had become a classic arms race. It had also become a security dilemma in the full sense of the term: the development of greater forces generated greater insecurity, which in turn created the need for more forces, thus creating a vicious cycle.

Under the impetus of the naval scare, Great Britain began to accelerate the pace of its naval production. "We want eight and we won't wait!" became a popular slogan. Yet there were those in the British government who disagreed. The Admiralty hoped to raise the original annual rate of four vessels to a new rate of six vessels. The left wing of the Liberal Party opposed this 50 percent increase. In the end, the parliament compromised: the original rate of four ships remained unchanged, but if German actions warranted, another four could be added. The British government proposed joint inspections of each nation's shipbuilding facilities to the Germans, in order to assess German behavior. This was, of course, rejected by Germany. The kaiser himself remarked, "The British must be crazy!" Parliament thereupon authorized the construction for four additional dreadnoughts on March 29. In response, Winston Churchill commented, "The Admiralty had demanded six ships, the economists offered four: and we finally compromised on eight."[62]

Germany responded with a fourth-generation dreadnought, the *Koenig* class, totaling four vessels. Keels were laid between October 1911 and May 1912. The ships entered service in August and September 1914. On average, each cost 45 million marks. Warships in this class displaced 25,800 tons of water, reached speeds of 21 knots, and carried five pairs of 30.5-centimenter guns arranged in a "center line" configuration. Yet even this class did not change Germany's losing position in the dreadnought competition. Arguably, the strides taken by Great Britain in 1909 were so great that Germany essentially already could not catch up. The "danger zone" anticipated by Tirpitz had lengthened. Originally, he had calculated that the greatest danger of a British preemptive strike would come in 1904–1905, with the danger decreasing after that period. He no longer held that belief by 1908. Instead, another problem rose to the fore that caused great difficulties for German naval expansion: finances.

German Domestic Divisions over Dreadnought Construction

The dreadnought competition was a classic example of an arms race. Both sides committed astronomical (according to the standards of the day) amounts of money, and enormous fiscal pressures in both countries limited naval construction. This situation was more severe in Germany.

Great Britain's shipbuilding industry and nautical design capabilities exceeded Germany's. Thus, even though each of the three generations of British dreadnoughts were more advanced than previous models, each also cost less than their predecessors. A first-generation dreadnought cost £1.783 million, a second-generation £1.765 million, and a third-generation £1.754 million. Germany experienced the reverse: a first-generation dreadnought cost 37.4 million marks, a second-generation 46.19 million marks, and a third-generation cost slightly less at 45 million marks. Within three years, the cost of a dreadnought had risen by 17.2 percent. By 1909, Germany had spent 20 percent more on dreadnoughts than Great Britain had. The cost of German battle cruisers, too, rose more quickly than the cost for British ones: within four years, the price tag had risen by 53.3 percent. The comparable figure for Great Britain was 23.7 percent. During the period between 1906 and the outbreak of war in 1914, German naval expenditures roles from 233.4 million marks to 478.96 million marks, for an increase of 105 percent over nine years. British naval expenditures only rose 28 percent in that period. Even more important, Germany (unlike Great Britain) could not concentrate solely on naval matters. Geography dictated that it had to maintain a strong army, too.

As a result, total military expenditures became a heavy fiscal burden. In 1905, Germany's military budget of 928.61 million marks was 35 percent less than Great Britain's 1.25726-billion mark budget. By 1914, Germany spent 2.24563 billion marks, exceeding Britain's expenditures of 1.6487 billion marks by 40 percent.

Although Germany had already surpassed Great Britain in steel and chemical production by the early twentieth century, its overall level of affluence still lagged behind. Under these circumstances, the dreadnought race would naturally severely strain Germany's finances. When Germany passed the Second Amendment to the Naval Law in 1908, the government was already 500 million marks in debt. During the period from the enunciation of the Tirpitz Plan in 1897 to the outbreak of war in 1914, naval expansion had added 1.04070 billion marks to the national debt. Arguably, Germany's tax collection system was hard-pressed to support the arms race from the beginning of the dreadnought competition in 1906. Once attempts to fundamentally restructure the tax system met with great resistance in the Reichstag, dreadnought production faced a crisis. Objectively speaking, these fiscal pressures were not fundamental problems for the Tirpitz Plan, nor were they the only reason that German policymakers began to oppose the naval arms race, but they do reveal a fundamental issue: Germany could not win this arms race. In 1908, Albert Ballin, the director of the Hamburg-America Line and friend of the kaiser, recognized: "We cannot let ourselves in for a Dreadnought competition with the much richer English."[63]

Among German policymakers, opposition to the Tirpitz Plan had been growing. Generally, those who held this view thought that the naval arms race with Great Britain was unwinnable, and the determination to expand the navy not only deepened the hostility between Great Britain and Germany, but also harmed Germany's diplomatic position. This had become apparent with the progress of events from the 1904 Anglo-French Entente to the 1907 Anglo-Russian Convention. Moreover, the claim that Germany needed a large navy also fell under suspicion. As hostility between Great Britain and Germany grew while German fiscal difficulties increased, some officials began to reconsider the issue of balancing and coordinating the army and the navy, given Germany's specific security environment. Holstein played an important role in this opposition group. Although he had resigned during the First Morocco Crisis, Chancellor Bülow had secretly remained in touch with him and relied on his advice on many foreign policy issues. Around a month after the passage of the First Naval Amendment in 1906, Holstein sent Bülow a memorandum that raised two core issues:

> (1) Can we ever, no matter how great our efforts, achieve naval parity with the combined fleets of England and France? In our own right? By alliance? (2) Will the sum total of German military strength be augmented or relatively diminished by an extreme program of fleet building.... We cannot conduct a war against the English without allies. No allies in sight. Against Japan we might perhaps proceed with America. Our conflicts with other Great Powers will be decided on land.[64]

Arguably, Holstein's questions touched on the crucial issues with the Tirpitz Plan and exerted an influence on Bülow. By 1908, Bülow had begun to change his mind and demanded that Tirpitz slow the pace of naval expansion in order to relax the increasingly intense relationship with Great Britain. He may even have considered reaching a naval agreement with Great Britain.

Faced with the chancellor's opposition, Tirpitz counterattacked. His opinions centered on several points. First, he did not believe that Great Britain could maintain its "two-power standard," and that the ratio of naval forces between the two countries could be 3:2 or 16:10. If Germany caved to Great Britain on the issue of naval construction at this moment, Germany would forever be stuck in the danger zone. Moreover, he considered making concessions to British threats to be tantamount to surrender and German humiliation. Second, the only way to reduce the danger of war with Great Britain was to continue following the construction plan and rely on force to cow Great Britain. Third, his proposal for any naval discussions with Great Britain were that, over the next ten years, Germany would limit itself to three new battleships a year and Britain to four. This 3:4 ratio would be favorable to Germany and would also be at the limits of British fiscal ability.[65]

This time, however, Tirpitz's reasoning did not impress Bülow and other German policymakers. Bülow assumed that Great Britain absolutely would not accept that condition. In the margins of a communication from Tirpitz, he even scrawled: "Then he ought to take it in hand himself! Let him try his luck with the British and see what he can get." [66] Instead, Bülow advocated greater German concessions on naval issues. The German Foreign Ministry generally supported Bülow's position and considered that proposing a 3:4 ratio to Great Britain would be tantamount to declaring war.[67] Tirpitz's hard-line reply was that, in response to British pressure, Germany's best course of action would be "to completely arm itself." He dismissed the notion that slowing the pace of German construction would result in British political concessions and considered British guarantees of neutrality to be meaningless. These conclusions grew from his belief that a British declaration of war was likely and that France and Russia would come to Great Britain's aid.[68] A high-level meeting was held at Bülow's official residence on June 3, 1909, during which the supporters of slowing the pace of naval expansion (including Theobald von Bethmann-Hollweg, who would soon replace Bülow as chancellor; the younger Helmuth von Moltke, the Army Chief of Staff; and Paul Wolff Metternich, ambassador to London) and advocates of continuing the arms race (Tirpitz and the head of the Navy Cabinet) engaged in a heated debate. Tirpitz, who had the kaiser's support, emerged with the upper hand. Not long after the meeting, Bülow was forced to resign. Divisions and arguments over naval expansion continued within the policymaking establishment, growing ever more intense.[69]

The Final Phase of the Tirpitz Plan

Efforts to Slow the Pace of German Naval Expansion

State Secretary for the Interior Bethmann replaced Bülow as chancellor of the German Empire in June 1909. Bethmann, nicknamed "the earthworm," was much more open and guileless than Bülow had been. Historian Gordon Craig provides this fairly balanced assessment of the new chancellor:

> He possessed all the best and worst qualities of the Prussian bureaucracy. He was a careful and energetic administrator, an efficient negotiator, and a man of courage and honor in time of crisis; but, like Caprivi, he lacked creative talent, and his intellectual and political horizons were narrow. His ignorance of foreign affairs was, as Bülow had said, profound, and his knowledge of military problems minimal; and this robbed him of any confidence in two fields that were crucial to Germany's future.[70]

He was one of the able servants of the post-Bismarckian era. Although he was able to recognize the mistakes in German policy, as well as the dangers these mistakes would bring, he was unable to do much about them. Much less was he able to reconstruct a balanced grand strategy. For example, he wrote in a letter about Germany's military expansion that "the whole policy is of a sort that I cannot co-operate with it. But I ask myself again and again whether the situation will not develop even more dangerously if I go and then probably not alone."[71] He was both clear-sighted and weak. As Germany's material power grew stronger while its strategic and decision-making problems grew deeper, he found himself pushed along by events.

Germany's international situation was already tense when Bethmann took office. The 1908–1909 Bosnia Crisis brought the European great powers close to the brink of war. Germany presented Russia with demands that sounded like a final ultimatum. Within German policymaking circles, it was commonly believed that an armed contest between the Austro-German alliance and the Franco-Russian alliance was unavoidable. This inspired some high officials, particularly those in the army and the foreign ministry, to seek a naval accord with Great Britain in order to reduce the tensions in that relationship. Such thoughts had led to the confrontation at Bülow's residence on June 3. Yet even after Bülow's dismissal from office, the army and the foreign ministry stuck to this point of view. In the words of Moltke the younger: "We had no chance whatsoever to fight a war with Britain with any success. An honorable understanding, perhaps on the basis of a slowing down of the building tempo, also appeared desirable to him. Thereby one should not conceal that the failure of attempts to seek an understanding could mean war."[72] This allowed Bethmann, a supporter of this point of view, to play a central role in this faction's efforts to reach some kind of accommodation with Great Britain by limiting naval expansion. This could also potentially result in British neutrality in the event of war. In August 1909, Bethmann's first foreign policy report to the kaiser discussed the possibility of British neutrality "if we are attacked by France and/or Russia, or if we have to assist Austria-Hungary on the strength of our alliance with her, if she is attacked by Russia."[73]

Bethmann's proposals were doomed to reach a dead end. A package deal of this kind clearly benefited Germany; Britain, which was ahead in the naval arms race, would not be inclined to accept it. Even more important, Bethmann was powerless to actually limit German naval armaments, for three important reasons. The first of these was social: naval expansion had become a nationwide movement, and neither the passions of the populace nor the prestige of the throne could accept this sort of end to it. Moreover, naval expansion created a large number of beneficiaries, particularly among the heavy industrialists. In 1912–1913, naval orders accounted for 12 percent of Krupp's business, for a total of 53 million marks.[74] Germany's large shipbuilding plans also affected employment in many other industries. One Foreign Ministry official remarked to the British ambassador that slowing the pace of naval construction would "throw innumerable men on the pavement, without their being able to find work elsewhere."[75] The second reason was political: under the German political system, the government and the military were completely separate; within the military, the army and navy each managed their own affairs. Thus, the chancellor as the head of government had no ability to interfere with naval issues, nor could the army bring any direct influence to bear on the navy. Wilhelm II, the highest authority in the land, supported naval expansion, while Tirpitz and the chief of the Navy Cabinet wielded immense influence in German politics. These factors made it very difficult for opponents of naval expansion to advance their agenda. The third reason was security: after the 1908 naval scare, the Anglo-German naval race had become a classic case of the security dilemma in which the increase in one side's power sparks countermeasures from the other side, creating an ever-increasing sense of insecurity. Within one year, Great Britain laid down the keels for eight battleships. Germany felt increased pressure on its own security, which required strengthening its own naval forces. From there it fell into a vicious cycle of wanting to stop but being unable to.

Thus, the Anglo-German negotiations promoted by Bethmann were rocky from the very start. German policymakers themselves held disparate views on these talks. Tirpitz and other supporters of a continued naval arms race refused to negotiate, and thus made demands that the British were bound to reject. For example, Bethmann hoped to exchange a slowing of German naval expansion for British neutrality in a continental war, yet Tirpitz proposed a dismantlement of the Anglo-French Entente and a 3:2 battleship ratio. The injection of Tirpitz's two demands into the negotiations made it difficult for talks to escape stalemate. For the British, it seemed that Germany plotted to achieve goals at the negotiating table that it could not through the arms race. Germany, at the same time, appeared to hope to overturn the most recent fruits of British diplomacy to nefarious ends.[76] The two sides quickly deadlocked. Great Britain demanded that Germany unconditionally reduce its navy before political reconciliation could be discussed, while Germany demanded that the two sides reach a comprehensive political reconciliation before making any concessions on naval armaments. Fitful negotiations occurred from August 1909 until June 1911 without reaching any conclusion.

Throughout this process, the struggle between the two factions within the German government continued. The 1908 Second Naval Amendment mandated the production of four battleships per year between 1908 and 1912, with the pace to drop to two per year after 1912. Thus, one of Tirpitz's main objectives after 1908 was to remedy the post-1912 deficit by raising production back to three ships annually. He announced two reasons publically. First, once production dropped from four ships to two in 1912, it would be difficult to raise this back to three unless a law was then passed. Second, if such a law was not passed, then the naval gap between Germany and Great Britain would stop shrinking, rendering the previous fourteen years of naval policy a waste.[77] At the same time, Tirpitz moved to obstruct the Anglo-German naval talks. With his support, Captain Wilhelm Widenmann, the German naval attaché in London, acted as a spoiler. Widenmann, for example, would claim that all British proposals were disingenuous and contained concealed ulterior motives. He also told the British that the German objective was to negotiate a 3:2 ratio. Bethmann, in response, saw this as giving the British "incorrect notions concerning the goals which German policy is currently pursuing relative to the question of an accord over the naval armament of the two Powers" and seriously undermining the trust of both sides. The kaiser, however, supported Widenmann. A dispute over the negotiations erupted between Metternich, the ambassador to London, and Widenmann in 1912. Metternich demanded Widenmann's recall, claiming that he harbored excessive hostility toward the British and was creating unnecessary difficulties for the bilateral relationship. Yet, in the end it was Metternich who was recalled. This incident accurately reflects the balance of power between the two groups within German policymaking circles. As the *Frankfurter Zeitung* assessed at the time, Metternich's recall symbolized the complete victory of Tirpitz's naval policy.[78]

The Second Morocco Crisis broke out in July 1911. Tirpitz acutely recognized that the passions unleashed by this crisis created an excellent opportunity to pass a new naval law. Thus he went back to work and proposed a Third Naval Amendment. Yet, at this moment, there was still a small chance of a breakthrough in the Anglo-German naval talks. As the crisis pushed the continent to the edge of war, some in the British government felt that overly tense relations with Germany were a liability, so they pressed for a thaw. Under pressure from the group, Foreign Secretary Edward Grey agreed to further explore naval issues with Germany. Lord Haldane visited Berlin in February 1912, ostensibly on a vacation, to hold talks on naval limitations. Arguably, the British had already made a concession this time: originally, they had insisted that Germany slow the pace of naval expansion before discussing other issues, while they now said that once Germany agreed to reduce its naval plans, a political agreement could be considered (without any promise of neutrality in a war between Germany and France, however) and colonial concessions could be mulled. Yet, from another perspective, the British did not attach too much importance to Haldane's mission. Grey's objectives were mainly to do enough to satisfy demands within his own government to make an effort at improving ties with Germany. In his own words, this mainly entailed "find[ing] out whether Germany's recent overture was serious or not."[79] Yet there was no way for Haldane to see this sort of sincerity. Bethmann and the German Foreign Ministry were anxious for an agreement with Haldane, yet Tirpitz (who was promoting his Third Naval Amendment) resolutely obstructed any substantive talks. Wilhelm II took a dim view of Haldane's visit from the very start. He saw German naval expansion as a purely domestic issue and equated British desires to limit German naval expansion with an interference in German sovereignty. As a result, the Haldane mission ended without an agreement.

The Third Naval Amendment and the End of the Naval Arms Race

Tirpitz's Third Naval Amendment passed the Reichstag in April 1912. This law authorized the construction of three battleships annually between 1912 and 1917, an increase from the previously mandated pace of two vessels a year. It also increased naval personnel by 15,000. At this rate of production, the German Navy would have 41 battleships (one flag ship, with the reminder divided into five squadrons), 28 cruisers (including battle cruisers) and 40 light cruisers. Total naval personnel would reach 100,500 sailors. Most important, this fleet would be maintained at a state of constant war-readiness.[80] The law's passage was a signal victory for Tirpitz, yet it would also be his last. The Second Morocco Crisis may have provided Tirpitz with the opportunity to pass this law, but it also created conditions for restricting naval expansion. During the final years of Bülow's chancellorship and the first years of Bethmann's, one important reason for opposing navy expansion was the need to strengthen the army. Bethmann had even made army expansion a condition for his agreement to navy expansion. Yet, with the strong support of the throne and political momentum generated by Tirpitz, the navy's share of the budget had grown without interruption: in 1898, it was 20 percent the size of the army's budget; in 1903, 34.1 percent; in 1909, 48.5 percent; and in 1911, at its peak, it was 54.8 percent.[81] After the Second Morocco Crisis, German policymakers believed that war was on the horizon. At this moment, the particularities of Germany's geography became policymakers' principal concern: Germany had land as well as maritime boundaries and battles on land would decide the nation's fate.

This consideration favored the army. The Prussian War Minister, Josias von Heeringen, proposed strengthening the existing three army groups in 1911. After Turkey's defeat in the First Balkan War of 1912, Germany lost a potentially powerful ally (the younger Moltke had always held this opinion), and the pressures for army expansion continued to rise rapidly. Heeringen, who feared that a large-scale expansion would damage the army's purity, proposed to Bethmann that the chancellor seek a new army bill. The Reichstag passed this bill in 1913, investing a further 898 million marks in the army and increasing its size by 136,000 soldiers. Thus the army reclaimed the favored position between 1911 and 1913 and increased its size by 175,000 men, or approximately 32 percent.[82] Naval expenditures, compared the army's budget, consequently began to fall: from 1911, when the navy budget equaled 54.8 percent of the army's budget, its share fell to 49.4 percent in 1912 and 32.7 percent in 1913.[83]

Diplomatically, Germany's naval arms race had also found itself at a dead end. After Winston Churchill took over as Lord of the Admiralty in October 1911, British naval policy exhibited greater decisiveness and aggressiveness. In response to Germany's Third Naval Amendment, Churchill declared in Parliament in March 1912 that Germany was Britain's only potential enemy at sea. The British government decided to build two battleships for every one built in Germany.

At the same time, Churchill undertook two important initiatives. The first was a reorganization of strategic deployments. Great Britain had already begun to redeploy its fleet to the North Sea after Fisher assumed leadership in 1904. Once Churchill took office, he began investigating further strategic reorientations. In May 1912, Churchill accompanied Prime Minister Herbert Asquith on a trip to Malta, Great Britain's most important Mediterranean naval base. He believed that, given the expansion of the Austro-German alliance's (including Turkey) naval power in the Mediterranean, Great Britain alone could not maintain command of that sea. Thus, talks began with France that produced quick results. In July 1912, Churchill announced a redeployment of the Royal Navy's Mediterranean Fleet to the North Sea. Ships based at Malta were moved to Gibraltar, and those at Gibraltar to the North Sea, in an effort to strengthen the home fleet. In September 1912, the French Atlantic Fleet was redeployed to the Mediterranean. British and French naval strategies became complementary, even in the absence of a written agreement. The French fleet would focus on control of the Mediterranean, while the British assumed responsibility for the defense of France's west coast in wartime. The two sides also worked out plans for joint military operations in the English Channel and the Mediterranean in April 1913. The Anglo-French Entente had transformed into a curious arrangement: although there were no overt political guarantees made between the two sides, and in theory both still enjoyed freedom of action, the technical details of their arrangements had already created an alliance relationship. Its planning and stipulations far exceeded those of the formal, written Austro-German alliance.

Churchill's second initiative was to increase the Royal Navy's strength. He saw Germany's Third Naval Amendment as a serious challenge with "no example in the previous practice of modern naval powers." In response, Churchill decided to build five *Queen Elizabeth*–class super-dreadnoughts in 1912. These were the first warships in British—and world—history to be powered by oil. They were the fastest battleships in the world, with a speed of 25 knots, and displaced between 31- and 33-thousand-tons of water. These ships were armed with 38-centimeter guns. Calculations had revealed that eight 38-centimenter guns had more firepower than ten 34.3-centimeter guns, thus the middle raised turret was removed for this class, and two pairs of guns were placed on the bow and the stern each. This, once again, gave Great Britain a lead in the naval arms race. Originally, the Germans had been unconcerned with Great Britain's adoption of 34.3-centimeter guns, believing the performance of their own 30.5-centimenter guns to be superior. Yet the advent of 38-centimeter guns left Tirpitz with no choice but to respond. The two *Bayern*-class warships that began construction in 1913 also incorporated four pairs of 38-centimeter guns. These ships were turbine-powered, displaced 28,600 tons of water, and had a maximum speed of 22 knots. They would be the last two dreadnoughts built by the German Empire.[84]

Moreover, Great Britain began to reconceptualize naval tactics. The British recognized that the development of mines, torpedoes, and other weapons had made close shore blockades much more costly. By 1912, the Royal Navy resolved to abandon that traditional strategy and replace it with a more distant form of open water blockade.[85] Foreign Secretary Grey explained to the Russians that the British fleet would not enter the Baltic Sea, as "assuming Germany to succeed in laying hands on Denmark and closing the exit from the Baltic, the British fleet would be caught in a mouse-trap. Accordingly, Great Britain would have to confine her operations to the North Sea."[86] Tirpitz's notion of wearing down the Royal Navy through engagements near the shoreline had become irrelevant.

In the face of British advantages, Tirpitz clung to his utter opposition to any measure that might moderate or slow naval expansion. His response to Churchill's 1913 proposal of a "Naval Holiday" was a classic example. The concept of the Naval Holiday was that both sides refrain from building battleships for an entire year. Churchill privately proposed this to the German military attaché in London. This official reported the proposal to Tirpitz first.

His immediate response was that, considering that domestically "long term reconciliation with Great Britain was a common desire," that the Reichstag and foreign ministry might accept this proposal—which would be unfortunate. Thus, the attaché must be as brief as possible in his report to Berlin, but must add his personal impression that Churchill hoped this move would delay and hinder the pace of German naval expansion, as Great Britain feared that it could no longer maintain its advantage at sea.[87] Afterward, Tirpitz passed a Navy Office report to the kaiser. The report began by proclaiming, "In respect to naval policy, the English are at the limit of their strength in terms of finances, politics, and naval technology."[88] Thus, Churchill's proposal went nowhere.

Tirpitz's actions, however, no longer affected the overall situation. By 1913, the majority of German elites had come to recognize that it would be impossible for the German Navy to catch up to the British. The great naval buildup that had begun in 1898 was in its final phase; the outbreak of war in 1914 would bring this enormous project to a sudden end. The efforts of Tirpitz and others had given German naval development an enormous push: the German Navy had ranked the sixth-strongest in the world in 1898, but second in 1914.[89]

This remarkable outcome came at a catastrophic price. Militarily, Germany's obsession with command of the sea created problems for its allocation of strategic resources. The army, which should have received investment, was overlooked. If Germany had foregone its plans for a massive navy and instead concentrated on its army, it could have at least assured victory for itself in any continental war: "As it was, when war came in 1914, the German dreadnoughts remained uselessly in harbor; the steel that had gone into them would have given Germany the heavy artillery and mechanized transport with which to win the war on land."[90] From a strategic perspective, the construction of the High Seas Fleet caused the regrouping of European powers into arrangements unfavorable to Germany. This was particularly true of the fundamental changes it wrought in Anglo-German relations. The post–World War I German diplomat Richard von Kuhlmann reflected that "Many years of political work in England before the war left me with the conviction that the rapidly increasing construction of a German war fleet was the ultimate motive that ranged England on the side of our enemies."[91] Before the Tirpitz Plan, Germany and Great Britain repeatedly clashed over colonies, security arrangements in the Mediterranean, and alliance negotiations, but Germany was not Britain's only opponent in Europe, nor was it Britain's most significant challenger. After the naval arms race began, however, Germany truly became Great Britain's primary enemy. This spurred Great Britain to compromise with its old enemies France and Russia, leaving Germany to face strategic encirclement. A final showdown between the rising power and the hegemon became increasingly unavoidable.

8

The Schlieffen Plan and the Retreat of Grand Strategy

"Everything depends upon fighting a decisive victory in the west."
Alfred von Schlieffen

THE SCHLIEFFEN PLAN, although itself only a blueprint for a military offensive, was representative of the entirety of German strategic thought before World War I. Its appearance symbolized the final demise of the harmonized diplomatic and military strategies that marked the era of Bismarck and the elder Helmuth von Moltke. The emergence of this plan signified the complete retreat of German policymakers from the concept of grand strategy. Tactical victories during wartime came to be seen as strategic goals in and of themselves.

The Creation of the Schlieffen Plan

When the elder Moltke had been head of the Prussian General Staff, German military strategy had focused on a two-front war. Strategy rested on the concept that the goal of military victories was to ensure favorable conditions for peace negotiations. The objective was limited victory. Germany adopted a policy of "strike first in the east and then in the west," which meant that German military forces would initially be concentrated on the eastern front to strike Russia's main force, while the western front would hold its position in prepared fortifications. Only once the eastern front was settled would troops be deployed in the west to force France out of the war. The essence of this strategy remained policy before 1891.

Schlieffen's Rejection of the Elder Moltke's Military Strategy

Upon taking over as chief of the General Staff in 1891, Alfred von Schlieffen expressed reservations about this strategy. His reasoning was threefold. First, it would be difficult to launch a successful attack in the east. At the end of the nineteenth century, Russian strongholds on its western frontier, including Brest-Litovsk and Warsaw, had been reinforced; the so-called Neuss defensive line ran right through the elder Moltke's planned avenue of attack. Second, the threat of a French offensive was not insignificant. Schlieffen took a French attack on the western front very seriously, much more so than his predecessors, the elder Moltke and Alfred von Waldersee. The elder Moltke had maintained that, if the situation required, the western front could be pulled back, and command of the battlefield could be reclaimed later by a counterattack along interior lines. Schlieffen, however, believed that France would attack through Belgium at the same time that it attacked Lorraine, leaving the German Army without enough space for such flexibility.[1] Third, Schlieffen argued that Moltke's strategy would result in a lengthy war of attrition, which would be impossible for the Austro-German alliance, with its smaller armies, to win. He wrote in 1891 that "our past victories were gained with superior numbers." If the elder Moltke's strategy was retained, however, then "German forces will have to shuttle between the fronts, pushing back the enemy here and there…[while] the war drags on with growing disadvantages and debilitation of our forces."[2]

Assessing this logic carefully, it becomes apparent that the first two reasons were essentially just foils, while the third reason was actually the critical one. This third point embodied the most elemental difference between the elder Moltke and Schlieffen as military planners. The elder Moltke held that a war with another great power, particularly France, could not be won quickly. Thus, Germany needed to prepare for the duration, and its military objectives needed to be limited. Military victories were only useful for creating favorable strategic trends that could benefit the nation's diplomatic and political standing. Schlieffen, by contrast, assumed that a lengthy war was no longer possible under prevailing conditions, because "in an age in which the existence of nations is based on the uninterrupted progress of trade and commerce…a strategy of exhaustion is impossible when the maintenance of millions necessitates the expenditure of [billions]."[3] More important, he considered military victory itself the only objective, a speedy victory to be the only route to that military victory, and the most reliable method for achieving speedy victory to be a large battle of annihilation. Thus, all of Schlieffen's thoughts circled around fighting a decisive battle of annihilation. This determined that he would, in the end, abandon the elder Moltke's "offensive in the east, defensive in the west" strategy.

In April 1891, as he was in the process of preparing his first memorandum as chief of the General Staff, Schlieffen revealed his intention to prioritize a western offensive and to seek a comprehensive yet quick victory.[4] By summer of the next year, he began consideration of a concentration of German military deployments on the western front. He emphasized that Germany must make full use of its geographical position between two adversaries by developing a capacity for speedy mobilization and rail transport, so that each opponent could be struck in turn. Given that French mobilization would be quicker than Russian, it was necessary for the German Army to strike it first. Schlieffen's concept had basically matured by December 1892. He doubted that an offensive against Russia could bring Germany the speedy, decisive victory that it needed. First, Russia had reinforced its westernmost fortifications, which would complicate the German advance. Second, even if the German Army overcame that obstacle, Russia's territory was vast and the distance between the German and Austrian Armies (between 375 and 450 kilometers) would inhibit German attempts to win a decisive victory:

> Should a German attack…be successful, the enemy would certainly not withdraw to the south into Austrian hands, but rather to the east, where the terminus of the railways upon which he is withdrawing are found. We would not succeed in fighting a decisive battle and in smashing the Russian army, but instead fighting a series of frontal battles against an enemy who is offered respite by a retreat into the heart of a powerful empire, while our own lines of communication would be poor and greatly endangered.[5]

An alternative eastern front–only plan was developed under Schlieffen's leadership, however. The plan anticipated French neutrality and the near-complete concentration of German military forces against Russia in the pursuit of a decisive battle. The objective would be the complete destruction of Russian military forces in the region. Yet the purpose of this plan was simply to validate Schlieffen's assessment that it would be impossible to defeat Russia decisively within a short period of time. In practice, Schlieffen never took this plan seriously.[6]

Conversely, Schlieffen devoted enormous attention to an attack on the western front. He supposed that if Germany concentrated its troops for an offensive against France, it could quickly win a decisive victory. Afterward, using its developed rail network, Germany could redeploy its army to the east before Russia was fully mobilized. The 1893–1894 war plan, developed in late 1892, embodied this concept. The plan demanded that three quarters of the German Army be deployed in the west. This would total 16 corps, 15 reserve divisions, and 6 cavalry divisions, organized into 4 army groups. Twelve and a half brigades of garrison troops (*Landwehr*) would also be added. This force of 54 divisions would be primarily concentrated on the Franco-German border in Alsace-Lorraine, from Diedenhofen (now called Thionville) in the north to Metz in the south, with the rear located in the western part of Strassburg. Only 4 corps, 6 reserve divisions, and 14 garrison brigades would be stationed in the east, for a total of 15 divisions. Of these, 11 would operate in coordination with the Austro-Hungarian Army to launch a limited attack from the Silesia region and southern Posen.[7]

The 1893–1894 war plan played a critical role in the pre–World War I reorientation of German strategy. Although this plan differed in many ways from what would later come to be the Schlieffen Plan—the allocation of forces between the two fronts had fewer disparities and an offensive was still planned in the east, among other differences—the foundational concepts were already in complete alignment. With this plan, the German General Staff discarded the elder Moltke's strategy of "defend in the west, attack in the east" and the pursuit of limited victory that it was based on. These were replaced with a strategy of "attack in the west, defend in the east," based on a quest for a quick, decisive victory as the core of the German battle plan.

Objectively, Schlieffen's decision to revise the elder Moltke's military strategy was not unjustified. Military plans are in a constant state of revision and change in response to conditions. Yet there was something else at work in the formulation of the 1893–1894 war plan: the General Staff began excluding political elements from military considerations. A single quick and decisive victory became the heart of the military's calculations; it was seen as a magic pill that could cure all problems. Once this tendency manifested itself, the direction of German military strategy (or, perhaps more accurately, German military planning) was set. The quest for a quick victory in a war between great powers necessarily meant seeking a battle of annihilation. The pure pursuit of a decisive battle of annihilation meant that Germany's strategic goals would grow ever more ambitious, and the demands for the concentration of forces ever more absolute, until in the end the plan became a single, massive strategic gamble. The development of the Schlieffen Plan would follow this road.

The Development of Schlieffen's Plans for a Two-Front War

As argued above, one primary reason Schlieffen called for an offensive against France was that he initially feared a French attack. Once decisive victory itself became the goal, however, he abandoned his earlier considerations and began to worry about the opposite: that France would not attack. As early as April 1891, he correctly predicted that France was not likely to launch an offensive on its own initiative, but would instead wait for a German attack on its prepared fortifications on the upper Moselle River and the Meuse River. This would result in a stalemate between the two armies, leaving Germany with the problem of figuring out how to seize the initiative within a short span of time.

Schlieffen concluded that Germany must rely on offensive attacks in order to maintain battlefield initiative. Yet the difficulty Germany faced was that France had fortified their shared border. This defensive system essentially constituted a "hermetically sealed" (in the words of the elder Moltke) line from Belfort in the south extending all the way to Epinal, where a small gap existed, and then from Toul to Verdun.[8] Overcoming this defensive line became the central issue for German military planning. It also became the turning point in the development of the Schlieffen Plan.

Overall, the Schlieffen Plan passed through three stages before its final formulation in late 1905. The period from the enunciation of the 1893–1894 war plan in 1892 through 1897 marked the first of these stages. In a July 1894 memorandum, Schlieffen first proposed encircling the French Army in the north. He anticipated that the best route of attack would be to force a crossing of the Meuse River near Verdun, as "French defensive works and troops are few" in this sector. Once this attack succeeded in a breakthrough, it would move south to outflank the rest of the French defensive line. In order to assure the success of this attack, the German Army would also need to attack simultaneously in strength between Verdun and Toul in order to aid the advance on Nancy.[9] This plan, however, was far from the decisive victory that Schlieffen sought. Thus, he continuously sought more soldiers in order to make a larger strategic attempt. Through his efforts, the Prussian Army agreed in 1896 to establish the basic framework for five armies, which would become five full armies at the outbreak of war. With these new troops, Schlieffen again expanded his strategic ambitions. In an August 1897 memorandum, he explained:

> The circumstances north of Verdun are the most favorable. The Meuse will certainly be occupied, but not with considerable strength. Ere, at least the right wing is free and there is the possibility of crossing the river by means of an envelopment. If this is successful, one can direct one's march against the rearward communications of the enemy and thus force the French army away from Paris.[10]

Yet more forces and greater strategic ambitions caused new problems: most significantly, the region between Belgium and Verdun was too small for a large army to pass. Sending an army through Belgium, however, would violate Belgian neutrality, which Germany and other nations had guaranteed. Faced with this, Schlieffen demonstrated the characteristics of a so-called pure soldier: fundamentally, he did not worry about the limits imposed by diplomacy. Belgium had reinforced fortifications along the German border (but lacked any defenses along its border with France), causing him to doubt its neutral status. More important, though, he saw military victory as more important than any other consideration. Anything that could hinder victory had to be pushed aside: "An offensive which seeks to wheel round Verdun must not shrink from violating the neutrality of Belgium as well as of Luxembourg."[11] Thus, in his August 1897 memorandum, he advocated for the first time the violation of Belgian neutrality in order to ensure enough space for German forces to envelope the northern end of the French defensive line. This memorandum, however, was not a plan for action, as available troop strength was insufficient. According to Schlieffen's own calculations, his plan would require an army comprising 25 divisions, plus two reserve divisions, as well as significant garrison forces. This would mean that no troops could be spared for defense of the eastern front.

The plan's second stage lasted from 1898 until 1904. During this period, Schlieffen's plans for an offensive did not take the form of systematic, complete memoranda, but instead were embodied in various staff rides, war games, and annual operational plans. Schlieffen strengthened his concept during this period, namely that in the early phases of a war, Germany needed to collect its forces to strike first at one opponent. For example, in a document he produced for the 1901 staff ride in the east, Schlieffen argued:

> Germany must strive, therefore, first to strike down one of the allies while the other is kept occupied; but then, when the one antagonist is conquered, it must, by exploiting its railways, bring a superiority of numbers to the other theater of war, which will also destroy the

> other enemy. The first blow must be delivered with the utmost power and a really decisive battle must take place; a Solferino will bring us nothing; a Sedan, or at least a Königgrätz, must be fought.[12]

Yet compared with the plan that would follow, Schlieffen had not fully decided to place his entire bet on a single roll of the dice—in other words, he did not yet place all of his hopes in a single, massive maneuver to outflank Germany's encirclement. Instead, these exercises and war plans had relatively limited objectives and were cautious in their approach, even to the point of warning German military commanders engaged in the outflanking maneuver not to penetrate too deeply into enemy territory. In the process of determining strategic objectives, these plans and exercises demonstrated significant flexibility, mandating that a counterattack begin the moment the French Army attacked Lorraine; if the French Army did not attack, then the Germans should make use of the momentum to initiate encirclement. For example, in the war plan of October 1898, Schlieffen anticipated two possibilities. The first was that the French Army would go on the offensive (the Germans required four weeks to mobilize, while the French only needed two or three, so the German General Staff thought it likely that the French would use that gap to launch an attack), but that the route of the attack would be through Belgium and Luxembourg. The German Army could defeat this strategy with a pincer attack. The second possibility was that the French Army would not attack. If this happened, the German Army would go on the offensive. The two army groups on the right, comprising eight corps, would force the crossing of the Meuse River at the northern end of the French fortifications. The Seventh Army Group (six reserve divisions) and the Third Army Group (four divisions and two reserve divisions) would cross the Meuse from the north and the south, respectively. In the center, the Fourth and Fifth Army groups (eight corps in total) would march on Nancy and push on to Toul. The Sixth Army Group (four corps and six reserve divisions) would screen the advance.[13] Evidently, what Schlieffen planned was still a limited battle of annihilation, and its objective was the encirclement of French defensive forces on the northern end of the Franco-German border.

Schlieffen continued to find problems with his concept. During the June 1904 General Staff's western staff ride, he doubted whether the encirclement of Mézières at the northern end of the French defensive line would be enough to force the French to abandon the entire line. Schlieffen felt that the French might continue to defend their line and the German advance might be split by that line into two parts. Thus, he began to consider a large-scale flank envelopment: "Another possibility is to by-pass the position entirely and to march with the whole army, or at least its main part, round Verdun. In other words, one would not attack the line Verdun-Belfort, but the line Verdun-Lille, because one must extend that far west in order to achieve the necessary freedom of maneuver."[14]

The Schlieffen Plan entered its third stage in 1905. During this stage, Schlieffen engaged in two major staff rides and war games, thus bringing the Schlieffen Plan into its final form. In the summer of 1905, the Prussian General Staff embarked on a western staff ride during which Schlieffen commanded the blue forces (representing the German Army), thus demonstrating his new concepts for warfare. During this exercise, Schlieffen made use of essentially the entire German fighting force. Five divisions were deployed from the Dutch border to the Metz line to act as the German right wing, while the Sixth Army Group moved from Metz to the border with France and Luxembourg to act as the German center, and the Seventh Army Group was sent to Alsace to act as the left wing. Schlieffen calculated that France had four army groups and that they were deployed further to the northwest than the 1898 German war plan had anticipated. The German plan was thus to go through the northern part of the French bases in order to encircle the main force of the French Army:

> After one has outflanked the [French] position from the north, one faces a new position, a complete fortified system along the Lille-Maubeuge line and behind this La Fère, Laon and Reims. Before one arrives at this line, one must pass Antwerp and one's advance is split by Liège and Namur. When one has overcome completely these considerable difficulties, one will find the entire French army before one. It is therefore advisable to bring the whole Germany army, or at least all of the active army corps, on to a line from Brussels to Diedenhofen. From here, the German plan of operations is self-evident: one must stand firm at Metz-Diedenhofen and wheel left with the entire army, thereby always advancing right in order to win as much territory to the front and to the north as possible and in order to envelop the enemy, wherever he may be. Such a maneuver can only be made when the left wing is covered. Metz serves this function, a large Metz with a strong southern front.[15]

Thus, the core of the Schlieffen Plan was formed: that a greatly strengthened German right flank (along a line from Diedenhofen to Brussels) would take responsibility for a flanking and encircling maneuver, forming a large wheel spinning left with its axis at the center front (the line from Diedenhofen to Metz). The main French fighting force would be pushed to destruction on the Franco-German border.

In November and December 1905, Schlieffen held a further set of war games to test deployment plans for responding to attacks on both fronts. These games differed from the summer's planning exercise: Germany's forces were divided equally in order to defend against both Russia and France. The games resulted a definite German victory. Yet two factors caused Schlieffen to abandon this plan. First, the probability that both adversaries would attack simultaneously was low, particularly given Russia's instability after its defeat by Japan. Second, the defensive works near Metz had been largely completed, meaning more German soldiers could be allocated to the offensive while still guaranteeing the effective defense of the axle of the German Army's right wing. A railroad to the German-Belgian border area had also been completed, giving Germany the ability to deploy a powerful right wing on short notice. These led Schlieffen to return to his original notion of encircling the main force of the French Army on the western front. Just before this, the Prussian General Staff produced a report that argued that the war with Japan had weakened Russian military power, leaving France only the option of adopting a defensive posture *vis-à-vis* Germany. Moreover, the report claimed, the French military had already anticipated the possibility of a German flanking of its defensive line, and thus was preparing to extend it northward. This report did little to change Schlieffen's thinking—and, instead, reinforced his belief that the right wing needed additional forces. Thus, by late 1905 and early 1906, Schlieffen had already completed his plans for war with France, the famous Schlieffen Plan.

The Main Contents of the 1905–1906 Schlieffen Plan

The Schlieffen Plan referred to the plans for war with France that the Prussian General Staff, under Schlieffen's direction, completed in late 1905 and early 1906. The plan is laid out in a detailed memorandum.

The memorandum began with the suggestion that France might remain on the defensive in a war with Germany, and that its defensive system would be difficult to break through with a frontal assault. It then proposed several options, such as attacking with the army's right wing across the Moselle River or attacking and occupying Nancy, but concluded that the likelihood of success was limited.

Schlieffen predicted that the French military would take counter-measures to prevent the envelopment of the northern end of its defensive line.

This would create additional difficulties for the attacking German troops. This could be counteracted, however:

> An attack from the northwest directed against the flanks at Mézières, Rethel, La Fère and across the Oise against the rear of the line appears more promising than a frontal attack with an envelopment of the left wing. For this to succeed, the Franco-Belgian border on the left bank of the Meuse, with the fortified areas of Hirson, Maubeauge, three small blocking forts, Lille and Dunkirk, has to be taken. To accomplish this, the neutrality of Luxemburg, Belgium, and the Netherlands has to be violated.[16]

In order to flank and envelope the French Army's left wing and then annihilate the main force of the French Army, Schlieffen concentrated forces in the Germany Army's right wing, in the line from Metz to Wesel, for a total of 23 army divisions, 12.5 reserve divisions, and 6 cavalry divisions. These would move left, like a wheel, crushing the French defensive line between Verdun and Dunkirk. Simultaneously, 3.5 army divisions and 1.5 reserve divisions would be left on the right hank of the Moselle River. These would pin down the French Army through an advance on Nancy, preventing this portion of the French Army from reinforcing the north. (If the French Army did not launch a counterattack from this spot, then two of these divisions could be diverted to the right wing to assist the offensive through Belgium.) Afterward, these forces would be tasked either with covering the left end of the right wing or with joining that main attack force. Metz, with its extensive fortifications and concentration of artillery, would form the fulcrum point of the entire German line.

The memorandum dictated that German victory depended on outflanking the French Army's side and rear—and that the right wing would be the key to this, and thus must be strengthened as much as possible. Eight army corps and five cavalry divisions from the Metz-Wesel line were to cross the Moselle River south of Liège, advancing toward the Brussels-Namur line. A ninth corps was to ford the Meuse River north of Liège and meet up with the main force. Seven reserve divisions followed, most of whom were to besiege Antwerp. The remainder were to guard the right flank. Six additional army divisions, one cavalry division, and one reserve division were to pass over the Meuse River between Mézières and Namur, thus giving the Germans a total of 15 to 17 corps on the left bank of the Meuse. Eight other divisions, accompanied by two cavalry divisions, were to strike the defenses between Mézières and Verdun, while five reserve divisions defended the German left wing at Metz. Ten brigades of territorial forces (used mainly to guard roads, rail lines, and infrastructure) would cross north from the Meuse, while sixwould proceed south across the same river, six would be stationed in Metz, 3.5 in the upper Rhine, and one in Lorraine.

Once the Germans broke the French defensive lines along the Meuse River, the army would, according to plan, turn to attack the left flank of French defensive positions at Mézières, Rethel, and La Fère. After pushing past fortifications on the French-Belgian border and the difficult terrain of the Ardennes Forest, the German Army would find itself in an advantageous position. Schlieffen thought that at this point the French Army might withdraw to the Somme River and take up defensive positions there, thus obligating the German Army's right wing to conduct a flanking maneuver in the direction of Amiens or even Abbeville further west. Yet he judged this to be only a small possibility, as the German Army coming from the Belgian border would be advancing from behind the French Army's left flank. The French would need to defend against this, too, or else they would be forced to retreat south of the Marne or Seine Rivers. Assuming the French did not want to lose all of northern France, the French Army would need to construct a defense between the Oise River, the Aisne River, and Paris.

At this point, Schlieffen calculated, the German Army would have used up a significant amount of its effective strength. Additionally, German troop strength would be dispersed by the need to besiege fortified points, defend lines of communication, and guard against British landings at Dunkirk or Calais. As the main French force withdrew into the French interior, increasing numbers of newly mobilized troops would enter the conflict, thus swelling the size of its army. German troop levels would clearly be insufficient. Schlieffen estimated that for his plan to be successful, the German Army would need to create eight additional army corps after mobilization began. These would be added to the offensive on the right flank. This would allow for the German Army facing French defenses between the Oise, the Aisne, and Paris to comprise 25 army corps, 2.5 reserve corps, and six newly created corps, for a total of 33.5 corps. Over one-third of these troops would besiege Paris: seven regular army corps would outflank the capital while the six new corps would attack it from the west and the south. Schlieffen specifically emphasized that the German Army must always remain on the offensive and absolutely not allow the conflict to degenerate into a Russo-Japanese War–style seesaw battle.

Schlieffen assumed that, once the French realized that the German Army had been deployed to the upper Rhine and the German-Belgian border, they would recognize the threat to Paris and would tread lightly around the German left flank. If the French Army were to venture an attack in that area, it would weaken their forces in the fortified areas, which would work in Germany's favor. In the best-case scenario, France would attack southern Germany through Switzerland, thus giving Germany another important ally. On the whole, a French attack on Germany would not require changes to Germany's general plan, because the moment the German right wing staged a breakthrough, any advancing French forces would have to be recalled to Paris. At the conclusion of his memorandum, Schlieffen again stressed the decisive nature of the German Army's right wing and that it must be as strong as possible.[17]

The Problems and the Strategic Meaning of the Schlieffen Plan

Overall, the 1906 Schlieffen Plan, as outlined in the form of a memorandum, was an operational plan with a grand strategic desire. Many subsequent soldiers and military historians have appraised it favorably. In particular, a number of German military officers who served in the war considered it to be a formula for victory. They blamed the failure of the plan in 1914 on Schlieffen's successor, the younger Helmuth von Moltke, who modified and failed to fully implement Schlieffen's original concept.[18] British military historian B. H. Liddell Hart argued that the Schlieffen Plan exemplified the strategy of the "indirect approach."[19] Nonetheless, a careful investigation of the plan reveals serious, even fatal, mistakes embedded in it. The existence of these problems not only foreshadowed the plan's failure in the opening stages of World War I, but also revealed that German strategic planning had already lost its comprehensive view and instead had resorted to a simplistic obsession with decisive victory.

Political and Diplomatic Problems

The first problems with the Schlieffen Plan were diplomatic and political. Compared with the previous heads of the General Staff such as the elder Helmuth von Moltke and Alfred von Waldersee, Schlieffen was a strictly apolitical and purely technical solider. He was proud of this fact. As a result, Schlieffen, unlike his predecessors, rarely came into conflict with civilian officials. Under his leadership, the General Staff became ever more closed and self-contained. Schlieffen believed that the quest for military victory was the military's only duty; politics and diplomacy were not within its sphere of concern. As a result, he had not a shred of doubt about violating Belgian neutrality.

This act would have serious consequences, however. Belgian neutrality was guaranteed by several great powers, Germany among them. Breaking its own pledge would damage Germany's moral reputation. Even more significantly, Belgian neutrality was critical for Great Britain, which had consistently opposed efforts of other great powers to control Belgium and the Netherlands. Thus, the Schlieffen Plan guaranteed British military involvement. Yet the Schlieffen Plan itself gave no consideration to this prospect. The early 1906 memorandum spoke only generally of the need to defeat a British expeditionary force, but in February 1906, Schlieffen specifically amended the 1905 memorandum to address this issue. Yet he only concluded that the British Army was inconsequential and would crumble under the assault of the German right wing.[20] In reality, this apolitical military view needed to be linked to politics and foreign policy. Unlike the era of the elder Moltke, this type of "victory above all" military thinking did not undergo a process of interaction with politics and foreign policy, and instead from its very inception demanded the compliance of politics and foreign policy. A classic example of this came in May 1905, when Schlieffen informed Friedrich von Holstein at the foreign ministry that, in the event of a two-front war, the General Staff did not wish to be limited by international treaties. He then asked for Holstein's opinion. After a long silence, Holstein replied: "If the Chief of the General Staff, particularly such a pre-eminent strategical thinker such as Schlieffen, considers such a measure imperative, then it is the duty of diplomacy to concur in it and to facilitate it in every manner possible."[21]

Military Problems

The Issue of Coordinating the Two Fronts

From a military perspective, the most obvious question revolved around the coordination of the two fronts. Or, in other words: What happens to the eastern front?

Schlieffen began from the same premise as the elder Moltke and Waldersee: Germany needed to be prepared for a two-front war with both Russia and France. Given his fears of a French attack and consequent desire to strike first on the western front, however, once Schlieffen began to search for a quick, decisive victory, overall consideration of the two-front war receded into the background. In 1899, he wrote on a document that: "The war on two fronts need not be taken into consideration at all. The war against France alone is quite enough to strain every nerve." Later he also wrote: "Enough of the war on two fronts! One front is ample."[22] To his mind, a two-front war was really two consecutive one-front wars, with the first war coming on the western front. Thus, throughout the development of the Schlieffen Plan between 1892 and 1905, the concentration of forces in the west continuously increased, until it reached a point of absolute concentration—or, in other words, the forces slated for offensive operations in the west included Germany's entire active-duty army. Only a portion of a reserve division would be left on the eastern front, not even enough to mount an effective defense. This created an enormous problem: if France and Russia went to war against Germany at the same time, what would happen to the eastern half of the country? In response, Schlieffen argued that: "Everything depends upon fighting a decisive victory in the west—if this is successful, one will see that which has been lost in the east won back again."[23] After retirement, Schlieffen hounded his successors with the warning that the fate of Germany's eastern provinces lay on the banks of the Seine, not the Vistula.[24] This victory in the west would determine the outcome of the war and even the fate of the empire. No bet could be larger.

Even if a decisive victory occurred on the western front, however, would the French simply then surrender and allow the German Army to deal with the Russians? The elder Moltke, based on his own experiences in war, believed that even after the main force of a great power suffered an annihilating defeat, it would continue to mobilize new armies and continue the struggle as long as its will to resist was not broken. Some within the German Army offered different advice to Schlieffen as well. For example, the commander of the Sixteenth Army, Field Marshal Gottlieb von Haeseler, commented: "You cannot carry away the armed strength of a great Power like a cat in a bag."[25] In fact, however, Schlieffen had never been especially confident about this. In 1905, during the last military exercises he commanded, Schlieffen wrote:

> Since the danger of a war with France and Russia is imminent, the theory of a decisive battle in the West plays a vital role. The theory runs approximately thus: we shall enter France with all forces, there engage in a decisive battle, which of course turns out in our favor, and on the evening of the battle, or at least the next morning, the trains are ready to carry the victors eastwards to give a new battle of decision on the Vistula, the Niemen, or the Narew. Wars are not waged in such a manner today. After battle, as may be read in the

> text-books, there follows the pursuit which sometimes lasts a very long time.... If we intend to wage war in France for months, we cannot, on the other hand, disregard the Russians completely. We cannot just watch them crossing the Vistula, Oder, Elbe and, in spite of that, continue to wage war in France. This is completely out of the question.[26]

Yet Schlieffen's solution was simply to return to his previous way of thinking and to trust in a miraculous battle of annihilation on the western front.

Alliance Coordination Issues

Schlieffen's stance on the eastern front naturally had implications for coordination with Germany's ally, Austria-Hungary. When the elder Moltke ran the General Staff, communication between the two empire's general staffs had been relatively robust. Schlieffen's focus on the western front, however, meant that he had little interest in military coordination with the Austro-Hungarian Empire. In the beginning, Schlieffen revised the war plan for the eastern front, changing the starting point of the German Army's line of march from eastern Prussia to Silesia, so that it could attack the Russian Army near Warsaw with the Austrian Army from Galicia. This reduced the objectives and scope of the German and Austrian Armies' outflanking maneuver. It should be pointed out that this revision occurred without the knowledge of the Austro-Hungarian General Staff—only after it was complete did Germany notify Austria-Hungary in August 1893. This naturally displeased Austria-Hungary. In May 1895, Germany again notified Austria-Hungary that it had reverted to the original staging point in East Prussia. Germany also demanded that Austria-Hungary shoulder the burden of significant new wartime responsibilities, such as unilaterally attacking Russian Army groups near Warsaw. This was obviously beyond the capabilities of the Austro-Hungarian Empire and was refused. On Christmas Eve 1895, Schlieffen changed plans again, informing his ally that the German Army would adhere to the plans devised by the elder Moltke and Waldersee, but with much lower troop levels. The ratio of German troops would drop from one in the east for every two in the west to one in the east for every four in the west (later, this would reach one in the east for every eight in the west). Thus, Austria-Hungary came to recognize that Germany had no intention of cooperating in a war on the eastern front, and that coordination between the two general staffs served little purpose. In 1896, Schlieffen simply terminated the dialogue between the general staffs. Each country began crafting its war plans alone.[27]

This created an interesting situation among the European great powers. The Anglo-French Entente was not a military alliance, yet the general staffs of the two countries coordinated closely and designed a synchronized plan for wartime. It was a comprehensive relationship, except for the lack of a formal political guarantee. The alliance between Germany and Austria-Hungary was the earliest of the great power alliances, but had no content beyond a formal political guarantee. The Schlieffen Plan brought even that aspect of the relationship into question. The 1879 treaty of alliance had stipulated that should "one of the two Empires be attacked by Russia, the High Contracting Parties are bound to come to the assistance one of the other with the whole war strength of their Empires," and that if one party was attacked by another power with the support of Russia, "then the obligation stipulated [above] for reciprocal assistance with the whole fighting force, becomes equally operative."[28] Yet the Schlieffen Plan dictated that, regardless of whether a war is instigated by a Russian attack or not, Germany should first smash France. Assistance to Austria-Hungary would only happen after that. According to Schlieffen, once Germany resolved its war with France on the western front, issues on the eastern front would naturally resolve themselves. The Austro-Hungarian Army could hold on alone until the Germans occupied Paris: "Austria need not worry: the Russian army intended against Germany will not march into Galicia before the die is cast in the West. And Austria's fate will be decided not on the Bug but on the Seine."[29] In making this assessment, he appeared to have completely forgotten a conclusion he had reached in 1891: that without German assistance, it was doubtful that Austria-Hungary could hold its defensive line.[30] Actually, neither of these conflicting judgments fully captured Schlieffen's true beliefs about his Austro-Hungarian allies. An examination of his overall attitude toward the eastern front (including Germany's easternmost provinces), shows that he was indifferent to Austria-Hungary as an ally and did not care if it collapsed before Germany had defeated France. A complete victory on the western front would be a magic pill that would solve all of these problems.

The damage done by the Schlieffen Plan to military coordination between Germany and Austria-Hungary did not end with Schlieffen's retirement. His successor, the younger Moltke, worked to repair the relationship with the Austro-Hungarian General Staff. Dialogue and cooperation were gradually resumed between the two militaries, but it was no longer at the level it had been during the elder Moltke's tenure. More important, the younger Moltke supported the basic framework of the Schlieffen Plan. This assigned the Austro-Hungarian military a second-act role in German military planning, making qualitative improvements in coordination between the two militaries impossible. In May 1914, Austro-Hungarian Chief of General Staff Franz Conrad von Hötzendorf asked the younger Moltke what would happen if the German Army did not win a quick victory on the western front. This question struck at the heart of the Schlieffen Plan. In response, the younger Moltke could only say: "I will do what I can. We are not superior to the French."[31] In fact, the two militaries never engaged in any joint war planning, much less discussed issues of unified military command, before the outbreak of the conflict in August 1914. On August 1, 1914, after Germany's mobilization and declarations of war against France and Russia, the German military attaché in Vienna recommended to the German General Staff that "it is high time that the two general staffs consult now with absolute frankness with respect to mobilization, jump-off time, areas of assembly and precise troop strength." This revealed the absence of any level of military coordination.[32]

The Issue of Troop Levels

The Schlieffen Plan had not been based on Germany's existing level of resources and strength. The plan's troop-level needs were a striking example of this. Schlieffen's logic was that Germany needed a decisive victory, a decisive victory required an offensive, and carrying out an offensive necessitated a particular level of troops. Whether or not such a number of troops actually existed was beyond the considerations of the Schlieffen Plan. Thus, from the very beginning, the Schlieffen Plan faced a serious manpower deficit.

This manpower deficit, as well as a comparatively insufficient budget, persisted throughout Schlieffen's tenure. The combined forces of Germany and Austria-Hungary were numerically inferior to the combined armies of France and Russia, as Schlieffen noted in a letter: "Our special enemies (Denmark not included) have almost double our strength. The relationship is something like 5:3.... For me, there is no doubt that this question cannot be put aside if Germany is not to collapse utterly."[33] The numerical superiority of French and Russian forces increased between 1897 and 1898, for a total of 1.56 million troops, compared to the German and Austro-Hungarian total of 888,000.[34] Two factors restricted Germany's ability to increase its army. The first was Germany's own program of naval expansion. Construction of the High Seas Fleet meant that, beginning in 1898, the naval budget grew rapidly, from 20 percent of the size of the army's budget in 1898 to 54.8 percent in 1911.[35] This expenditure squeezed the army's budget, slowing its growth between 1898 and 1911. The second was the German Army's system and mission. Under the German Empire, the German Army was foremost the army of the royal house, and only secondarily the army of the nation. One of its important missions was the maintenance of domestic stability, particularly the leading role of the Hohenzollern dynasty. Given this, the army was particularly sensitive to its "purity." The Army Cabinet and War Ministry opposed a large expansion, believing that this would lead political unreliable individuals to infiltrate the ranks and the officer corps. This would weaken the army as a pillar of established authority.

This made it difficult for Schlieffen's troop-level needs to be satisfied. Under the impetus of Chancellor Leo von Caprivi in 1893, Germany passed an army bill that increased the military by 66,000 men, the largest expansion since unification. At the same time, the number of heavy artillery troops was also increased.[36] Schlieffen felt that this was far from enough, and demanded more troops and the organization of new armies. The Prussian Ministry of War, responsible for soldiers and logistics, refused. War Minister Heinrich von Gossler steadfastly clung to his belief that such an expansion of the army in peacetime would weaken its political reliability. It might even lead to a democratization of the military. The General Staff and the Army Ministry reached an agreement in the end, with the Army Ministry permitting the creation of the basic framework of five additional armies in 1898, which could become full armies upon the outbreak of hostilities.

This compromise was wholly inadequate for Schlieffen's designs. In 1899, he asked for seven additional corps. The War Ministry ultimately agreed to three, but they would be organized out of already-existing troops. Total German forces would only increase by 23,377 men (reduced by 7,000 when eventually passed by the Reichstag).[37] Schlieffen, however, compelled the War Ministry to agree to create the full seven corps he had asked for before the outbreak of war. Yet, the final formulation of the Schlieffen Plan in 1905 led to a significant increase in demands for troops. According to the plan, total German strength on the western front was to be 33.5 corps, of which seven would be needed to encircle Paris from the west and five or six needed to attack the city. The troops assigned to these two tasks would exceed one-third of the entire German Army deployed on the western front. Yet, these critical forces did not exist during Schlieffen's tenure, and the entire fighting force of the German Army measured only twenty corps. Even including the seven additional "paper" corps promised by the War Ministry in the event of war, a deficit of seven corps still existed. This equaled 21 percent of the anticipated attack force. Any consideration of deploying defensive forces to the eastern front would only increase this gap. Thus, the Schlieffen Plan made force demands only in theory, and gave little thought to whether or not they could be met in reality. In other words, the problem of this troop deficit was foisted off on his successors. Even Schlieffen's most loyal follower, Erich Ludendorff, admitted that this was a serious flaw in the Schlieffen Plan.[38] Even on the eve of World War I, this problem would remain unsolved.

The Uncertainty of War Planning

As a war plan, the Schlieffen Plan was exhaustively detailed and tightly organized. It provided precise plans for the entire course of the war. In this respect, it departed greatly from the traditions of the Prussian General Staff.

Traditional German (or, more accurately, Prussian) war planning had placed particular emphasis on the uncertainty of war. Clausewitz termed this "friction in war."[39] Karl Wilhelm von Grolmann, who led Prussia's General Staff after the Napoleonic Wars, emphasized: "In the dispositions and plans for a future war, only the first general order, with regard to the exact knowledge of the theater of war, should be fixed. The preparations of offensive as well as defensive must be made. We must limit ourselves to theses; to design a plan of operation of years from the office-table is nonsense and belongs to the sphere of military novel."[40] The elder Moltke, who planned and commanded Germany's wars of unification, agreed with this. He held that from the beginning of military action:

> Our will soon meets the independent will of the enemy.... The material and moral consequences of any larger encounter are, however, so far-reaching that through them a completely different situation is created, which then becomes the basis for new measures. No plan of operations can look with any certainty beyond the first meeting with the major forces of the enemy.... The commander is compelled during the whole campaign to reach decisions on the basis of situations that cannot be predicted. All consecutive acts of war are, therefore, not executions of a premeditated plan, but spontaneous actions, directed by military tact. The problem is to grasp in innumerable special cases the actual situation that is covered by the mist of uncertainty, to appraise the facts correctly and to guess the unknown elements, to reach a decision quickly and then to carry it out forcefully and relentlessly.... It is obvious that theoretical knowledge will not suffice, but that here the qualities of mind and character come to a free, practical, and artistic expression, although schooled by military training and led by experiences from military history or from life itself.[41]

Yet, this intense awareness of the uncertainty of war was completely abandoned in the Schlieffen Plan, as was the premise that the enemy, too, enjoys independent will. At its heart, the Schlieffen Plan was an attempt to use the German Army's superior planning, command, and war-making abilities to devise a comprehensive, finely detailed plan that would force the enemy to behave reactively.[42] Under these conditions, Prussian traditions of broad and flexible planning were replaced by finely detailed, step-by-step instructions. These instructions incorporated a healthy dose of wishful thinking, and essentially overlooked potential problems that might arise.

First, the plan gave no consideration to the fundamental disparity of the forces. Planned German troop strength on the western front was 33.5 corps. The French Army that was to be encircled comprised at least 19 corps and perhaps three British corps. Yet when it came to a consideration of relative French and German troop strength, the plan was less robust than it could have been.

Second, it did not consider the effects of a French counterattack. In his 1905–1906 memorandum, Schlieffen considered the possibility of a French counterattack several times, but only in a very simplistic manner. His conclusion each time was that "this counterattack will meet with defeat." In fact, French counterattacks would be an important cause of the plan's failure in World War I.

Third, it gave little thought to the immense difficulty of carrying out such a large flanking maneuver. According to the Schlieffen Plan, the French Army would completely lack independent will. Instead, it would accept its defeat passively. In fact, there was a critical problem with this large-scale flanking maneuver: the French Army could use its rail network, centered on Paris, to reinforce its left flank, making it difficult for the German Army to complete its encirclement. Or it could mass troops for a counterattack against the flanking forces. Schlieffen thought this unlikely, as such a plan would extend and weaken the French line, allowing for the German Army to stage a breakthrough. Yet he failed to consider the simple fact that French troop strength was not limited to those stationed on the border with Germany. While Germany was fighting on the Aisne or the Marne, French reserve forces from the east of the country would concentrate in Paris, threating the German right flank. What would Germany do in such a situation? Neither Schlieffen nor his successors had an answer. This exact situation occurred in 1914, during the Battle of the Marne. It forced the spear tip of the German Army's right flank—the First and Second Army Groups—to turn and defend. The September 5, 1914, order from the German headquarters to its commanders began with the claim that the opposing forces had evaded the German flanking offensive. The true meaning of this was that the original battle objectives were now being deliberately discarded.[43] In other words, the Schlieffen Plan had already failed.

Fourth, the plan did not consider logistical issues. Schlieffen's force-level requests were derived from his plan for a large battle of annihilation. He did not even consider whether or not it would be possible to move such a massive body of troops. Arguably, existing German logistical capabilities could not support such a long-distance deployment of an army of this size. This was particularly true for the nearly million-man force in the right flank that would squeeze through Belgium during a time when the French and Belgian militaries could be counted on to sabotage railways, thus reducing Germany's logistical supply abilities. Schlieffen's calculations of ammunition requirements were already forty years out of date. During an offensive managed according to his plans, German troops would not be able to be effectively resupplied with ammunition; participation in any decisive battle would thus be complicated. One military scholar later concluded that: "the sheer size and weight of the German Army in 1914 proved wholly out of proportion to the means of tactical transportation at its disposal."[44] These deficiencies were spotted, and partially ameliorated, by Schlieffen's successor, the younger Moltke. After taking control of the General Staff, the younger Moltke held a number of logistics and communications drills that justified his concerns. As a result of his significant investment in logistical arrangements, the initial phases of the Schlieffen Plan, namely the advance to the Marne, became possible when the plan was actually put to use in 1914.[45] Yet even British military historian B. H. Liddell-Hart, who had a favorable appraisal of the plan, admitted that:

> by the time the Germans reached the Marne they bore the air of beaten troops—beaten by hard marching on an empty stomach. If Moltke had avoided his much condemned subtractions, and used larger numbers on this far-advancing right wing, their state would have been worse. The long over-looked lesson of the American Civil War was repeated—that the development of railways, and armies' dependence on such communications, both fixed and fragile, fostered the deployment of larger numbers than could be maintained in long-range operations without risk of breakdown."[46]

Overall, the Schlieffen Plan contained serious strategic, battlefield, and tactical mistakes. One scholar quipped in the 1930s that the Schlieffen Plan could only have resulted in victory if the German Army had been commanded by God or the French Army by fools.[47] After World War II, another German military scholar, Gerhard Ritter, claimed: "The great Schlieffen Plan was never a sound formula for victory. It was a daring, indeed an over-daring, gamble whose success depended on many lucky accidents. A formula for victory needs a surplus of reasonable chances of success if it is to inspire confidence—a surplus which tends quickly to be used up by 'frictions' in the day-to-day conduct of war."[48]

All of these points made above, however, describe the problems inherent in the plan itself. Yet the fact that this problematic plan was adopted by Schlieffen's successors after his retirement, and that this plan would come to constitute Germany's only plan for war or for responding to crises, was not solely the fault of the plan or of its creator. Instead, blame lies on the entire German Army and on Germany's policymakers. The strategic implications of the Schlieffen Plan were that, regardless of what occurs, Germany only had two military options: do nothing or fight a total war. Inside the German policymaking system, the autonomous nature of each department and the extreme lack of coordination between them made strategic planning impossible. None of the leaders inside the system saw the necessity for this kind of planning. Any awareness of strategy as a concept had vanished. The future of Germany's rise, and the fate of the German Empire, increasingly rested with a single military gamble.

The Schlieffen Plan and the Obsessive Nature of German Military Thought

The question that arises here is: why was the Schlieffen Plan retained in (more or less) its original state after Schlieffen's retirement in 1906?

German military leaders could have significantly revised this plan during the years between 1906 and 1914. To a certain extent, this would have avoided the disastrous consequences of 1914. The problem was that Schlieffen's point of view, and to a certain extent the Schlieffen Plan itself, reflected contemporary German military thought. Schlieffen's own influence simply further strengthened pre-existing tendencies. Schlieffen held his position in the General Staff for sixteen years, during which he attached great importance to the General Staff's ability to educate and direct the entire army. He made wide use of publications to promote his military concepts. After retirement, while he may no longer have had direct influence on the General Staff, the officers there (who had been trained according to Schlieffen's methods) arguably carried on his legacy. His reputation within the German Army remained high, and his writings remained fodder for discussion within the ranks. This illustrated the extent to which the kind of military thinking represented by Schlieffen permeated the army and created an intellectual model. According to this line of thinking, the Schlieffen Plan was a classic that could be revised and perfected, but not overturned. It would be treated as a binding military "last will and testament."

Depoliticizing the Military

Military historians have often overestimated the extent of Clausewitz's influence on the German military. B. H. Liddell Hart, for example, claimed that "accepting the Prussian philosopher of war, Clausewitz, as their master, [German military thinkers] blindly swallowed his undigested aphorisms." He termed such strategists the "unthinking disciples" of Clausewitz.[49] In reality, Clausewitz exerted only limited influence within the German Army. This was particularly true for the era after Schlieffen took command of the General Staff. This can be most clearly seen in the understanding of the connection between politics and the military.

Clausewitz repeatedly emphasized that the military was subordinate to politics. In his view, "war is not merely a political act, but also a real political instrument, a continuation of political commerce, a carrying out of the same by other means."[50] Thus, military strategy during wartime must follow political needs. This point of view, however, was greatly discounted within the German military, particularly the Prussian General Staff. The elder Moltke was the most important military strategist and thinker during the period between the Napoleonic Wars and World War I. On the whole, he agreed with Clausewitz's point of view. The elder Moltke's 1869 "Instructions for the Senior Troop Commanders" explained that the "objective of war is to implement the government's policy by force." In a post–Franco-Prussian War essay, entitled "On Strategy," the elder Moltke qualified this concept to a certain extent: "Political considerations can be taken into account only as long as they do not make demands that are militarily improper or impossible."[51]

By the time Schlieffen took command, the notion that military concerns should be subservient to political concerns had fallen into abeyance. Schlieffen himself was a "pure" soldier—or, to use other words, he strictly followed an "apolitical" path and resolutely remained aloof from political issues, concentrating all of his energy on the military itself. He was hardworking and demonstrated a spirit of self-sacrifice toward the army. Germany's most important World War I–era commander, Erich Ludendorff, deeply admired Schlieffen and called him "one of the greatest soldiers who ever lived."[52] This intense focus on the military, however, comes at the cost of the complete separation of the political world and the military world. War planning during Schlieffen's tenure did not include consideration of any non-military factors. Arguably, this was a war plan made up of simple calculations of distance, troop levels, firepower, and other statistics in the vacuum created by the exclusion of politics and diplomacy. In the end, diplomacy and politics could do nothing but follow this plan. An example of this can be found in the plan's focus on France to the exclusion of any consideration of Belgian neutrality. Moreover, this Schlieffenesque depoliticization manifested itself in a disregard for domestic politics as well as international politics. This was clear in the plan's consideration of troop levels. Schlieffen took a "pure military" or "purely technical" standpoint when proposing troop levels and did not consider the domestic situation comprehensively. The War Minister from 1903 to 1908, Karl von Einem, complained that the General Staff could "comfortably" close its doors and make abstract, impractical suggestions, while other departments had to take responsibility for turning these ideas into reality.[53] Under Schlieffen's influence, this unpolitical tendency became more pronounced within the German military. Increasing numbers of officers were proud of the label "unpolitical," and the complete separation of military issues and political issues became a common concept within the German Army.[54]

The Absolute Nature of Security Assessments

During Schlieffen's tenure, the mental practice of seeing Germany's security environment through the lens of the "worst possible scenario" became deeply entrenched. Originally, the worst possible scenario was a standard for battlefield commanders assessing the enemy's situation. This had been a tradition within the German military. Even in 1933, Germany's national defense army regulations emphasized the necessity of analyzing the enemy's "ability to prevent the friendly intent."[55] Once this mental model is raised from the tactical or operational level to the strategic level, however, it creates problems. It causes strategy to deadlock, and could even transform a worst-case scenario into a self-fulfilling prophecy.

Bismarck's immediate successor, Caprivi, was the first to take the worst-case scenario as a definite assessment. He predicted that a general war between the Austro-German alliance and the Franco-Russian alliance was "unavoidable."[56] The tendency to use the worst-case scenario to assess Germany's security environment became more pronounced after Schlieffen's appointment to the General Staff. The clearest example of this comes from the General Staff's war games and plans, which without exception focused on the worst case scenario of a two-front war. Any other possible scenario was excluded.

After his retirement, Schlieffen penned a famous essay on Germany's security environment, entitled "War Today," which was published anonymously in January 1909. In this essay, beyond describing his views on modern war and tactics, he painted an alarming picture of Germany and Austria-Hungary's encirclement. He pointed to the series of defensive fortifications constructed in Holland, Belgium, and France on Germany's western borders, as well as similar facilities in Italy on Germany's southern border (despite the existence of an alliance between the countries) and Russian installations, reinforced by rivers and swamps, on Germany's eastern border. To the north, the Danes had transformed Copenhagen into an arsenal that controlled access to the Baltic, while Britain's Royal Navy could appear on the German coasts at any time. Germany and its Austro-Hungarian ally were surrounded by an iron ring. Great Britain, France, and Russia all harbored deep hatred for, and jealousy of, Germany. Even Italy harbored territorial designs. Schlieffen believed that this shared hatred might lead these nations to attack Germany: "At a given moment, the gates will be opened, the drawbridges lowered, and the million-man armies will flow out over the Vosges, the Maas, the Konigsau, the Niemen, the Bug, as well as over the Isonzo and the Tyrolean Alps, laying waste and destroying as they go." Yet he also claimed in the essay that the hostile, encircling powers might not make such rash use of direct methods. Instead, they could use secret, concealed means. The Entente powers, given that they had encircled Germany, held the advantage. They might instead exert pressure and manufacture crises to force German concessions and submission. Dissension between Germany and Austria-Hungary would be instigated, as would domestic conflicts within each nation, in order to weaken central Europe's two great powers. Schlieffen proposed closer coordination between the two allies to deal with this situation, coupled with "a large, strong, and powerful army, which is guided by a sure hand and full of confidence."[57]

In this sketch of the future, Schlieffen's essential point was that war is unavoidable. His reasoning was simplistic, and even suppositional, such as his belief in the hatred that other countries harbored toward Germany. This was particularly apparent in his assessment that Anglo-German conflict was inevitable. He took no account of the naval arms race, focusing instead only on commercial competition between the two countries, claiming that "the powerful expansion of Germany's industry and trade had earned her another implacable enemy" in Great Britain. It was "questions of debit and credit which determine the level of resentment" that made such conflict unavoidable. Holstein's assessment, by contrast, was significantly more objective. He acknowledged that the impact of German economic growth on British commerce had generated hostility, but believed that such hostility would not automatically develop in extreme directions and thus conflict was not inevitable. Great Britain, after all, faced economic competition from the United States as well. The British well understood that an Anglo-German war would clear the two most important economic competitors from the path of the United States.[58]

Yet for most—including those in the army—Schlieffen's blunt assessment was easier to accept. "War Today" not only reflected the collected views of the German Army, but it also strengthened the tendencies that led to those views. Before its publication, drafts had circulated among the army's upper echelons. Readers included the younger Moltke and War Minister Einem, both of whom agreed with the book. The younger Moltke particularly approved, even claiming that Schlieffen's text "would be read and taken to heart by thousands." Wilhelm II admired it as well, and read it aloud at his New Year's feast with army corps commanders on January 2, 1909.[59] Under such circumstances, the essentializing tendencies of Schlieffen's security assessment penetrated deeply into the minds of the German Army's soldiers and officers. The sense that war was inevitable became widespread throughout the army, and estimates about the future became ever more pessimistic. In 1911, the German military theorist Friedrich von Bernhardi's newly published book, *Germany and the Next War*, baldly asserted that Germany would "either become a world power or be annihilated." This extreme strategic choice indicated the prevalence of essentialized security assessments within the army ranks. Flexible strategies could not be generated under such conditions. All thought was wrapped up in the notion of total war. The premise that "war is inevitable" soon led to the dangerous conclusion that "the earlier war begins, the better."

Historical Determinism

The idea of inevitability appears frequently in Schlieffen's worldview. Many of his thoughts are expressed through the formulation that "it is inevitable that…". This is connected to his deterministic concept of history.

The Prussian and Germany Armies traditionally placed great emphasis on military history. The elder Moltke had even established a research institute for military history within the Prussian General Staff. The study of history (and especially military history), he believed, was an important aspect of the training of commanding officers. Its principal function was to obtain wisdom from the study of the past and to enhance the quality of their minds. He opposed the notion that ready-made answers or universal laws could be derived from history. Schlieffen, however, thought differently. He did not share the elder Moltke's deep interest in literature and history (the elder Moltke had once spent his spare time translating Edward Gibbon's six-volume *The Rise and Fall of the Roman Empire* into German and had been considered "essentially a humanist of the post-Goethe era").[60] Instead, Schlieffen focused on statistics and technical issues and emphasized pragmatism. He was a complete pragmatist in his view of history. He believed that the purpose of historical study was to find solutions to practical problems, and thus he sought universal laws through historical research.[61] Even more significantly, these laws "must be obeyed" and "cannot be changed." Schlieffen frequently tried to inject these ideas into the military. During the dedication ceremonies for the elder Moltke's monument, for example, he claimed that the elder Moltke has "learned from the book of the past what might come and must come." At the centennial of the Prussian Military Academy, he claimed that the study of military history revealed "the knowledge [of] how everything has come, how it had to come and will come again."[62]

This deterministic theory manifested itself with great clarity in Schlieffen's study of the Battle of Cannae. During this battle, which occurred in 216 BC, Carthaginian general Hannibal had used an encircling maneuver to annihilate a numerically superior Roman Army. In the process, Rome lost 50,000 men at the cost of only 6,000 Carthaginians. Schlieffen greatly admired this battle and published an article on it in a 1909 edition of the General Staff's quarterly publication. From then until his death, Schlieffen published a series of historical articles. These essays all shared a similar purpose: to demonstrate that all of the famous generals in history had made the complete destruction of the enemy their objective. The process by which they all sought to achieve this was through flanking and envelopment maneuvers. Schlieffen emphasized that the "practical use" of his research was that the German Army could again adopt this "unalterable law" in pursuit of a future victory:

> A battle of annihilation can be carried out today according to the same plan devised by Hannibal in long forgotten times. The enemy front is not the goal of the principal attack. The mass of the troops and the reserves should not be concentrated against the enemy front; the essential is that the flanks be crushed. The wings should not be

> sought at the advanced points of the front, but rather along the entire depth and extension of the enemy formation. The annihilation is completed through an attack against the enemy's rear.[63]

Schlieffen's method of using history according to his needs was undoubtedly problematic. Bernhardi, author of *Germany and the Next War* and an accomplished military scholar in his own right, had criticized him for tailoring history to suit his own purposes even before the publication of his essay on Cannae. Retired military commander Sigismund von Schlichting, another critic, commented that "the defect of Schlieffen's doctrine is that he always generalizes lessons and experiences that suit his particular case." In other words, he doubted the applicability of this ancient battle to modern warfare.[64] Schlieffen's followers, however, defended his method of historical research. They admitted to some mistakes in his work, such as the wishful thinking and factual mistakes evident in his discussion of the elder Moltke's strategy at the Battle of Sadowa contained in an essay on Cannae. Yet, they maintained that Schlieffen's historical research was merely meant to elaborate the methods of "applied strategy" (as distinct from Clausewitz's "theoretical strategy"). The purpose of this was to guide the German Army in the prosecution of present and future wars and, particularly, how to initiate a battle of annihilation. Thus, his flawed uses and interpretations of history were not particularly significant. In their eyes, he was not a teacher of military history, but a strategist and a promoter of "applied strategy" and, as such, could twist history to support his view—even to the point of "revising" geography or numbers.[65]

Due to Schlieffen's status, and perhaps due to the inertia of this mindset, his ideas became prevalent throughout the army. Many high-ranking officers were unwilling to think deeply about such abstract and contentious issues in military theory. They were easily taken in by Schlieffen's simplified, "pragmatic" methods. The younger Moltke, Schlieffen's successor, encouraged his own son to forgo reading Clausewitz's *On War* in favor of Schlieffen's writing on Cannae while preparing for his military academy entrance examination. Some commanders saw it as a virtue never to read Clausewitz.[66] As this vision of history became widespread, Schlieffen's strongly deterministic thought process naturally became mainstream within the German Army. Its claims of "unchangeable laws" and "necessarily occurring events" had been repeatedly "proven" by history and thus its reliability was undoubtable. In this intellectual atmosphere, the Schlieffen Plan—which was the essence of

Schlieffen's mindset made concrete—could not be questioned in the army or, especially, the General Staff.

Essentialization and Dogmatism in Operational Doctrine

The clearest example of the obsessive nature of German military thinking was apparent in operational doctrine. If any single phrase could sum up the operational doctrine of Schlieffen and his followers, it would be "battle of annihilation." According to Schlieffen, wars were determined by decisive battles. This mindset essentially accorded with Prussian military traditions, yet differed from them in extent. Clausewitz had emphasized main force battles, but he left space open for other possibilities in his analysis and advocated a dialectical approach to problems. For instance, he suggested that war "does not consist of a single instantaneous blow," and wondered if "whether, through the loss of a great battle, forces are not perhaps roused into existence, which otherwise would never have come to life."[67] Schlieffen, by contrast, pushed the concept of "decisive battle" to its logical extreme, to the extent that he essentially equated it with war itself. Thus, a decisive battle of this sort could only be achieved through the complete destruction of the enemy's main force. Through, in other words, a battle of annihilation.

The only model of war that had any value for Schlieffen, therefore, was the battle of annihilation. In a letter dated September 18, 1909, Schlieffen stated: "the battle of annihilation alone is the desirable battle."[68] As chief of the General Staff, he repeated tried to inject this notion—that the complete annihilation of the enemy's main force is the highest command objective and that any victory that does not accomplish this is incomplete—into the army. He considered the elder Moltke's victory at Sadowa to have been "incomplete," as it did not fully destroy the Austrian main force, whereas the victory at Sedan in the Franco-Prussian War was a "complete victory."

In terms of concrete methods, Schlieffen believed that the secret to winning a battle of annihilation was attacking the enemy's flank. As argued above, he clung to the belief that history demonstrated that, from ancient times down to the present day, flank and rear attacks were the only method for accomplishing this. It was an unalterable law. Through his efforts, this vision was spread throughout the army and other types of offenses were discounted—in particular frontal attacks and breakthroughs, which were commonly held to result only in "regular victories." Schlieffen's ideas did encounter resistance from some high-ranking officers, such as Bernhardi, who considered them mistaken and dangerous because they restricted a commander's ability to react flexibly to battlefield developments, and because they made it easy for enemy commanders to predict and counteract German plans.[69] Others held that, while flanking and envelopment attacks were important military tactics, they were not the only important military tactics. Commanding officers should study how to correctly assess conditions and how to flexibly use a variety of tactical methods in response. Some ranking officers even criticized Schlieffen's development of an "envelopment mania" within the army.[70] Overall, however, these critiques did not have much effect, and Schlieffen's ideas remained dominant. According to researchers, initiating a battle of annihilation through flank and rear attacks became standard operational procedure during Schlieffen's tenure. The classic example of this was the 1904–1907 German colonial war in Southwest Africa. This war was fought to repress a popular uprising. German troop levels and logistics in Southwest Africa were insufficient for a battle of annihilation, yet the Germans repeatedly attempted to use this tactic.[71]

The command style Schlieffen championed was even more dogmatic than his strategies or operational doctrines. In modern war, given the size of armies and battlefields, fights and battles are distant from one another; the highest authority should give army commanders precise instructions, just as in the past, battlefield commanders gave precise orders to unit commanders. Thus, in his view, wars were simply battles writ large. This is why the Schlieffen Plan was conceived of as a large-scale military campaign. When it came to concrete strategic command, Schlieffen believed that the highest commanding officer was the most important, "all army commanders should fully acquaint themselves with the plan of the supreme commander, and one thought alone should permeate the whole army." At the same time, planners from the General Staff were simply the supreme commander's "chessmen," guaranteeing that the supreme command could concentrate on precisely ordering an army of over a million troops. The powerful right flank called for by the Schlieffen Plan was supposed to march through Belgium as if on "battalion drill."[72] Once the supreme command sets the route for the offensive and orders the army into action, however, there is essentially nothing left to do. Once the machinery of the army has been set in motion, its operations should become automatic. The role of the supreme commander then would be to transmit orders to his armies and then only to "urge the armies and corps already engaged in action to new exertions, to keep in their direction of march those not yet engaged, or to direct them into new ones if the situation has changed."[73]

The concepts that undergirded Schlieffen's method of strategic command cannot be ascribed to Prussian or German traditions. The elder Moltke had emphasized that a rigid, dogmatic adherence to operational plans could be fatal. Supreme commanders therefore must encourage subordinate commanders at all levels to act proactively and independently. In terms of concrete operational command, the elder Moltke proposed that commanding officers must, as much as possible, restrict themselves to issuing only the most necessary orders: "An order shall contain everything that a commander cannot do by himself, but nothing else." As a wartime commander, the elder Moltke very rarely interfered with action at the tactical level, and was ready to change his overall plan at a moment's notice based on his subordinates' tactical victories. During the opening weeks of the Franco-Prussian War, for example, he realigned his pre-existing plans once they had been rendered void by the precipitous actions of overly enthusiastic subordinates. Building on their successes, he was soon able to achieve victory at Sedan.[74] Given the existence of this tradition, Schlieffen's mechanical theory met with a certain resistance within the German Army. Bernhardi, for instance, denounced the notion as "mechanistic," arguing that this kind of warfare "can scarcely be any longer called an art" and would diminish commanding officers to acting as mere "mechanics." Even the younger Moltke harbored doubts about this kind of centralized, detailed style of command.[75] Resistance and doubt, however, only exerted a limited influence overall. All of the General Staff's pre-war planning exercises and war games operated under this mechanistic principle. The younger Moltke, as head of the General Staff, would similarly demand that planned routes and schedules be rigidly adhered to in war games.

Finally, Schlieffen believed that spiritual aspects lay at the core of fighting a large-scale, decisive battle of annihilation. He recognized the difficulty and risk of fighting such battles, including the one anticipated by the Schlieffen Plan. This led him to set high standards for the army's morale and willpower. He demanded that soldiers develop a fearless, heedless optimistic spirit, decisiveness unwavering in the face of danger, and unwillingness to entertain any doubts about the prospects of victory. During his tenure, he systematically injected his vision of willpower, extreme courage, optimism in the face of danger, and a naïve kind of action at all costs into a new generation of General Staff officers, which had a tremendous influence on the whole army. In a speech, his successor, the younger Moltke, noted that Schlieffen had directed everyone's attention to a single objective: "All energy should be directed to this highest goal, and the will that leads to it was the will to victory. This unrelenting, emotional will to victory is the legacy that [Schlieffen] has left to the General Staff. It is up to us now to hold it sacred." In all fairness, demands for high military morale and spirit are common, and Schlieffen's emphasis on this was not excessive. The problem, however, was that these demands were made against the backdrop of his extreme idealization of battles of annihilation. Thus, errors crept in: Schlieffen's calls for high morale shifted, to a great extent, into encouragement of excessively optimistic belief in his operational methods and strategic objectives. Doubt was repressed. In his diary, the crown prince of Bavaria wrote: "It was a false mental orientation, especially visible in Prussian military circles, that one did not want to hear doubts. Anyone who expressed doubts or an opinion different from what was desirable was all too easily taken to be a pessimist, weakling, or faint-hearted, and if possible was removed."[76]

In conclusion, Schlieffen was the most authoritative military theorist after the elder Moltke, and exerted a significant impact on German military theory and mindsets. His views on the links between the military and the political, on security assessments, and on operational thought all, in fact, reflected a dead-end or single-minded tendency within the German military. This was a step backward for German military thinking. At the same time, the German military increasingly fell under the control of two entirely opposed emotions: desperation caused by a feeling of entrapment and extreme self-confidence brought about by the feeling that they held the key to victory. Under the influence of this bipolar intellectual tension, the Schlieffen Plan ultimately became the German Army's only choice.

9

Crisis Management on the Path to World War, 1908–1914

"And if the chance of one battle—that is, a particular cause—has brought a state to ruin, some general cause made it necessary for that state to perish from a single battle."
Montesquieu

As reflected in both the Tirpitz Plan and the Schlieffen Plan, Germany no longer had a grand strategy—or anything close to it—by 1908. Ever since Bismarck's fall in 1890, Germany's ability to plan for or utilize its strength had declined, even as its material power continued to grow apace. The result of this was that, by 1908, foreign pressures had reached catastrophic proportions, and the whole of Europe had entered an era of crisis and conflict. It was possible for Germany to be drawn into a final reckoning with another power at any moment. Effective crisis management had become Germany's last remaining tool to prevent disaster. Yet, in a certain sense, crisis management is also an extension of grand strategy. In the absence of a grand strategy, German crisis management fell prey to the whims of foreign and domestic pressures. In the end, it facilitated a final reckoning with foreign pressures: World War I. This shattered Germany's rise.

The Bosnia Crisis and its Consequences

The Pre-Crisis Situation

After the Anglo-French Entente and Anglo-Russian Convention, Germany's encirclement became common knowledge. By 1908, ties between the Triple Entente powers were drawn even closer. That May, the French president received a warm welcome on a visit to Great Britain. The next month, King Edward VII of Great Britain visited Reval and met with the czar. He was accompanied by First Sea Lord Jackie Fisher, Foreign Office Permanent Undersecretary Charles Hardinge, and other prominent officials, who held talks with Russian Prime Minister Peter Stolypin and Foreign Minister

Alexander Izvolsky. During these meetings, Hardinge emphasized to Izvolsky that, due to the "unnecessarily large increase in the German naval program," Great Britain placed no faith in Germany's future intentions. As the German naval plan moved toward completion, he warned,

> in seven or eight years' time a critical situation might arise, in which Russia, if strong in Europe, might be the arbiter of peace, and have much more influence in securing the peace of the world than at any Hague Conference. For this reason it was absolutely necessary that England and Russia should maintain toward each other the same cordial and friendly relations as now exist between England and France.[1]

These actions naturally served to deepen Germany's fears. From Germany's perspective, the frequent summits between the leaders of the Entente countries, particularly the Reval meeting, were steps toward the tightening of Germany's encirclement. Although both the British and the Russian governments assured the Germans that they had not concocted any anti-German plans at that meeting, few in Germany were convinced. At the same time, Germany's only ally, Austria-Hungary, appeared weaker and weaker. In 1906, the Austro-Hungarian Empire experienced a constitutional crisis over its dual monarchical system, based on the connections between the Hapsburg dynasty and the Hungarian royal house. Demands for independence from Slavs within the empire continued to rise as well. Common opinion across Europe held that the Austro-Hungarian Empire was held together only by the person of the eighty-year-old emperor, Franz Joseph II—and once he passed, so too would the empire. French and British newspapers frequently broached the topic of Austria-Hungary's imminent collapse. This served to make Germany's assessment of the current situation even more pessimistic, and its support for Austria-Hungary more unconditional. Chancellor Bernhard von Bülow's memorandum of June 25 was a good reflection of this. In this lengthy document, Bülow laid out his understanding of the Entente powers' opposition to Germany. He noted that although their arrangement was a defensive one, he feared that they might attack as they gained in strength. Bülow also noted that Austria-Hungary was much weaker than Germany, and thus much more likely to become a target. Thus, Germany's general policy should be one of loyal cooperation with Austria-Hungary while maintaining a low-profile program of military preparation.[2]

Neither Austria-Hungary's Chief of General Staff Franz Conrad von Hötzendorf nor Foreign Minister Alois Lexa von Aehrenthal were inclined for their country to be merely Germany's junior partner. They believed that a series of forceful diplomatic actions could revive their empire's fortunes. Both believed that the roots of Slavic national liberation movements within the Austro-Hungarian Empire lay in Serbian encouragement and support. A determined strike at this would-be Piedmont of the Slavs would resolve the empire's nationality problem.[3] The national liberation movements then active in Bosnia-Herzegovina seemed to provide a perfect occasion to test this theory. The 1878 Treaty of Berlin had assigned sovereignty over this region to the Ottoman Empire, while also authorizing Austrian occupation and administration. As national consciousness grew among Slavs in the territory, calls for union with Serbia also rose. This led Aehrenthal to consider simply annexing the territory, in order to squash this notion and, at the same time, damage Serbian prestige. Russian Foreign Minister Izvolsky, too, had been seeking a dramatic foreign policy victory, particularly one that would open the Black Sea Straits to the Russian Navy. This raised the possibility of a secret accommodation between the two sides.

The Bosnia Crisis and German Management

On July 2, 1908, Izvolsky offered Austria-Hungary a bargain: Russian support for its annexation of Bosnia in exchange for Austrian support of Russian naval access to the Black Sea Straits. The foreign ministers of the two empires met at Buchlau on September 15, where they reached a secret accord to this effect. During the talks, Austrian Foreign Minister Aehrenthal promised that he would inform the Russian government before taking any concrete action.

Yet, to the Austrians, it was not particularly important to respect this agreement *per se*; instead, it was important that the Austrian action both humiliate Serbia and establish Austrian superiority in the Balkans. On October 6, Bulgaria declared independence with Austrian support, thus violating the terms of the 1878 Treaty of Berlin, which had established Bulgaria as a self-governing state under Ottoman suzerainty. The stage was set for the crisis. Aehrenthal, in response to this event, claimed that "now we and Germany have Bulgaria in our hands."[4] A day after the Bulgarian declaration, Austria-Hungary took the significant step of formally announcing the annexation of Bosnia. This incited a heated international reaction, thus igniting the crisis in earnest.

Three parties had particularly furious reactions to Austria's announcement: the Ottoman Empire, Serbia, and Russia. The Ottoman Empire's domestic situation was extremely unstable, the country having just experienced the "Young Turk" revolution in July 1908 that overthrew the sultan's autocratic rule. The annexation was another blow to the country's prestige, and the Young Turks organized a nationwide boycott of Austro-Hungarian products.

Emotions in Serbia were even more intense, and popular opinion violently criticized the move as a violation of the Treaty of Berlin and called for a war to the death against Austria-Hungary. The Serbian government made preparations for a general mobilization, while irregular "Comitadji" units armed themselves. At the same time, the government called on other European countries to intervene, while demanding "territorial compensation" for Serbia.[5]

For Russia—and Izvolsky in particular—anger and a sense of betrayal were mixed together, making the reaction especially intense. After his secret agreement with his Austrian counterpart, Izvolsky concluded that the Black Sea issue had implications for the Treaty of Berlin, and thus it would be appropriate for him first to gain the approval of the other signatory nations. He embarked on a trip to canvass for support in Paris and London, but before he got underway, Austria-Hungary announced the annexation and Serbia appealed for Russian help. Izvolsky was caught unprepared. He soon learned that both France and Great Britain (the latter in particular) were fundamentally opposed to Russian access to the straits. Although Great Britain and Russia had reached an agreement in 1907, considerable British dissatisfaction with Russian actions remained. Consequently, the British saw opposition to Russia in this instance as the only means of enforcing Russian compliance with the agreement.[6] Pan-Slavists within Russia denounced Izvolsky for betraying Slavic interests to Aehrenthal. In this situation, Izvolsky could do nothing other than quickly change his tune. He suddenly became a staunch supporter of Serbia, claimed that he had never agreed to the Austro-Hungarian annexation, and demanded an international conference on the Bosnian issue. Austria firmly opposed this. Thus, the Bosnia Crisis quickly transformed into a diplomatic struggle between Russia and Austria-Hungary.

Up to this point, Germany was not yet involved in the dispute. Moreover, Germany was displeased with Austria-Hungary's impetuous actions, which were taken without any advance notice given to Germany. Wilhelm II was incensed, calling Austrian actions and explanations "laughable."[7] His initial reaction was that Germany needed to oppose the Austro-Hungarian action, so that no one else would believe that it had been taken with German support. Even more important, Germany had invested a significant amount of capital in the Ottoman Empire and had essentially already pulled it into

Germany's strategic orbit. Austria's actions had now upset that calculus. From Germany's perspective, its current ally had just bullied its prospective ally. It was in an embarrassing situation: it could neither oppose its ally nor protect its prospective ally. Wilhelm II expressed this succinctly in his notes on a telegram from Bülow:

> I only regret that Aehrenthal's fearful stupidity has brought us into the dilemma of being unable to protect and stand by the Turks who are our friends, seeing that my own ally has injured them. And now I must look on at England taking my place in Turkey with her advice and protection, and doing so with arguments based on International Law, which are incontestable and really after my own heart. Thus my Turkish policy, so carefully built up for 20 years, is thrown away! A great triumph over us for Edward VII![8]

Yet this was not the mainstream judgment among German policymakers. For the German government, suffering from the encirclement of other powers, nothing was more frightening than the loss of Austria-Hungary as an alliance partner. Thus, Bülow had attempted to mollify the kaiser in a long October 7 telegram that laid out his views on the proper German reaction to the crisis. In this document, Bülow undertook a defense of Austria-Hungary's actions, which he claimed originated in anxieties about Serbian and Croatian nationalism. An impatient German attitude would not help matters. Moreover, Austria-Hungary's understanding of Balkan affairs was much greater than Germany's, and its interests in the region much more profound. Bülow reminded the kaiser of Austria-Hungary's loyal support of Germany at the Algeciras Conference and during the 1908 summer naval exercises. Germany should endeavor to reciprocate.[9] Wilhelm II was soon persuaded. Thus Germany had essentially committed itself to support for Austria-Hungary in the early phase of the crisis.

Once the crisis transformed into a diplomatic showdown between Russia and Austria-Hungary, Germany's position changed as well. Germany began to see a connection between the Bosnia Crisis and the earlier strengthening of the Triple Entente. German leaders soon conceptualized the crisis as a contest between the Austro-German alliance and the entente—and as an opportunity to weaken Russia. Bülow stated this directly in a memorandum: "Since Russia demonstratively joined England at Reval, we could not give up Austria. The European situation was so changed that we must be more reserved to Russian wishes than we used to be."[10] At the same time, Germany expressed forceful, and virtually unconditional, support for Austria-Hungary. On October 20, Bülow wrote to Aehrenthal, stating that Austria could deal with Serbia as it saw fit: "'I shall regard whatever decision you come to as the appropriate one."[11] This, essentially, gave Austria a blank check—and this would play a critical role in the development of the crisis. Austria-Hungary was convinced that Germany would foot the bill for the risks it ran; thus, it stuck to a hard-line position and even prepared for war with Serbia. Aehrenthal replied with his thanks in a December 12 letter that also expressed Austria's willingness to take an even greater risk of war:

> If in the course of the next two months Serbia's attitude gives us cause again for serious complaint, we should have then to make a final decision. You may be assured, honored friend, that I should inform you of this in good time. If this happens I intend, in order to prevent a further extension of the conflict, to declare definitely to the other Powers that we are merely performing an act of clear necessity, but that we do not mean to attach the independence and territorial integrity of Serbia and Montenegro. I may hope that a quick military action combined with this declaration will prevent the dangers of which I have spoken.[12]

By early 1909, Germany's blank check to Austria had extended from diplomatic issues to military ones. In January, Chief of the Austrian General Staff Conrad sent a letter to the younger Moltke, asserting that a war with Serbia was probable. He predicted that once war broke out, Russia would join the Serbian side and that Germany, according to the 1879 treaty of alliance, should then assist Austria-Hungary. France, however, might then enter the war as well, or Germany might have to launch a preemptive war to forestall a French strike on the German rear. Austria-Hungary's General Staff thus needed to know where Germany would focus its military efforts, as this would have implications for its own planning. Conrad's letter, generally speaking, was vague in its content and phrasing, but was clearly intended to suss out Germany's strategic bottom line in an emergency. Bismarck, or another practitioner of Europe's various diplomatic traditions, would have replied indirectly or have demanded clarification. By this time, however, Germany's pressing need to rein in its Austro-Hungarian ally had eclipsed all other concerns. The younger Moltke did not deny Austria-Hungary's assumptions and did not demand an explanation of Austro-Hungarian intentions. Instead, he completely accepted the Austro-Hungarian rhetoric and gave an extremely clear response: If Russian interference gave Germany the cause for war, then Germany would mobilize as soon as Russia mobilized.[13] The reply was sent on January 21, after first having obtained the kaiser and the chancellor's approval. This essentially represented a blank check in military affairs; Conrad understood the younger Moltke's words as "binding written agreements."[14] Even more important, during this phase of the Bosnia Crisis, the nature of the Austro-German alliance changed dramatically. When Bismarck built the alliance in 1879, he asserted that it was defensive in nature and guided entirely by Germany. This would prevent Germany from being needlessly dragged into danger by Austro-Hungarian expansionism. During the December 1887 Bulgaria Crisis, Bismarck's blunt response to an Austro-Hungarian feeler was: "For us Balkan questions can in no case constitute a motive for war."[15] Beginning with Bülow's letter of October 30 and the younger Moltke's of January 21, the Austro-German alliance diverged from Bismarck's original intention, becoming an expansionary alliance. Even more important, Austria-Hungary could write whatever it wanted on the blank check provided by Germany and thus could activate the alliance whenever, and for whatever purpose, it chose. In other words, control of the alliance had slipped from German into Austro-Hungarian hands.

When Germany gave its complete support to Austria-Hungary's dealings with Serbia and Russia, it naturally also needed to focus on the actions of the other two members of the Triple Entente: Great Britain and France. Germany's desire was to conciliate with these powers in order to concentrate forces exclusively against Russia. Of the two, France was the easier to deal with. No major crisis had erupted between Germany and France since the First Morocco Crisis. Neither Wilhelm II nor Bülow had any remaining interest in Morocco itself. Just before the outbreak of the Bosnia Crisis, there had been a diplomatic scuffle between the two countries in which the German consulate in Casablanca attempted to aid the desertion of six foreign national French soldiers. French troops not only caught the deserters, but also beat the consular secretary and several German soldiers. The German government had no heart for further entanglement in the Moroccan Question, and thus was uninterested in allowing the situation to expand from the beginning. After the outbreak of the Bosnia Crisis, Germany fervently wished to rid itself of this issue. Wilhelm II himself admitted in a letter that the demands of the German public could not be fulfilled, and that an accommodation with France on this issue should be the most important policy goal.[16] On February 9, 1909, Germany and France signed an agreement on the Morocco issue. France promised not to damage German economic interests, while Germany acknowledged France's leading role in Morocco, thus temporary stabilizing the relationship between the two countries.

Great Britain, however, would not be so simple. First, Anglo-German ties were already strained by the naval arms race. Great Britain saw Germany as its principal competitor, and its handling of the Bosnia Crisis contained elements of a balancing policy against Germany. Second, Great Britain intended to use the situation to increase its own influence in Turkey and the Balkans. Third, Anglo-Russian relations had been rocky since the 1907 convention between the two countries, so Great Britain was looking to strike a blow against its erstwhile ally. Thus, in the Bosnia Crisis, Great Britain did not seek to replicate the firm support it had given France in the First Morocco Crisis. It did not offer words of support for Russia. The British, moreover, excelled at effectively cloaking their own national interests with the rhetoric of universal justice. (The United States, in more recent times, has never been able to excel at this to the same level.) During the Bosnia Crisis, the British packaged their own interests in two seemingly irrefutable notions: first, that international law and international treaties should be respected, and second, that injured parties should be compensated. The implication of the first was that the Black Sea Straits would not be opened to Russia, that Austria-Hungary could not unilaterally annex Bosnia, and that Bulgaria could not proclaim itself independent. Yet it did not suggest specific means of redress, allowing for flexibility and latitude. The second generated goodwill in Turkey and Serbia, but Great Britain itself would not have to pay for their compensation. These stances not only allowed Great Britain to take the moral high ground in the crisis, but also preserved its room for maneuver in terms of concrete actions.

Without French and British support, Russia was at a disadvantage in facing the combined pressure of Germany and Austria-Hungary. Russian military strength still had a long road to recovery from defeat in the Russo-Japanese War, and the danger of domestic revolution still existed. These factors determined Russia's bottom line: under no circumstances could it fight a war with Austria-Hungary and Germany. Izvolsky's hard-line position could only be surface-deep under these conditions. As the crisis developed, Great Britain became worried about the risk of a war between Austria-Hungary and Serbia. British Foreign Secretary Edward Grey circulated a note to Germany, France, and Italy on February 19, 1909, calling on the four nations to cooperate in preventing an Austrian declaration of war against Serbia. Germany's position, however, had already been set: it would not act as a "middleman" of any kind, not would it undertake any kind of mediation (these were exactly the roles that Bismarck had adopted); instead, everything would be directly decided by the countries involved.[17] In other words, Germany was encouraging a great-power showdown. Once Germany's position became clear, the British efforts naturally fizzled out and Austro-Serbian and Austro-Russian tensions grew. The Bosnia Crisis increasingly came to resemble a game of chicken that could only end with one side's complete retreat. On February 26, France expressed the view to Russia that events in Bosnia were "a question in which the vital interests of Russia are not involved" and that "French public opinion would be unable to comprehend that such a question could lead to a war in which the French and Russian armies would have to take part."[18] The French had declared that the Franco-Russian alliance did not apply to the Bosnia Crisis.

France's position made Russia's predicament even worse. In March 1909, Austria-Hungary began war preparations, and the danger of conflict with Serbia rose. In the face of this, the Serbian government maintained its uncompromising, hard-line attitude. On March 10, Serbia circulated a diplomatic note to the powers, protesting the annexation of Bosnia and claiming that all signatories to the Treaty of Berlin needed to respond to this event. Russia clearly understood that, given its inability to aid Serbia at this moment, Serbia would be crushed by Austria-Hungary's superior might. As a consequence, Russia's position and prestige in the Balkans would suffer disastrous blows. Thus, Russia demanded an international conference even as it grew more desperate to rein in Serbia, demanding that it "maintain self-restraint." Against this backdrop, Germany proposed on March 14 that, through the exchange of notes, Austria-Hungary invite the great powers to agree to an Austro-Ottoman convention and annul the clause of the Treaty of Berlin relevant to Bosnia. Russia, however, would have to signal its agreement before Austria issued its invitation.[19] All things considered, Germany's proposal was in fact a demand that the other great power acknowledge and legitimize Austria-Hungary's violation of an international treaty after the fact. Although this action would work entirely in Austria-Hungary's favor, it would also allow the other great powers to preserve face. This led to changes in British and Russian stances. The British expressed their dissatisfaction with Serbia's March 10 note to Germany. The Germans took this to indicate that "Europe's sympathy had cooled off so much that even in the lamentable event of a collision there was reason to hope that the conflict might be localized."[20] Russian Foreign Minister Izvolsky still hoped to hold out, but others in the Russian government had already prepared to fold. On March 17, the Russian cabinet decided against military intervention in the Austria-Serbia dispute. Izvolsky himself came under pressure from Austria. He had long painted himself a protector and supporter of Serbia and the southern Slavs, so Aehrenthal threatened to release documents from their secret negotiations at Buchlau that would prove his complicity in the annexation of Bosnia.[21]

By this point, the crisis was approaching resolution. Germany and Austria-Hungary, however, seemed to feel that they had not yet inflicted enough humiliation on their opponents. Great Britain proposed allowing Serbia to distance itself from the issue. Austria-Hungary rejected this and demanded Serbian acknowledgment of Austria-Hungary's authority to annex Bosnia. While the Russian foreign minister hesitated in making a decision on whether or not to pressure Serbian compliance with this harsh demand, Germany again pressured Russia in an unnecessary tone that sounded like a final ultimatum: "We expect an answer—yes or no; we must regard any evasive, conditional or unclear answer as a refusal. We should then draw back and let things take their course. The responsibility for further events would then call exclusively on M. Izvolsky, after we had made a last sincere effort to help him clear up the situation in a way which he could accept."[22]

Russia could only surrender. Although the British were unwilling, in the end they, too, pressured Serbia in accordance with Austria-Hungary's demand. On March 30, 1909, the ambassadors from Great Britain, France, Russia, and Italy presented the Serbian government in Belgrade with a joint note demanding Serbian acceptance of the Austro-Hungarian demand. The next day, the government formally declared:

> Serbia recognizes that she has not been affected in her rights by the *fait accompli* created in Bosnia, and that consequently she will conform to the decisions that the Powers may take in regard to Article 25 of the Treaty of Berlin. In deference to the advice of the Great Powers, Serbia undertakes to renounce the attitude of protest and opposition which she has adopted since last autumn with regard to the Annexation. She undertakes, moreover, to modify the direction of her present policy toward Austria-Hungary, and to live in future on good neighborly terms with the latter.[23]

The crisis had ended with a complete victory for the Austro-German alliance.

Consequences of the Crisis

The consequences of the crisis proved harmful for Germany. Overall, the European situation had grown increasingly tense. During the crisis, the Triple Entente and the Austro-German alliance were locked into fully oppositional stances, and the danger of all-out war arose for the first time.

Even more important, Germany had become the entire center of the dispute. Originally, the crisis had been instigated by the Austro-Hungarians; Germany had no part in it. Yet Germany's hard-line stance during the crisis made other nations suspect that it was the puppet master behind the scenes. During a 1910 visit to Austria-Hungary, Wilhelm II exaggeratedly claimed that Germany had stood at Austria's side in the moment of danger "like a knight in shining armor."[24] This simply fueled the suspicions of other powers. The stance of the Triple Entente toward Germany also became more hard-line as a result. From the British perspective, the Bosnia Crisis coincided with the height of the Anglo-German naval competition. The "naval scare" had occurred in 1908, and Germany had already become Great Britain's greatest and most direct threat. The British believed that Germany's goal was to use the crisis to splinter the entente and establish itself as a continental hegemon. The only available route for Great Britain, then, was to solidify ties with France and Russia. During the crisis, Grey wrote that "if we sacrifice the other Powers to Germany we shall eventually be attacked."[25] It was Russia, however, that had been humiliated the most during the crisis, and the impact was correspondingly large. Pan-Slavic newspapers in Russia engaged in long-term, fierce criticisms against Germany. They openly predicted that a war between the Slavic race and the Teutonic race was "unavoidable." Russia's policymakers found the roots of this failure in Russia's insufficient military preparations, which led them to decline the Austro-German challenge. Thus, Russia embarked on a program of military expansion, strengthened its ties with Great Britain and France, and resolved itself not to back down in the next crisis. The recommendations of the Russian ambassador in Paris were representative:

> Foreseeing the further development of the European situation, many newspapers come to the conclusion that precisely as Germany and Austria have now achieved a brilliant victory, so must the two Western Powers, together with Russia, now pay their attention to the systematic development of their forces in order to be able, once they are in a position not to fear a challenge of the Triple Alliance—and in this case Italy would separate herself from the Triple Alliance—to set up on their part demands which would restore the political balance which has now been displaced in favor of Germany and Austria...all these circumstances show how necessary it is for us to bind ourselves still more closely to France and England in order to oppose in common the further penetration of Germany and Austria in the Balkans.[26]

Serbia, too, felt deeply humiliated and had set its heart on vengeance. Serbian determination to promote national liberation in the Balkans intensified, and underground organizations like the Black Hand increased their activities. This planted the seeds for Archduke Franz Ferdinand's assassination in 1914.

From the perspective of the Austro-German alliance, Germany found itself in an uncomfortable position. Fears of losing Austria-Hungary as an ally had driven it to offer support regardless of cost during the crisis, including taking the lead in opposing Russia. Even more important, Germany had given Austria-Hungary its blank check. This was an offer of unconditional German support for any Austro-Hungarian action, including war. The balance within the alliance had clearly tilted toward Austria-Hungary; the weaker nation was leading the stronger. Afterward, German policymakers appeared to regret this course of action. Not long after the crisis was resolved, Chancellor Bülow resigned and reportedly told the kaiser: "Do not repeat the Bosnian affair."[27] A year later, Germany's ambassador to Vienna wrote:

> Germany is not a Balkan Power. During the past year, for reasons of higher policy, we threw the weight of our political influence into the scales in favor of Austria. In my opinion we should do well to prevent, as far as possible, a repetition of this procedure. For the future, we ought to preserve a free hand for ourselves, and allow ourselves to be drawn as little as possible into Balkan questions, so that we shall be able at the psychological moment to choose our policy freely or to use it as profitably as possible.[28]

Over the following years, however, Germany's fear of encirclement overwhelmed its calculations of interests; regret and reflection had no time to have an impact on policy. The motives and logic that had been apparent in the Bosnia Crisis would be replicated in the July Crisis of 1914. The difference was that the stance of Germany's opponents would not be the same, and the final results would be completely different.

The Second Morocco Crisis

The Pre-Crisis Situation

The Bosnia Crisis had cast a momentary shadow of general war over Europe. History, however, does not develop in a straight line. Although Russia embarked on an expansion of its military and vowed not to back down in the next crisis, its relationship with Germany did not continue to deteriorate after the crisis. In September 1910, Russian Foreign Minister Izvolsky was transferred to the ambassadorship in Paris and replaced as foreign minister by Sergey Sazonov. Russo-German ties began to thaw. In November, Sazonov met with Chancellor Theobald von Bethmann-Hollweg and German Secretary of State for Foreign Affairs Alfred Kiderlen in Potsdam, where the two sides reached an agreement on the Baghdad Railway under construction by Germany and Persia. This Potsdam meeting was a setback for Great Britain, which had tried to prevent unilateral deals between France or Russia and Germany over the railway issue. In anger, Grey even claimed that he would resign in favor of a foreign secretary who could reach a naval understanding with Germany, so that an Anglo-German alliance could oppose Russian expansion in Persia and Turkey.[29] The other member of the Triple Entente, France, had struck an independent bargain with Germany over Morocco. Of course, neither Russian nor French deal-making behind Great Britain's back implied a betrayal of the entente. Yet it demonstrated that the entente was far from being iron-clad, and that opportunities existed for Germany to break out of its encirclement.

This potential was reflected most clearly with regard to France. As long as Alsace and Lorraine remained in German hands, Franco-German relations would also remain deadlocked, to be sure. "Deadlock," however, did not mean that France was determined to fight a war, much less that it wanted to recover its lost territories by force. Conversely, at the same time that the naval arms race had decidedly worsened Anglo-German ties, there were signs of a thaw in Franco-German relations. Finance capitalists and a number of heavy industrial capitalists in the two countries hoped to work together to increase their monopolies. French Finance Minister (and later prime minister) Maurice Rouvier represented these forces in French politics. Major German steel companies Thiessen and Krupp inked an agreement with the French company Schneider-Creusot to cooperatively develop mines in Morocco, the focus of a crisis in 1905. This, in essence, was a joint monopolization of Moroccan iron mining.

The momentum for improved ties, however, was unstable. Inside Germany, some forces were displeased by this cooperation over Morocco. The German Colonial Society and the Pan-German League had always resented Germany's defeat in the First Morocco Crisis, and believed that the government was sacrificing Germany's interests in the country. Some smaller steel manufacturers were dissatisfied with the monopolization of Moroccan mines by larger companies. Such companies joined hands with the Colonial Society and the Pan-German League to promote their position as the defenders of the national interest. These pressures were direct attacks on Franco-German cooperation. At the same time, they made the German government increasingly nervous about dealing with Moroccan affairs.

Germany's Crisis Management

In March 1911, an anti-French uprising broke out in Fez, Morocco. The French used this as a pretext to dispatch an army and occupy the country's cities, including Fez. This placed the entire country under the French sword and rendered the Algeciras agreement null. France promised the signatories on that accord that, once order was restored, it would withdraw its troops. The European nations all understood, however, that the restoration of order would take an indefinite period of time. Thus began the Second Morocco Crisis.

The German principally responsible for managing the crisis was Kiderlen. He had entered the German diplomatic service in 1879 and had demonstrated promise. He gave a number of apt nicknames to important German political figures, dubbing Bülow "the eel" and Bethmann "the earthworm." He had adopted hard-line methods and could be pompous. He authored the final ultimatum to Russia issued during the final stages of the Bosnia Crisis. Kiderlen became foreign minister in 1910, after which he became even more self-confident and proud, to the point where he rarely communicated with his superior, the chancellor. This further fragmented the German Empire's decision-making systems. These issues would all deeply mark Germany's handling of the Second Morocco Crisis.

Germany reacted to France's abrogation of the agreement reached at Algeciras. On April 28, 1911, Kiderlen warned France that it would be easier to occupy Fez than to vacate it. If the French Army remained in Fez, Germany would consider the sultan's sovereignty null and void. Given that the Algeciras understanding was no longer operative, Germany was free to take independent action.[30] What would such action entail? Kiderlen initially hoped to block French annexation of Morocco, but was opposed by Wilhelm II. The kaiser had not wanted to be dragged into Moroccan affairs in 1905, and was even less willing to cross France over this issue again, given the results of the last crisis there. Thus, when reminded that Germany was a signatory to the Algeciras agreement, the kaiser took exception: "If it suited their policy the French would coolly ignore such Agreements in spite of protests by others and then we might whistle for it since we did not want a war over Morocco."[31]

Yet the German government could not remain aloof from the Moroccan Question. Greed may have played a part, but the most significant factor was German public opinion. From the moment the French occupied Fez, the German government came under enormous pressure at home. This was the major difference between the two Morocco Crises. During the first crisis, the German government was invested but the population was not; essentially, the government pushed public opinion along. In the wake of that crisis, after being subjected to the repeated educational efforts of the government and the propaganda of the Colonial Society and Pan-German League, German public opinion had been fully awakened. Many ordinary Germans had already come to see Morocco as an important factor in Germany's future development. Thus, when the second crisis broke out, German public opinion became more invested than the government; public opinion now pushed the government. In May 3 memorandum, Kiderlen pointed out: "Our public opinion, saving only the Social Democratic Party, would reproach the Government severely, if it simply let things in [Morocco] go on as they please; whereas it is certain that material results would turn the votes of many dissatisfied electors and perhaps influence not inconsiderably the approaching Reichstag election." The importance of the memorandum lay not only in its partial explanation of Germany's motives, but also for its detailed display of German outlook and policy considerations. It clearly states:

> In all probability by the force of circumstances sooner or later the provisions of the Act of Algeciras will no longer hold good, however great the pretense. The Sultan, who can only maintain his authority in the land with the help of French bayonets, no longer provides guarantees for the independence of his country, and this was the whole object of the Act of Algeciras.

Given the treaty's nullification, freedom of action reverted to the signatory nations. The question for Germany was how to make use of this. As the memorandum notes, the occupation of Fez paved the way for the French annexation of the entire country. Germany would gain nothing from protesting and could, instead, suffer a moral defeat. Thus, given that France could deploy troops to protect its citizens in Morocco from harm, so too could the Germans dispatch warships to Adagir and Mogador. Once the navy entered those ports, it would obtain some kind of "pledge" and Germany should "look confidently on at the further development of affairs in Morocco and see whether France will offer us proper compensation in her own colonial possessions, in return for which we could abandon the two ports."[32]

After winning Wilhelm II's approval, Kiderlen set about to trying to wrest tangible advantages from France. His basic calculations were quite clear: focus on France alone, rather than attempting a multilateral strategy. He did not propose concrete conditions, but instead hoped to force France to offer compensation proactively. He ignored Great Britain, although his reason for selecting these two Atlantic ports as Germany's objectives was their distance from the Mediterranean. This, he thought, meant that Great Britain would not mind. There were three gaps in his considerations. First, although bilateral talks would have been effective in 1905, 1911 would be different, given the existence of the Triple Entente. Second, the Anglo-German naval competition was at its peak, so moves to acquire an Atlantic port would touch a nerve in Great Britain and might be met with fierce opposition. Third, in the wake of the Bosnia Crisis, the British government would not ignore Franco-German negotiations. In fact, on May 22, British Foreign Secretary Grey had told the German ambassador in London that while Great Britain had freedom of action in other areas, in Morocco it was bound by the entente to support France.[33] Germany paid no heed to this warning, and continued to press France. France, however, had no intention of providing any compensation to Germany, and merely feigned civility when Germany hinted at its desire. On June 20, Franco-German talks finally began at Kissingen. Kiderlen maintained his reticence during the negotiations, thus the meeting concluded with French hints of compensation for Germany. Both sides, however, claimed the need for greater authorization from their governments.

After the Kissingen negotiations, the French dragged their feet, failing to suggest any concrete compensation for Germany. Germany grew impatient. Kiderlen felt that it was time for Germany to take strong measures. On July 1, 1911, the German destroyer *Panther* anchored in Agadir harbor, ostensibly to protect German citizens. Suddenly, the situation had become tense. This turned out to be an extremely inopportune moment for Germany to take a hard-line stance. The relatively pro-German Joseph Caillaux had just become France's prime minister, creating hopes for an increasing thaw between the two nations. Faced with Germany's forceful actions, however, Caillaux's relatively pro-German faction had even less maneuvering room to make concessions than France's anti-German groups. He was vulnerable to criticism as an appeaser, even a traitor. Thus, France sought help separately from Great Britain and Russia. Russia's response was repayment for the French position on the Bosnia Crisis—it claimed that the Franco-Russian alliance would be "inoperative" in the event of a war begun by colonial disputes. Great Britain's reaction, however, was very different. The British interpreted this as another German attempt to tear the Triple Entente apart. Moreover, it was also an attempt to obtain a large naval base on the Atlantic. Great Britain could accept neither of these things. Thus, as Grey thought, Great Britain needed "to give to France such support as would prevent her from falling under the virtual control of Germany and estrangement from us."[34] The French Foreign Ministry asked for a Royal Navy vessel to be dispatched to Agadir as well; although Grey agreed, the cabinet vetoed the notion. In the end, Great Britain decided merely to issue Germany a warning. On July 4, Grey met with the German ambassador to London and conveyed three messages. First, Great Britain considered Germany to have created a new situation by sending a gunboat to Agadir. Two, if Moroccan affairs continued to develop in this way, it would attract greater British attention. Three, Great Britain could not permit any new agreements that it was not a party to.[35]

The British response transformed the crisis. Previously it had been primarily a hidden contest between France and Germany. From then on, however, Great Britain would take center stage, and its disputes with Germany would come to the fore, superseding the Franco-German tensions. After Great Britain took this foreign policy stance, the French government notified Germany on July 6 that the presence of the *Panther* made the resumption of negotiations very difficult. Germany paid no notice to this refusal and continued to press France. On July 9, Kiderlen held another meeting with the French ambassador. There had been no changes to either side's thinking. Germany was still unwilling to put all of its cards on the table, while the French were happy to delay things further. Each side waited for the other's proposals. In the end, this negotiation was the diplomatic equivalent of going around in circles: both men claimed to need further instructions from home before the talks could continue. This seesaw-style diplomacy caused the kaiser to lose his patience. He jotted in the margins of a report from the chancellor that: "Now I should like to know what further authority is needed. Mine was given 4 weeks ago. The whole thing was brought before me a second time at Kiel quite superfluously by Kiderlen in the Chancellor's presence and my approval was asked for again and granted at once. What the devil is to happen now? It is pure farce! They negotiate and negotiate and nothing comes of it."[36] Kiderlen was unable to remain calm in this situation. French patience, too, had been worn down to the point that France floated proposals for compensation.

On July 15, two weeks after the *Panther* had anchored itself at Agadir, the French ambassador sought out Kiderlen with the proposal that France cede the border region of its colony in Congo as territorial compensation. Kiderlen put all of his cards on the table this time: a portion of French Congo was unacceptable; only the whole of it would do. This surprised the French ambassador, who explained that even relinquishing part of the Congo would be difficult to explain to the French people. The French government had thought of a number of possibilities, including asking the Germans to cede a small piece of colonial territory in return. There was no precedent for the wholesale surrendering of a colony, however. In the end, they rejected the German proposal. Faced with France's stance, splits appeared within the German government. Kiderlen believed that Germany should continue to push its proposal, and moreover, "we must continue to act very strongly, if we were to get a favorable result." Chancellor Bethmann, however, thought that the French rejection was understandable. Asking for an entire colony as compensation was not realistic; Germany, if needed, could also cede a portion of colonial territory to France as compensation.[37] Kiderlen handled the negotiations on his own, however, and essentially ignored Bethmann's views. Kiderlen judged that the original notion of holding Agadir as a pledge had become impractical, as an actual occupation of the port could easily lead to conflict with Great Britain. Germany's only escape route was to obtain as much compensation as possible through a tough negotiating stance.[38] Public opinion within Germany had now reached flood tide, with every party except the Social Democrats and left-wing progressive groups holding high hopes for the compensation that could result from this crisis. The Pan-German League and other like-minded groups openly called for Germany to risk war. Confronted with these pressures, the German government naturally found it difficult to turn away from its hard-line policy. It could only go forward.

In reality, the space for Germany's hard-line policy during the Second Morocco Crisis was already diminishing. The French negotiating position had slowly hardened, as France could reject any German claim without being harmed unless Germany actually decided to go to war. The pressure from Great Britain, too, was increasing. Kiderlen's insistence on bilateral negotiations sparked British fears that their interests might be sacrificed in any Franco-German compromise that resulted from them. Germany had never revealed its true intentions to Great Britain, and had never explained that it was not actually seeking an Atlantic naval base, causing British doubts to grow. On July 21, 1911, British Foreign Secretary Grey summoned the German ambassador and directly inquired about Germany's intentions. He expressed misgivings that a Franco-German deal was in the works, and was particularly worried about Germany obtaining an Atlantic port. Yet the German ambassador failed to provide a clear response. On the same day, Chancellor of the Exchequer David Lloyd George made a public address at the London mayor's residence. He displayed a rarely-seen hard-line stance:

> I would make great sacrifices to preserve peace. I conceive that nothing would justify a disturbance of international good-will except questions of the gravest national moment. But if a situation were to be forced upon us in which peace could only be preserved by the surrender of the great and beneficent position Britain has won by centuries of heroism and achievement, by allowing Britain to be treated, where her interests were vitally affected, as if she were of no account in the Cabinet of nations, then I say emphatically that peace at that price would be a humiliation intolerable for a great country like ours to endure.[39]

Lloyd George's shocking speech was the first major event of the Second Morocco Crisis. It was rare for a cabinet member to make such forceful remarks, so this speech had a strong impact on public opinion in Great Britain, France, and Germany. In Great Britain and France, anti-German feelings swelled at once, and newspapers of all kinds attacked Germany. Inside Germany, these remarks created a tide of anti-British sentiment. Political parties and forces of all stripes called the speech humiliating to Germany and demanded a powerful response from the government. Moreover, Lloyd George had long held moderate views on Anglo-German ties, to the extent that he could be seen as the leader of a peace faction. The harsh words of such a figure naturally shocked the German government deeply. Thus, the German government concluded that Lloyd George had been carefully selected by the British government to present this view in order to demonstrate that the cabinet was united on this issue.[40] When Germany protested this speech, Grey displayed a similarly hard-line stance, arguing that Lloyd George's words had been "suitable to the occasion" and that he had "no means of allying the public anxiety as to our alleged intentions regarding Agadir."[41]

Confronted by both Britain's hard-line stance and the German public's aroused nationalistic sentiments, the German government was left with little room to maneuver. It could only bullheadedly continue to follow its own hard line of pressuring France to indicate that "the dignity of Germany would compel her to secure by all means full support by France for German treaty rights."[42] "All means" included war. In fact, Kiderlen had considered going to war, but the kaiser refused to support a war over Morocco. Given that war was actually off the table, German insinuations that it would resort to war to achieve its aims were not effective. Instead, they led to two unanticipated results. The first was the danger of an Anglo-German war. Germany's threats had been aimed at France, yet there was no indication that a Franco-German war was in the offing. The British, however, actually began preparing for war, and the odds of an Anglo-German conflict rose. At the end of July, the Royal Navy was ready for war and, even more significantly, the Admiralty had begun planning the transport of the British Army to the continent. The outlines of World War I were already becoming apparent. By August, Lloyd George openly called for his compatriots to pay attention to the risk of war, thus inspiring a bellicose mood in the British population. Railway workers ended a major strike in response. The second result was that feelings among the German public intensified. Once the Second Morocco Crisis began, the public had pressured the government to take a hard-line position. By July, public sentiment was out of control. Some extremist organizations called openly for war with Great Britain and France. The government's own stance and hints of war after Lloyd George's speech gave the German public even more confidence that their government would continue to take a hard-line position, even to the point of war. The whole country experienced war fever, and seemingly the entire population was ready to welcome this battle. These two results undoubtedly made it more difficult for the German government to walk back from the precipice. As this was happening, the German stock market dropped precipitously on fears of war, and France demanded payment on short-term loans to Germany. A fiscal crisis resulted.[43] By this point, Kiderlen's hard-line strategy had reached a dead end.

Germany finally agreed to compromise with France in September. Germany accepted that the Algeciras agreement had been voided and that Morocco was now a French protectorate. In compensation, the French ceded two long, narrow parcels of land in the French Congo. On November 4, the two sides signed the agreement and the *Panther* left Agadir at the end of that month. The crisis was now over.

Effects of the Crisis

The Second Morocco Crisis had brought Europe closer to war than either of the preceding major crises. Although none of the four continental powers began concrete preparations for war, Britain's Royal Navy had done so. This was the first time since German unification that any European power had begun to put itself on a wartime footing. Viewed macroscopically, the main consequence of the Second Morocco Crisis was that it further increased the hostility between the two alliance systems. Policymakers in all of the powers were left with an even deeper impression that war was unavoidable.

For the Entente powers, this crisis spurred closer military cooperation between France and Great Britain. In terms of written documentation, of course, no alliance at all existed between the two countries, and both denied any military obligations to the other. The British and French General Staffs had begun effective military consultations after the First Morocco Crisis, however, and an alliance had already been built at the operational level rather than the policymaking level. After the Second Morocco Crisis, operational cooperation increased, with a number of concrete policy implications. In July 1912, the Royal Navy recalled its fleet from the Mediterranean in order to strengthen its naval force in the North Sea. Simultaneously, the French Navy transferred its Atlantic fleet to the Mediterranean. This, in effect, created a strategic division of labor between the two countries. Under this arrangement, France essentially abandoned the defense of its Atlantic coastline. Great Britain would shoulder an inescapable moral duty to protect this region. Although there was no treaty, the Royal Navy would have to undertake this responsibility in wartime, perhaps even to the extent of intervening in a continental war.[44]

The Franco-Russian alliance was reinforced at around this time, too. In July 1912, the two countries reached a secret naval agreement that stipulated mutual support in the event of war. Now the entire armed forces of both countries were linked by formal treaty obligations. Even more important, both had strengthened their resolve to confront the Austro-German alliance. During the 1908 Bosnia Crisis, France had declined to back Russia, claiming that the Balkans were not a core interest of France. During the Second Morocco Crisis, the Russians naturally repaid this treatment in kind. Yet after that crisis, the two countries apparently realized that they needed to provide greater mutual support, at least in terms of relations with the Austro-German alliance. French Prime Minister Raymond Poincaré said as much during a 1912 visit to Russia. A Russian record reported him explaining that "public opinion in France would not permit…military action for the sake of purely Balkan questions if Germany did not take part." For situations in which Germany became involved, however, Russia "could certainly count on France for the exact and complete fulfilment of her obligations."[45] A month later, Poincaré told Izvolsky, now serving as ambassador to Paris, that "if conflict with Austria brought intervention by Germany, France would fulfil her obligations."[46]

For Germany, the crisis provided further impetus to take military risks in the next crisis. During the crisis, German public opinion had been completely mobilized. A fervor permeated the nation, to the point that, to a certain extent, the people were already psychologically prepared for war. Yet the resolution had left the population disappointed. It seemed to many that the demands of the people and of the nation had been exchanged for two bits of swamp-filled, jungle-covered land in the French Congo. The German colonial secretary dismissed these tracts of land as essentially "useless."[47] The chasm between the emotions and the results of the crisis led the public to vent its anger at the government. The newspapers, speaking essentially with one voice, castigated the weakness of the government and of the kaiser, who they dubbed "Wilhelm the Peaceful." In the Reichstag, parties of all affiliations voiced their displeasure. On November 9, 1911 (five days after the agreement had been signed), the Reichstag held three days of debate, during which Bethmann was twice forced to take the floor in his own defense. Conservatives blamed the government for making concessions in Morocco and thus sacrificing German prestige, as well as for making only a weak response to Lloyd George's speech. The leader of the National Liberals accused the government of fearing war. He claimed that the German people had been ready, but that they had been let down by the cowardice of their government and their kaiser, who should take complete responsibility for this diplomatic humiliation.[48] During each of these attacks, the crown prince applauded in support, putting the government under even greater pressure. The Pan-German League openly attacked Wilhelm II, while others filed a complaint against Kiderlen on the grounds that his compromise was "treason." Nothing like this had happened since the founding of the German Empire. It seemed as if "Germany experienced a sort of national revolution, an 'awakening.'"[49]

These relentless pressures deeply unsettled German policymakers and reinforced their resolve to face their next test without backing down. The younger Moltke expressed these feelings clearly in a letter:

> If we creep out of this affair with our tails between our legs, if we cannot be aroused to an energetic set of demands which we are prepared to enforce by the sword, then I am doubtful about the future of the German Empire. And I will resign. But first I will propose that we abolish the army and place ourselves under the protection of Japan. Then we will be able to make money without interference and to become imbeciles.[50]

Overall, the experiences of the Second Morocco Crisis strengthened German tendencies to adopt hard-line policies even at the risk of war. It proved to be a psychological dress rehearsal for the outbreak of war two years later.

The July Crisis and the Coming of War

The Situation on the Eve of the Crisis

If one could combine the 1908 Bosnia Crisis and the 1911 Second Morocco Crisis, the result would essentially be a rough outline of the July Crisis in 1914, which led to the outbreak of war. Arguably, these two crises provided opportunities for different actors to rehearse their roles: the Austro-German alliance and Russia in 1908 and the Anglo-French Entente and Germany in 1911. Instead, there are always changes that leave gaps and possibilities. Those with the ability, and the courage, can grasp hold of these short-lived opportunities to transform the fate of an individual or a nation.

After the Second Morocco Crisis, hostility between the two alliance systems increased, militaries in all countries expanded, and the possibility of world war grew. Yet historical gaps still existed. In 1913, Germany and Great Britain had at long last reached a compromise over the Baghdad Railway. The two countries also concluded an agreement over the fate of Portugal's colonies. Likewise, they acted relatively cooperatively during both the First and the Second Balkan Wars in order to prevent the conflicts from escalating. In 1914, the two nations experienced a brief conflict over Middle Eastern oil, but found a solution in March that resulted in a joint Anglo-German oil company.[51] Calls within the British government for improved Anglo-German ties gained in strength. Chancellor of the Exchequer Lloyd George declared: "Our relations are very much better than they were a few years ago.... The two great Empires begin to realize they can co-operate for common ends, and that the points of co-operation are greater and more numerous and more important than the points of possible controversy."[52] In France, forces opposed to greater military spending and to the alliance with Russia gained the upper hand in the April 1913 elections; a Franco-German thaw seemed near, too. Doubts also emerged within the German government about the value of the Austro-Hungarian alliance. The German ambassador to Vienna wrote in May 1914 that "I constantly wonder whether it really pays us to bind ourselves so tightly to this phantasm of a State which is cracking in every direction, and to toil any further at dragging it along with us." He suggested that consideration be given to German policy in event of the dual monarchy's dissolution.[53]

These were only tiny sprouts, however. None of Germany's political or military leaders at the time seized upon or even noticed them. Instead, they increasingly focused on what was seen as an inevitable war. Within the German policymaking establishment, a growing number of people began to see war as an acceptable choice. Even Chancellor Bethmann, who had never advocated war, began to shift his opinion. Wilhelm II discovered that "even the Chancellor now appears to be accustomed to the idea of a war, although he had said only a year ago that he would never be capable of advising war."[54] The German military had become uneasy with the pace at which the militaries of the Entente powers, particularly Russia, had been growing. Military commanders came to believe that the Austro-German alliance was at an increasing disadvantage. Russia was in the process of constructing a rail network in its western territories. Once completed (which the Germans estimated would happen in 1916), it would be of immense value to the Russian military machine. It would also make conditions on the ground even less favorable for the Schlieffen Plan. Given this assessment, the logic of the German military was easy to understand: Given that war was unavoidable, it should be started before Germany's advantages disappeared entirely. The younger Moltke made this clear to his Austro-Hungarian counterpart in a May 12, 1914, letter: "We are ready, the sooner the better for us."[55]

Germany's willingness to risk war rose in tandem with the increasing military collaboration between the Entente powers. Between 1913 and 1914, continuing the trend begun by the Franco-Russian naval accord, Russia demanded a naval understanding with Great Britain, so that the Royal Navy would force open the Black Sea Straits in the event that they were closed in wartime (during the war, this thinking would lead to the 1915 Gallipoli campaign). The June 1914 Anglo-Russian naval talks held in London were discovered by a German spy in the Russian Embassy. This information shook the German government. Bethmann reported that "whereas up till now it was only the most extreme pan-Germans and militarists in Germany who insisted that Russia was deliberately scheming to attack us, now calmer politicians as well are beginning to incline to that opinion."[56] The majority of German policymakers took this as a sign that Germany's encirclement was being drawn even tighter. Breaking out of this encirclement now became a pressing task.[57] This provided the psychological backdrop to the July Crisis.

Germany's Response to the Crisis

On June 28, 1914, Archduke Franz Ferdinand, heir to the Austro-Hungarian throne, was assassinated by a Serbian nationalist. This event shook the entire continent and raised the curtains on the July Crisis.

Paradoxically, Franz Ferdinand had been among the most enlightened Austrian political leaders on the issue of nationalities. He promoted increased political rights for Slavs and advocated the transformation of the empire from a dual monarchy in which power was jointly shared by Germans and

Hungarians into a triple monarchy that included the Slavs. He also opposed war. In March 1914, the German ambassador in Austria-Hungary specifically identified the archduke as the pro-war faction's main opponent.[58] Thus, not only did his assassination give Austria-Hungary the perfect excuse to settle the score with Serbia, but it also cleared away this obstacle to war. The pro-war faction quickly became ascendant within Austria-Hungary. The course of events then pushed Austria-Hungary's ally, Germany, to the center of the stage.

The German reaction—and, in particular, the reaction of Wilhelm II—to the assassination was to encourage Austria-Hungary to take strong measures during the time that it still retained the sympathies of other European nations. German foreign policy, by contrast, remained cautious. On June 30, German ambassador to Vienna Heinrich von Tschirschky advised the Austrians to remain calm and to determine their objectives carefully, keeping in mind that Austria was not the only country in the world. It would therefore need to consider its ally and the entire European situation, particularly the stances taken by Italy and Romania toward Serbia. Wilhelm II's annotations on this document, however, suggested the exact opposite: "Now or never. Who authorized him to act that way? That is very stupid! It is none of his business, as it is solely the affair of Austria, what she plans to do in this case. Later, if plans go wrong, it will be said that Germany did not want it! Let Tschirschky be good enough to drop this nonsense! The Serbs must be disposed of, and that right soon!"[59]

Wilhelm II's impulse would ultimately come to have an important influence on the course that the crisis took. Yet, between June 30 and July 5, German handling of the crisis continued to follow the course set by the foreign ministry. On July 2, for example, Austro-Hungarian Foreign Minister Leopold Berchtold again spoke to the German ambassador about the Serbian threat and demanded German support. Yet Tschirschky responded that German support had never included specific guarantees, due to the Austrian insistence of speaking only in principle rather than in terms of concrete plans of action. Only once such a detailed plan was proposed could Berlin consider giving its full support.[60] In other words, Germany would not provide a blank check for Austria to use as it wished. On July 4, the German Foreign Ministry was still working on Austria-Hungary, demanding that it maintain restraint. The Austrian ambassador in Berlin reported back to Berchtold that "Zimmerman [German Under-Secretary of State for Foreign Affairs] assured me that he would consider decisive action on the part of Austria, with whom the whole civilized world today was in sympathy, quite comprehensible, but still he would recommend the greatest caution, and advise that no humiliating demands be made upon Serbia."[61]

On July 5, the situation began to change. The kaiser met the Austrian ambassador for lunch, during which he was given a handwritten note from the Austro-Hungarian Emperor Franz Joseph II. It read in part:

> After the last frightful events in Bosnia, you too will be convinced that a friendly settlement of the antagonism which divides Austria from Serbia is no longer to be thought of, and that the peace policy of all European monarchs is threatened so long as the source of criminal agitation in Belgrade lives on unpunished.

He further proposed building a new Balkan alliance on the basis of strengthened ties with Bulgaria and Romania.[62] This was nothing less than an attempt by Austria-Hungary's highest authority to force Germany's highest authority to take a position. By this point, however, the kaiser's reaction had become much more constrained than it had been during the crisis's first days. He made a cautious response, explaining that while he hoped that Austria-Hungary would take serious actions against Serbia, the current proposals were likely to lead to a serious European conflict. Thus, he could not make any definitive replies before conferring with his chancellor. Later, however, the kaiser's attitude seemed to change again and his emotions got the upper hand. He told the Austrian ambassador that Austria-Hungary would receive Germany's complete support on this issue. With regard to actions against Serbia, he urged the Austrians to act quickly, regardless of what they were planning to do. Russia, he believed, was not yet ready for war, and so would weigh its response carefully.[63] The historical documentation of this conversation is exceptionally murky; the kaiser's words and the Austrian ambassador's own inferences are lumped together, making any precise analysis difficult. One point, however, is clear: the kaiser had expressed Germany's full support for Austria-Hungary. In other words, Wilhelm II had provided the blank check that his foreign ministry had been unwilling to supply.

Bethmann prepared a formal version of the blank check. On July 6, he wrote in his instructions that Germany would help Austria-Hungary win over Romania and Bulgaria. On the issue of Serbia, "His Majesty [the Kaiser] will faithfully stand by Austria-Hungary, as is required by the obligations of his alliance and of his ancient friendship."[64] From the beginning of the crisis, Germany surrendered control over events and allowed Austria to take action

Not only did Wilhelm II and Bethmann give Austria-Hungary complete freedom of action, but they also encouraged Austria-Hungary to go to war against Serbia. They believed that as long as Austria-Hungary took action while memories of the assassination remained fresh, other powers would find it morally difficult to respond forcefully. Austria-Hungary could then easily win a military victory. Moreover, German assessments indicated that Russian military preparations were incomplete. Russia thus would not run the risk of war by supporting Serbia. An Austro-Serbian war would therefore be a localized war, and Germany would not be drawn in. Based on this assessment, Germany made no preparations for war on July 6, and the kaiser returned to his sailing vacation on the North Sea.

Once Germany's opinion had reached the Austrian emperor, it became a powerful weapon in the hands of the pro-war faction. They used it to pressure Hungarian Prime Minister István Tisza, who had advocated the pursuit of a diplomatic victory only, to consent to issue demands "that would be wholly impossible for the Serbs to accept." The situation would then be solved by military force.[65] On July 14, he agreed to send a final ultimatum to Serbia. No obstacles to war remained within the Austrian government. On July 20, Austria-Hungary secretly shared its ultimatum with the Vienna-based ambassadors of the other great powers. It was conveyed to Serbia on July 23 and to the other great powers on the following day. Between July 6 and July 28, Germany essentially left Austria-Hungary to its own devices. It offered only tactical suggestions, such as Foreign Ministry Secretary Gottlieb von Jagow's advice on July 11 to "collect sufficient material to show that there exists a Greater-Serbia agitation in Serbia which threatens the Monarchy, in order that European public opinion should be convinced of the justice of Austria's cause as far as possible. It would be best to publish this material—not in parts, but as a whole—shortly before submitting the demands, or the ultimatum, to Serbia."[66] Austria-Hungary would, in fact, ignore this piece of advice.

Even more important, Germany remained in the dark about Austria-Hungary's ultimate objective. On the one hand, Germany knew the basic contents of the final ultimatum, and understood that Serbia would find them unacceptable, thus leading to an Austro-Serbian war.[67] On the other hand, however, Germany was unclear about what Austria-Hungary ultimately hoped to achieve. In particular, it was uncertain whether or not Austria-Hungary intended to partition Serbian territory. On July 17, Jagow demanded that the German ambassador in Vienna figure out what empire's "plans" actually were and "where the road is likely to lead us."[68] Regardless, however, Germany's crisis management strategy had been to follow the path of supporting Austrian settling of accounts with Serbia. Germany's leaders believed that it was entirely possible for such a war to remain localized. As long as Germany did not mobilize, and Austria-Hungary engaged in only a partial mobilization (that, in particular, precluded mobilization in the border regions with Russia), then forceful diplomatic action would be enough to keep the Russians out of the war.[69] The more that Germany supported Austria-Hungary, the less likely it was that Russia would intervene, making a localized war even more possible. Foreign Ministry Secretary Jagow explained this assessment in a July 18 letter to the German ambassador to Great Britain:

> The maintenance of Austria, and, in fact, of the most powerful Austria possible, is a necessity for us both for internal and external reasons.... The more determined Austria shows herself, the more energetically we support her, so much more quiet Russia will remain.... If we can not attain localization (of the conflict) and Russia attacks Austria, a *casus foederis* will then arise; we could not throw Austria over then...I still hope and believe, even today, that the conflict can be localized.[70]

It should be pointed out that lurking behind Germany's confidence in a localized conflict was another baseline consideration: even if the war proved impossible to localize and the Austro-German alliance was drawn into a wider war, Great Britain would remain neutral. As early as November 1912, the Austrian ambassador in London had inquired of Foreign Secretary Grey whether or not Great Britain would remain neutral in an Austro-Serbian war. Grey remained silent, which was taken as a tacit indication of neutrality.[71] In July 1914, British King George V told German Prince Henry that Great Britain would remain neutral in a continental war. Based on this information, Jagow stated on July 26 that "we are certain Great Britain will remain neutral." Bethmann, too, agreed with this assessment. Arguably, Germany's handling of the crisis before July 26 had been based on the assumption of British neutrality.[72]

This assessment, like so many others in post-1890 Germany, was entirely wishful thinking. Even though Great Britain's ultimate policy stance was still unclear, the tendencies had long been evident. On December 2, 1912, during the early phase of the First Balkan War, Bethmann emphasized in a speech to the Reichstag that if Austria-Hungary were attacked by "a third partner" and "if her existence were thus threatened," Germany would aid its ally. Germany would also "fight, in order to preserve our position in Europe and to defend our future and security." On the following day, British Secretary of State for War Richard Haldane told the German ambassador that Great Britain desired to maintain the balance of power, thus could "not tolerate under any circumstances the defeat of the French." Nor could Great Britain accept "one block of continental powers under the leadership of one single power." Two days later, Foreign Secretary Grey also raised the topic of Bethmann's speech with the German ambassador. He warned the ambassador that Germany should not expect that Russia would back down in the face of German pressure in the next crisis, and that Great Britain had a strong interest in preventing another French defeat by Germany. This hinted that if the situation on the continent escalated into a Franco-German war, Great Britain would not remain neutral. Wilhelm II, upon hearing this, became so incensed with Great Britain that he "saw" the Anglo-Saxons would stand with the Slavs and the Latins in a coming confrontation with the Teutons.[73]

Thus, Germany's (and, in particular, Bethmann's) handling of the July Crisis was tainted by self-delusion and false confidence. On July 23, 1914, Austria-Hungary delivered its final ultimatum to Serbia and demanded a reply within 48 hours. The following day, after Austria-Hungary shared the contents of its ultimatum with the other powers, Germany declared that it had no advance knowledge of the ultimatum's contents. It also, however, announced at the same time its complete support for Austria-Hungary's actions and emphasized the importance of keeping the dispute between Austria-Hungary and Serbia localized. The Entente powers, Russia in particular, saw Germany's action as being extremely heavy-handed, and it was understood to indicate that Austria-Hungary's moves had been instigated by Germany. At this point, the Russians reacted exactly in the manner that Grey had warned about in 1912: they resolved not to back down and considered war to be unavoidable. In this tense situation, Austria-Hungary declared that Serbia's response (which had been given within 48 hours) was unacceptable. It then cut diplomatic ties with Serbia. Within an hour of this announcement, Austria-Hungary withdrew all of its diplomatic personnel from Belgrade. The July Crisis had entered a new phase. The countdown to an Austro-Serbian war had begun. Emotions ran high within Russia's pro-war faction, which demanded military mobilization in support of Serbia. On July 26, Great Britain warned Germany that a localized Austro-Serbian war was "wholly impossible, and must be dropped from the calculations of practical politics."[74]

By this point, there was very little possibility that Germany could limit the war to Austria-Hungary and Serbia alone. The time for crisis management was running out. On July 26, Germany became aware of two trends. The first was that Russia had begun military preparations at dawn that day. The second was that, in the afternoon, the British had proposed a high-level conference with Germany, France, and Italy in order to prevent further escalation of the crisis. Germany did not see either of these trends as beneficial. The Russian mobilization naturally inspired German nervousness, as Germany's advantage lay in the speed of its own mobilization. If Russia mobilized while Germany did nothing, then Germany would quickly lose its advantage. This led Bethmann to telegraph the Russians, warning that "maintenance of European peace depends upon Russia alone. Confiding in Russia's love of peace and in our long-established friendly relations, we trust that she will take no step that will seriously endanger the peace of Europe."[75] He also demanded that Great Britain and France pressure Russia, but neither responded. Germany was also resistant to Great Britain's suggested four-power conference. On the surface, it appeared to be a fair "court of law": of the four countries, two were Austrian allies (Germany and Italy) and two were Russia's partners (Great Britain and France). In fact, however, Italy had been leaning toward the Entente powers for a long time, making it likely that the balance of power within the conference would be three against one. A meeting of ambassadors, moreover, would not put an end to the preparations for war. Russia could continue to mobilize, while Germany's advantage in mobilization speed would be dissipated by this so-called international conference. If negotiations broke down, the Austro-German alliance would find itself in a deeply disadvantageous military situation. Thus Germany rejected Great Britain's proposal. On the same day, even as Bethmann, Germany's highest civilian official, half-heartedly pursued the localization of the conflict, the German military came to its own assessment. The younger Moltke returned to Berlin and, believing that war was now inevitable, drafted a final ultimatum to Belgium. This would begin the implementation of Germany's only war plan—the Schlieffen Plan.

On July 27, the kaiser ended his North Sea cruise and returned to Potsdam. He was surprised to discover the extent to which Austria-Hungary had overdrawn his "blank check." As war approached, Wilhelm II seemed to shrink back from the conflict. On the morning of July 28, he saw the response Serbia had given to Austria-Hungary's ultimatum three days earlier and could not contain his enthusiasm: "A brilliant performance for a time-limit of only forty-eight hours. This is more than one could have expected! A great moral victory for Vienna; but with it every reason for war drops away."[76] He envisioned for Austria-Hungary to occupy a portion of Serbia, including Belgrade, as a guarantee to ensure that Serbia would live up to its commitments. Regardless of whether this notion was laughable or practical, however, time had already run out. On the same day, Austria-Hungary declared war on Serbia, pushing the crisis to a much more dangerous level. Russia was again faced with the choice between war and humiliation. The dominoes leading to war had already begun to fall.

Yet Germany's policies continued to attempt to balance full-throttled support for Austria-Hungary with a half-hearted acceptance of a continental war in which Great Britain, it still believed, would remain neutral. Thus, even after the July 28 declaration of war, Germany did not exert pressure on Austria-Hungary. After the kaiser floated his notion of a guarantee, Bethmann attempted to mediate on this basis. He demanded that Austria-Hungary satisfy itself with "stopping at Belgrade." His attitude, however, was noticeably equivocal:

> You will have to avoid very carefully giving rise to the impression that we wish to hold Austria back. The case is solely one of finding a way to realize Austria's desired aim, that of cutting the vital cord of the Greater-Serbia propaganda, without at the same time bringing on a world war, and, if the latter cannot be avoided in the end, of improving the conditions under which we shall have to wage it, in so far as is possible.[77]

The final sentence in particular revealed Bethmann's acceptance of a wider war. Thus, after July 28, Germany focused its diplomatic efforts on preventing Russia's entry into the war. There were three reasons for this. First, Germany did not want to offend Austria-Hungary. Second, Germany believed that Russia could again be cowed into submission (as it had been in the 1908 Bosnia Crisis) by a strong German position. Third, if Russia did enter the conflict, responsibility for the war could be placed on Russia, thus improving the conditions for conducting the war.

On July 29, Germany attempted to sway Russia. The kaiser directly telegraphed the czar at 1:45 a.m., expressing his hope that the joint efforts of the two countries could maintain the peace. At around the same time, the czar telegraphed the kaiser with a similar message. Yet these were merely sentimental appeals for peace. This "hot line" between heads of state did not, and could not, result in any concrete, actionable plans for resolving the crisis. Neither side was willing to budge in its support for its ally. On the same day, Russia began mobilizing for war, and Germany's options contracted further. Austria-Hungary now began pressuring Germany: once Russia began its mobilization, Austria-Hungary started to feel military pressure on their common border. Yet it was unwilling to back down in Serbia, and so requested

German military assistance. Austrian Foreign Minister Berchtold was clearly calling for an Austro-German mobilization in response to Russia's move.[78] In addition to this request from an ally, the opinion of Germany's own military played a critical role. The General Staff submitted a report to the chancellor on July 29 that noted that mobilization and the structure of the alliance were an automatic, mechanical series of interconnected processes. Austria-Hungary's intervention in Serbia, combined with Russia's partial mobilization, necessitated a host of linked responses that would culminate in a European war.[79]

Germany increased its pressure on Russia. Bethmann sent what was, in essence, a final ultimatum on July 29 at 12:50 p.m. He stated that if Russia continued to mobilize, then it would force Germany to do the same and "in that case a European war could scarcely be prevented."[80] Several hours later, the kaiser sent another telegram to the czar that read "military measures on the part of Russia which could be looked upon by Austria as threatening would precipitate a calamity we both wish to avoid, and jeopardize my position as mediator which I readily accepted on your appeal to my friendship and my help."[81] Czar Nicholas II was weak-willed and, faced with this exhortation based on appeals to blood ties and the threat of a final ultimatum, he sought to backtrack. He immediately rescinded the general mobilization order and replaced it with a partial mobilization on the Austrian border alone. None of his ministers concurred, however. The foreign minister was unwilling to make diplomatic concessions, while the military emphasized that technical issues meant that a change in the mobilization order would create chaos. Even more important, the next rounds of Russo-German diplomatic contact revealed that the rift between the two countries could not be healed. These included Germany's demand that Russia accept Austria's empty proclamation of "respect for Serbia's territorial integrity" (which meant that the partial Austrian occupation of Serbia would only be temporary). Russia, of course, absolutely could not allow Serbia to be reduced to an Austro-Hungarian protectorate. Thus, Russian suspension of mobilization only created the most fleeting of opportunities. Once Germany ended its restraint of Austria-Hungary, the wheels of war began to turn again.

From Germany's own perspective, it had made some efforts to preserve the peace. Yet, it had not taken the one critical step of directly pressuring Austria-Hungary at any time during the entire month before July 29. In the words of the French deputy foreign secretary, it was this alone that could have prevented general war.[82] Thus, Germany's diplomatic efforts should be understood as an attempt to win another diplomatic victory for the Austro-German alliance rather than as an attempt to prevent general war. Once a diplomatic victory became impossible, Germany hoped for a localized military victory. By July 29, however, it suddenly became clear that this policy, too, would be difficult to maintain. That day, Great Britain formally issued a warning to Germany: if the conflict were limited to Russia and Austria-Hungary, Great Britain could remain neutral; if Germany and France were drawn in, however, Great Britain would not find it "practicable to stand aside and wait for any length of time."[83] This information came in a report from the German ambassador to Great Britain that reached Berlin at 9:12 p.m. on July 29. It instantly shattered German illusions about British neutrality, and "the foundation of their policy during the crisis collapsed."[84] Bethmann discovered that the crisis could result in a general European war, rather than just a continental war. Germany had placed too high a bet. At 1:30 a.m. on July 30, a telegraph from Vienna informed Germany that Austria-Hungary would not accept its suggestion to "stop at Belgrade."

Anxiously, Bethmann finally took the critical step of directly pressuring Austria-Hungary. At 2:55 a.m. on July 30, he forwarded the telegram he had received from the ambassador in London to the German ambassador in Vienna. He appended a new telegram that read:

> As a result we stand, in case Austria refuses all mediation, before a conflagration in which England will be against us; Italy and Romania to all appearances will not go with us, and we two shall be opposed to four Great Powers. On Germany, thanks to England's opposition, the principal burden of the fight would fall. Austria's political prestige, the honor of her arms, as well as her just claims against Serbia, could all be amply satisfied by the occupation of Belgrade or of other places.... Under these circumstances we must urgently and impressively suggest to the consideration of the Vienna Cabinet the acceptance of mediation on the above-mentioned honorable conditions. The responsibility for the consequences that would otherwise follow would be an uncommonly heavy one for both Austria and us.[85]

Five minutes later, he sent another telegram, warning Austria-Hungary: "We are, of course, ready to fulfill the obligations of our alliance, but must decline to be drawn wantonly into a world conflagration by Vienna, without having any regard paid to our counsel." He ordered the ambassador to "please talk to Count Berchtold at once with all impressiveness and great seriousness."[86]

It was already too late for these steps. Hostility between Austria-Hungary and Serbia, backed by Russia, had passed the point of no return. Germany, however, continued its efforts. On July 30, the younger Moltke, under pressure from the kaiser and the chancellor, sent a message to Conrad at the Austro-Hungarian General Staff that argued Russian mobilization was not sufficient cause for German mobilization, unless Austria-Hungary and Russia actually entered a state of war. By this time, however, the opinion of German policymakers began to shift. The earlier predisposition to shrink from war had disappeared, to be replaced with an inclination to welcome it. Bethmann announced in a July 30 meeting of the Prussian cabinet that the emphasis had shifted from pressuring Austria-Hungary to make concessions to allowing the Russians to take responsibility for initiating hostilities. This might entice the traditionally anti-war Social Democrats to support the war.[87] The German military believed that events were already in motion that could not be stopped. The younger Moltke became increasingly anxious and, on the afternoon of July 30, he ignored the foreign ministry entirely and directly contacted Austro-Hungarian military officials in order to request their mobilization against Russia. He assured them, too, of Germany's support.[88] Simultaneously, Bethmann was still advising Austria-Hungary to make concessions and accept mediation. The splintered nature of the German policymaking system was again on full display. Austrian Foreign Minister Berchtold could not resist complaining: "What a joke! Who rules in Berlin?"[89] In point of fact, no one had the final say in the Germany of 1914. In Germany, as in the other European great powers, the strictures of alliance obligations, military mobilizations, and war plans forced politics into the service of strategic needs and subordinated strategy to tactical requirements. All were placed on a conveyor belt to war.

At 6:00 p.m. on July 30, the czar renewed the mobilization order. The machine of war had been set into motion. A series of mobilizations and declarations of war followed, seemingly automatically. Austria-Hungary declared a general mobilization eighteen hours later. Germany, pressed for time by the demands of the Schlieffen Plan, ordered preparations for general mobilization on July 31. The following day, August 1, Germany announced a general mobilization in earnest and declared war on Russia. France mobilized the same day. On August 3, Germany declared war against France and presented a final ultimatum to Belgium that demanded passage for the German Army. Great Britain issued its own ultimatum to Germany on August 4, insisting that Germany respect Belgian territorial integrity. At midnight the same day, the two nations entered into a state of war. World War I had broken out. After four years of bitter war, the German Empire would collapse, marking an end to Germany's rise as a world power.

Notes

Translator's Note

1. Tang Taizong (r. 626–649), speaking of Wei Zheng. This English translation is cited from Howard Wechsler, *Mirror to the Son of Heaven: Wei Cheng at the Court of T'ang T'ai-tsung* (New Haven, Conn.: Yale University Press, 1974), frontispiece. The Chinese original appears in the biography of Wei included in Liu Xu, et al., *Jiu Tang Shu* [Old History of the Tang], Vol. VIII (Beijing: Zhonghua shuju, 1975), p. 2561.
2. Michael Pillsbury, to cite one example, has constructed an alarmist portrayal of Chinese foreign policy on the basis of this insight. Michael Pillsbury, *The Hundred-Year Marathon: China's Secret Strategy to Replace America as the Global Superpower* (New York: Henry Holt, 2015).
3. William Kirby, *Germany and Republican China* (Stanford, Calif: Stanford University Press, 1984), p. 147.
4. See the original formulation of this thesis in Graham Allison, "Thucydides's trap has been sprung in the Pacific," *Financial Times*, August 22, 2012; and a slightly revised version in Graham Allison, "Obama and Xi Must Think Broadly to Avoid a Classic Trap," *New York Times*, June 6, 2013.
5. *The Next Great War? The Roots of World War I and the Risk of U.S.-China Conflict*, Richard Rosecrance and Steven E. Miller, eds. (Cambridge, Mass.: The MIT Press, 2015).
6. For one example, see Xi's comments during a conversation with members of the Berggruen Institutes 21st Century Council in late 2014, "The Most Powerful Leader in the World: A Conversation with Chinese President Xi Jinping." Available at http://berggruen.org/topics/a-conversation-with-president-xi-at-big-s-understanding-china-conference (accessed on August 12, 2015).
7. Sheena Chestnut Greitens, "Lost in Translation: Problematic Metaphors in Contemporary U.S.-China Relations," in Melanie Hart, ed., *Exploring the Frontiers of U.S.-China Strategic Cooperation: Visions for Asia-Pacific Security Architecture* (Washington, D.C.: Center for American Progress, 2014). For scholarly explorations of this reading of Thucydides, see Richard N. Rosecrance, "Allies, Overbalance, and War," and Charles S. Maier, "Thucydides, Alliance, Politics, and Great Power Conflict," in Rosecrance and Miller, eds., *The Next Great War?*
8. Andrew S. Erickson, Testimony before the House Committee on Foreign Affairs Subcommittee on Asia and the Pacific, *Hearing on America's Security Role in the South*

China Sea, 114th Congr., 1st sess., July 23, 2015.

9. The Chinese version of *Fragile Rise* has, as of July 2016, gone through two editions for a total print run of 15,600 copies. Beyond the book itself, Xu has also presented a popular sixteen-part online lecture series on Wilhelmine Germany. This series has garnered nearly 115,000 views for the introductory lecture and several tens of thousands for many of the other lectures. It is available at http://v.qq.com/cover/l/lnbzuelgyjn7zab.html (accessed July 12, 2016).

10. Christopher Clark, *The Sleepwalkers: How Europe Went to War in 1914* (New York: Penguin Books, 2012).

Preface

1. Thucydides, *The Peloponnesian War*, trans. Richard Crawley and rev. trans. T. E. Wick (New York: Modern Library College Editions, 1982), p. 199.

Chapter 1. A Low-Posture Rise

1. Paul Kennedy, *The Rise and Fall of the Great Powers: Economic Change and Military Conflict from 1500 to 2000* (London: Unwin Hyman, 1988), p. 187.

2. Translator's Note: Here the author is using a famous term from recent Chinese foreign policy—*taoguang yanghui* [literally, "hiding strength and biding time"]. The phrase is commonly attributed to Deng Xiaoping, China's leader during the early phases of the reform era, and indicates a deliberate attempt to assume an international role smaller than a nation's size or economy might warrant.

3. John Mearsheimer, *The Tragedy of Great Power Politics* (New York: W.W. Norton, 2001), pp. 68–69.

4. L.S. Stavrianos, *The World since 1500: A Global History* (Englewood Cliffs, N.J.: Prentice Hall, 1971), p. 223.

5. Koppel S. Pinson, *Modern Germany: Its History and Civilization* (Prospect Heights, Ill.: Waveland Press, 1989), p. 158.

6. D. G. Williamson, *Bismarck and Germany 1862–1890*, 2nd ed. (New York: Addison Wesley Longman, Ltd., 1998), p. 45.

7. Pinson, *Modern Germany*, p. 158.

8. Otto von Bismarck, *Bismarck: The Man & The Statesman, Being the Reflections and Reminiscences of Otto, Prince von Bismarck, Written and Dictated by Himself after his Retirement from Office*, A.J. Butler, et al., trans., Vol. I (New York: Harper and Brothers Publishers, 1899), p. 324.

9. Imanuel Geiss, *German Foreign Policy 1871–1914* (London: Routledge and Kegan Paul, 1976), p. 5.

10. Cited in James Joll, *The Origins of the First World War*, 2nd ed. (New York: Longman, 1992), p. 56.
11. Otto Pflanze, *Bismarck and the Development of Germany*, Vol. III (Princeton: Princeton University Press, 1990), p. 12.
12. Ralf Dahrendorf, *Gesellschaft und Demokratie in Deutschland* (München: Piper and Co. Verlag, 1965), pp. 43–59.
13. Gordon A. Craig, *Germany 1866–1945* (Oxford: Oxford University Press, 1981), pp. 103–105.
14. Otto von Bismarck, *Bismarck: The Man & The Statesman*, Vol. II, p. 292.
15. Quoted in Paul M. Kennedy, *The Rise of the Anglo-German Antagonism, 1860–1914* (London George Allen and Unwin, 1980), p. 25.
16. George Earle Buckle and W. F. Moneypenny, *The Life of Benjamin Disraeli, Earl of Beaconsfield*, Vol. V (New York: MacMillan Company, 1920), pp. 133–134.
17. Ibid., pp. 421–422.
18. Edmund Fitzmaurice, *The Life of Granville George Leveson Gower, Second Earl of Granville*, Vol. II (London: Longmans, Green, 1904), pp. 111–114.
19. *Waijiao shi* [Diplomatic History], ed. B. M. He-wo-si-tuo-fu [V. M. Khvostov], trans. Gao Changrong, Sun Jianping (Beijing: Sanlian shudian, 1979), di er juan shang, 45.
20. Bismarck, *Bismarck: The Man & The Statesman*, Vol. II, p. 275.
21. Pflanze, *Bismarck and the Development of Germany*, Vol. II, p. 248.
22. Bismarck, *Bismarck: The Man & The Statesman*, Vol. II, pp. 290–294.
23. Fitzmaurice, *The Life of Granville George Leveson Gower*, Vol. II, p. 74.
24. An English translation of this treaty can be found in Basil Dmytryshyn, ed. *Imperial Russia: A Source Book, 1700–1917* (Hinsdale, Ill.: Dryden Press, 1974), pp. 289–290.
25. Fitzmaurice, *The Life of Granville George Leveson Gower*, Vol. II, p. 113.
26. Pflanze, *Bismarck and the Development of Germany*, Vol. II, p. 266.
27. Ibid., p. 265.
28. Ibid., p. 266.
29. *Die große Politik der Europäischen Kabinette 1871–1914: Sammlung der Diplomatischen Akten des Auswärtigen Amtes* [The Foreign Policy of the European Cabinets, 1871–1914: Collection of diplomatic documents of the Foreign Office], Johannes Lepsius, et al., eds., Vol. I (Berlin: Deutsche verlagsgesellschaft Für Politik und Geschichte, 1922–1927), p. 249.
30. Gordon A, Craig, *The Politics of the Prussian Army 1640–1945* (Oxford: Oxford University Press, 1955), pp. 216–220.
31. The British made this point even before this. E. T. S. Dugdale (selected and translated), *German Diplomatic Documents 1871–1914*, Vol. I (New York: Harper and Brothers, 1928), pp. 3–5.

32. This is the mainstream view of the "War in Sight" Crisis held by historians. See, for instance, A. J. P. Taylor, *The Struggle for Mastery in Europe, 1848–1918* (Oxford: Clarendon Press, 1954), pp. 225–227; and Gordon A. Craig, *Germany*, pp. 107–108. Yet a minority holds that Bismarck truly desired to launch a preventive war against France. See Immanuel Geiss, *German Foreign Policy*, p. 28.
33. Edward Crankshaw, *Bismarck* (London: MacMillan, 1981), pp. 324–325.
34. Dugdale, *German Diplomatic Documents*, Vol. I, p. 10.
35. Pflanze, *Bismarck and the Development of Germany*, Vol. II, pp. 268–269.
36. George Earle Buckle, ed., *The Letters of Queen Victoria, Second Series*, Vol. II (London: John Murray, 1926), pp. 313–314.
37. Dugdale, *German Diplomatic Documents*, Vol. I, pp. 3–5.
38. *Die groβe Politik*, Vol. I, p. 272.
39. Dugdale, *German Diplomatic Documents*, Vol. I, p. 10.
40. Buckle, *The Letters of Queen Victoria*, Vol. II, pp. 394–395.
41. Waijiao shi, ed. He-wo-si-tuo-fu, di 2 juan shang, 62.
42. Dugdale, *German Diplomatic Documents*, Vol. I, pp. 6–7.
43. Ibid., pp. 8–10.
44. Erich Eyck, *Bismarck: Leben und Werk*, Vol. III (Erlenback-Zurich: Eugen Rentsch Verlag A. G., 1944), p. 174.
45. Alan Palmer, *Bismarck* (New York: Scribner, 1976), pp. 183–184.
46. Arnold Toynbee, *A Study of History: Abridgement of Volumes I–VI by D.C. Somervell* (Oxford: Oxford University Press, 1946), pp. 217–230.
47. After Austria's 1866 defeat at Prussia's hands, the empire underwent a vast re-organization. Hungarians obtained equal status (or, in some realms, more than equal status) with Austrian Germans. After this point, the empire became a "dual monarchy" referred to as the Austro-Hungarian Empire. This, however, created the issue of the status of other ethnicities (who, collectively, outnumbered the combined German and Hungarian populations) within the empire. Germans and Hungarians each numbered about nine million people, while there were approximately ten million Czechs and Slovaks, four million Poles, and three million Southern Slavs living within the empire's boundaries, as well as three million Romanians and seven hundred thousand Italians. René Albrecht-Carrié, *A Diplomatic History of Europe since the Congress of Vienna* (New York: Harper and Row, 1958), p. 167.
48. Norman Rich, *Friedrich von Holstein: Politics and Diplomacy in the Era of Bismarck and Wilhelm II*, Vol. I (London: Cambridge University Press, 1965), p. 96.
49. Ibid.
50. The Austrian and Russian versions of this agreement differ. Initially, this agreement was kept secret from Germany; Bismarck learned of its existence from Andrássy only in September. *Die groβe Politik*, Vol. II, pp. 45–47.

51. Ibid., p. 76.
52. This agreement, too, was kept secret from Germany.
53. This is a famous example that illustrates the principle that public opinion is an unreliable basis for making policy decisions.
54. An English translation of the treaty can be found in *The European Concert in the Eastern Question and Other Public Acts* (Oxford: Clarendon Press, 1885), pp. 335–348.
55. Rich, *Friedrich von Holstein*, Vol. I, p. 100.
56. German interests were fewer than French interests, as France had a relatively greater economic stake in the region. Britain, Russia, and Austria all had a strategic interest in the area.
57. Norman Rich and M. H. Fisher, eds., *The Holstein Papers*, Vol. III (Cambridge, UK: Cambridge University Press, 1955–1963), p. 43.
58. Bismarck, *Bismarck: The Man & The Statesman*, Vol. II, pp. 290–291.
59. *Die große Politik*, Vol. II, pp. 31–34.
60. Ibid., Vol. I, pp. 207–208.
61. Taylor, *The Struggle for Mastery in Europe*, p. 271.
62. *Die große Politik*, Vol. II, p. 29.
63. Pflanze, *Bismarck and the Development of Germany*, Vol. II, p. 419.
64. *Die große Politik*, Vol. II, pp. 149–151.
65. Ibid., pp. 152–153.
66. Cited in Pflanze, *Bismarck and the Development of Germany*, Vol. II, p. 431.
67. *Die große Politik*, Vol. II, p. 53.
68. Cited in Gordon A. Craig, *The Politics of the Prussian Army*, p. 264.
69. Cited in Taylor, *The Struggle for Mastery*, p. 239, n. 2.
70. Bismarck, *Bismarck: The Man & The Statesman*, Vol. II, p. 234.
71. *Die große Politik*, Vol. II, pp. 180–182.
72. France declined this thankless job. Waddington proposed that, if Bismarck was unable to chair, then the task should fall to Gorchakov. This was unacceptable to Britain and Austria. Ibid., pp. 219–220.
73. W. N. Medlicott, *The Congress of Berlin and After* (Hamden, Conn.: Archon, 1963), p. 37.
74. Gwendolen Cecil, *Life of Robert Marquis of Salisbury*, Vol. II (London: Hodder and Stoughton, 1921), pp. 286–287.
75. The English language text of this treaty can be found in Edward Hertslet, ed., *The Map of Europe by Treaty; which have taken place since the general peace of 1814, Volume IV: 1875–1891* (London: Her Majesty's Stationery Office, 1891), pp. 2759–2798.

Chapter 2. "Active Shaping" and the Foundation of a Grand Strategy

1. Bismarck's personal prestige and political astuteness allowed him to avoid domestic political attacks. From beginning to end, he followed his vision of Germany's national interest to promote a stable, comprehensive strategy. This strategy cannot be seen in any specific historical documents, nor did Bismarck ever clearly state a fully formed plan. An analysis of Germany's policies between 1871 and 1890, however, reveals that there indeed was a kind of global planning and coordination. The stable, underlying layer of this planning and coordination can be taken as this grand strategy.
2. Imanuel Geiss, *German Foreign Policy 1871–1914* (London: Routledge and Kegan Paul, 1976), p. 12.
3. Otto Pflanze, *Bismarck and the Development of Germany*, Vol. II (Princeton: Princeton University Press, 1990), pp. 247–249.
4. A. J. P. Taylor, *The Struggle for Mastery in Europe, 1848–1918* (Oxford: Clarendon Press, 1954), p. 294.
5. Bismarck, in an 1857 letter, wrote that "we cannot exist in the center of Europe in a state of passivity, devoid of any plan and glad only to be left alone; such a course might be as dangerous to us today as it was in 1805, and we shall have to serve as the anvil if we do nothing to become the hammer." Otto von Bismarck, *Bismarck: The Man & The Statesman, Being the Reflections and Reminiscences of Otto, Prince von Bismarck, Written and Dictated by Himself after his Retirement from Office*, A.J. Butler, et al., trans., Vol. I (New York: Harper and Brothers Publishers, 1899), p. 204.
6. E. T. S. Dugdale (selected and translated), *German Diplomatic Documents 1871–1914*, Vol. I (New York: Harper and Brothers, 1928), pp. 54–55.
7. Henry Kissinger, *A World Restored: Metternich, Castlereagh, and the Problems of Peace, 1812–22* (Boston: Houghton Mifflin, 1957), p. 247.
8. Bismarck, *Bismarck: The Man & The Statesman*, Vol. II, p. 255.
9. Ibid., pp. 262–263.
10. Ibid., p. 282.
11. Ibid., p. 256.
12. Ibid., p. 246.
13. C. J. Lowe, *The Reluctant Imperialists: British Foreign Policy, 1878–1902* (London: Routledge, 1967), p. 24.
14. Norman Rich, *Friedrich von Holstein: Politics and Diplomacy in the Era of Bismarck and Wilhelm II*, Vol. I (London: Cambridge University Press, 1965), p. 108.
15. Pflanze, *Bismarck and the Development of Germany*, Vol. II, p. 492. Although on the whole domestic political considerations only played a small role in this alliance. Bismarck's conservative turn after 1879 served to further strengthen the alliance. For this view, see Geiss, *German Foreign Policy*, pp. 22 and 35.

16. Bruce Waller, *Bismarck at the Crossroads: The Reorientation of German Foreign Policy after the Congress of Berlin, 1878–80* (London: Athlone Press, 1974), pp. 192–193.
17. This hope originated from Wilhelm I himself, who felt that if the alliance with Austria were to be complete, it should be directed against the revenge-seeking French. Alan Palmer, *Bismarck* (New York: Charles Scribner's Sons, 1976), p. 211.
18. Cited in Patricia A. Weitsman, *Dangerous Alliances: Proponents of Peace, Weapons of War* (Stanford, Calif.: Stanford University Press, 2004), p. 73.
19. Denys Myers and J. G. Paul (trans.), *The Secret Treaties of Austria-Hungary*, Vol. I (Cambridge, Mass.: Harvard University Press, 1920), pp. 24–31.
20. Taylor, *The Struggle for Mastery in Europe*, p. 261.
21. This was an important difference between Bismarck and his successors: he saw the alliance with Austria as a tool to obtain other goals, while they saw it as an end in and of itself. This was perhaps linked to the Russian threat promoted by Bismarck to persuade Wilhelm I of the treaty's value. *Die große Politik*, Vol. III, pp. 92–99. Friedrich von Holstein, who would later manage Germany's foreign policy, was left with a deep impression of the threat posed by Russia during this process, and the anti-Russia aspects of the Austro-German alliance became a central part of his strategic thinking. Rich, *Friedrich von Holstein*, Vol. I, p. 107.
22. *Die große Politik der Europäischen Kabinette 1871–1914: Sammlung der Diplomatischen Akten des Auswärtigen Amtes* [The Foreign Policy of the European Cabinets, 1871–1914: Collection of diplomatic documents of the Foreign Office], Johannes Lepsius, et al., eds. Vol. IV (Berlin: Deutsche verlagsgesellschaft Für Politik und Geschichte, 1922–1927), pp. 3–4.
23. *Die große Politik*, Vol. IV, pp. 7–10.
24. *Die große Politik*, Vol. IV, pp. 11–12.
25. William Langer, *European Alliances and Alignments, 1871–1890,* 2nd ed. (New York: Alfred A. Knopf, 1966), p. 188.
26. Taylor, *The Struggle for Mastery in Europe*, p. 266.
27. Quoted in Pflanze, *Bismarck and the Development of Germany*, Vol. II, p. 509.
28. Bismarck, *Bismarck: The Man & The Statesman*, Vol. II, pp. 276–277.
29. Rich, *Friedrich von Holstein*, Vol. I, p. 108.
30. Palmer, *Bismarck*, p. 214.
31. Paul Kennedy, *The Rise of the Anglo-German Antagonism 1860–1914* (London: George Allen and Unwin, 1980), p. 157.
32. W. N. Medlicott, *Bismarck, Gladstone, and the Concert of Europe* (London: Athlone Press, 1956), p. 171.
33. Taylor, *The Struggle for Mastery in Europe*, p. 269.
34. *Die große Politik*, Vol. IV, pp. 211–212.
35. Geiss, *German Foreign Policy*, p. 40.

36. Cedric J. Lowe and Frank Marzari, *Italian Foreign Policy 1870–1940* (London: Routledge and Kegan Paul, 1975), pp. 13–27.
37. Geiss, *German Foreign Policy*, p. 42.
38. William Langer, *European Alliances and Alignments*, p. 244.
39. Rich, *Friedrich von Holstein*, Vol. I, p. 110.
40. Norman Rich and M. H. Fisher, eds., *The Holstein Papers: Correspondence 1861–1896*, Vol. III (London: Cambridge University Press, 1961), p. 62.
41. Cited in Taylor, *The Struggle for Mastery in Europe*, p. 283, n. 1.
42. Cited in ibid., p. 275.
43. Italy added an additional statement to the effect that the stipulations of the treaty were not directed against Great Britain.
44. Bismarck, *Bismarck: The Man & The Statesman*, Vol. II, pp. 290–294.
45. Cited in Taylor, *The Struggle for Mastery in Europe*, p. 282.
46. British "reforms" mainly consisted of abolishing Morocco's status as a protectorate. This system had been established by treaty between Britain, Spain, and Morocco. It stipulated that Moroccans serving British and Spanish diplomatic entities did not have to pay taxes to the Moroccan government and would not be subject to Moroccan criminal law. By the 1870s, this system had expanded greatly, thus diminishing the Moroccan government's finances and ability to maintain order. The main British architect of this plan was John Drummond Hay. Louisa Annette Edla Drummond-Hay Brooks, *A Memoir of Sir John Drummond Hay* (London: John Murray, 1896), pp. 321–323.
47. Palmer, *Bismarck*, p. 138.
48. Cited in Taylor, *The Struggle for Mastery in Europe*, p. 287.
49. Rich, *Friedrich von Holstein*, Vol. I, p. 124.
50. Information on the desire to placate France can be found in *Die große Politik*, Vol. III, p. 394. For keeping Egypt as a point of contention, see Taylor, *The Struggle for Mastery in Europe*, pp. 290–291.
51. Rich, *Friedrich von Holstein*, Vol. I, p. 124.
52. Ibid., p. 125.
53. Dugdale, *German Diplomatic Documents*, Vol. I, p. 158.
54. Rich and Fisher, *The Holstein Papers*, Vol. II, pp. 259–260.
55. Of course, the British occupation was not instigated by Bismarck, but was part of the British government's own pre-existing strategy. It was merely an issue of timing. On September 18, 1882, Queen Victoria claimed in a letter that the Egyptian crisis was a gift from heaven, as it would create a chance for "securing for ourselves such a position in Egypt as to secure our Indian Dominions and to maintain our superiority in the East." Cited in C. J. Lowe, *The Reluctant Imperialists: British Foreign Policy 1878–1902* (New York: Macmillan, 1969), pp. 52–53.

56. George Earle Buckle, ed., *The Letters of Queen Victoria, Second Series,* Vol. II (London: John Murray, 1926), pp. 546–547.

57. Ibid., p. 549.

58. Ibid., pp. 549–550.

59. Rich, *Friedrich von Holstein*, Vol. I, p. 126.

60. Ibid.

61. Rich and Fisher, *The Holstein Papers*, Vol. III, p. 69.

62. Ibid., p. 68.

63. Ibid., p. 69.

64. Ibid.

65. Martin Van Creveld, *Command in War* (Cambridge, Mass.: Harvard University Press, 2003), p. 149.

66. Helmut Boehme, ed., *The Foundation of the German Empire: Selected Documents* (London: Oxford University Press, 1971), p. 16.

67. Gordon A. Craig, *The Politics of the Prussian Army, 1640–1945* (Oxford: Oxford University Press, 1955), p. 224.

68. Koppel S. Pinson, *Modern Germany: Its History and Civilization* (Prospect Heights, Ill.: Waveland Press, 1989), p. 308.

69. Palmer, *Bismarck*, p. 267.

70. Craig, *The Politics of the Prussian Army*, p. 208.

71. Peter Paret, *Clausewitz and the State: The Man, His Theories, and His Times* (New York: Oxford University Press, 1976), p. 369.

72. Craig, *The Politics of the Prussian Army*, p. 216.

73. Bismarck, *Bismarck: The Man & The Statesman*, Vol. II, p. 103.

74. Gerhard Ritter, *The Schlieffen Plan: Critique of a Myth* (New York: Frederick A. Praeger, 1958), p. 18.

75. Gunther E. Rothenberg, "Moltke, Schlieffen, and the Doctrine of Strategic Envelopment," in Peter Paret, ed., *Makers of Modern Strategy from Machiavelli to the Nuclear Age* (Princeton: Princeton University Press, 1986), p. 307.

76. Craig, *Politics of the Prussian Army*, p. 275.

77. Ritter, *The Schlieffen Plan*, p. 19.

78. Ibid., 19–20.

79. Rothenberg, "Moltke, Schlieffen, and the Doctrine of Strategic Envelopment," p. 308.

80. Craig, *The Politics of the Prussian Army*, p. 276.

81. Ibid., pp. 274–275.

82. Holger H. Herwig, "Strategic Uncertainties of a Nation-State: Prussia-Germany, 1871–1918," in Williamson Murray, et al., eds., *The Making of Strategy: Rulers, States, and War* (Cambridge, UK: Cambridge University Press, 1994), p. 250.

83. Frederick Engels, “The Role of Force in History,” *Karl Marx, Frederick Engels: Collected Works*, Vol. XXVI (New York: International Publishers, 1990), p. 494.
84. The later years of World War I validate the potential of this strategy. On the western front, allied offensives were relatively unsuccessful, while on the eastern front, German advances scored surprising gains.
85. Ka-er Ai-li-xi Bo-en [Karl Erich Born], et al., *Deyizhi shi di 3 juan* [Handbuch der deutschen Geschichte, Vol. 3], Zhang Zaiyang, et al., trans. (Beijing: Shangwu yinshuguan, 1991), shang 383 and 403.
86. These figures are taken from a chart in Taylor, *The Struggle for Mastery in Europe*, p. xxvii.
87. These figures are from John Mearsheimer, *The Tragedy of Great Power Politics* (New York: W.W. Norton, 2001), p. 71.

Chapter 3. Working to Maintain the Grand Strategy

1. Douglass C. North, *Structure and Change in Economic History* (New York: Norton, 1981), pp. 45–58.
2. Xing Yue, “Yishixingtai zai duiwai zhengce zhong de zuoyong [The use of ideology in foreign policy],” *Taipingyang xuebao*, 2009, p. 9.
3. North, *Structure and Change*, p. 49.
4. Louis Althusser, *Lenin and Philosophy and Other Essays* (New York: Monthly Review Press, 1971), p. 172.
5. The concept of imperialism used here is not the same as Lenin’s notion of imperialism as the highest stage of capitalism. Instead, William Langer’s definition—“the rule or control, political or economic, direct or indirect, of one state, nation, or people over other similar groups, or perhaps one might better say the disposition, urge or striving to establish such rule or control”—is adopted. William L. Langer, *The Diplomacy of Imperialism 1890–1902* (New York: Alfred A. Knopf, 1935), p. 67.
6. Boyd C. Shafer, *Nationalism: Myth and Reality* (New York: Harcourt, Brace and Company, 1955), p. 105.
7. Leften Stavros, *A Global History: From Prehistory to the 21st Century* (New York: Pearson, 1998), pp. 264–267.
8. E. J. Hobsbawm, *The Age of Empire, 1875–1914* (New York: Vintage, 1989), 142–144.
9. Langer, *The Diplomacy of Imperialism*, p. 246.
10. Paul Kennedy, *The Realities behind Diplomacy: Background Influences on British External Policy, 1865–1980* (London: George Allen and Unwin, 1981), p. 51.
11. Otto Pflanze, *Bismarck and the Development of Germany*, Vol. III (Princeton: Princeton University Press, 1990), p. 116; and Paul Kennedy, *The Rise of the Anglo-*

German Antagonism 1860–1914 (London: George Allen and Unwin, 1980), pp. 167–169.

12. Klaus J. Bade, *Friedrich Fabri und der Imperialismus in der Bismarck-zeit* (Freiburg: Atlantis Verlag A. G., 1975), pp. 21–24.

13. Zhang Guangzhi and Zhang Guangyong, *Shixue, wenhua zhong de wenhua—wenhua shiye zhong de xifang shixue* [Historiography, the Culture within Culture—Western Historiography from a Cultural View] (Hangzhou: Zhejiang renmin chubanshe, 1990), p. 409.

14. Frederick Engels, "The Role of Force in History," *Karl Marx, Frederick Engels: Collected Works*, Vol. XXVI (New York: International Publishers, 1990), p. 483.

15. E. J. Hobsbawm, *The Age of Capital, 1848–1875* (London: Abacus, 1975), p. 91.

16. Historians are divided in their appraisals of Bismarck's colonial activities in the 1880s. Hans-Ulrich Wehler has argued that Bismarck's colonial interests did not arise from expediency, but from an interest in creating a "social imperialism" that would distract the public from domestic political disputes and create an atmosphere of cooperation in the imperial center. Hans-Ulrich Wehler, "Bismarck's Imperialism, 1862–1890," *Past and Present*, Vol. 48 (August 1970), pp. 122–123. Most historians (including the author of this book), however, do not accept this argument and instead consider the concept of "social imperialism" to be a better fit for the era of Wilhelm II. See, for example, Paul M. Kennedy, "German Colonial Expansion: Has the 'Manipulated Social Imperialism' been Antedated?" *Past and Present*, Vol. 54 (February 1972), 134–141. In general, the historians who agree with Kennedy make a fundamentally similar argument: Bismarck's interest in colonies was an act of political expediency adopted to achieve short-term goals. The differences arise from disagreements over the exact nature of those short-term goals. Gordon Craig described those goals as political, stemming from a need to strengthen the National Liberal Party in the 1884 elections and a desire to mollify free traders unhappy with protective tariffs imposed in 1879. See Gordon A. Craig, *Germany 1866–1945* (Oxford: Oxford University Press, 1981), p. 167. A. J. P. Taylor instead emphasized the anti-British objectives of the colonial policies that was designed to prevent against "the triumph of liberalism." A. J. P. Taylor, *Germany's First Bid for Colonies* (London: Macmillan, 1938), p. 6; and A. J. P. Taylor, *The Struggle for Mastery in Europe, 1848–1918* (Oxford: Clarendon Press, 1954), pp. 292–293. Otto Pflanze, by contrast, focused on their economic importance. Pflanze, *Bismarck and the Development of Germany*, Vol. III, pp. 121–122.

17. Bismarck apparently accepted the 1868 views of Rudolph Delbruck, who had worked for him during the period of Bismarck's alliance with liberalism. Delbruck believed that the notion that colonies would promote German industrial development was an "illusion" and that "the losses would outweigh the gains" in any colonial effort. Ibid., p. 114.

18. Ibid., p. 115.

19. Edmond Fitzmaurice, *The Life of Granville George Levenson Gower*, Vol. II: (London: Longmans, Green, 1905), p. 337.

20. Bade, *Friedrich Fabri*, pp. 121–133.

21. Pflanze, *Bismarck and the Development of Germany*, Vol. III, p. 124.

22. See, for example, Taylor, *The Struggle for Mastery in Europe*, pp. 295–296; and Alan Palmer, *Bismarck* (New York: Charles Scribner's Sons, 1976), pp. 225–226.

23. E. T. S. Dugdale (selected and translated), *German Diplomatic Documents 1871–1914*, Vol. I (New York: Harper and Brothers, 1928), p. 174.

24. Ibid., p. 175.

25. Ibid., p. 176.

26. Ibid.

27. C. J. Lowe, *The Reluctant Imperialists: British Foreign Policy 1878–1902* (New York: Macmillan, 1969), p. 61.

28. Fitzmaurice, *The Life of Granville George Levenson Gower*, Vol. II, p. 359.

29. Dugdale, *German Diplomatic Documents*, Vol. I, pp. 178–180.

30. Craig, *Germany*, p. 115.

31. Norman Rich, *Friedrich von Holstein: Politics and Diplomacy in the Era of Bismarck and Wilhelm II*, Vol. I (London: Cambridge University Press, 1965), p. 147.

32. Dugdale, *German Diplomatic Documents*, Vol. I, p. 176.

33. Pearl Boring Mitchell, *The Bismarckian Policy of Conciliation with France, 1875–1885* (Philadelphia: University of Pennsylvania Press, 1935), p. 152.

34. Cited in Taylor, *The Struggle for Mastery in Europe*, p. 294.

35. Kennedy, *The Rise of the Anglo-German Antagonism*, 201.

36. Mitchell, *The Bismarckian Policy of Reconciliation with France*, p. 154.

37. Norman Rich and M. H. Fisher, eds., *The Holstein Papers: Correspondence 1861–1896*, Vol. III (London: Cambridge University Press, 1961), p. 130.

38. Lowe, *The Reluctant Imperialists*, p. 63.

39. *Die große Politik der Europäischen Kabinette 1871–1914: Sammlung der Diplomatischen Akten des Auswärtigen Amtes* [The Foreign Policy of the European Cabinets, 1871–1914: Collection of diplomatic documents of the Foreign Office], Johannes Lepsius, et al., eds. Vol. IV (Berlin: Deutsche verlagsgesellschaft Für Politik und Geschichte, 1922–1927), pp. 77–78.

40. Herbert von Bismarck explained, "When we started colonial policy, we had to face a long reign by the Crown Prince, during which English influence would predominate. In order to forestall this, we had to launch colonial policy, which is popular and can produce conflicts with England at any moment." Cited in Taylor, *The Struggle for Mastery in Europe*, p. 293. According to Holstein, Bismarck made a similar statement about the purpose of his colonial policy to Russian Czar Alexander III. Rich and

Fisher, *The Holstein Papers,* Vol. II, p. 161.

41. A. J. P. Taylor, *Bismarck: The Man and the Statesman* (New York: Random House, 1967), p. 221.

42. *Die große Politik*, Vol. V, pp. 10–12. See also Rich and Fisher, *The Holstein Papers*, Vol. II, p. 385.

43. Ibid., pp. 13–15.

44. Ibid., Vol. IV, pp. 264–265.

45. Palmer, *Bismarck*, p. 232.

46. William L. Langer, *European Alliances and Alignments 1871–1890* (New York: Alfred A. Knopf, 1950), pp. 368–369.

47. Rich and Fisher, *The Holstein Papers,* Vol. II, p. 267.

48. Bismarck, *Bismarck: The Man & The Statesman*, Vol. II, pp. 276–277.

49. Craig, *Germany*, pp. 125–126.

50. *Die große Politik*, Vol. V, pp. 136–140.

51. Rich, *Friedrich von Holstein*, I:185.

52. Rich and Fisher, *The Holstein Papers,* Vol. II, pp. 290–292.

53. Dugdale, *German Diplomatic Documents*, Vol. I, pp. 249–251.

54. Ibid., p. 251.

55. Ibid., pp. 253–255.

56. Ibid., pp. 263–264.

57. Cited in Taylor, *The Struggle for Mastery in Europe*, p. 309.

58. Craig, *Germany*, p. 129.

59. Langer, *European Alliances and Alignments*, p. 382.

60. Dugdale, *German Diplomatic Documents*, Vol. I, pp. 266–267.

61. *Die große Politik*, Vol. V, p. 96.

62. Ibid., p. 211.

63. Taylor, *The Struggle for Mastery in Europe*, p. 316.

64. *Waijiao shi*, ed. He-wo-si-tuo-fu, di 2 juan, p. 326.

65. Denys Myers and J. G. Paul (trans.), *The Secret Treaties of Austria-Hungary*, Vol. I (Cambridge, Mass.: Harvard University Press, 1920), pp. 275–280.

66. Dugdale, *German Diplomatic Documents*, Vol. I, pp. 286–288.

67. Lowe, *The Reluctant Imperialists*, p. 111.

68. *Die große Politik*, Vol. IV, p. 304.

69. Bismarck emphasized to the Austrians Germany's lack of interests in the Balkans. Thus, if Austria sought to prevent Russia from seizing Bulgaria, it would have to turn to Great Britain for support. Even if Austria did not actually obtain British military support, its reputation would be enough to discourage any Russian challenges. *Die große Politik,* Vol. IV, pp. 323–324.

70. Alfred Francis Pribram, *The Secret Treaties of Austria-Hungary* (Lenox, Mass.:

HardPress, 2013), pp. 102–103.
71. Pribram, *The Secret Treaties of Austria-Hungary*, pp. 99–101.
72. Lowe, *The Reluctant Imperialists*, p. 117.
73. Cited in Taylor, *The Struggle for Mastery in Europe*, p. 320.
74. Dugdale, *German Diplomatic Documents*, Vol. I, pp. 345–348.
75. Ibid., pp. 359–361.
76. *Die große Politik*, Vol. VI, p. 61.
77. Ibid., pp. 12–13.
78. Cited in Taylor, *The Struggle for Mastery in Europe*, p. 322.
79. Craig, *The Politics of the Prussian Army*, p. 269.
80. Craig, *The Politics of the Prussian Army*, pp. 266–270.
81. *Die große Politik*, Vol. VI, pp. 59–62.
82. Taylor, *The Struggle for Mastery in Europe*, pp. xxix–xxx.
83. Palmer, *Bismarck*, p. 138.
84. Bismarck, *Bismarck: The Man & The Statesman*, Vol. II, p. 290.
85. Craig, *Germany*, p. 126.
86. Henry Kissinger, *A World Restored: Metternich, Castlereagh, and the Problems of Peace, 1812–22* (Boston: Houghton Mifflin, 1957), pp. 247–248.
87. Bismarck, *Bismarck: The Man & The Statesman*, Vol. II, p. 199.
88. Craig, *The Politics of the Prussian Army*, pp. 227–230.

Chapter 4. Entering the Post-Bismarckian Era

1. Bismarck's retirement in 1890 brought forth strong responses throughout Europe. The British satirical magazine *Punch* ran a cartoon entitled "Dropping the Pilot," that expressed the view and emotions of the European countries toward this historical event.
2. Holger H. Herwig, *"Luxury" Fleet: The Imperial German Navy 1888–1918* (London: Ashfield Press, 1980), p. 19.
3. Gordon A. Craig, *Germany 1866–1945* (Oxford: Oxford University Press, 1981), p. 127.
4. *Die große Politik der Europäischen Kabinette 1871–1914: Sammlung der Diplomatischen Akten des Auswärtigen Amtes* [The Foreign Policy of the European Cabinets, 1871–1914: Collection of diplomatic documents of the Foreign Office], Johannes Lepsius, et al., eds. Vol. VII (Berlin: Deutsche verlagsgesellschaft Für Politik und Geschichte, 1922–1927), pp. 3–4.
5. Norman Rich, *Friedrich von Holstein: Politics and Diplomacy in the Era of Bismarck and Wilhelm II*, Vol. I (London: Cambridge University Press, 1965), pp. 309–310.

6. *Die große Politik*, Vol. VII, pp. 4–10.

7. Rich, *Friedrich von Holstein*, Vol. I, p. 315.

8. Ibid., p. 314.

9. E. T. S. Dugdale (selected and translated), *German Diplomatic Documents 1871–1914*, Vol. II (New York: Harper and Brothers, 1928), pp. 2–3.

10. *Die große Politik*, Vol. VII, pp. 24–27; and ibid., pp. 352–353.

11. William L. Langer, *The Diplomacy of Imperialism 1890–1902* (New York: Alfred A. Knopf, 1935), p. 9.

12. Paul Kennedy, *The Rise of the Anglo-German Antagonism 1860–1914* (London: George Allen and Unwin, 1980), p. 201.

13. Ibid., p. 206.

14. According to Salisbury's daughter, consideration of a second invasion of Sudan had already become a priority in Britain's Africa policy by 1889. Gwendolen Cecil, *Life of Robert Marquis of Salisbury*, Vol. IV (London: Hodder and Stoughton, 1921), pp. 239–240.

15. Langer, *The Diplomacy of Imperialism*, pp. 106–107.

16. A. J. P. Taylor, *The Struggle for Mastery in Europe, 1848–1918* (Oxford: Clarendon Press, 1954), pp. 329-330, n. 3.

17. Paul Kennedy has compared the 1890 Heligoland-Zanzibar Treaty and the 1905 Anglo-French Agreement, noting that while the latter became the starting point for an alliance, the former did not perform that function. He argued that this demonstrated that Anglo-German disputes and conflicts could not be reconciled. Kennedy, however, failed to see that the 1890 treaty itself increased, rather than reduced, the difficulty of bridging the differences between the two countries. Kennedy, *The Rise of the Anglo-German Antagonism*, p. 205.

18. C. J. Lowe, *The Reluctant Imperialists: British Foreign Policy, 1878–1902* (London: Routledge, 1967), p. 8.

19. Cecil, *Life of Robert Marquis of Salisbury*, Vol. IV, pp. 374–375.

20. Erich Brandenburg, *From Bismarck to the World War: A History of German Foreign Policy, 1870–1914* (London: Oxford University Press, 1927), p. 30.

21. Cited in Langer, *The Diplomacy of Imperialism*, p. 7.

22. Taylor, *The Struggle for Mastery in Europe*, pp. 336–337.

23. Langer, *The Diplomacy of Imperialism*, pp. 27 and 31.

24. Ibid., p. 32.

25. "The Franco-Russian Alliance Military Convention (August 18, 1892)," available online at http://avalon.law.yale.edu/19th_century/frrumil.asp (accessed July 25, 2015).

26. J. L. Garvin, *The Life of Joseph Chamberlain*, Vol. II (London: Macmillan, 1933), p. 457.

27. Cecil, *Life of Robert Marquis of Salisbury*, Vol. IV, p. 302.

28. Dugdale, *German Diplomatic Documents*, Vol. II, pp. 145–146.
29. Ibid., pp. 144–145.
30. Ibid., pp. 169–170.
31. Ibid., p. 175.
32. Ibid., pp. 191–192.
33. Ibid., pp. 236–237.
34. Ibid., p. 239.
35. Ibid., pp. 240–242.
36. G. P. Gooch and H. W. Temperley, eds., *British Documents on the Origins of the War 1898–1914*, Vol. II (London: His Majesty's Stationary Office, 1926–1938), p. 288.
37. William L. Langer, *The Franco-Russian Alliance 1890–1894* (Cambridge, Mass.: Harvard University Press, 1929), pp. 360–362.
38. Ibid., p. 379.
39. Brandenburg, *From Bismarck to World War*, p. 42.
40. Dugdale, *German Diplomatic Documents*, Vol. II, pp. 281–282.
41. A. J. P. Taylor believes that Germany's desire was to force a British alliance with Austria-Hungary. Taylor, *The Struggle for Mastery in Europe*, pp. 349–350. This is incorrect. At that moment, Germany was still unwilling to let colonial problems affect European affairs. As early as April, Adolf von Marschall, the German secretary of state for foreign affairs, commented that "if it is to England's interests to oppose the French aspirations, it is always possible for the British Government to make proposals, which will show proper consideration for Germany's legitimate desires." Dugdale, *German Diplomatic Documents*, Vol. II, 285–286. Caprivi, the chancellor, noted that "it remains to decide what diplomatic means are at our disposal to bend England to our wishes. I assume that we should not do well to change our general policy of the Anglo-Italian friendship, but I think there could be no objection to our marking our colonial policy by turning more away from England and nearer to France. England's new treaty with the Congo State can easily be a reason for this." Ibid., p. 291. Hatzfeldt also proposed using this treaty to apply pressure on Britain and force its position on Samoa to become "more amenable." Ibid., pp. 292–294. The Germans desired to manage colonial issues and European issues separately; it was Great Britain that linked them.
42. *Die große Politik*, Vol. VIII, p. 455.
43. *Die große Politik*, Vol. VIII, pp. 455–456.
44. Thus Taylor's conclusion that Germany changed course because of Rosebery's threats is unsubstantiated. Taylor, *The Struggle for Mastery in Europe*, p. 351.
45. Dugdale, *German Diplomatic Documents*, Vol. II, p. 318.
46. Ibid., p. 318.
47. Langer, *The Franco-Russian Alliance*, pp. 389–390.
48. Rich, *Friedrich von Holstein*, Vol. I, p. 397.

49. Gordon A. Craig, *The Politics of the Prussian Army, 1640–1945* (Oxford: Oxford University Press, 1955), pp. 244–245.
50. *Die große Politik*, Vol. VII, pp. 243–244.
51. Rich, *Friedrich von Holstein*, Vol. I, p. 358.
52. *Die große Politik*, IX, p. 109.
53. Craig, *Germany*, p. 238.
54. *Die große Politik*, Vol. IX, p. 253.
55. Brandenburg, *From Bismarck to World War*, p. 60.
56. Dugdale, *German Diplomatic Documents*, Vol. II, pp. 327–328.
57. Ibid., pp. 329–331.
58. Langer, *The Diplomacy of Imperialism*, p. 198.
59. Dugdale, *German Diplomatic Documents*, Vol. II, pp. 331–332.
60. Ibid., pp. 332–335.
61. Ibid., pp. 335–336.
62. Langer, *The Diplomacy of Imperialism*, p. 209.
63. Taylor, *The Struggle for Mastery in Europe*, p. 359.
64. For an example of that claim, see Wang Shengzu, ed., *Guoji guanxi shi* [A History of International Relations] (Beijing: Shijie zhishi chubanshe, 1995), juan 3, p. 154.
65. Dugdale, *German Diplomatic Documents*, Vol. II, pp. 349–351; and ibid., pp. 368–369.
66. Langer, *The Diplomacy of Imperialism*, p. 204.
67. *Die große Politik*, Vol. X, p. 203.
68. Cited in Taylor, *The Struggle for Mastery in Europe*, p. 362.
69. *Die gross Politik*, Vol. XI, p. 67.
70. Dugdale, *German Diplomatic Documents*, Vol. II, pp. 373–374.
71. Su-si-man-nuo-wei-qi [Unidentified Soviet author], *Diguozhuyi dui Feizhou de guafen* [Imperialism's Partition of Africa], trans. Wen Zhiling (Beijing: Shijie zhishi chubanshe, 1962), p. 103; and Kennedy, *The Rise of the Anglo-German Antagonism*, pp. 219–220.
72. Germany had dominant positions in local commercial and financial activity. Germans monopolized the marketplaces for whiskey and dynamite. Krupp, Siemens, and Deutsche Bank had branch offices in Transvaal. Germany accounted for 20 percent of the total foreign investment in the country. See Craig, *Germany*, p. 245.
73. Dugdale, *German Diplomatic Documents*, Vol. II, pp. 371–372.
74. Ibid., pp. 376–377.
75. Ibid., p. 370.
76. Ibid., pp. 378–379.
77. Ibid., p. 387.
78. *Die große Politik*, Vol. XI, p. 41.

79. George Earle Buckle, ed., *The Letters of Queen Victoria, Third Series*, Vol. III (London: John Murray, 1931), p. 22.
80. Taylor, *The Struggle for Mastery in Europe*, pp. 365–367.
81. Dugdale, *German Diplomatic Documents*, Vol. II, pp. 403–406.
82. Langer, *The Diplomacy of Imperialism*, p. 243.
83. Ibid., pp. 245–246.
84. Ibid., p. 239.
85. Taylor, *The Struggle for Mastery in Europe*, p. 364.
86. Langer, *The Diplomacy of Imperialism*, p. 244.
87. Buckle, *The Letters of Queen Victoria*, Vol. III, pp. 17–18.
88. Dugdale, *German Diplomatic Documents*, Vol. II, p. 399.
89. Ibid., p. 404.
90. Ibid., pp. 401–403; and ibid., pp. 403–406.
91. Langer, *The Diplomacy of Imperialism*, p. 253.
92. Buckle, *The Letters of Queen Victoria*, Vol. III, p. 33.
93. The costs of this expedition were not borne by Great Britain itself, but by the Egyptian treasury. Egyptian finances, however, were under the control of a six-nation debt commission and thus Britain's plan needed the support of the six nations. France and Russia would cast dissenting votes, Italy would obviously vote in favor, and Austria would follow Germany's lead—meaning that Germany could decide whether or not Britain would receive majority support.
94. Cited in Taylor, *The Struggle for Mastery in Europe*, pp. 367–368.

Chapter 5. Institutions, Society, Popular Opinion, and Grand Strategy

1. Hans-Ulrich Wehler, *The German Empire 1871–1918*, trans. Kim Traynor (Leamington Spa, N.H.: Berg, 1985), p. 62.
2. Otto von Bismarck, *New Chapters of Bismarck's Autobiography*, trans. Bernard Miall (London: Hodder and Stoughton, 1920), p. 248.
3. For more on Prince Eulenburg, see Ekkehard-Teja D. W. Wilke, *Political Decadence in Imperial Germany: Personnel-Political Aspects of the German Government Crisis 1894–97* (Urbana: University of Illinois Press, 1976).
4. J. C. G. Röhl, *Germany without Bismarck: The Crisis of Government in the Second Reich 1890–1900* (Berkeley: University of California Press, 1967), p. 161.
5. Ka-er Ai-li-xi Bo-en [Karl Erich Born], et al., *Deyizhi shi di 3 juan* [Handbuch der deutschen Geschichte, Volume 3], Zhang Zaiyang, et al., trans. (Beijing: Shangwu yinshuguan, 1991), shang 421–422.
6. On October 28, 1908, the British newspaper *Daily Telegraph* published an interview with Wilhelm II. In it, the kaiser claimed that he was Great Britain's friend,

that he had prevented the emergence of an anti-British alliance during the Boer War, and that he proposed a war plan to Britain that was similar to the one eventually adopted by the British. This was seen in Great Britain as arrogance, and it sparked public anger. In Germany, public opinion had sympathized with the Boers and the kaiser's words caused a controversy. German political parties accused the kaiser of damaging German diplomacy. Even the pro-monarchical Conservative Party was openly critical and demanded that the kaiser speak in a more restrained manner. Under enormous pressure, the kaiser promised on November 17 to respect constitution procedures in the future. This became known as the *Daily Telegraph* incident.

7. George Monger, *The End of Isolation: British Foreign Policy 1900–1907* (London: Thomas Nelson and Sons Ltd., 1963), p. 94.

8. Holger H. Herwig, "The Dynamics of Necessity: German Military Policy during the First World War," in Allan R. Millett and Williamson Murray, eds., *Military Effectiveness*, Vol. I (Boston: Allen and Unwin, 1988), p. 91.

9. Gordon A. Craig, *The Politics of the Prussian Army, 1640–1945* (Oxford: Oxford University Press, 1955), p. 240.

10. Herwig, "The Dynamics of Necessity: German Military Policy during the First World War," p. 82.

11. Holger H. Herwig, *"Luxury" Fleet: The Imperial German Navy 1888–1918* (London: Ashfield Press, 1980), pp. 22–23.

12. Jack Snyder, *Myths of Empire: Domestic Politics and International Ambition* (Ithaca, N.Y.: Cornell University Press, 1991), pp. 31–32.

13. Ibid., pp. 43–46.

14. Thucydides, *The Peloponnesian War*, p. 126.

15. Samuel P. Huntington, *Political Order in Changing Societies* (New Haven, Conn.: Yale University Press, 1968), pp. 195–196.

16. Otto Pflanze, *Bismarck and the Development of Germany*, Vol. III (Princeton: Princeton University Press, 1990), p. 12.

17. Gordon A. Craig, *Germany 1866–1945* (Oxford: Oxford University Press, 1981), p. 250.

18. Koppel S. Pinson, *Modern Germany: Its History and Civilization* (Prospect Heights, Ill.: Waveland Press, 1989), p. 602.

19. This remained the case until the Nazis took power in 1933.

20. Wehler, *The German Empire*, p. 40.

21. Otto von Bismarck, *Bismarck: The Man & The Statesman, Being the Reflections and Reminiscences of Otto, Prince von Bismarck, Written and Dictated by Himself after his Retirement from Office*, A.J. Butler, et al., trans., Vol. I (New York: Harper and Brothers Publishers, 1899), p. 268.

22. Ka-er Di-te-li-xi Ai-er-de-man [Karl Dietrich Erdmann], *Deyizhi shi di 4 juan*

[Handbuch der deutschen Geschichte, Volume 4] Gao Niansheng trans. (Beijing: Shangwu, 1986) shang 6.

23. Craig, *Germany*, p. 118.

24. Bo-en [Born], et al., *Deyizhi shi di 3 juan*, shang 410. Translator's Note: This quotation is a translation of the Chinese translation of a German text that does not have its own published English language translation.

25. Mildred S. Wertheimer, *The Pan-German League 1890–1914* (New York: Octagon, 1924), p. 101.

26. Wertheimer, *The Pan-German League*, p. 198.

27. Eckart Kehr, *Schlachtflottenbau and Parteipolitik 1894–1901* (Berlin: Ebery, 1930), p. 169.

28. A. J. P. Taylor, *The Struggle for Mastery in Europe, 1848–1918* (Oxford: Clarendon Press, 1954), pp. 519–520.

29. Henry Cord Meyer, *Mittleuropa in German Thought and Action 1815–1945* (The Hague: International Scholars Forum, 1955), pp. 101–102.

30. John C. G. Röhl, *From Bismarck to Hitler: The Problem of Continuity in German History* (Harlow: Longmans, 1970), pp. 65-67.

31. Fritz Fischer, *War of Illusions: German Policies from 1911 to 1914*, trans. Marian Jackson (New York: Norton, 1975), p. 233.

32. Imanuel Geiss, *German Foreign Policy 1871–1914* (London: Routledge and Kegan Paul, 1976), p. 80.

33. Hans-Ulrich Wehler, *The German Empire*, p. 176.

34. Geoff Eley, "Reshaping the Right: Radical Nationalism and the German Navy League, 1898–1908," *Historical Journal*, Vol. XXI (1978), p. 333.

35. Paul Kennedy, *The Rise of the Anglo-German Antagonism 1860–1914* (London: George Allen and Unwin, 1980), p. 384.

36. Ibid., p. 382.

37. Emil Ludwig, *Bismarck: The Story of a Fighter* (Boston: Little, Brown, and Company, 1927), p. 619.

38. Wilke, *Political Decadence in Imperial Germany*, pp. 203–204.

39. Ibid., p. 205.

40. E. J. Hobsbawm, *The Age of Empire, 1875–1914* (New York: Vintage, 1989), p. 106.

41. Bismarck, *Bismarck: The Man & The Statesman*, Vol. I, p. 204.

42. http://en.wikiquote.org/wiki/Otto_von_Bismarck.

43. http://en.wikiquote.org/wiki/Otto_von_Bismarck.

44. Kennedy, *The Rise of the Anglo-German Antagonism*, p. 361.

45. Craig, *Germany*, pp. 246–248.

46. Joll, *The Origins of the First World War*, p. 131.

47. Kennedy, *The Rise of the Anglo-German Antagonism*, p. 365

48. Ibid.

49. Röhl, *Germany without Bismarck*, pp. 129–130.

50. Dugdale, *German Diplomatic Documents*, Vol. III, pp. 119–120.

51. Kennedy, *The Rise of the Anglo-German Antagonism*, p. 240.

52. Ibid., p. 367. At the instigation of liberal groups, Prussia attempted to unify Germany during the 1848 revolutions, but Prussian King Frederick Wilhelm IV backed away from this position and surrendered to the Austrians. On November 29, 1851, Prussia signed a compromise agreement with Austria at Olmutz, which became a symbol of Prussian (and German) humiliation.

53. Fritz Fischer, *War of Illusion: German Politics from 1911 to 1914* (London: Chatto and Windus, 1975), pp. 89–90.

Chapter 6. From *Weltpolitik* to Encirclement

1. Imanuel Geiss, *German Foreign Policy 1871–1914* (London: Routledge and Kegan Paul, 1976), p. 69.

2. Holger H. Herwig, *"Luxury" Fleet: The Imperial German Navy 1888–1918* (London: Ashfield Press, 1980), p. 20.

3. Gordon A. Craig, *Germany 1866–1945* (Oxford: Oxford University Press, 1981), p. 244.

4. Otto Pflanze, *Bismarck and the Development of Germany*, Vol. III (Princeton: Princeton University Press, 1990), p. 116; and Paul Kennedy, *The Rise of the Anglo-German Antagonism 1860–1914* (London: George Allen and Unwin, 1980), pp. 167–169.

5. Ka-er Di-te-li-xi Ai-er-de-man [Karl Dietrich Erdmann], *Deyizhi shi di 4 juan* [Handbuch der deutschen Geschichte, Volume 4] Gao Niansheng trans. (Beijing: Shangwu, 1986) shang 6.

6. E. J. Hobsbawm, *The Age of Empire, 1875–1914* (New York: Vintage, 1989), pp. 69-70; and Volker Durr, Kathy Harms, and Peter Hayes, eds., *Imperial Germany*, (Madison: The University of Wisconsin Press, 1985), p. 121.

7. Ibid.

8. J. C. G. Röhl, *Germany without Bismarck: The Crisis of Government in the Second Reich 1890–1900* (Berkeley: University of California Press, 1967), pp. 246–247.

9. Ibid., p. 252.

10. James Joll, *The Origins of the First World War*, 2nd ed. (New York: Longman, 1992), p. 111.

11. Kennedy, *The Rise of the Anglo-German Antagonism*, p. 225.

12. Geiss, *German Foreign Policy*, p. 69.

13. Craig, *Germany*, p. 262.

14. Norman Rich, *Friedrich von Holstein: Politics and Diplomacy in the Era of Bismarck and Wilhelm II*, Vol. II (London: Cambridge University Press, 1965), p. 501.

15. Craig, *Germany*, p. 274.

16. Jonathan Steinberg, *Yesterday's Deterrent: Tirpitz and the Birth of the German Battle Fleet* (New York: MacMillan, 1965), pp. 61 and 69.

17. *Die große Politik der Europäischen Kabinette 1871–1914: Sammlung der Diplomatischen Akten des Auswärtigen Amtes* [The Foreign Policy of the European Cabinets, 1871–1914: Collection of diplomatic documents of the Foreign Office], Johannes Lepsius, et al., eds. Vol. XV (Berlin: Deutsche verlagsgesellschaft Für Politik und Geschichte, 1922–1927), p. 420. Translator's Note: This quotation, though originally in German, was translated directly from Chinese to English.

18. Ivo Nikolai Lambi, *The Navy and German Power Politics 1862–1914* (Boston: Allen and Unwin, 1984), p. 177.

19. *Die große Politik*, Vol. XV, pp. 516–517.

20. Ibid., p. 522. Translator's Note: This quotation, though originally in German, was translated directly from Chinese to English.

21. George Monger, *The End of Isolation: British Foreign Policy 1900–1907* (London: Thomas Nelson and Sons, Ltd., 1963), p. 10.

22. Ibid., p. 12.

23. William L. Langer, *The Diplomacy of Imperialism 1890–1902* (New York: Alfred A. Knopf, 1935), p. 513.

24. Ibid., p. 508.

25. Ibid., p. 499.

26. *Die große Politik*, Vol. XIV, pp. 204–207.

27. Rich, *Friedrich von Holstein*, Vol. II, p. 598.

28. Langer, *The Diplomacy of Imperialism*, p. 659.

29. Monger, *The End of Isolation*, pp. 36–37.

30. Ibid., p. 15.

31. Ibid., p. 17.

32. G. P. Gooch and H. W. Temperley, eds., *British Documents on the Origins of the War 1898–1914*, Vol. II (London: His Majesty's Stationary Office, 1926–1938), p. 7.

33. Langer, *The Diplomacy of Imperialism*, p. 705.

34. Ibid., pp. 714–716.

35. Ibid., p. 722.

36. *Die große Poltik*, Vol. XVII, pp. 14–16.

37. Cited in Rich, *Friedrich von Holstein*, Vol. II, p. 630.

38. *Die große Politik*, Vol. XVII, p. 22.

39. He reported to his home government that the proposal had originated from Lansdowne, but it is now commonly thought that Eckardstein himself first advocated

it and that he misled Germany about this fact. Langer, *The Diplomacy of Imperialism*, pp. 728–729.

40. G. P. Gooch and H. W. Temperley, *British Documents*, Vol. II, p. 65.

41. Ibid., p. 66.

42. Ibid., pp. 68–69.

43. *Die große Politik*, Vol. XVII, pp. 295–296.

44. Ibid., pp. 341–342.

45. Kennedy, *The Rise of the Anglo-German Antagonism*, p. 246.

46. *Die große Politik*, Vol. XVII, p. 332.

47. In August 1901, King Edward VII of Great Britain visited Germany. In preparation, the British government drafted several briefing memorandums on Anglo-German relations. These documents claimed that the two countries had similar policies on Morocco and expressed hope that the situation continue. This was merely meant as reference material, but Edward VII mistakenly passed it to his German interlocutors, who did not spot this mistake but offered the sentence quoted here in response. G. P. Gooch and H. W. Temperley, *British Documents*, Vol. II, pp. 94–96.

48. Ibid., pp. 122–123.

49. Norman Rich, *Friedrich von Holstein: Politics and Diplomacy in the Era of Bismarck and Wilhelm II*, Vol. II (London: Cambridge University Press, 1965), p. 668.

50. Langer, *The Diplomacy of Imperialism*, pp. 774–775.

51. Monger, *The End of Isolation*, pp. 62–63.

52. Langer, *The Diplomacy of Imperialism*, p. 776.

53. Monger, *The End of Isolation*, p. 63.

54. Ibid., p. 82.

55. Julian Amery, *The Life of Joseph Chamberlain 1901–1903*, Vol. IV: (London: MacMillan, 1951), pp. 163–164.

56. Cited in Monger, *The End of Isolation*, p. 145.

57. E. T. S. Dugdale (selected and translated), *German Diplomatic Documents 1871–1914*, Vol. III (New York: Harper and Brothers, 1928), pp. 171–172.

58. *Die große Politik*, Vol. XVII, p. 344.

59. Ibid., p. 348.

60. Lambi, *The Navy and German Power Politics*, p. 178.

61. *Die große Politik*, Vol. XVII, pp. 567–570.

62. Ibid.

63. Kennedy, *The Rise of the Anglo-German Antagonism*, p. 269.

64. *Die große Politik*, Vol. XX, Part 1, pp. 23–24; and ibid., p. 211.

65. *Die große Politik* Vol. XVII, Part 1, p. 68.

66. *Die große Politik* XIX, Part 1, p. 132.

67. Ibid., pp. 303–304.

68. Ibid., pp. 62–63.

69. Dugdale, *German Diplomatic Documents*, Vol. III, pp. 220–221.

70. Monger, *The End of Isolation*, 106.

71. Ibid., pp. 161–162.

72. Eugene N. Anderson, *The First Moroccan Crisis, 1904–1906* (Hamden, Conn: Archon, 1966), p. 183.

73. G. P. Gooch and H. W. Temperley, *British Documents*, Vol. III, p. 76.

74. *Die große Politik*, Vol. XX, Part 2, pp. 297–299; and ibid., pp. 301–303.

75. Rich, *Friedrich von Holstein*, Vol. II, p. 700.

76. *Die große Politik*, Vol. XX, Part 2, p. 313.

77. Rich, *Friedrich von Holstein*, Vol. II, pp. 693 and 702, n. 1.

78. *Die große Politik*, Vol. XX, Part 2, p. 339.

79. Rich, *Friedrich von Holstein*, Vol. II, p. 708.

80. *Die große Politik*, Vol. XX, Part 2, pp. 490–492.

81. Taylor, *The Struggle for Mastery in Europe*, p. 433.

82. *Die große Politik*, Vol. XX, Part 2, p. 662.

83. *Die große Politik*, Vol. XX, Part 2, p. 531.

84. Taylor, *The Struggle for Mastery in Europe*, p. 441.

85. Lambi, *The Navy and German Power Politics*, pp. 259–260.

86. Monger, *The End of Isolation*, pp. 206–207.

87. G. P. Gooch and H. W. Temperley, *British Documents*, Vol. III, pp. 170–171.

88. Monger, *The End of Isolation*, p. 251.

89. Winston Churchill, *The World Crisis*, rev. and abbr. ed. (New York: Free Press, 2005), p. 19.

90. Geiss, *German Foreign Policy*, p. 121.

91. Lambi, *The Navy and German Power Politics*, p. 188.

92. *Die große Politik*, Vol. XXI, Part 2, p. 361.

93. Cited in Joll, *The Origins of the First World War*, p. 56.

94. G. P. Gooch and H. W. Temperley, *British Documents*, Vol. III, p. 267.

95. This is a reference to the construction of the Berlin-to-Baghdad Railway, backed by German capital since the late nineteenth century. This project brought Germany into the Persian Gulf, which traditionally lay with the British and Russian spheres of influence. There are numerous references to this project in British diplomatic correspondence about the Anglo-Russian Entente. In the scheme of things, however, the impact of this project on Anglo-German or Russo-German relations was not all that great. A compromise had already been reached between the parties by the eve of World War I.

96. Monger, *The End of Isolation*, p. 282.

97. Alexander Izvolsky, *Recollections of a Foreign Minister*, trans. Charles Louis Seeger (Garden City, N.Y.: Doubleday, Page, and Company, 1921), p. 73.

98. Monger, *The End of Isolation*, p. 95.
99. Joll, *The Origins of the First World War*, pp. 45–46.
100. G. P. Gooch and H. W. Temperley, *British Documents*, Vol. III, p. 416.
101. Ibid., p. 420.
102. *Die große Politik*, Vol. XXI, Part 2, pp. 507–509.
103. Ibid., Vol. XXV, Part 2, p. 45.
104. Ibid., Vol. XXIV, p. 27.
105. Ibid., 68-76.
106. Ibid., XXV, Part 2, pp. 466–467. The first sentence has been translated from German to English; the remainder of this quotation is from John C. G. Röhl, *Wilhelm II: Into the Abyss of War and Exile, 1900–1941* (Cambridge, UK: Cambridge University Press, 2014), p. 618.
107. Norman Rich and M. H. Fisher, eds., *The Holstein Papers: Correspondence 1861–1896*, Vol. IV (London: Cambridge University Press, 1961), p. 551.

Chapter 7. An Obsession with Command of the Seas

1. Holger H. Herwig, *"Luxury" Fleet: The Imperial German Navy 1888–1918* (London: Ashfield Press, 1980), p. 16.
2. Bismarck's assessment of Tirpitz's plans for naval expansion was that they contained the intention to make war against Great Britain and as such were extremely dangerous. Rolf Hobson, *Imperialism at Sea: Naval Strategic Thought, The Ideology of Sea Power and the Tirpitz Plan, 1875–1914* (Boston: Brill Academic Publishers, 2002), pp. 297–299.
3. Many ascribe the construction of the High Seas Fleet to the rapid growth of overseas trade. Even Tirpitz himself made this claim in a speech to the Reichstag. Yet this is not a persuasive claim, as many policymakers during Wilhelm II's reign had begun thinking about the navy much earlier. Tirpitz, for instance, had formed his views as early as 1871. Patrick Kelly, "Strategies, Tactics and Turf Wars: Tirpitz and the Oberkommando der Marine, 1892–1895," *Journal of Military History*, Vol. 66, No. 4 (October 2002), pp. 1049–1050.
4. Patrick Kelly, "Strategies, Tactics and Turf Wars," pp. 1054–1055.
5. Portugal adopted a five-year naval construction plan in 1895, the Netherlands passed a ten-year plan in 1900, Mexico enacted a plan in 1901, and Spain announced a long-term program of naval construction in 1908.
6. Jonathan Steinberg, *Yesterday's Deterrent: Tirpitz and the Birth of the German Battle Fleet* (New York: MacMillan, 1965), p. 164.
7. Martin Kitchen, *The German Officer Corps, 1890–1914* (Oxford: Clarendon, 1968), pp. 5, 22, and 24.

8. Jonathan Steinberg, "The Kaiser's Navy and German Society," *Past and Present*, Vol. 28 (July 1964), pp. 105–106.

9. In today's language, this reflected a demand for social mobility. Moreover, both the middle class and liberal intellectuals understood the navy as a symbol of a unified Germany and as a historical manifestation of liberal ideals. The reasons for this date back to the 1848 revolutionary era. At the Frankfort Conference organized by German liberals, one of the few actions taken was a proposal to establish a German Navy. Thus, from its very inception, the German Navy was a unified national force, unlike the army, which belonged to the various states and would only fall under the unified command of the kaiser in event of war.

10. William L. Langer, *The Diplomacy of Imperialism 1890–1902* (New York: Alfred A. Knopf, 1935), p. 429.

11. Ibid., p. 656.

12. Ibid., pp. 437–438.

13. Ivo Nikolai Lambi, *The Navy and German Power Politics 1862–1914* (Boston: Allen and Unwin, 1984), p. 34.

14. Herwig, *"Luxury" Fleet*, p. 17.

15. Lambi, *The Navy and Germany Power Politics*, pp. 35–36.

16. Before Tirpitz took office in 1897, the naval official with the greatest influence over the kaiser was Gustav Freiherr von Senden-Bibran, chief of the Navy Cabinet from 1889 to 1906. He believed that Germany needed a large fleet centered on battleships and repeatedly emphasized to the kaiser the need for large publicity efforts to stir up national interest in the Navy. After Tirpitz took office, Senden-Bibran continued to play an important role as a promoter of German naval construction.

17. Steinberg, *Yesterday's Deterrent*, pp. 89-90.

18. Ibid., p. 41.

19. Herwig, *"Luxury" Fleet*, p. 40.

20. *Waijiao shi*, ed. B. M. He-wo-si-tuo-fu, di er juan shang 491–492. Translator's Note: The original Chinese edition quoted directly from this speech at length, based on the version that appears in this Chinese translation of a Russian textbook. The original speech could not be identified, thus only a paraphrase of its contents has been provided.

21. Lambi, *The Navy and German Power Politics*, p. 139.

22. Steinberg, *Yesterday's Deterrent*, p. 209.

23. Lambi, *The Navy and German Power Politics*, p. 142.

24. Herwig, *"Luxury" Fleet*, p. 38.

25. Tirpitz calculated that a ratio of two German ships to three British ones would be enough. Hobson, *Imperialism at Sea*, pp. 254–255.

26. Paul Kennedy, *Strategy and Diplomacy 1870–1945* (Boston: George Allen and Unwin, 1983), p. 133.

27. The earliest mention of this was an August 19, 1897, report from the German naval attaché in London, but Tirpitz "made no attempt to verify it." Instead, it was used as a political weapon. Lambi, *The Navy and German Power Politics*, pp. 144–145.

28. In 1807, the British fleet launched a sneak attack, without declaring war, on the Danish capital and seized its entire navy.

29. Herwig, *"Luxury" Fleet*, p. 37.

30. Kennedy, *Strategy and Diplomacy*, p. 132.

31. Alfred Thayer Mahan, *The Influence of Sea Power on History, 1660–1783* (Boston: Little, Brown and Company, 1891), p. 29.

32. Cited in Kennedy, *The Rise of the Anglo-German Antagonism*, p. 421.

33. There are two main views about the level of Mahan's influence on the German Navy. The first of these argues that Mahan's ideas formed the theoretical basis of German naval expansion. For an example, see Volker R. Berghahn, *Der Tirpitz Plan: Genesis und Verfall einer innenpolitischen Krisenstrategic unter Wilhelm II* (Dusseldorf: Droste Verlag, 1971), pp. 145 and 421. The second argument is that his influence was not significant and points to German misreadings of Mahan, claiming that Wilhelm II and Tirpitz cut and pasted portions of Mahan's theories to fit their own needs while ignoring the intellectual content of these theories. For an example of these, see Holger Herwig, "The Failure of German Sea Power, 1914–1915: Mahan, Tirpitz, and Raeder Reconsidered," *International History Review*, Vol. X (1988), pp. 68–105. This author tends toward the later argument—that Mahan mainly served as a propaganda tool and was merely one part of the ideology behind the High Seas Fleet. If Tirpitz and others had truly understood what they read in Mahan, they would have known that their challenge to British naval supremacy would be fruitless.

34. Langer, *Diplomacy of Imperialism*, p. 435.

35. Lambi, *The Navy and German Power Politics*, p. 144.

36. Lambi, *The Navy and German Power Politics*, p. 149.

37. Rich and Fisher, *The Holstein Papers*, Vol. IV, p. 28. Translator's Note: The quotation used in the Chinese edition could not be located, so a thematically similar one has been substituted.

38. Ibid., p. 50.

39. Lambi, *The Navy and German Power Politics*, p. 156.

40. Ibid., p. 147.

41. Kennedy, *The Rise of the Anglo-German Antagonism*, p. 251.

42. Monger, *The End of Isolation*, p. 63.

43. Ibid., pp. 68–69.

44. Ibid., p. 69.

45. Ibid., p. 82.

46. The "two-power" standard was that British naval power should equal the combined naval power of the next two largest powers. This was first used in 1889 and abandoned in 1912.

47. Arthur J. Marder, *Fear God and Dread Nought: The Correspondence of Admiral of the Fleet Lord Fisher of Kilverstone*, Vol. II (London: Cape, 1956), p. 20.

48. Herwig, *"Luxury" Fleet*, p. 37.

49. Kennedy, *The Rise of the Anglo-German Antagonism*, p. 420.

50. *Die große Politik der Europäischen Kabinette 1871–1914: Sammlung der Diplomatischen Akten des Auswärtigen Amtes* [The Foreign Policy of the European Cabinets, 1871–1914: Collection of diplomatic documents of the Foreign Office], Johannes Lepsius, et al., eds. Vol. XIX, Part 1 (Berlin: Deutsche verlagsgesellschaft Für Politik und Geschichte, 1922–1927), p. 292.

51. Ibid., p. 359.

52. Jonathan Steinberg, "The Copenhagen Complex," *Journal of Contemporary History*, Vol. 1, No. 3 (July 1966), pp. 35 and 38.

53. Lambi, *The Navy and German Power Politics*, p. 275.

54. Ibid., pp. 275–276.

55. Tirpitz first suggested this in his 1919 memoirs and later expanded upon it in other publications. Many historians have accepted this assessment, although Volker Berghahn refutes it in *Der Tirpitz Plan*.

56. Herwig, *"Luxury" Fleet*, pp. 55–57.

57. Lambi, *The Navy and German Power Politics*, p. 270.

58. Herwig, *"Luxury" Fleet*, pp. 59–60.

59. Ibid., pp. 64 and 69.

60. *Die große Politik*, Vol. XXIV, p. 27.

61. Taylor, *The Struggle for Mastery in Europe*, p. 458.

62. Herwig, *"Luxury" Fleet*, p. 70.

63. Ibid., p. 61. Statistics are cited from ibid., pp. 61, 63, and 70–71.

64. Rich and Fisher, *The Holstein Papers*, Vol. IV, pp. 427–428.

65. Lambi, *The Navy and German Power Politics*, pp. 297–298.

66. E. T. S. Dugdale (selected and translated), *German Diplomatic Documents 1871–1914*, Vol. III (New York: Harper and Brothers, 1928), p. 342.

67. *Die große Politik*, Vol. XXVIII, p. 81.

68. Ibid., pp. 78–79.

69. J.C.G. Röhl, "Admiral von Muller and the Approach of War," *Historical Journal*, Vol. 12, No. 4 (1969), pp. 651–673.

70. Craig, *Germany*, p. 287.

71. Cited in Taylor, *The Struggle for Mastery in Europe*, p. 460.
72. Lambi, *The Navy and German Power Politics*, p. 301.
73. Geiss, *German Foreign Policy*, p. 130.
74. Jack Snyder, *Myths of Empire: Domestic Politics and International Ambition* (Ithaca, N.Y.: Cornell University Press, 1991), p. 108.
75. G. P. Gooch and H. W. Temperley, eds., *British Documents on the Origins of the War 1898–1914*, Vol. X, Part 2 (London: His Majesty's Stationary Office, 1926–1938), p. 736.
76. Ibid., Vol. VI, pp. 309–310.
77. Lambi, *The Navy and German Power Politics*, p. 369.
78. Craig, *The Politics of the Prussian Army*, pp. 296–297.
79. Sidney Bradshaw Fay, *Origins of the World War*, Vol. I (New York: MacMillan Company, 1928), p. 303.
80. Herwig, *"Luxury" Fleet*, pp. 77–78.
81. Ibid., p. 75.
82. *Waijiao shi*, ed. He-wo-si-tuo-fu, p. 1058.
83. Herwig, *"Luxury" Fleet*, p. 78.
84. Ibid., pp. 80-82.
85. Churchill, *The World Crisis*, pp. 77-80.
86. Fay, *Origins of the World War*, Vol. I, p. 327.
87. Craig, *The Politics of the Prussian Army*, p. 298.
88. Lambi, *The Navy and German Power Politics*, pp. 379–380.
89. Kennedy, *Rise and Fall of the Great Powers*, p. 212.
90. Taylor, *The Struggle for Mastery in Europe*, pp. 461–462.
91. Pinson, *Modern Germany*, p. 301.

Chapter 8. The Schlieffen Plan and the Retreat of Grand Strategy

1. Gordon A. Craig, *The Politics of the Prussian Army, 1640–1945* (Oxford: Oxford University Press, 1955), p. 279.
2. Gunther E. Rothenberg, "Moltke, Schlieffen, and the Doctrine of Strategic Envelopment," in Peter Paret, ed., *Makers of Modern Strategy from Machiavelli to the Nuclear Age* (Princeton: Princeton University Press, 1986), p. 312.
3. Craig, *The Politics of the Prussian Army*, p. 281.
4. Gerhard Ritter, *The Schlieffen Plan: Critique of a Myth* (New York: Frederick A. Praeger, 1958), p. 22.
5. Robert T. Foley (trans.), *Alfred von Schlieffen's Military Writings* (London: Frank Cass, 2003), pp. 144–145.
6. The younger Moltke formally suspended this plan in 1913, making the Schlieffen Plan the German military's only strategic plan. On August 1, 1914, when the kaiser

demanded that he deploy the main force of the German Army to the east in order to prevent France from being dragged into the war, the younger Moltke claimed that it would be impossible for technical reasons. Ritter, *The Schlieffen Plan*, pp. 34–37.

7. Foley, *Alfred von Schlieffen's Military Writings*, p. 145.
8. Ibid., p. 146.
9. Ibid.
10. Ibid., p. 149.
11. Ritter, *The Schlieffen Plan*, pp. 41 and 80.
12. Jehuda L. Wallach, *The Dogma of the Battle of Annihilation: The Theories of Clausewitz and Schlieffen and Their Impact on the German Conduct of Two World Wars* (Westport, Conn.: Greenwood, 1986), p. 55. In the battle of Solferino, Napoleon III's Franco-Sardinian Alliance defeated the Austrian Army. The battle of Sedan, however, was a decisive Prussian victory of the Franco-Prussian War. The battle of Königgrätz, also known as the battle of Sadowa, was a decisive Prussian victory of the Austro-Prussian War. Schlieffen considered the battle of Sedan to be a "compete victory," while seeing the battle of Königgrätz as incomplete.
13. Foley, *Alfred von Schlieffen's Military Writings*, pp. 152–153.
14. Ritter, *The Schlieffen Plan*, pp. 44.
15. Foley, *Alfred von Schlieffen's Military Writings*, p. 155.
16. Ibid., p. 165.
17. Ibid., pp. 165–174.
18. Ritter, *The Schlieffen Plan*, p. 5.
19. B. H. Liddell Hart, *Strategy*, 2nd rev. ed. (New York: Meridian, 1991), p. 153.
20. Foley, *Alfred von Schlieffen's Military Writings*, pp. 175–177.
21. Gordon A. Craig, *Germany 1866–1945* (Oxford: Oxford University Press, 1981), p. 317.
22. Ritter, *The Schlieffen Plan*, p. 33.
23. Foley, *Alfred von Schlieffen's Military Writings*, p. 153.
24. Rothenberg, "Moltke, Schlieffen, and the Doctrine of Strategic Envelopment," p. 319.
25. Wallach, *The Dogma of the Battle of Annihilation*, p. 118, n. 44.
26. Ibid., pp. 58–59.
27. Gunther E. Rothenberg, *The Army of Francis Joseph* (West Lafayette, Ind.: Purdue University Press, 1976), pp. 112–117.
28. Denys Myers and J. G. Paul (trans.), *The Secret Treaties of Austria-Hungary*, Vol. I (Cambridge, Mass.: Harvard University Press, 1920), pp. 25–31.
29. Ritter, *The Schlieffen Plan*, p. 32.
30. Ibid., p. 28.

31. Holger Herwig, "The Dynamics of Necessity: German Military Policy during the First World War," in Allan R. Millett and Williamson Murray, eds., *Military Effectiveness*, Vol. I (Boston: Allen and Unwin, 1988), p. 89.
32. Gordon A. Craig, "The World War I Alliance of the Central Powers in Retrospect: The Military Cohesion of the Alliance, *Journal of Modern History*, Vol. 37, No. 3 (September 1965), p. 338.
33. Craig, *The Politics of the Prussian Army*, p. 243.
34. Holger Herwig, "Strategic Uncertainties of a Nation-State: Prussia-Germany, 1871–1918," in Williamson Murray, et al., eds., *The Making of Strategy: Rulers, States, and War* (Cambridge, UK: Cambridge University Press, 1994), p. 255.
35. Herwig, *"Luxury" Fleet*, p. 75.
36. Craig, *The Politics of the Prussian Army*, p. 244–245.
37. Foley, *Alfred von Schlieffen's Military Writings*, p. 151.
38. Ritter, *The Schlieffen Plan*, p. 61.
39. Carl von Clausewitz, *On War*, J. J. Graham, trans. (London: N. Trubner and Company, 1873), pp. 39–41.
40. Wallach, *The Dogma of the Battle of Annihilation*, p. 54.
41. Hajo Holborn, "The Prusso-German School: Moltke and the Rise of the General Staff," in Peter Paret, ed., *Makers of Modern Strategy from Machiavelli to the Nuclear Age*, p. 289.
42. Dennis E. Showalter, "Total War for Limited Objectives: An Interpretation of German Grand Strategy," in Paul Kennedy, ed., *Grand Strategies in War and Peace* (New Haven, Conn.: Yale University Press, 1991), p. 112.
43. Luo-si-tu-nuo-fu [Unidentified Soviet Author], *Di yi ci shijie da zhan shi* [History of the First World War], trans. Zhong Shi (Shanghai: Shanghai Yiwen chubanshe, 1982), pp. 321–322.
44. Martin van Creveld, *Supplying War: Logistics from Wallenstein to Patton* (London: Cambridge University Press, 1977), pp. 140–141.
45. Creveld, *Supplying War*, pp. 119–21.
46. Liddell Hart, *Strategy*, p. 156.
47. Luo-si-tu-nuo-fu, *Di yi ci shijie da zhan shi*, p. 179.
48. Ritter, *The Schlieffen Plan*, p. 66.
49. Liddell Hart, *Strategy*, p. 208.
50. Clausewitz, *On War*, p. 12.
51. Rothenberg, "Moltke, Schlieffen, and the Doctrine of Strategic Envelopment," p. 298.
52. Erich Ludendorff, *Ludendorff's Own Story*, Vol. I (New York: Harper and Brothers, 1919), p. 28.
53. Showalter, "Total War for Limited Objectives," p. 112.
54. Wallach, *The Dogma of the Battle of Annihilation*, pp. 37–38.

55. Bruce Condell and David T. Zabecki, ed. and trans., *On the German Art of War: Truppenfuhrung* (Boulder: Lynne Rienner, 2001), p. 29.
56. Hobson, *Imperialism at Sea*, p. 121.
57. Foley, *Alfred von Schlieffen's Military Writings*, pp. 202–205.
58. Rich and Fisher, *The Holstein Papers*, Vol. I, pp. 159–167.
59. Foley, *Alfred von Schlieffen's Military Writings*, p. 186.
60. Rothenberg, "Moltke, Schlieffen, and the Doctrine of Strategic Envelopment," p. 297.
61. Wallach, *The Dogma of the Battle of Annihilation*, p. 36.
62. Ibid., p. 46.
63. Foley, *Alfred von Schlieffen's Military Writings*, p. 189.
64. Ibid.
65. Wallach, *The Dogma of the Battle of Annihilation*, p. 37.
66. Herwig, "Strategic Uncertainties of a Nation-State," p. 252.
67. Clausewitz, *On War*, pp. 4 and 148.
68. Wallach, *The Dogma of the Battle of Annihilation*, p. 41.
69. Ibid, p. 45.
70. Foley, *Alfred von Schlieffen's Miltary Writings*, p. 190.
71. Isabel V. Hull, *Absolute Destruction: Military Culture and Practices of War in Imperial Germany* (Ithaca, N.Y.: Cornell University Press, 2005), p. 168.
72. Ritter, *The Schlieffen Plan*, pp. 53–54.
73. Wallach, *The Dogma of the Battle of Annihilation*, p. 53.
74. Hajo Holborn, "The Prusso-German School," pp. 290–291.
75. Antulio Echevarria, *After Clausewitz: German Military Thinkers before the Great War* (Lawrence: University of Kansas Press, 2001), pp. 197–198.
76. Hull, *Absolute Destruction*, pp. 170–171.

Chapter 9. Crisis Management on the Path to World War, 1908–1914

1. Edward Grey, *Twenty-five Years 1892–1916*, Vol. I (New York: Frederick A. Stokesco, 1925), p. 205.
2. *Die große Politik der Europäischen Kabinette 1871–1914: Sammlung der Diplomatischen Akten des Auswärtigen Amtes* [The Foreign Policy of the European Cabinets, 1871–1914: Collection of diplomatic documents of the Foreign Office], Johannes Lepsius, et al., eds., Vol. XXV (Berlin: Deutsche verlagsgesellschaft Für Politik und Geschichte, 1922–1927), pp. 474–479.
3. Piedmont is a region in northern Italy. The kingdom of Sardinia-Piedmont, based in this region, played a central role in the unification of the Italian peninsula. As an indicator of the region's historical significance, the crown prince of post-unification

Italy was designated as the Prince of Piedmont. Marx and Engels penned an essay about the defeat of the Piedmontese Army.

4. E. T. S. Dugdale (selected and translated), *German Diplomatic Documents 1871–1914*, Vol. III (New York: Harper and Brothers, 1928), p. 303.

5. Sidney Bradshaw Fay, *The Origins of the World War* (New York: MacMillan Company, 1928), pp. 378–379.

6. A. J. P. Taylor, *The Struggle for Mastery in Europe, 1848–1918* (Oxford: Clarendon Press, 1954), p. 452.

7. *Die große Politik*, Vol. XXVI, Part 1, p. 39.

8. Dugdale, *German Diplomatic Documents*, Vol. III, p. 306.

9. Ibid., pp. 304–306.

10. Taylor, *The Struggle for Mastery in Europe*, p. 453.

11. Ibid.

12. Dugdale, *German Diplomatic Documents*, Vol. III, pp. 317–318.

13. Craig, *The Politics of the Prussian Army*, pp. 288-89.

14. Ibid.

15. Ibid., p. 289.

16. *Die große Politik*, pp. 440–41.

17. *Die große Politik*, Vol. XXVI, Part 1, pp. 222–223.

18. Taylor, *The Struggle for Mastery in Europe*, p. 455.

19. *Die große Politik*, Vol. XXVI, Part 2, pp. 669–670.

20. Dugdale, *German Diplomatic Documents*, Vol. III, pp. 321–322.

21. In the end, Izvolsky demanded that Germany persuade Austria against releasing these documents; German pressure worked.

22. Fay, *The Origins of the World War*, Vol. I, p. 391.

23. Ibid., p. 393.

24. Michael Balfour, *The Kaiser and His Times* (London: Cresset Press, 1964), p. 295.

25. G. P. Gooch and H. W. Temperley, eds., *British Documents on the Origins of the War 1898–1914*, Vol. VI (London: His Majesty's Stationary Office, 1926–1938), p. 261.

26. Fay, *The Origins of the World War*, Vol. I, pp. 398–399.

27. Taylor, *The Struggle for Mastery in Europe*, p. 456.

28. Fay, *The Origins of the World War*, Vol. I, p. 405.

29. Taylor, *The Struggle for Mastery in Europe*, p. 464.

30. *Die große Politik*, Vol. XXIX pp. 97–98.

31. Dugdale, *German Diplomatic Documents*, Vol. IV, p. 2.

32. Ibid., pp. 2–4.

33. *Die große Politik*, Vol. XXIX, p. 119.

34. Taylor, *The Struggle for Mastery in Europe*, p. 470.

35. *Die große Politik*, Vol. XXIX, p. 167.
36. Dugdale, *German Diplomatic Documents*, Vol. IV, pp. 10–11.
37. Ibid., pp. 11–12.
38. *Die große Politik*, Vol. XXIX, p. 189.
39. Edward Grey, *Twenty-five Years*, Vol. I, p. 216.
40. Churchill, *The World Crisis*, p. 30.
41. Dugdale, *German Diplomatic Documents*, Vol. IV, p. 15.
42. Churchill, *The World Crisis*, p. 30.
43. Craig, *Germany*, pp. 328–329.
44. Churchill, *World Crisis*, p. 66.
45. Fay, *The Origins of the World War*, Vol. I, pp. 335–336.
46. Taylor, *The Struggle for Mastery in Europe*, p. 488.
47. *Die gross Politik*, Vol. XXIX, p. 406.
48. Fritz Fischer, *War of Illusion: German Policies from 1911 to 1914* (London: Chatto and Windus, 1975), pp. 89–90.
49. Fritz Fischer, *Germany's Aims in the First World War* (London: Chatto and Windus, 1967), p. 25.
50. Craig, *Germany*, p. 329.
51. In the early twentieth century, the importance of oil grew, as did its strategic implications, particularly once the Royal Navy began using it to power warships. German interest in oil increased as well. Great Britain principally extracted its Middle Eastern oil from southern Persia, while German oil came from Mesopotamia. Competition between the two nations for Middle Eastern oil grew fierce. Later, when the American Standard Oil Company planned to enter the Middle East, the two countries quickly reached an agreement in March 1914 (negotiations had been broken off in 1912, but had resumed in February 1913) to create a joint company to extract Mesopotamian oil. Deutsche Bank, representing German oil interests, provided only 25 percent of the company's capital, thus illustrating the constrained nature of German resources.
52. Taylor, *The Struggle for Mastery in Europe*, p. 513.
53. Dugdale, *German Diplomatic Documents*, Vol. IV, p. 369.
54. Geiss, *German Foreign Policy*, p. 143.
55. Ibid., p. 149.
56. Dugdale, *German Diplomatic Documents*, Vol. IV, p. 370.
57. Joll, *The Origins of the First World War*, p. 35.
58. Geiss, *German Foreign Policy*, p. 157.
59. Karl Kautsky, et al., eds., *Outbreak of the World War: German Documents Collected by Karl Kautsky*, trans. Carnegie Endowment for International Peace (New York: Oxford University Press, 1924), p. 61.

60. Fay, *The Origins of the World War*, Vol. II, p. 199.
61. Ibid.
62. Ibid., pp. 201–203.
63. Ibid., p. 203.
64. Karl Kautsky, et al., *Outbreak of the World War,* p. 78.
65. Ibid., pp. 92–94.
66. Ibid., p. 95.
67. J. C. G. Röhl, "Admiral von Muller and the Approach of War, 1911–1914," *Historical Journal*, Vol. 12, No. 4 (December 1969), p. 668.
68. *Outbreak of the World War,* p. 122.
69. Ibid., pp. 616–620.
70. Ibid., pp. 131–132.
71. P. H. S. Hatton, "Britain and Germany in 1914: The July Crisis and War Aims," *Past and Present*, Vol. 36 (April 1967), p. 141.
72. Jack S. Levy, "Preferences, Constraints, and Choices in July 1914," *International Security*, Vol. 15, No. 3 (Winter 1990–91), pp. 163–166.
73. Cited in Geiss, *German Foreign Policy,* pp. 141–142.
74. Karl Kautsky, et al., *Outbreak of the World War,* pp. 230–231.
75. Ibid., p. 209.
76. Ibid., pp. 250–254.
77. Ibid., pp. 288–289.
78. Fischer, *Germany's Aims in the First World War*, pp. 73–75.
79. Karl Kautsky, et al., *Outbreak of the World War,* pp. 306–308.
80. Ibid., p. 302.
81. Ibid., p. 315.
82. Fischer, *Germany's Aims in the First World War*, pp. 57-64.
83. Karl Kautsky, et al., *Outbreak of the World War,* pp. 321–322.
84. Fischer, *Germany's Aims in the First World War*, p. 78.
85. Karl Kautsky, et al., *Outbreak of the World War,* pp. 344–345.
86. Ibid., pp. 345–346.
87. The Social Democratic Party was the leading anti-war force inside Germany. The party, however, viewed the czar as the symbol of reaction, leading many German elites to conclude that it would not oppose a war directed at Russia.
88. Fay, *The Origins of the World War*, 506–511.
89. Taylor, *The Struggle for Mastery in Europe*, p. 524.

About the Author

Xu Qiyu is Deputy Director of the Institute for Strategic Studies at National Defense University in Beijing, China. He is also an advisor to the Chinese Ministry of Defense, as well as a researcher at the Academy for Military Sciences and at Peking University. Additionally, he has been a visiting scholar at the Institute for Security and Development Policy in Stockholm, Sweden.

Xu received his MA from National Defense University and his Ph.D. from the Chinese Academy of Social Sciences. He participated in the U.S.-China Young Leaders Forum of the National Committee on U.S.-China Relations in 2003, and was elected a member of the Eleventh Committee of the All-China Youth Federation in 2010.

Contributors

Graham Allison is Director of the Belfer Center for Science and International Affairs and Douglas Dillon Professor of Government at the John F. Kennedy School of Government at Harvard University. The "founding dean" of the modern Kennedy School, Allison has served as a special advisor to the secretary of defense under President Ronald Reagan and as an assistant secretary of defense under President Bill Clinton. His first book, *Essence of Decision: Explaining the Cuban Missile Crisis*, ranks among the all-time best-sellers with more than 450,000 copies in print. His latest book, *Lee Kuan Yew: The Grand Master's Insights on China, the United States, and the World*, coauthored with Robert D. Blackwill, has been a best-seller in the United States and abroad.

Joshua Hill is Assistant Professor of History at Ohio University. A historian of modern China, Hill earned his Ph.D. at Harvard University and held an appointment as a postdoctoral scholar at the University of California, Berkeley in the Center for Chinese Studies.

Index

Adowa, 125
Aehrenthal, Alois Lexa von, 185, 260–264, 267
Afghanistan, 41, 101, 186
Agadir Crisis, 274–278
agriculture, 6, 135-136
Albania, 24, 115
Albedyll, Emil von, 90, 192
Albert II (Belgian), 110
Alexander I (Russian), 37
Alexander II (Russian), 14, 18, 40, 44
Alexander III (Russian), 85, 105
Algeciras Conference, 173, 182, 184–185, 263, 272–273, 278
"all-big-gun" battleship, 210–211
Alsace-Lorraine, 4, 10, 11, 14, 17, 61, 63, 84, 159, 163, 183, 188, 228, 230, 233, 234, 237, 271
Andrássy, Count Gyula, 23–24, 39, 40
Anglo-French Entente, 131, 161, 173–174, 178, 180, 181, 187, 208, 216, 220, 223, 242, 259, 280. *See also* Triple Entente
Anglo-German alliance, 163–173, 271
Anglo-German competition, 82–83, 101, 188, 210–218, 220, 221, 225, 265, 269, 274
Anglo-German relations, 12, 75, 99, 100, 102–103, 105–108, 110–111, 117, 121–124, 158, 186, 194, 196, 204, 209, 220, 225, 251, 252, 265, 271, 277, 281
Anglo-German Yangzi Agreement, 166–168
Anglo-Japanese alliance, 171, 176
Anglo-Russian Convention, 187, 216, 259
Anglo-Russian Entente, 182–189. *See also* Triple Entente
Anglo-Russian relations, 14–15, 27, 29, 43, 53, 114, 173–174, 266, 282
anti-German alliance, 9, 27, 29, 31–32, 36–38, 76, 81, 105, 185, 187, 192, 201
anti-Russian alliance, 39–41, 79, 86, 96, 167–168
arms races, 146, 188, 200, 202, 210–218, 218–222, 222–226
Austro-German alliance, 39–41, 41–45, 45–49, 89, 219, 223–224, 228, 250, 263, 265, 268–269, 279, 280–281, 286, 288, 290. *See also* Triple Alliance
Austro-Hungarian Army, 230, 242
Austro-Hungarian Empire, 6, 13, 23, 39, 42, 78–81, 100, 184, 241, 260–261
Austro-Hungarian Foreign Ministry, 47, 79, 80, 88, 99, 112, 117, 261, 283, 289, 292
Austro-Hungarian General Staff, 241, 242, 243, 291
Austro-Prussian War, 46, 96
Austro-Russian tensions, 44–45, 79, 80–82, 85, 266
Austro-Serbian tensions, 266
Austro-Serbian war, 284–287

balance of power, 10, 18, 23, 30, 106, 113, 133, 135, 137–139, 221, 286, 288
Balfour, Arthur, 125, 165, 206

Balkans, 13, 18, 22–28, 42–44, 53, 69, 76, 78–82, 84, 86, 88–89, 99, 110, 112, 116–118, 185, 261, 263, 265–267, 269, 270, 279, 284
Balkan Wars, 222, 281, 286
Ballin, Albert, 129, 160, 216
Baltic Sea, 9, 196, 224, 251
battleships, 123, 160, 163–164, 193, 199, 203–205, 210–214, 217, 220, 222–224
Belgium, 17, 61, 63, 228, 232–233, 236, 239, 247, 251, 256, 288, 292
Berchtold, Leopold, 283, 289, 291, 292
Berlin Conference, 26–27, 28, 30–32, 33, 45, 78, 80, 92, 102, 111, 115, 159
Bernhardi, Friedrich von, 144, 252, 254, 257
Bethmann-Hollweg, Theobald von, 138, 218–223, 270, 272, 276, 280–282, 284, 286–291
bipolarity, 6, 136, 157, 258
Bismarck, Herbert von, 55, 56, 81, 96, 97
Bismarck, Otto von, 1, 2, 7, 9, 16, 53, 56, 57, 67, 71, 72, 91–94, 98–100, 122, 131, 136, 139, 140, 143, 148, 149, 185, 192, 201, 204, 259, 264, 266
  and Austria-Hungary, 13, 25, 31–32, 39–40, 43, 44, 46, 48, 49, 79, 82, 83, 87, 88, 90, 162, 265
  Bismarck revelations, 148–149
  and Britain, 10, 12, 14, 20, 21, 25, 28, 29, 41, 43, 49, 50, 54, 55–56, 74, 75–78, 82, 83, 87, 89, 102
  and the Bulgaria Crisis, 78–82, 84, 85, 90, 91, 265
  and colonial policies, 72–78, 157
  disagreements with other politicians, 7–8, 58, 59–63, 63–65, 147
  dismissal from office, 67, 95, 96, 97–100, 127, 128, 130, 137, 158, 259
  and the Egyptian Crisis, 51–56
  and France, 17, 19, 49–51, 54, 75, 83, 84
  and the Kissingen Dictation, 33–37, 43, 52
  and the League of Three Emperors, 14, 22, 29, 38, 41–44, 45, 50, 78, 82, 85, 87
  and the Near East Crisis, 27–30, 30–32, 53
  and Russia, 11, 12, 14, 18, 20–21, 28, 29, 31–32, 38, 42, 43, 44, 45–47, 49, 79, 81, 82, 85–87, 90, 97, 149, 162
  Thoughts and Reminiscences, 4–5, 12, 150
  and the Triple Alliance, 47–49, 50
  and the "War in Sight" Crisis, 18–20, 21, 22, 59, 84
Bismarckian era, 9, 65, 72, 136, 140, 144, 158, 178, 182, 192. *See also* post-Bismarckian era
Black Sea, 11, 12, 26, 31, 35, 36, 43–44, 53, 74, 89, 101, 109, 262
Black Seas Straits, 87, 89, 98–99, 101, 116, 125, 261, 266, 282
blank check, 263–265, 270, 283–284, 288
Boer Republics, 69, 119, 166, 195
Boer War (1899–1902), 152, 163, 177
Bosnia Crisis (1908–1909), 219, 259–261, 261–268, 268–270, 272, 274, 279, 280, 289
Bosnia-Herzegovina, 23–28, 31, 261–268, 268–270, 283

British Army, 52, 125, 162, 171, 239, 246, 277
British Empire, 101, 123, 172, 173, 187, 208
British Foreign Ministry, 20, 23, 41, 55, 70, 74–75, 76, 107, 169, 176, 183, 185, 274, 276
British foreign policy, 80, 115, 123, 187
British General Staff, 183, 278
British naval scare/panic, 213–215, 220, 269
British Navy, 52, 55, 104, 108–109, 125, 164, 192–193, 195, 199–200, 203, 205, 206, 207, 208, 209, 210–213, 213–215, 215–218, 223, 224, 225. *See also* Royal Navy
Bulgaria, 24–27, 31, 39, 45, 46, 59, 78–85, 85–86, 88, 89, 90–91, 112, 155, 261, 265, 266, 284
Bulgaria Crisis, 59, 78–85, 85–86, 88, 90–91, 265
Bülow, Bernhard von, 6, 129, 137, 151, 152, 155, 157, 159–160, 162–163, 168–171, 174, 175, 181, 184, 187, 188, 189, 200, 202, 203, 204, 209, 216–218, 219, 222, 260, 262–263, 265, 270, 272

Caprivi, Leo von, 96–99, 101, 108, 111–113, 137, 140, 149, 155, 159, 218, 244, 250
cartelization, 133–135, 136, 137, 139–143, 153
Catholic Centre Party (German), 16, 100, 136, 137, 146
Catholics, 5, 6, 15–18, 46, 48, 136, 185
Centre Party (German), 136, 138
Chamberlain, Joseph, 106, 123, 125, 165, 166, 168, 171–172, 173, 174
China, 76, 114, 118, 151, 155
Churchill, Randolph, 83
Churchill, Winston, 183, 215, 223–225
Clausewitz, Carl von, 58, 245, 249, 254
Cleveland, Grover, 122–123
Concert of Europe, 43, 54, 55
Congo, 75, 77, 110, 111, 118, 155, 275, 278–279
Conrad, Franz von Hötzendorf, 185, 243, 260, 264, 291
Continental League, 113–116, 117–118, 119–120, 124, 162, 177, 202,
continental war, 220, 225, 279, 286, 288, 291
"Copenhagen-style" attack, 200, 207–208, 208–210, 319 n28
Crimean War, 24, 25, 26, 30, 39
cruisers, 123, 160, 163, 199, 203, 204, 211–213, 214, 215, 222

Daily Telegraph incident, 130, 138, 153
Dardanelles, 36, 44, 86, 88, 116, 117, 126
democracy (national liberalism), 68, 70, 72, 134, 144,
Derby, Lord, 20, 21, 23
diplomacy, 7, 19, 31, 33, 50, 56–59, 61, 64, 68, 70, 87, 90, 93, 95, 100, 102, 118, 148, 163, 170, 171, 184, 187, 189, 196, 200, 220, 232, 239, 250, 275
Disraeli, Benjamin, 10, 23, 26, 29, 41, 43, 52, 54, 72,
domestic politics, 2, 16, 43, 51, 67, 68, 70, 72, 77, 78, 83–84, 93, 101–102, 112, 115, 124, 127, 134–136, 140–142, 144, 148, 155, 157–158, 184, 189, 197, 204, 250,

Dreadnought battleships, 188, 210–218, 224, 225

East Prussia, 62, 63, 241
Eastern Question, 23, 43, 69, 82, 88, 99,
Egypt, 28, 35, 36, 50, 51–56, 74–77, 87, 101, 106, 116, 118, 121, 124–126, 162, 177,
encirclement (German), 124, 142, 149, 155, 182–189, 226, 233, 251, 259, 260, 263, 270, 271, 282

First Morocco Crisis, 141, 182–185, 187, 216, 265, 266, 271, 278
First Naval Amendment, 212, 217
First Naval Law, 202–204, 205
Fisher, John "Jackie," First Sea Lord, 183, 207–211, 223, 259
Franco-German relations, 11, 15–18, 44, 75–77, 84, 85, 92, 103–105, 119, 162, 178–181, 183, 229–230, 271, 274–276, 277, 281, 287
Franco-Prussian War, 10–12, 14, 17, 18, 19, 21, 37, 58, 60, 63, 96, 104, 171, 249, 255, 257
Franco-Russian alliance, 45, 47, 49, 76, 85, 87, 93, 98, 100, 103–104, 105, 107–109, 111–113, 117–118, 148, 156, 158, 161, 162, 169, 170, 171, 174–175, 178, 181, 183, 184, 198, 206, 219, 250, 267, 274, 279
Franz Ferdinand, Archduke, 269, 282
French Army, 60, 63, 231–235, 236–238, 246, 248, 272
French Empire, 51
French Foreign Ministry, 19, 103, 104, 151, 177–178, 179, 274
French General Staff, 103, 278
French Navy, 279
French Revolution, 10, 69

German Army, 3, 8, 56, 57, 61, 62, 65, 84, 94, 130–132, 141–142, 208, 228–231, 233–235, 237, 238, 240, 241, 243, 244, 246–250, 252–254, 257–258, 292
    Army Bill, 83–84, 111, 223, 244
    Army Cabinet, 90, 94, 131, 244
German Empire, 1–4, 5, 8, 9, 12, 127, 139, 141, 145, 161, 166, 185, 196, 198, 218, 224, 243, 248, 272, 280, 292
German Foreign Ministry, 84, 97, 120, 148, 165, 176, 217, 222, 283
German foreign policy, 35, 48, 50, 75, 96–97, 137, 158–159, 161, 283
German General Staff, 3, 230, 233, 243
German grand strategy, 1, 2, 9, 33, 56, 59–63, 65, 67, 72, 75, 78, 85, 90, 91–94, 95, 99, 127, 133–134, 137, 142, 153, 155, 159, 191, 218, 227, 260
German Navy, 132, 141–142, 160, 172, 192–196, 200, 201–202, 202–203, 206–208, 212, 222, 225
    Navy Cabinet, 131–132, 160, 203, 218, 220
    Navy General Staff, 132, 160, 194
German War Ministry, 130–131, 244, 250, 252
Germany and the Next War (1911), 144, 252, 254
Giers, Nikolay, 45, 80, 85, 98, 103, 104, 105

Gladstone, William, 25, 43, 106
Gorchakov, Alexander, 11, 14, 17–18, 20, 24, 28, 29
great powers, 1, 9, 12, 13, 18, 19, 20–22, 22–27, 27–28, 31–32, 34, 36, 37, 43, 50–52, 60, 65, 76, 79, 80, 91, 113–114, 116–117, 124, 161, 164, 166, 177, 182, 184, 193, 201, 210, 217, 219, 230, 239, 242, 251, 267, 268, 285, 291, 292
Greater Bulgaria, 26, 31, 78, 80
Greater Germany, 34, 39, 144
Grey, Sir Edward, 183, 185, 187, 221, 224, 266, 269, 271, 274, 276, 277, 286, 287

Haldane, Lord Richard, 183, 221–222, 286
Hamilton, George, 166, 172
hard-line policies, 79, 120, 124, 127, 141, 143–144, 146, 147, 150, 152–153, 178, 182, 183, 194, 217, 264, 266–268, 268–269, 272, 274, 276–278, 280
Hatzfeldt, Paul von, 82, 83, 107–108, 115–116, 156–157, 165–166, 170
hegemony, 1, 10, 33–34, 64, 102, 124, 145, 156, 173, 186, 191, 202, 226, 269
Heligoland, 100, 101–102, 103, 106, 196, 199
"hide and bide," 1, 12, 15, 22, 33
High Seas Fleet, 151, 152, 156, 158, 161, 189, 191, 192–196, 198, 212, 225, 243
Hindenburg, Paul von, 57
Hohenlohe-Schillingsfürst, Chlodwig zu, 113, 119, 137, 159–160, 193–194, 205
Hohenzollerns, 5, 34, 57, 151, 153, 244
Holland, 29, 206, 251. *See also* the Netherlands
Holstein, Friedrich von, 27, 48, 81, 93, 96–98, 100, 106, 112, 113, 115–116, 118, 121, 124, 129, 149, 162, 166, 170, 171, 174–176, 178–180, 189, 203, 204, 209, 216–217, 239, 252
Holy Alliance, 13, 22
House of Commons (British), 10, 165
House of Lords (British), 20, 74

ideology, 26, 37, 68, 69, 72, 144, 146, 193
Imperial Admiralty, 96, 132
Imperial Navy (German), 132, 141, 152, 161, 194, 195, 197, 202
imperialism, 68, 69, 70–72, 113, 144–146, 193
India, 51–53, 101, 107, 118, 120, 166, 167, 186, 187
industrialization, 6, 63, 71, 91, 113, 123, 135–138, 139–141, 157, 158, 164, 193, 194, 198, 219, 271
institutions, 3, 8, 16, 65, 70, 93, 127–128, 131, 134–135, 139
Italy, 15, 18, 20, 21, 45–47, 47–49, 51, 79, 84, 87–89, 98, 104–105, 106–107, 110–111, 115–118, 121, 125, 155, 170, 174, 177, 179, 182, 251, 266, 268–269, 283, 287, 288, 291
Izvolsky, Alexander, 186, 260–262, 266–268, 270, 279

Jagow, Gottlieb von, 285–286
Jameson Raid, 119–120
Japan, 114, 156, 164–165, 167–168, 171, 173, 176, 178, 181, 182, 186, 207, 208, 210–211, 217, 235, 280
Japanese Army, 114
Japanese Foreign Ministry, 114

July Crisis (1914), 270, 280–282, 287
Junker landlords, 4, 6, 113, 136–138, 157, 194

Kálnoky, Count Gustav (Austrian), 79, 88, 99
Kennan, George, 187
King Edward VII (British), 95, 259, 263
Kissingen Dictation, 33–34, 43, 50, 52, 274
Kissinger, Henry, 37, 93
Königgrätz, 233. *See also* Sadowa
Kruger Telegram, 119–121, 122–124, 125, 148, 151, 155, 158, 162, 163, 194
Kuhlmann, Richard von, 174, 177, 225
Kulturkampf, 15–16, 18, 48

Lansdowne, Lord, 168–170, 173, 176, 178
Lascelles, Frank, 120, 173, 206–207
League of Three Emperors, 14, 22–23, 27, 29, 38, 39, 41–45, 49, 50, 76, 78, 80, 82, 84, 85, 87, 89
Lenin, Vladimir, 156
Leveson-Gower, George Granville, 55, 75
Liddell Hart, B.H., 238, 247, 249
Lloyd George, David, 276–277, 280, 281
Lobanov, Aleksey, 114, 117
Ludendorff, Erich von, 58, 245, 249
Luxembourg, 232, 233, 234, 236

magic pill, colonies as, 73, 230, 242
Mahan, Alfred, 193, 195, 197, 201–202
Marriage of iron and rye, 136–137, 139
Marschall, Adolf von, 96, 110–111, 119–121, 124, 130, 160
Mediterranean Agreements, 85, 87–90, 99
Meditteranean Sea, 26–27, 35, 42, 49, 50, 53, 87–88, 99, 104, 107, 108, 110, 115- 116, 125–126, 177, 196, 207, 223, 225, 273, 278, 279
Metternich, Klemens von, 13, 22, 36–37, 93
Metternich, Paul Wolff, 174, 187, 188, 209, 218, 221
middle road, 161–173
Moltke, Helmuth von (the elder), 91, 253
  as Chief of Prussian General Staff, 14, 17, 19, 58–59, 90, 156, 227, 241
  and Schlieffen, 227–230, 231, 239, 240, 255, 258
  strategic philosophy of, 61, 62, 63–65, 227–230, 231, 240, 245, 249, 254, 256–257
Moltke, Helmuth von (the younger), 218, 219, 238, 242–243, 247, 252, 264–265, 280, 282, 288, 291–292
Moroccan Question, 176–177, 272
Morocco crisis *see* First Morocco Crisis, Second Morocco Crisis

Napoleonic Wars, 36, 51, 60, 69, 115, 188, 214, 245, 249
National Liberal Party (German), 138, 145–146, 153, 280
nationalism, 2, 4, 24, 68, 69, 70, 72, 144–146, 152, 263
naval arms race, 146, 188, 200, 202, 210–216, 218, 219–220, 222–226, 251, 265, 271
Navy, German, 132, 160, 172, 192–196, 200, 201–202, 202–208, 212, 222, 225,
Nazi period, 139
Near East Crisis, 22–32, 34, 53

the Netherlands, 193, 236, 239. *See also* Holland
new course, 97–100, 103–111, 112–113, 155, 158
Nicholas II (Russian), 112, 148, 176, 290
Nile River, 101–102, 125–126, 162
North Sea, 9, 33, 100, 101, 199, 207–208, 209, 212, 223, 224, 279, 285

one-front war, 240
open-door policy, 178–179
Ottoman Empire, 23–25, 28, 42, 44, 54, 55, 80, 84, 115–116, 261, 262. *See also* Turkey

Pan-German League, 141, 144–146, 150–151, 153, 271, 272, 276, 280
pan-Slavism, 24, 26, 45, 80, 87, 262, 269
patriotism, 146–147
peace, 8, 14, 19, 20–21, 26, 28–30, 36, 42, 45, 48, 59–63, 65, 81, 89, 109, 114, 120, 124, 125, 132, 142, 150, 172, 181–182, 184, 188, 204, 227, 260, 276–277, 284, 287–290
Poland, 5, 62, 63
Poles, 5–6, 16, 45, 105, 117
Portugal, 75, 120, 193, 281
post-Bismarckian era, 97–102, 111, 112, 118, 127–128, 130, 137, 146, 158, 218
post–Great Man effect, 147–150
Praetorian societies, 134–135
preemptive war, 49, 59, 84, 91, 264
preventive war, 17, 19–20, 21, 59, 83, 90
Prince Alexander of Battenberg (Bulgarian), 78–80, 87
Prince Philipp Friedrich Alexander Eulenberg (Prussian), 129, 149
Protestants, 5–6, 15–16, 18, 136, 185
Prussian Army, 8, 10, 96, 171, 194, 231
Prussian General Staff, 3, 8, 14, 17, 18–19, 56, 58–59, 132, 156, 227, 234–235, 245, 249, 252
Prussian Ministry of War, 56, 57, 222, 244
public opinion, 25, 32, 46, 70, 73, 78, 84, 94, 101, 123, 125, 127, 134, 140–141, 143–147, 147–153, 157, 175, 177, 195, 267, 272–273, 276–277, 279, 285

Qing dynasty, 114, 164, 168
Queen Victoria (British), 20, 54, 108, 123, 165, 195

Radowitz, Joseph Maria von, 17–19, 93, 98
Rhodes, Cecil, 71, 119
risk theory (Tirpitz), 199, 202, 205, 212
Romania, 24, 31, 45–46, 98, 112, 155, 159, 283, 284, 291
Roosevelt, Theodore, 179
Rosebery, Lord (Archibald Primrose), 107, 111, 121
Royal Navy (British), 26, 163, 164, 191, 195, 199, 200, 205–210, 212, 223–224, 251, 274, 277, 278, 282
Russell, Lord Odo, 10, 20
Russian Army, 25, 31, 62, 63, 105, 168, 178, 208, 229, 241–242
Russian Empire, 62
Russian Foreign Ministry, 11, 80, 85, 98, 114, 117, 163, 186, 261, 267, 268, 270
Russian Navy, 108, 208, 209, 261
Russo-Austrian relations, 29, 30, 76, 82
Russo-German Reinsurance Treaty, 85–87, 97–100

Russo-German relations, 17, 32, 42, 53, 60, 86, 87, 97, 99, 105, 113, 148, 175, 181, 185, 270, 290
Russo-Japanese War, 175, 176, 208, 211, 238, 266

Sadowa, 48, 58, 254, 255. *See also* Königgrätz
Salisbury, Lord Robert, 10, 41, 52, 77, 87, 89, 100–102, 106, 107, 115–117, 123–125, 167, 168, 170
Schlieffen, Alfred von, 183, 209, 232, 234–235, 236, 238, 241, 244, 245, 246, 250, 252, 254, 255, 256, 258. *See also* Schlieffen Plan
and Moltke the elder, 227–230, 231, 239, 240, 255, 258
Schlieffen Plan, 63, 189, 235–238, 248–258, 259, 282, 288, 292. *See also* Schlieffen, Alfred von
creation of, 227–238
problems with, 238–248, 248–252, 253–254, 255–258
versus Moltke the elder's strategy, 61, 64, 227–230, 239, 253
Schweinitz, Lothar von, 98, 103
Second Morocco Crisis, 141, 153, 221, 222, 270–280, 281
Second Naval Amendment, 213–214, 220
Second Naval Law, 202, 204–208, 212
Second Reich, 95, 145
security dilemma, 214, 220
Sedan, 76, 233, 255, 257
Selborne, First Sea Lord (William Palmer), 164, 172, 206, 208
Senden, Admiral (Gustav von Senden-Bibran), 160, 203
Serbia, 18, 23, 24–25, 31, 78–79, 86, 155, 261–268, 269, 282–292
Skobelev, Mikhail, 45–46, 47
Slavs, 23–25, 260–261, 262, 267, 269, 282, 287. *See also* pan-Slavism
Social Darwinism, 70, 144, 193
Social Democratic Party (German), 136–137, 147, 149, 157, 273
Socialism, 68
Solferino, 233
South Africa, 69, 74, 101, 119, 122, 166, 171, 205
Southwest Africa, 77, 110, 152, 256
sovereignty, 2, 3, 31, 89, 177, 222, 261, 272
Spain, 51, 106, 165, 179, 193, 194, 205
sphere of influence, 101
Austrian, 86
German, 165
Russian, 78–80, 86, 164, 165
stalemate, 83, 113, 136, 220, 231
State Secretaries (German), 4, 7, 96, 132, 141, 157, 218
Strassburg, 61, 63, 230
Suez Canal, 26, 51, 54, 55
sultan, Moroccan, 106, 170, 177, 179, 273
sultan, Ottoman, 52, 54, 79, 83, 115

tariffs, 77, 136, 137, 140, 155
Third Naval Amendment, 221–222, 222–226
Thirty Years' War, 5, 6, 185
Thoughts and Reminiscences (Bismarck), 4–5, 12, 150
Three Eastern Monarchies, 38, 39
Thucydides, 134
Tirpitz Plan, 156, 189, 202, 204, 216, 217, 218–226, 259
Tirpitz, Alfred von, 132, 141, 152, 156, 160–161, 165–166, 191, 197–201, 201–202, 202–204, 204–208, 209–210, 212, 213, 214, 215, 217, 218, 259
risk theory, 199, 202, 205, 212
Tirpitz memorandum, 198

Transvaal, 119–120
Treaty of Berlin, 80, 261–262, 267, 268
Treaty of Frankfurt, 10, 11, 17
Treaty of Madrid, 51, 178–179
Treaty of San Stefano, 26–27, 31
Treitschke, Heinrich von, 71, 145
Triple Alliance, 47–49, 50, 98, 99, 103–105, 105–109, 111, 112, 115, 116, 117–118, 119–121, 125, 168, 170, 174, 182, 188, 269
Triple Entente, 143, 175, 259, 263, 265, 268, 269, 271, 274
Triple Intervention, 114, 155
Turkey, 24, 25, 27, 36, 83, 86, 112, 222, 223, 263, 266, 271. *See also* Ottoman Empire
two-front war, 59–60, 84, 105, 109, 227, 231–235, 239, 251
two-power standard, 207, 217

Ukraine, 44, 53
unification of Germany (1871), 1–2, 4–6, 7, 8, 9–12, 15, 19, 29, 33, 46, 56, 58, 59, 65, 69, 72, 92, 112, 126, 135, 144, 145, 148, 150, 182, 192, 193, 244, 245, 278
United States, 71, 110, 122, 164, 165, 167, 175, 179, 193, 194, 205, 211, 252, 266

Waldersee, Alfred von, 90–91, 94, 155, 156, 167, 228, 238, 239, 241
Wallis Bay, 74, 110
"War in Sight" Crisis, 15–22, 34, 59, 84, 153
Weber, Max, 145, 197
Weimar Republic, 141
Weltpolitik (world policy), 146, 149, 151, 155–161, 163, 174, 175, 184, 189, 191
Wilhelm I (German), 14, 20, 29, 40, 45, 91, 95, 149
Wilhelm II (German), 77, 95–96, 100, 148, 153, 180, 188, 195, 202, 252, 279, 280, 281, 283, 287, 288
  and Bismarck, 57, 71, 75, 91, 95, 97
  and Bülow, 160, 263, 265
  and Hohenlohe, 159, 160
  and the German Navy, 195–197, 204, 208, 209, 220, 222
  political actions of, 3, 103, 108, 112–113, 114, 117, 127,128–130, 130–133, 137, 138–139, 163, 167, 171, 177, 178, 183, 262, 265, 268, 272, 273, 284
Wilhelmine Germany, 77, 135, 137, 139, 140, 141, 142, 144, 146, 147, 150, 151, 153
World War I, 3, 11, 29, 75, 142, 147, 157, 238, 246, 249, 259, 292
  pre–World War I, 157, 227, 230, 245, 249, 277
  post–World War I, 210, 225

Belfer Center Studies in International Security

Published by The MIT Press
Sean M. Lynn-Jones and Steven E. Miller, series editors
Karen Motley, executive editor
Belfer Center for Science and International Affairs
John F. Kennedy School of Government, Harvard University

Acharya, Amitav, and Evelyn Goh, eds., *Reassessing Security Cooperation in the Asia-Pacific: Competition, Congruence, and Transformation* (2007)

Agha, Hussein, Shai Feldman, Ahmad Khalidi, and Zeev Schiff, *Track-II Diplomacy: Lessons from the Middle East* (2003)

Allison, Graham, and Robert D. Blackwill, with Ali Wyne, *Lee Kuan Yew: The Grand Master's Insights on China, the United States, and the World* (2013)

Allison, Graham T., Owen R. Coté Jr., Richard A. Falkenrath, and Steven E. Miller, *Avoiding Nuclear Anarchy: Containing the Threat of Loose Russian Nuclear Weapons and Fissile Material* (1996)

Allison, Graham T., and Kalypso Nicolaïdis, eds., *The Greek Paradox: Promise vs. Performance* (1997)

Arbatov, Alexei, Abram Chayes, Antonia Handler Chayes, and Lara Olson, eds., *Managing Conflict in the Former Soviet Union: Russian and American Perspectives* (1997)

Bennett, Andrew, *Condemned to Repetition? The Rise, Fall, and Reprise of Soviet-Russian Military Interventionism, 1973–1996* (1999)

Blackwill, Robert D., and Paul Dibb, eds., *America's Asian Alliances* (2000)

Blackwill, Robert D., and Michael Stürmer, eds., *Allies Divided: Transatlantic Policies for the Greater Middle East* (1997)

Blum, Gabriella, and Philip B. Heymann, *Laws, Outlaws, and Terrorists: Lessons from the War on Terrorism* (2010)

Brom, Shlomo, and Yiftah Shapir, eds., *The Middle East Military Balance, 1999–2000* (1999)

Brom, Shlomo, and Yiftah Shapir, eds., *The Middle East Military Balance, 2001–2002* (2002)

Brown, Michael E., ed., *The International Dimensions of Internal Conflict* (1996)

Brown, Michael E., and Sumit Ganguly, eds., *Fighting Words: Language Policy and Ethnic Relations in Asia* (2003)

Brown, Michael E., and Sumit Ganguly, eds., *Government Policies and Ethnic Relations in Asia and the Pacific* (1997)

Carter, Ashton B., and John P. White, eds., *Keeping the Edge: Managing Defense for the Future* (2001)

Chenoweth, Erica, and Adria Lawrence, eds., *Rethinking Violence: States and Non-State Actors in Conflict* (2010)

de Nevers, Renée, *Comrades No More: The Seeds of Change in Eastern Europe* (2003)

Elman, Colin, and Miriam Fendius Elman, eds., *Bridges and Boundaries: Historians, Political Scientists, and the Study of International Relations* (2001)

Elman, Colin, and Miriam Fendius Elman, eds., *Progress in International Relations Theory: Appraising the Field* (2003)

Elman, Miriam Fendius, ed., *Paths to Peace: Is Democracy the Answer?* (1997)

Falkenrath, Richard A., *Shaping Europe's Military Order: The Origins and Consequences of the CFE Treaty* (1995)

Falkenrath, Richard A., Robert D. Newman, and Bradley A. Thayer, *America's Achilles' Heel: Nuclear, Biological, and Chemical Terrorism and Covert Attack* (1998)

Feaver, Peter D., and Richard H. Kohn, eds., *Soldiers and Civilians: The Civil-Military Gap and American National Security* (2001)

Feldman, Shai, *Nuclear Weapons and Arms Control in the Middle East* (1996)

Feldman, Shai, and Yiftah Shapir, eds., *The Middle East Military Balance, 2000–2001* (2001)

Forsberg, Randall, ed., *The Arms Production Dilemma: Contraction and Restraint in the World Combat Aircraft Industry* (1994)

George, Alexander L., and Andrew Bennett, *Case Studies and Theory Development in the Social Sciences* (2005)

Gilroy, Curtis, and Cindy Williams, eds., *Service to Country: Personnel Policy and the Transformation of Western Militaries* (2007)

Hagerty, Devin. T., *The Consequences of Nuclear Proliferation: Lessons from South Asia* (1998)

Heymann, Philip B., *Terrorism and America: A Commonsense Strategy for a Democratic Society* (1998)

Heymann, Philip B., *Terrorism, Freedom, and Security: Winning without War* (2003)

Heymann, Philip B., and Juliette N. Kayyem, *Protecting Liberty in an Age of Terror* (2005)

Howitt, Arnold M., and Robyn L. Pangi, eds., *Countering Terrorism: Dimensions of Preparedness* (2003)

Hudson, Valerie M., and Andrea M. Den Boer, *Bare Branches: The Security Implications of Asia's Surplus Male Population*

Kayyem, Juliette N., and Robyn L. Pangi, eds., *First to Arrive: State and Local Responses to Terrorism* (2003)

Kokoshin, Andrei A., *Soviet Strategic Thought, 1917–91* (1998)

Lederberg, Joshua, ed., *Biological Weapons: Limiting the Threat* (1999)

Mansfield, Edward D., and Jack Snyder, *Electing to Fight: Why Emerging Democracies Go to War* (2005)

Martin, Lenore G., and Dimitris Keridis, eds., *The Future of Turkish Foreign Policy* (2004)

May, Ernest R., and Philip D. Zelikow, eds., *Dealing with Dictators: Dilemmas of U.S. Diplomacy and Intelligence Analysis, 1945–1990* (2007)

Phillips, David L., *Liberating Kosovo: Coercive Diplomacy and U.S. Intervention* (2012)

Rosecrance, Richard N., and Steven E. Miller, eds., *The Next Great War? The Roots of World War I and the Risk of U.S.-China Conflict* (2015)

Shaffer, Brenda, *Borders and Brethren: Iran and the Challenge of Azerbaijani Identity* (2002)

Shaffer, Brenda, ed., *The Limits of Culture: Islam and Foreign Policy* (2006)

Shields, John M., and William C. Potter, eds., *Dismantling the Cold War: U.S. and NIS Perspectives on the Nunn-Lugar Cooperative Threat Reduction Program* (1997)

Tucker, Jonathan B., ed., *Toxic Terror: Assessing Terrorist Use of Chemical and Biological Weapons* (2000)

Utgoff, Victor A., ed., *The Coming Crisis: Nuclear Proliferation, U.S. Interests, and World Order* (2000)

Weiner, Sharon K., *Our Own Worst Enemy? Institutional Interests and the Proliferation of Nuclear Weapons Expertise* (2011)

Williams, Cindy, ed., *Filling the Ranks: Transforming the U.S. Military Personnel System* (2004)

Williams, Cindy, ed., *Holding the Line: U.S. Defense Alternatives for the Early 21st Century* (2001)

Xu Qiyu, *Fragile Rise: Grand Strategy and the Fate of Imperial Germany, 1871–1914*, trans. Joshua Hill (2016)

Zoughbie, Daniel E., *Indecision Points: George W. Bush and the Israeli-Palestinian Conflict* (2014)

Belfer Center for Science and International Affairs

Graham Allison, Director
John F. Kennedy School of Government, Harvard University
79 JFK Street, Cambridge MA 02138
Tel: (617) 495-1400 | Fax: (617) 495-8963
http://www.belfercenter.org | belfer_center@hks.harvard.edu

The Belfer Center is the hub of the Harvard Kennedy School's research, teaching, and training in international security affairs, environmental and resource issues, and science and technology policy.

The Center has a dual mission: (1) to provide leadership in advancing policy-relevant knowledge about the most important challenges of international security and other critical issues where science, technology, environmental policy, and international affairs intersect; and (2) to prepare future generations of leaders for these arenas. Center researchers not only conduct scholarly research, but also develop prescriptions for policy reform. Faculty and fellows analyze global challenges from nuclear proliferation and terrorism to climate change and energy policy.

The Belfer Center's leadership begins with the recognition of science and technology as driving forces constantly transforming both the challenges we face and the opportunities for problem solving. Building on the vision of founder Paul Doty, the Center addresses serious global concerns by integrating insights and research of social scientists, natural scientists, technologists, and practitioners in government, diplomacy, the military, and business.

The heart of the Belfer Center is its resident research community of more than 150 scholars, including Harvard faculty, researchers, practitioners, and each year a new, international, interdisciplinary group of research fellows. Through publications and policy discussions, workshops, seminars, and conferences, the Center promotes innovative solutions to significant national and international challenges.

The Center's International Security Program, directed by Steven E. Miller, publishes the Belfer Center Studies in International Security, and sponsors and edits the quarterly journal, *International Security*.

The Center is supported by an endowment established with funds from Robert and Renée Belfer, the Ford Foundation, and Harvard University, by foundation grants, by individual gifts, and by occasional government contracts.